BUSINESS COMMUNICATION for the 21st Century

Marguerite P. Shane Joyce

With Contributions by

Doris Christopher
Dan Frise
Christine Irvine

KENDALL/HUNT PUBLISHING COMPANY
4050 Westmark Drive Dubuque, Iowa 52002

ISBN: 0–7872–4184–9

Printed in the United States of America

10 9 8 7 6 5 4 3 2 1

To my husband, Lionel L. Joyce, Sr., my son, Jeffrey N. Shane,
and in loving memory of my parents
Mary Louise Gorman Mays and Robert Cephus Mays.

CONTENTS

CALIFORNIA STATE UNIVERSITY, LOS ANGELES
School of Business and Economics
Department of Management

MEMORANDUM

To: **MGMT 301 Students**
From: **Dr. Marguerite P. Joyce, Professor**
Date: **September 1, 1997**
Subject: **Custom Business Communication Textbook**

This custom textbook is a collaboration among some of the instructors of MGMT 301. This textbook was written with you in mind in hopes that your individual needs would be addressed to help you develop and enhance your communication skills.

The content, application exercises, and Jeopardy Quizzes were carefully written to challenge your intellectual skills. We are sure you will find the textbook both interesting and timely.

Please share with the author your views on the content, application exercises, etc. as you progress throughout the quarter. You may use E-mail to send a message to the author.

I wish each of you the very best in the MGMT 301 class. Remember your instructors are available to help you improve your communication skills.

Dr. James M. Rosser, who previously has held senior administrative positions in two major universities and one statewide university system, has served as President of California State University, Los Angeles since 1979, where he holds academic appointment as Professor of Health Care Management.

President Rosser's many tasks as the leader of a preeminent and diverse urban university include delivering numerous speeches to students, faculty and staff—addressing the campus at special events such as Commencement, Honors Convocation and Fall Faculty Day in addition to his participation in open forums and meetings intended to facilitate dialogue and clarify important issues.

As this University is part of a larger system, the President receives information and directives from the Chancellor's Office which he in turn, must interpret and disseminate to the campus in order to comply with the requirements of The California State University. President Rosser understands the importance of having excellent communication skills, both oral and written. The increasing emphasis of a technological age places greater demand on one's communication skills in the effort to continually share information through very rapid forms of media. Dr. Rosser must frequently interact with the numerous and diverse constituencies that Cal State L.A. serves including, but not limited to, many local community organizations and business enterprises as well as numerous national educational agencies.

President Rosser is the consummate communicator. A charismatic orator who delivers his message with a clarity and precision that fosters universal understanding. His message to you, students of the Management 301 Business and Communications course, is to dedicate yourselves to continually developing and enhancing your written and communication skills. These skills are vitally important to your success personally and professionally. Your ability to exhibit excellence in communication will be one of your most important assets and honing this ability is, undoubtedly, a lifelong process.

It is my hope and the expectation of President Rosser and the School of Business and Economics that this course, and others like it, will provide the foundation for developing the essential communication skills that you, as students and ultimately as professionals, will need to ensure success.

We thank you for choosing California State University, Los Angeles.

Best wishes for your continued success!
MCW (4–17–97)

PART I

THE COMMUNICATION PROCESS AND YOU

CHAPTER 1

Dr. James M. Rosser, President, California State University, Los Angeles

Fundamentals of Business Communication

Objectives

After reading this chapter and doing the application exercises, you should be able to:

1. Explain the role of communication in relations to a manager's tasks.
2. Articulate the concept that people or employees cannot function without communication.
3. Explain the parts in the communication decision tree.
4. Name five audiences/communication realms with whom you may correspond.
5. Define the term "business communication."
6. Identify types of internal and external communication.
7. Explain the acronym OSHA and what is its purpose.
8. Explain the concept that "meaning is in the mind."
9. Identify the types of noise that interfere with the communication process.
10. Illustrate by an example the importance of feedback.

Strong communication skills are required in all professions, but never has the need for effective communication been more critical in view of today's culturally diversed workplace. You will be expected to have good communication skills regardless of your profession or position. Malra Treece states that no other ability will be more valuable to you than the ability to relate effectively and harmoniously with other people through communication.[1] The goal of this textbook is to help you enhance your communication skills so that you can become an effective and efficient communicator.

Organizations need people to perform jobs and tasks to carry out its goals. People work in organizations to achieve their own goals as well as the goals of the organization. An organization can be defined as an entity of people working together to achieve common goals. An organization cannot exist without people. These people are essentially the employees of the organization. Employees need information to perform their tasks; they need feedback regarding their performance. Employees need to be kept abreast of the organization's goals and its performance relative to goal achievement. Communication plays an important role in the organization, whether it is an employee talking to a customer or client, an employee talking to a supervisor, employees talking to each other, or a supervisor talking to an employee. It is this communication that forms people's impressions of the organization.

Communication in business is sometimes informal and sometimes formal; then, too, communication between and among employees is spontaneous as well. Employees in an organization are all involved in doing their own tasks; as a result, they are constantly involved in a number of functions of a typical manager. A manager plans, organizes, directs, and controls the activities of the organization. Good communication is the key to accomplishing all of these functions.

Communication in Business

Every organization has a product or service to sell. You may be involved in developing new products or services; you may be involved in servicing customers or clients; you may be directly involved in operations management or personnel management; you may be involved in marketing operation; you may be involved in the accounting or financial management of the organization; or you may be responsible for management of information systems. Whatever the case, you will have to exhibit your communication skills.

Planning. You as an employee will be given various tasks to perform; as a result, you will have a number of decisions to make. You will need to prioritize the tasks that need to be done unless your tasks are repetitious. These tasks may need to be done by you or perhaps you will need to ask for assistance from others; you will need to communicate. Whether you are setting goals, determining objectives, researching a problem, making decisions and/or working with other people to achieve company objectives or goals, communication plays a major role.

Organizing. A manager is responsible for making sure employees follow policies and procedures for accomplishing job tasks. Typically, the physical arrangement of the workplace and the flow of work within the organization need to be reviewed on a timely basis to ensure an optimum employee performance level. Inherent in this function is a manager's ability to scrutinize the situation, investigate possible solutions, choose the best solution, and implement the solution, and later evaluate the situation. All of these abilities require constant communication.

Staffing. The culmination of your years of study hopefully will result in getting your degree. With your degree in hand, you will become a staff member in some organization but not without exhibiting your communication skills. Communication is a vital part of hiring, training, evaluating, and promoting employees. Prospective applicants are hired based on their potential value to the organization; in most instances today, an applicant's communication skills are considered just as important as one's specialty skills, which are sometimes called hard skills. While communication skills are sometimes referred to as soft skills, this fact does not negate the importance of communication skills.

Directing. A manager needs intensive human relations skills. After all, a manager directs the employees in the organization. Much of a manager's ability to accomplish organization goals is done with and through employees.

Employee performance will depend on the manager's communication skill and the organization's climate. As a manager, you will be called upon to make oral presentations or perhaps to critique some documents written by others for your signature. Needless to say, as a manager, you will be writing most of your documents. A manager needs to exhibit good oral and written skills because employees will glean from the manager the importance of communication skills. As a manager moves up the corporate ladder, his or her interpersonal communication skills become more and more important.

Controlling. A manager frequently seeks to coordinate and/or control the performance of employees or the manufacture of a product or service; in any of these instances, the need for good communication skills is clear. Standards must be established in order to measure performance and to take the necessary corrective action. When actual performance does not measure up to established standards, the results must be communicated to upper management. Strong, effective communication skills are needed in presentations to this level.

All management functions require good written and oral presentation skills. It is the combination of employees exhibiting good communication skills, people skills, and specialty skills of marketing, finance, computer information systems, and accounting that enable an organization to achieve its highest growth.

Importance of Communication

Communication is such an integral part of our daily lives that we cannot function adequately without it. Communication is all encompassing—it involves hearing, listening, speaking, writing, thinking, analyzing, reading, as well as perceiving. No two people receive and perceive communication exactly the same. We all have our own theory of the world in our heads; we tend to view the world according to our expectations, our backgrounds, our experiences, and our cultures. This is why communication is so important as well as necessary. As we begin to study communication, and specifically business communication, we need to focus on the receiver of our communications. We need to create in the mind of the listener or reader a communicator who is concerned about the image and effect of his or her communication, whether it is oral or written.

Communication Guidelines

Before we approach any writing task, we need to ask ourselves the following questions: What kind of document have I been asked to prepare or do I need to prepare? To whom am I writing? What is the purpose of my message? What is the best arrangement for the type of information in my message? Figure 1.1 shows a Communication Decision Tree which helps in organizing the content of the message.

Each of these guidelines will be discussed in more detail in the proceeding chapters, but for now we need to focus on communication in general.

We communicate basically to develop, maintain, or nurture relationships. We communicate to inform, convince, or entertain others. In the workplace, we give and receive information in order to do our jobs; we give and receive information to convince others to do certain tasks; and we sometimes give and receive humorous information to enliven our interactions with others.

Since you are taking this business communication course, let us begin by introducing you to the environment of which you are a part. Businesses depend upon communication. In fact,

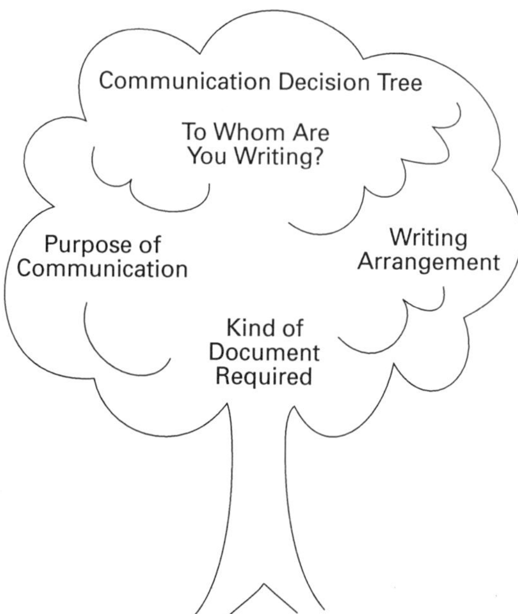

Figure 1.1.

the success of all organizations is directly related to its communication process. It is the quality of those communications that affect employees, customers, clients, consumers, and society. To this extent, business people do not communicate in a vacuum.

Definition of Communication

Business Communication can be defined as the exchange of information within a business environment. That business environment may be a university, a bakery, a nursery, a grocery store, a coin dealer, a corporation, a manufacturing company, a shopping center, a retail outlet, etc. Information must be moved from one mind to another's mind for it to be useful.

The term "communication" comes from the Latin word "communicare" which means to share or to have in common. Communication in organizations is encompassing. Employees communicate with one another, departments communicate with each other, and management communicates will all factions—within and outside the organization. Whether you are communicating to another peer person within the organization, to a superior, to a client or customer, or to a person outside the organization, your communications are important. You should exercise care in the preparation of your business messages which may be sent internally or externally. The use of communication technology helps you to perform your job tasks easier and faster as well.

Internal communications consist of memorandums, telephone calls, fax messages, e-mail, reports, meetings, and letters. External communications include letters, reports, and news releases, fax messages, e-mail, etc. These communication media will be discussed in greater detail in succeeding chapters.

Ergonomics

Ergonomics is the study of the office environment and its impact upon the worker. The workplace of some twenty-five years ago was plagued with over-sized equipment that had slow processing capabilities, subdued colors that abounded in offices, and non-body conforming furniture which did little to facilitate worker comfort. Little attention was placed on worker comfort because it was expected of people to make do with what they had; it was thought at the time that the environment had little if any relevance to productivity.

The advent of computer technology in the 1970s brought about a wealth of concerns regarding the office and the worker. It was evident that job tasks could be improved, performance could be enhanced, and tasks could be done faster, thereby ensuring increased worker productivity. Technology does not necessarily make office workers better workers; however, people using technology in the performance of their jobs become better workers and their productivity rises.

The Occupational Safety and Health Act (OSHA) was passed by Congress in 1971 to oversee human resource management. Safety and health problems seriously affect both productivity and the quality of work life. New technology, ergonomic furniture, and better health and safety procedures are contributing to a more comfortable workplace.

Theory of Communication

Communication informs, persuades, and entertains through the use of verbal and nonverbal cues. Verbal communication means communicating with spoken or written words; nonverbal communication means communicating without words. Communication is sometimes classified as intrapersonal, which is communicating within one's mind. Interpersonal communication is a conversation between two persons with others present or interacting, and group communication is communicating to masses of people by radio, newspapers, or television with little or no chance of feedback. In today's society we certainly have cultural communication which is symbolized by the cars, clothing, homes, morals, and languages—all characteristic of a culture or a given set of beliefs and values.

We communicate with words and symbols. Words have no meaning in and of themselves. People attach meaning to words; therefore, meaning is in the mind. Words have a denotative (dictionary) meaning as well as a connotative (affective) meaning. Connotative meanings add feelings. The word "house" refers to an object, but a person may attach personal meaning by referring to the house as a "home."

Approximately one million words make up the complete English vocabulary. Of the 500 most commonly used words in the English language, each one has about 30 definitions. Is it any wonder people learning English find it difficult? Then, too, even native English speakers are still wrestling with speaking and writing correct English.

Many new words have been added to the English language such as e-mail, electronic bulletin boards, internet, ethernet, etc. Similarly, some old words now have new meanings. For example, input now refers to keying in information on a computer. These and other changes in our language are due to new technologies.

Process of Human Communication

The process of human communication is complex as well as complicated. It involves our senses, our experiences, our feelings, our intelligence, and our perceptions. In fact, our communication is reflective of our intellectual capacity. We communicate with words or symbols in hope that people will understand our messages exactly as we intended, to gain a desired receiver response, and to build and/or maintain favorable relationships.

The elements involved in human communication consists of the sender, the message, the medium, the channel, and the receiver. Figure 1.2 is an illustration of a communication's model which includes formation source, encoding process, channel, decoding process, destination, and feedback.

The sender is the message formulator who draws upon his or her own experiences and background to convey a communication (made up of words or bits of information). In addition to formulating the message, the sender also acts as the encoder, speaker, or writer. Encoding involves selecting and organizing bits of information into an understandable and meaningful message.

The message is made up of words (bits of information) stored in our brain which becomes the input for the information source. The information source is the human mind which in actuality contains all our living experiences.

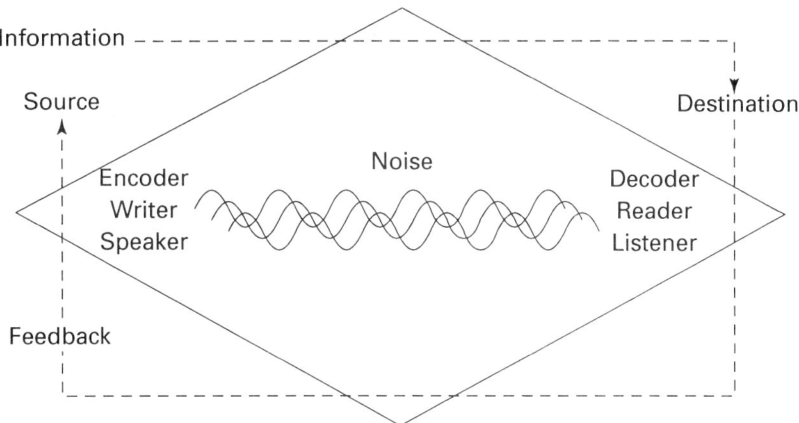

Figure 1.2. Model of Process of Human Communication.

The channel is the means of conveying the message by print (text), touch, sound, or air. Media are the methods used such as a memo, letter, report, telephone, fax machine, e-mail, or computer.

The receiver is the person to whom our message is directed. The receiver interprets the message of the sender. The destination is where decoding takes place—in the receiver's mind. Feedback is the return message or reaction from the receiver of the original message. Once feedback is received, modifications or adjustments of the intended message are frequently needed.

The message received must be reasonably similar to the intended message; otherwise, effective or intended communication has not occurred. Anything that hinders, prevents, or alters the communication process is called noise. Types of noise that occur in the transmission of a message are semantic, psychological, and mechanical. Semantics means variations in word meanings. We must remember that words in and of themselves have no meaning—people attach meaning to words. For example, the word "fast" and "bad" probably conjure up a meaning in your mind; but your fellow classmate probably has his or her own meaning for "fast" and "bad." Language thus shapes our perceptions. Let us focus on the following words, for example.

Sushi—this is raw fish; why don't you call it that?
Escargot—these are snails; why don't you call them that?
Caviar—this is fish eggs; why don't you call it that?
Chitterlings—these are pig intestines; why don't you call them that?
Calamary—this is squid; why don't you call it that?

Psychological noise deals with our feelings and emotions. For instance, you are told that you will have a speaker today in class on the subject of abortion, euthanasia, or AIDS. Automatically, you experience pangs of anxiety, etc. depending upon how you view the subject and your feelings. Your feelings and/or emotions will interfere with your reception of the message. Your feelings and emotions will probably become more intense if the speaker's viewpoint is contrary to yours.

Mechanical noise involves errors in grammar, punctuation, sentence structure, verb tense, spelling, voice, etc. Any error tends to force the reader or listener to concentrate on the error rather than the message. We should not rationalize the severity of an error; we must make every effort to make sure our communication is free of errors. Do not be fooled into thinking that no one (reader or listener) is going to spot the error or that no one really cares or will pay any attention to it. Your communication and signature on the document reflect YOU. People will form a mental image of you as well as your company based upon the communications they receive.

Your goal is to become an effective communicator; nothing short of perfection is acceptable. Communication is effective if it is understandable in a single reading or hearing. Consider the following incidents that happened in our society. Federal income tax forms had to be reprinted because people could not understand them. People could not decipher what the questions on the form were asking; the problem here could have been semantics. Whatever the case, taypayers ended up having to pay for the reprinting of these new tax forms. Social Security checks were issued to deceased recipients for several years. Taxpayers had to pay for these errors. Whose image is tarnished?

Communication Roadblocks

Communication is often distorted because the perception in the mind of the receiver differs from that in the mind of the sender. When two people see an accident, each will see something different because of their perceptions. Similarly, when two people visit an art museum, each may be attracted to different pictures because of their own perceptions. Truly, "beauty is in the eye of the beholder."

Confusing gestures, faddish clothing, inappropriate vocabulary, and poor voice qualities also cause miscommunication to occur. Frequently, we give conflicting communications. For example, we may be wishing someone well while our facial expression reflects a frown. You are what you wear; so if you wear faddish clothing, perhaps you are rather young and easily influenced. A business graduate goes for an interview and every other word he or she utters is a slang expression. What image does this reflect in the eyes of the receiver or are these examples of reinforced communication?

Communication roadblocks also occur by the way we see ourselves, other people, and the world about us. Seldom will we perceive every situation exactly as the other person does, but we can show empathy by making an honest effort to appreciate his or her point of view in order to achieve more meaningful communication.

Other barriers or roadblocks to communication include the following:

Lack of interest. At times, we must do things for which we feel a lack of interest. Your noninterest impedes your perception and reception of the message. Perhaps you delayed taking this course as long as you could because you did not relish the idea of having to take a business writing course. Maybe you feel uneasy about your ability to write or that this course will certainly challenge you. If you have areas in writing with which you feel you need help, view them as opportunities for improvement and growth. A positive attitude and a willingness to *really* work at improving your writing will enhance your performance.

Distractions. All too often our minds are clouded with tasks that we must do or unpleasant experiences. We think constantly of how we will accomplish them with our limited time or how we will cope with stressful situations. This thinking process hampers our ability to truly concentrate on the matter at hand.

Nonsophistication. Sometimes we read or hear information that is unfamiliar or about which we feel less knowledgeable. At times, we may need to do some extra reading or research to help familiarize ourselves with the topic. The learning process is a lifelong process and one not limited to life as a student in the classroom.

Blunders. Writers or speakers often contribute to their reader's or listener's inability to focus on a topic if their presentation—oral or written—in unorganized or appears to be haphazardly presented. It is difficult to concentrate on communications which are unclear and unorganized.

Personal asides. Some of our personal qualities also tend to hamper our communication abilities. Our emotions, which are often deep seated, surface on occasion, thereby causing us not to focus on the communication. Our personality types can impact our relationships in the workplace and perhaps hinder our ascent up the corporate ladder. Being pessimistic, argumentative, and antagonistic to peers, supervisors, etc. only serve to lessen one's chances for promotability.

Prejudices. The United States is a culture pluralistic society. It is the richness of different peoples' values, customs, etc. that make it an exciting place. No one is perfect, yet some people feel they are since they have a tendency to judge others based on their own standards. Yes, prejudices sometime hinder our ability to accept information from others unlike us as well as to receive information from others dissimilar to us. With our culturally diversed society, it is incumbent upon all of us to be accepting of others regardless of social, economic, and ethnic origins.

Communication Realms

In business writing, we will communicate regularly with a number of audiences or realms.[2] These audiences include customers and clients, subordinates, team members, and superiors. Our communication tasks will involve sending memos to people within the organization, writing letters to people outside the organization such as customers and clients, sending reports to various governmental agencies, being on teams to complete projects, and communicating with superiors. These communication realms or audiences will be discussed in greater detail in Chapter 2. In preparation for these various writing assignments, we must first assess our critical thinking and analysis skills.

Critical Thinking and Analysis

We often times must make decisions which will require a major financial outlay. Do we just buy the item or do we make an informed decision? Let us consider for example that we are going to purchase a new car. Where do we begin? How do we begin? Some people may look at the classified ads in the newspaper for the car, some people may visit dealerships, and still some people will look at *Consumer Reports Buying Guide* for specific information on the best performance cars. We are just beginning, and we have not even thought about the manufacturer, color, size, cubic engine, two door or four door, etc. Once we have gathered all information, we now must synthesize and compare all the information and weigh the costs with the product. This is where our critical thinking skills and analysis come into play. We want the best car for the money. The critical thinking process is one of asking questions, more questions, etc. The more questions we ask, the better we will be prepared to make an informed decision on which car to buy.

Similarly, if you were planning your wedding or an anniversary celebration, how would you begin? Where would you begin? You would need to ask yourself numerous questions; for example, how many people do you anticipate inviting? What is the date and who has the date available? Or do you want to have it at a church, hotel, or reception hall? Is this a sit-down meal function or buffet style? Is the event to be catered? Do you have a budget for this wedding or anniversary celebration? These questions will need to be answered and comparisons made to determine the best food, location, etc. for the cost.

Critical thinking is needed for each writing task. You will determine why you are writing, what information you want to include in the document, and how the information is to be arranged. In each of these instances, your critical thinking and analysis skills are exhibited.

An element common to all who seek to be business professionals is the need to make timely and effective decisions in a dynamic and uncertain environment. You should be open-minded and not locked into existing ideas or solutions. Strive to explore new arrangements in which the facts combine to create new and innovative ways of meeting the needs of clients and customers. Critical thinkers must ensure intellectual and ethical honesty by making their beliefs explicit and accounting for the moral implications of their actions.

Your writing should be reader-centered; that is, write with the reader in mind. You should tell readers what they want to know in a way that is useful to them. Some familiar examples of writer-centered rather than reader-centered documents are insurance policies and Internal Revenue Service tax forms.

As the environment for communication becomes more and more increasingly complex, so do the communication challenges faced by all business communicators.

Now, that the fundamentals of business communication have been presented, we need to look at organizational communication.

References

1. Treece, Malra. (1994). SUCCESSFUL COMMUNICATION FOR BUSINESS AND THE PROFESSIONS, Allyn and Bacon, 1.
2. Locker, Kitty O. (1995) BUSINESS AND ADMINISTRATIVE COMMUNICATION, Irwin, 58.
3. Hisker, William J. (1993). CRITICAL THINKING GUIDE, McGraw-Hill.

Questions

1. Define the word "organization."
2. Why is communication important in an organization?
3. Discuss the functions of a typical manager.
4. Explain the processes involved in communication.
5. Describe the branches of the decision tree.
6. Why do we communicate?
7. Define the term "business communication."
8. Discuss the statement "Meaning is in the mind."
9. Give examples of internal and external communication.
10. What are the elements involved in human communication?
11. Describe the three types of noise that can occur in the communication process.
12. Name three communication roadblocks that you have experienced.
13. Describe the four main communication realms with whom you will most likely communicate in an organization.
14. Discuss the need for critical thinking skills.

Applications

1. Arrange to interview a professor in your field and a business person in a job for which you will be seeking after graduation. Ask these two people to share with you the specific communication skills they use in the performance of their work.
2. Get a current copy of the *Los Angeles Times* and look in the Classified Ads for the number of jobs in your field that ask for communication skills. Identify the type of skills.
3. Locate a current article in a journal (*Business Communication Quarterly, The Journal of Business Communication*, etc.) that discusses communication skills and share it with the class.
4. Find a copy of a current annual report of a company in which you would like to own stock some day. Analyze the report in terms of ethnic representativeness, pictures included, and the company's corporate culture.
5. Find an article on a company or its employees in which negative publicity has surfaced. Share the article with the class and discuss the communications issues this company must face.
6. Interview two Human Resource Managers to get their opinion on specific communication skills they seek and how they assess these skills in an interview.
7. Find the definition for the following words and use each of them in two sentences:

   proclivity
   attribute
   tenacity
   pretentious

8. Read the following document and circle any errors you find.

Memoranda

To: **Roberta Warren, Director**
From: **Taylor Shane, Chair**
date **1/21/97**
subject: **Need for Picture IDs**

starting today january 15 97 all employes must display a picture id while on the jobs. Since there our many peoples working on the premises doing various construction jobs, we need to be able to identity everyone.

If you need a picture id please come to Room 145 Main bldg. thankyou.

9. Choose the more positively worded sentence below:
   a. Macy's will close at 9 p.m. on Friday.
   b. Macy's will be open until 9 p.m. on Friday.
10. Rewrite the sentences below to make them shorter.
   a. All too often this same problem happens.
   b. It is not necessary for you to lay off the program staff.

• • • MINI-CASE SCENARIOS • • •

1. You have a family member who is thinking about opening his or her own business. Based upon having read this chapter, what key issues would you share with the person relative to opening a business?
2. As a followup to Case 1, if you were opening a business, what skills would you feel are necessary in this venture? Would you want to hire some employees from the start or are there other options?

Name ______________________________ Date ____________

JEOPARDY QUIZ #1

1. The answer is: An entity of people working together to achieve common goals.

   What is ______________________________?

2. The answer is: Resources needed to perform jobs and tasks in the organization.

   What is ______________________________?

3. The answer is: What an organization has to offer its customers and/or clients.

   What are ______________________________?

4. The answer is: A type of skill needed by every person regardless of his or her profession.

   What is ______________________________?

5. The answer is: Planning, Organizing, Staffing, Directing, and Controlling.

   What are ______________________________?

6. The answer is: It involves hearing, listening, speaking, writing, thinking, reading, and perceiving.

   What is ______________________________?

7. The answer is: To whom you are writing, purpose of the communication, writing style arrangement, and kind of document required.

   What are ______________________________?

8. The answer is: Communicating without words.

   What is ______________________________?

9. The answer is: Words and symbols.

   What are ______________________________?

continued

10. The answer is: The message formulator who draws upon his or her experiences to convey a message.

    Who is ____?

11. The answer is: The return message or reaction from the receiver.

    What is ____?

12. The answer is: Semantic, psychological, and mechanical.

    What are ____?

13. The answer is: Confusing gestures, faddish clothing, inappropriate vocabulary, distractions, etc.

    What are ____?

14. The answer is: Customers, clients, subordinates, team members, and superiors.

    What are ____?

15. The answer is: The processing of asking questions and more questions to become better informed to make a decision.

    What is ____?

CHAPTER 2

Dr. Marguerite P. Shane Joyce, Professor
Computer Information Systems Department

ızational ıunication

Objectiv

After r' . the following activit

1. Define tı ıd give two examples.
2. Draw a diagram illustrating :ation at three organizational levels.
3. Explain the five audiences or communication realms with which most organizations must deal.
4. Discuss the difference between upward and downward communication.
5. Describe the concepts of channels and mediums.
6. Give an example of an informal communication channel in the workplace and at school.
7. Determine what should be your guide in selecting a writing style.
8. Discuss the need for open communication between employees and upper management.

While numerous books have been written on organizational communication, only a brief overview is presented here to emphasize the importance of the communication flow and process in organizations. An organization's culture is its attitudes, values, perceptions, and philosophies which are sometimes revealed in the allocation of money, power, and space.

Organizational communication is sometimes regarded as the activity of writing documents such as letters to customers and/or clients and other organizations. Additionally, memos, reports and the presentations to internal groups and other entities can be added to this definition.

Every organization has a flow of communication. This flow is usually dependent upon the chain of command particularly based upon the hierarchial chart or the organizational chart. The two organizational charts (Figure 2.1 and Figure 2.2) portray the typical flow of information in an organization.

In Figure 2.1, the flow of communication shows upward, downward, lateral, and diagonal movement. Information comes into the organization in terms of state and Federal regulations; information goes out of the organization in the form of letters and reports to governing bodies, stockholders, the public, and other entities.

Figure 2.2 shows the flow of communication in an organization more familiar to students attending a higher education institution. A university is made up of schools such as the School of Arts and Sciences, the School of Natural and Social Sciences, the School of Business and Economics, etc. Similarly, a college is made up of departments. Let us look closely at the organizational chart in Figure 2.2.

Staff is available at each level to assist in the dissemination of information, university policies and procedures. While students appear to be at the bottom of the organizational chart, they are the most important reason why a higher educational institution exists. Students are the customers and/or clients that the institution serves.

Upper management personnel usually forward information down to middle management personnel who then share information with subordinates. Information is also sent to several audiences or realms which will be discussed in detail later in this chapter:

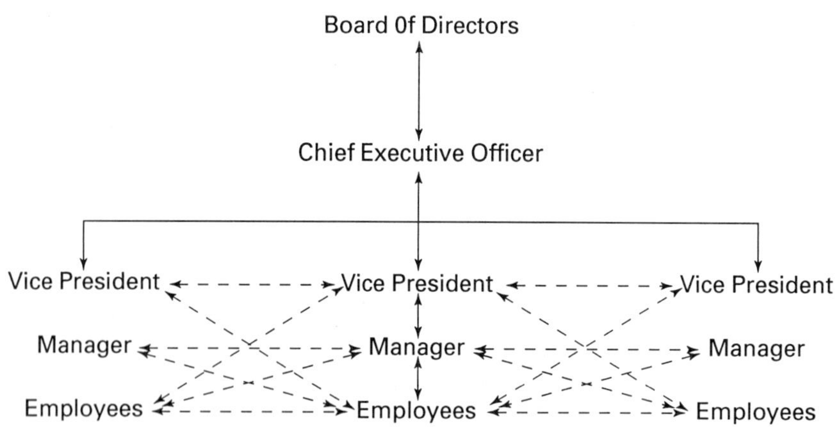

Figure 2.1. Typical Organizational Chart.

1. Communication to employees within the organization
2. Communication with customers, clients, and other organizations outside the organization
3. Communication with labor organizations
4. Communication with government and community, and
5. Communication with prospective employees

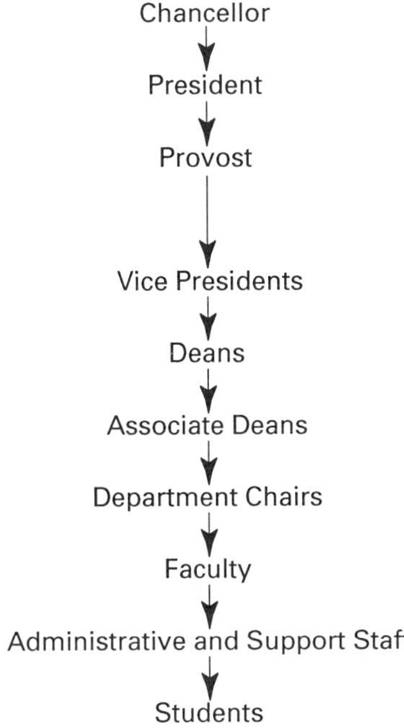

Figure 2.2. Higher Education Institution.

Organizational communication consists of the documents that are produced within the organization—a memo, a letter, or a report. Organizational communication also involves the oral messages that filter throughout the organization and can also be called those communications that are sanctioned by the organization, that is, those that are dictated by the formal channel. Of course, an informal communication channel is the grapevine.

Flow of Communications in Organizations

The earlier flow of communication in organizations some 30 years ago included only a three way flow—information coming into and information going out of the organization as well as information sent downward in the organization. Rarely did subordinates have the opportunity to send information upward nor to express their views on job tasks procedures or redesign of job procedures. The issue then was whether or not management took employees seriously or merely patronized them. However, the need for information at all levels in the organization has never been more important. Within the past fifteen years, there has been a concentrated effort by upper level management to involve all employees in the information flow. The typical organization engages in a variety of communication activities daily; these activities can be categorized as downward, upward, lateral, diagonal, and external.

Downward communication. Upper management passes information such as policies and procedures, instructions, plans, decisions, etc. to those employees who will carry them out. Superiors relate these types of information to subordinates. Additionally, superiors communicate information to employees about their job tasks and responsibilities, performance, fringe benefits and employment packages. Downward communication is necessary to instruct workers, to maintain employee morale and goodwill toward management and the organization, to keep operations and activities running smoothly, and to solicit upward communication or feedback. Downward communicationn may come in the form of newsletters, memos, letters, brochures, and may be informal conversations. The downward flow of information may directly impact employees' attitudes. Failure on the part of management to keep employees informed about the organization will result in unhappy and unproductive employees, rumors, misunderstandings, or miscommunication. The happy, productive employee is one who is evaluated fairly, who is fully informed by superiors about the organization, its goals and objectives, and its responsibility to society.

Upward communication. The most common medium for the upward flow of communication in an organization is the report, which is often used in management decision making. Reports are written by employees at various levels in the organizational structure to provide feedback to upper management on the operations of the organization and the implementation of policies and plans, performance levels, and decisions. These reports can be formal reports, surveys, suggestion slips, form reports, or perhaps informal conversations or meetings. Also, this upward communication allows employees to share information and concerns, and also to express their opinions regarding the administration. Upward communication is an important vehicle for conveying to employees their value to the organization by soliciting their ideas and feelings. After all, an organization wants its employees to achieve its goals; so employees who truly feel a part of the organization will continually perform to their maximum.

Lateral communication. All levels of the organizational chart are interdependent and must work together to accomplish the organization's goals. For instance, in the higher educational institution organizational chart, deans and department chairs may continually communicate with each other to keep abreast of university policies and procedures and/or to share happenings in their departments or at their levels. Depending upon the size of the organization, reports and/or meetings are often used to alert others of actual performance. Lateral communication is a vehicle used mostly to help coordinate performance.

Diagonal communication. Information continually moves across levels within an organization. It may criss cross, that is, different levels may communicate with each other outside of a particular school environment. For example, the dean from the School of Arts and Letters may communicate with a department chair in the School of Business and Economics or with students who take courses in a school other than the one offering their major. Employees are often required to communicate with a variety of people in the performance of their tasks; they will engage in writing to different realms or audiences.

Communication Realms: Internal and External

The first type of audience or communication realm organizations communicate with are their customers and/or clients. An organization provides a product or a service for its customers and/or clients. They become the buyers of that organization's product or service. The organization survives on its customer/clients base. The organization must continue to make a good product or offer a good service in order to reach its bottom line—net profit.

The first communication with *customers or clients* may be the phone if the organization is at a distance from its customers or clients. Or the only contact with customer or clients may be by written correspondence. Another type of contact with customers or clients may be in person. The main point is that the communicator must be cordial and friendly with all of the company's customers and clients. The employees represent the company and that representation may be the only contact that the customer or client has in order to form a mental image of the company. Establishing goodwill among its customers and clients is very important to a company's survival.

Communication with *subordinates* is another category of communication realms. Supervisors and managers must keep employees informed of their performance as it relates to accomplishing the company's goals. Then, too, this group of management personnel is sometimes the only link with upper management. Their ability to communicate and to maintain employee satisfaction and morale impact the company's attainment of its goals. Employees need to know their job tasks and how these tasks relate to both their goals and the goals of the organization. Some companies permit employees' involvement in participative management opportunities such as administrative decision making. Open communication is needed so that employees can feel free to express their views, suggestions, and concerns. Of course, management needs effective communication skills when dealing with employees. A sense of fairness and respect for all employees is key to maintaining good morale.

A third type of communication activity or realm involves *teamwork* within the organization. Many projects and reports cannot be done solely by one person; therefore, many people are needed to prepare certain parts of the project or the report. The fact that interrelated parts produce a total effect greater than the sum of each of the parts working independently is called synergy. Another example of synergy would be an symphony orchestra playing in concert. For example, the formula could easily be 1 + 1 = 3. As culturally diverse as most of the organizations are today, effective communication skills and people skills are essential. Teamwork requires the ability to get along with and work with all types of people; knowledge of group dynamics, a good sense of humor, and the ability to compromise are needed.

Just as management needs effective communication skills when dealing with employees, so do employees need effective communication skills when dealing with *superiors*. In most instances, employees usually respond in the manner they have been accustomed. For example, if an employee asks and gets permission in advance for time off to attend a special family engagement but on that particular day he or she is now told to finish an assignment, the element of trust is broken. While there are miscommunications sometimes and problems that do occur within the organization, employees will respect authority as long as they feel they have been treated fairly and with respect. This fourth type of communication realm involves commitment from both employees and others within the organization.

A fifth type of communication realm is *labor organizations*. Some companies have unions, and management must interpret and enforce contract provisions. While lower level employees make up the labor force within the organization, the union is another vehicle to ensure fair treatment, fair wages, and fair performance expectations. A union contract usually sets the terms for employment, job responsibilities, authority, pay scales, and accountability. A union serves as an entity with which to handle complaints and grievances brought by employees against the organization. Management's view of the union and its relationship with the union can cause the company to succeed or fail. For example, consider what happened to Eastern Airlines. Communication among the pilots, flight attendants, mechanics, and management all went awry; even the arbitrators could not get the units at the bargaining table to compromise. What was once a leading airline exists no longer.

Every organization must deal with government regulations and laws on a daily or frequent basis, so *governmental agencies* are another communication realm. All companies must submit tax returns and interpret and enforce laws that pertain to employment hiring decisions and the workplace. While most of this type of communication results in detailed information such as facts and figures, upper management would do well to keep in mind that submission of these timely, accurate reports are for its own protection.

Communication with the *community* is another communication realm. If the organization is located in the community where most of its employees reside, the image of the company will be determined by the employees. The positive image of the company wherein it is housed is important. Happy, content employees will reflect a positive image to others. On the other hand, malcontents usually will portray a negative image of the company. Here is why keeping the lines of communication open at all levels can often nix negative employees' perception before they have a chance to root.

Communication with *prospective employees* is the last communication realm. An organization cannot survive without employees. Hiring good employees is critical to the organization's success or failure. Numerous opportunities exist at this stage in wooing prospective employees. As will be discussed in a later chapter, the employment process is quite encompassing. A company must know which jobs need replacement, what qualifications are needed, which job descriptions need updating, and what realistic pay scales prevail, before beginning the job recruitment process. The various stages of the employment process, from the job posting to the interview process, are all important in selecting and hiring the most compatible, qualified person to fit in with the organization's purposes. Once employees are hired, they represent the company in a variety of communication tasks such as presentations or document writing.

For a thorough view of the communication realms or audiences that an organization must deal with, see Figure 2.3.

Communication Media and Networks

A message is the oral, written, or nonverbal communication that the speaker or sender transmits to an audience. Every message is transmitted through a channel and medium

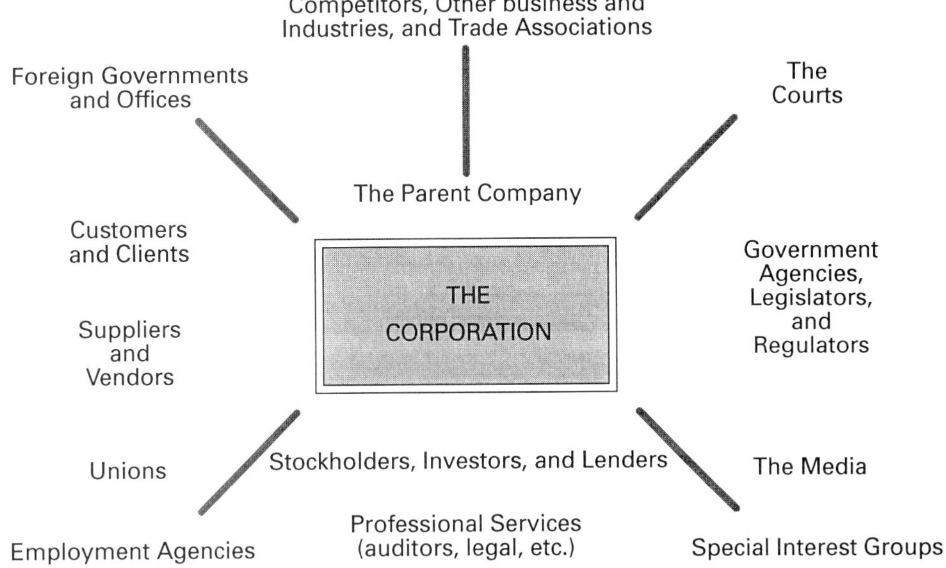

Figure 2.3. An Organization's Realms of Communication.

through which the message sender and the message receiver communicate. Types of media include memos, letters, reports, phone calls, meetings, TV ads, electronic mail, meetings, billboards, bulletin boards, fax machines, Internet, and videoconferencing. Electronic media will be discussed in more detail in Chapter 4 on Communication Technology.

Both formal and informal communication networks exist within every sizable organization. As an employee, you will have a supervisor to whom you should direct your concerns and problems; this supervisor in turn also has a direct superior. Business savvy dictates that you address your concerns and problems to your supervisor. Only in rare and extreme cases should a subordinate go to his or her supervisor's boss.

The routine, daily conversations that employees carry on with each other is usually morale building or an opportunity to see what others are doing in the organization. For the most part, these are pleasant conversations that provide employees a sense of belonging. The formal communication network is the one sanctioned by the organizational chart.

The informal communication network is the grapevine, a source of company information. This informal network may carry far more information, some of it perhaps factual and the message moves faster. Other information that surfaces along the grapevine is gossip, half-truth, and rumor. Malcontents in the organization are quick to spread half-truths and rumors based on their perception of the situation. While there is information that must be contained until the precise moment is at hand to disseminate it, secrecy must be maintained. If employees truly feel they are a part of the organization and feel that management can be trusted, they have confidence in the organization and may not rely on the grapevine.

Many executives want to squash the grapevine, but research has shown that filtering the right information to the right people will squelch any untrue rumors. Executives should use the grapevine to their advantage; that is, find out who are the leaders of the grapevine and get the correct information to them rather than fear the grapevine. For example, have you asked other students about courses and what instructor to choose? Was the information you were given accurate or inaccurate? A grapevine exists in practically all organizations. It is human nature to search out the grapevine and then use that information in your own decision-making process.

Communication Channels

A communication channel is the means used to transmit the signals that carry a message. Verbal and nonverbal media are the methods used most often. The verbal message can be either written or spoken, and the nonverbal message is the body language—gestures and actions that surface consciously or unconsciously—that also transmit messages. Nonverbal cues always accompany verbal messages.

Verbal messages—written or spoken. Written business communication can consist of correspondence or reports. Internal correspondence such as written messages—memos—are sent to employees within the organization. External correspondence such as written messages—letters—are sent to people outside the organization. These types of messages will be discussed in detail later in Chapters 7 and 8.

Reports can be written in a variety of formats: memo, letter, formal, short, proposal, or manuscript. Basically, reports can either communicate a decision or ask for a decision, and reports can communicate information or decisions for others to use in their job. For example, policy manuals or employee handbooks contain information for employees to follow.

Even oral messages shared in meetings, in telephone conversations, etc. all help to convey information for others to use in the performance of their work. That is why choosing the right message medium is just as important as the message itself and the environment. Communicators need to focus on the impact of their messages based on the receivers' anticipated reaction.

Business Communication Psychology

Business messages can be prepared in three different formats; namely, positive, negative, or persuasive. The writer must always keep in mind how the reader will respond to the message. It is human nature to always want to hear good news and to have all our wants and desires fulfilled. However, that is not always the case. In business writing, the writer needs to focus on the receiver of the document. The writing style should be chosen based on the receiver's anticipated reaction to the message. As a company employee, you will always want to maintain the customer's goodwill if possible. Consider the following scenarios:

Mari Baldwin, a loyal customer of yours, would like a credit card, but the Credit Department has determined that her credit rating is not good. How do you tell her the bad news? Should you tell her "no" in the first paragraph? Or do you take her step by step through the decision you have reached in hopes of retaining her as a cash customer? The best solution would be to use the inductive writing style for conveying the bad news. In this style, a buffer is presented in the first paragraph followed by reasons leading up to the decision, then stating the decision, and ending on a positive close. In most instances, the reader will read the entire message due to the arrangement of the information rather than throwing the letter away if the "no" is stated in the first paragraph.

Sam Mays operates a tax preparation business. He is seeking more clients. Should he focus on what his company can do for the prospective client or does he focus on what the client will gain by subscribing to his tax preparation service?

The best solution is for Sam to use the persuasive writing style to first get the reader's attention, create interest in the tax service, describe reader benefits (desire) and to request reader's action. Presenting the information in this format helps to gain the client's goodwill.

You are considering going to graduate school after the completion of your bachelor's degree. After talking with a few of your professors and others about which universities to attend, you have decided to write to several universities seeking admission and financial aid information. What should you say in your letter? What writing style should you use?

The best solution is to use a deductive writing style in which the main idea (you are requesting a graduate application, housing, and financial aid) is put in the first paragraph followed by details about when you plan to start graduate school, etc. and end on a positive close.

Your company is downsizing, and you have to let go three good employees. This is a difficult situation, but you have to do as your superior directs you. How should you begin? What format do you use? Where should you communicate this bad news? Do you think these employees have any idea they will be terminated?

A best solution probably does not exist for this situation as no one wants to hear he or she is being terminated, regardless of the circumstances. Ideally, it is hoped that upper management has done its job in terms of company responsibility particularly if the company has a union. Then the next step would be to tell each of the employees in a private conversation in his or her office the decision of company in terms of downsizing. As the employee's supervisor, perhaps you can tell them what provisions have been made for helping them find another job, how long the present health benefits remain in effect, their last day of employment, etc. As the bearer of bad news, you should anticipate and be prepared for emotional reactions. Sometimes having counselors on company premises is a good idea. This oral conversation should be followed up thereafter with a memo to the employee and a copy put in the employee's file.

Writing letters to customers and clients and conveying information to employees is very important in terms of maintaining and nurturing the goodwill of the customers, clients, and employees. After all, customers and clients are the ones who keep the organization in business, and employees are the peoplepower that perform their duties that help achieve the goals of the organization. Extra care and preparation should be used in writing every business letter to people outside the organization. As stated earlier, sometimes the only contact the customer or client has is through the letter that he or she receives. The writing style should be chosen based on the impact the reader will have from your message. Writing styles and types of messages will be discussed in more detail in Chapters 8, 9, and 10.

QUESTIONS

1. Explain what is meant by the term "organizational communication."
2. Discuss the flow of communication in today's organization. Use Cal State Los Angeles as an example.
3. Describe the five different audiences or communication realms in which information is sent.
4. Explain the difference between upward and downward communication.
5. Describe the formal communication network.
6. How reliable is the information from the grapevine?
7. What is the difference between a medium and a channel?
8. Discuss what is meant by "business communication psychology."

APPLICATIONS

1. Input a 6-8 line paragraph on your perception of information you have received from the grapevine.
2. Revise the following memo in terms of the inductive writing style. Renumber the sentences/paragraphs and turn it in to your instructor.

MEMORANDUM

To: Aletha Wilson
From: Viola Hill
Date: November 13, 1996
Subject: Refund for Ticket

I cannot grant your request for a ticket refund. It is against company policy.

In order to refund you the ticket money, the ticket must be returned two days before the event. You turned in the ticket one day before the event was to be held.

Since this was a discount ticket anyway, the full ticket price would not be granted anyway.

The play "Man of LaMancha" was even more exciting than before and we are sorry you were not able to attend.

We hope you will be able to attend the next showing of "Man of LaMancha" which is scheduled in late August 1997.

3. Input a memo to your professor describing your perception of how you are or have been treated by this University as a customer. Cite example(s).
4. Read the paragraph below and circle errors you find.

   I has a spelling checker as you can sea.
   I ran it though as you ask. But my checker did not find an error as you can planely sea.
   Of coarse you tolled me sew.
5. If you are working or have worked, with which audiences or realms have you communicated?
6. Look up the definitions and then use each word below in a sentence.

   aggregate scrutinize affinity
7. Circle the sentence which is grammatically correct.
   a. I go to store often.
   b. I go to the store often.
8. Choose the incorrect wording in the sentences below.
   a. The staffs is engaged in volunteer work.
   b. The staff is engaged in volunteer work.
9. Cross out the excess words in the sentence below.

   It has come to my attention that a fee hike is imminent.
10. Using a writing analysis software program, retrieve the paragraph from Application 3 and run it through Rightwriter or another writing analysis package.

• • •MINI-CASE SCENARIOS •

1. A staff member in your department continually chit chats with your immediate supervisor. Although she has not shared any information regarding your department or problems, etc., you think her behavior is out of line in terms of the chain of command in organizational communication levels. What issues are present here?
2. You have been in your present position as a Manager for three years. You were told by the former Division Head that your picture would appear in the Annual Report as an administrative team member; now the Annual Report has come out and your picture is not in it. What should you do? You really wanted to see your picture in it as you had told several family members.

Name ______________________________ Date ____________

JEOPARDY QUIZ #2

1. The answer is: A diagram of positions and reporting levels.

   What is ______________________________?

2. The answer is: Information moves upward, downward, lateral, and diagonal.

   What is ______________________________?

3. The answer is: An informal information channel in every organization.

   What is ______________________________?

4. The answer is: Policies and procedures, instructions, plans, decisions, etc.

   What are ______________________________?

5. The answer is: The combined efforts of individuals are greater than their individual parts in task accomplishment.

   What is ______________________________?

6. The answer is: Unhappy employees who spread negative information about the organization.

   What are ______________________________?

7. The answer is: The oral, written, or nonverbal communication that a speaker or sender transmits to an audience.

   What is ______________________________?

8. The answer is: Memos, phone calls, TV ads, meetings, billboards, Internet, etc.

   What are ______________________________?

9. The answer is: The means used to transmit the signals that carry a message.

   What are ______________________________?

continued

10. The answer is: The need to always write positive letters and maintain goodwill of customers and/or clients.

    What is ____?

CHAPTER 3

Mrs. Rhoda James, Lecturer
Department of Management

Intercultural, International, and Global Communication

Objectives

After reading the chapter and doing the exercises, you should be able to:

1. Give a rationale for the importance of developing intercultural, international, and global communication skills.
2. Cite an example of ethnocentrism.
3. Define the term "language."
4. Distinguish between culture and subculture.
5. Discuss 5 to 6 factors that affect international communication.
6. Identify the reasoning behind English being the official language of international business.
7. Analyze the difference between low-context and high-context cultures.
8. Compare the difference in context in letters written in foreign languages.
9. Determine his or her own value system in relations to decision making in business ventures.
10. Evaluate his or her feeling on gender hindrances or preferences relative to the U. S. or a foreign work force.

U. S. companies create and sell $81 billion in good and services in Japan. Is that part of the U.S. economy or the Japanese economy? Of course, they all are part of one economy, the global economy, and that economy is on a booming course as it races toward the year 2000.[1]

A study of intercultural, international, and global communication is important because of the following facts: 1) Many leading American corporations earn approximately half of their profits from their operations abroad; 2) Over thirty percent of American corporate executives have international business management experience; 3) the United States is becoming heavily involved in world trade at a rapid pace, and 4) the work place is becoming global—a mixture of native and immigrant workers nationally and internationally[2].

The American Assembly of Collegiate Schools of Business (AACSB) has long supported the internationalization of the business school curriculum. This need to internationalize the business school curriculum is mainly a result of companies expanding multinationally and internationally. The prospective business graduate must be able to communicate in any culture effectively. Of course, communications technology, global trade, and transportation systems all have contributed to making the world appear smaller. Since global competition abounds, the ability to function in an international and intercultural environment is paramount.

Globalization and International Trade

The growth of international trade has increased the importance of international business communication. International trade is beneficial because of differences in the productive capabilities of various countries. Approximately 6,000 American companies have foreign operations, and 20,000 or more American firms continue to export products or services abroad3. Our present leading trading partners include Japan and what was once Western Europe; due to recent trade agreements such as NAFTA, Canada and Mexico have now joined the ranks. German unity as well as the dramatic changes in the former U.S.S.R. have had an impact on international business. Also, many foreign national companies have operations in the United States. Many graduates will work for a foreign-owned organization. These valuable statistics may suggest that since United States firms have been doing so much business abroad, there is no need for students to develop cross-cultural communication skills — it can just be "business as usual" no matter what the country. Your intercultural communication skills are of great importance so that you can be prepared to work in any of these environments.

The economic world is undergoing major changes. In 1992, the European Economic Community eliminated economic barriers among its twelve member countries; and in 1997, Hong Kong will be under China's leadership. These two events open up new arenas for business relationships. Those who understand foreign markets and cultures will have an opportunity for exciting career experiences.

Another study indicated that 43 percent of top-level executives—CEO's, Presidents, and Vice Presidents—have worked abroad for an average of three years each[4]. This percentage has risen even more with more global competition. Executives and employees can no longer ignore the influence of the Far East or Europe, culturally or economically.

According to Andrews and Andrews[5], you can BUY in any language; but you SELL in the culture of the market. Consider the following quote:

> The North American manufacturer goes to a potential market with the product, shows all its excellent qualities and particularly its central selling feature—in essence, stressing why the buyer should have the product. The Japanese manufacturer, on the other hand, goes to the potential buyer and listens while the buyer describes what is needed—the product, its delivery, after-purchase service, etc. The Japanese manufacturer also consults with the various departments of the manufacturing firm that are involved, then returns to the potential buyer with an offer to sell what will meet the buyer's stated need. (p. 2)

Many of you will be involved either in international business activities or in intercultural activity that necessitates the need to communicate across all cultures.

Now, let us look at some factors that have a bearing on our ability to communicate across cultures.

Culture

Culture means many things to people. It can be defined as the sum total of one's living experiences or the way of life of a group of people. Culture is also the beliefs, values, attitudes, behaviors, and symbols that are accepted within a given society. Peter S. Adler[6] describes the development of culture in the following way:

> Nation, culture, and society exert tremendous influence on each of our lives, structuring our values, engineering our view of the world, and patterning our responses to experiences. No human being can hold himself apart from some form of cultural influence. No one is culture free. Yet, the conditions of contemporary history are such that we may now be on the threshold of a new kind of person who is socially and psychologically a product of the interweaving of cultures in the twentieth century. (p. 86)

Understanding People and Language

Cultures can be categorized as low-context or high-context; information that is inferred from the context of a message, not necessarily explicitly stated, is characteristic of high-context cultures such as Japan, Latin America and Arabic. In low-context cultures, context is less important; most information is spelled out explicitly. A few low-context cultures include North American, German, and Scandinavian.

Victor[7] points out that high- and low-context cultures value different kinds of communication and have different attitudes toward oral and written channels. Business communication practices in the United States reflect these low-context preferences.

Subcultures exist within various cultures. African-Americans, Hispanics, Latinos, Asians, etc. and females are a few of the subcultures present in the United States. Other subcultures can be Jews and Protestants, Northerners and Southerners, rural residents and urban residents.

Culture touches every aspect of our daily lives. It is often referred to as the thread that binds groups of people who share a common bond—our perceptions, our language, and our knowledge. Our perceptions are built upon our past, present, and future expectations of those around us and with whom we feel comfortable. Likenesses breed compatibility and convenience. We sometimes tend to imitate our parents because we learned from them initially; however, in actuality, many people tend to avoid imitating parents while retaining many values learned from parents.

Our knowledge is made up of life and educational experiences—it is the sum total of all that we know or have learned over time. Language, the words and/or symbols that we use to communicate, is the glue that binds nations, countries, and people together. Language, like art, is an expression of culture. More specifically, language can be thought of as a direct expression of the thought patterns common to a group of people. Thinking styles are different from country to country.

Cultural pluralism, the presence of nonnative Americans and immigrants, is certainly evident in the United States. All countries have their own pockets of people from different cultures. But the United States is truly atypical in that of all the different cultures that are represented, they each contribute to the cultural richness of this great country. One excellent example of cultural richness is the student body population at California State University, Los Angeles!

Accepting Cultural Differences

Now, what can you do to be a better communicator interculturally? The first step is to accept and respect cultural differences. People are unique; they come in different shapes, sizes, and shades. They all have the same desires and aspirations as most people do—a good life for their children and families. You must acknowledge your own assumptions of universality based on your own culture and experiences. Of utmost important is for you to know that a difference does NOT indicate a deficiency. More specifically, you can be enriched by this cultural diversity.

Ethnocentrism

Ethnocentrism is often referred to as the tendency of people to view all other people by using their own culture as a guide to interpreting others' values, customs, gesture, etc. Even in the United States and other foreign cultures, there are many differences within, between, and among groups of people. Ethnocentrics prefer to judge others based on their own cultural identities. To preserve the dignity of all individuals you encounter, you must recognize your own biases so you can deal with them and take appropriate, deliberate actions to change them. You will be respected by others when you show respect for them and their culture. You should be willing to tolerate the cultural mistakes of others. Learning to accept the beliefs, practices, and values of other cultures is really important.

Scenario: You have been asked to go abroad to one of four countries, China, Japan, Colombia, or Mexico to represent your company in a business transaction. What country will you choose? Are there factors you should before your departure that could affect international business communication?

Factors Affecting International Business Communication

While there are numerous books you could read to learn about various countries and the factors that affect communicating in the international environment, the literature purports that perceptions of time, space, clothing, gift giving, body chemistry, directness, management style, religious customs and laws, gender, education, and nonverbal communication are major factors that impact your ability to communicate successfully.

Time. Time, sometimes referred to by social scientists as "chronemics," is viewed differently among cultures. To Americans, time is money. They tend to be very time-conscious and are fervent about punctuality. They expect business meetings to begin on time. How would you respond to the question, "Does time revolve around you?" or "Do you revolve around time?" To emphasize this even more, answer the question "Do you have on a wristwatch?" When was the last time you looked at your watch or the clock? Time in some cultures, particularly Mexico, some parts of the Middle East (Arab countries), and some South American countries, is viewed in a casual manner as most of the businesspersons usually will not show up on time. However, the French expect punctuality but may make you wait so they can care resolve any other business beforehand so there are no interruptions during your meeting. The Japanese businesspeople feel it necessary to take as much time as possible to nurture business relationships and to establish trust. In the Latin American culture, their concept of time is that if it cannot be done today, there is always tomorrow.

Space. The word "proxemics" is used to refer to zones of territory in which people operate. How would you like to "breathe the breath of your conversant"? This would be most common and acceptable in Saudi Arabia. Americans demand space depending upon the situation and level of acquaintanceship. They feel most uncomfortable when crowded together in trains, buses, or elevators; but crowdedness is common in Latin America, the Middle East, China, Bangladesh, and Taiwan. In Japan, crowdedness on public transit is due to necessity, but their desirable social distance is larger than Americans.

Naturally, closeness is fine where intimacy is concerned, but you also have a need for personal space, usually 2 to 3 feet. This is called your comfort zone which is the distance between people who know and like each other. However, when you are in elevators, you may feel uncomfortable because your "bubble" (a distance of 18 inches) has been invaded. Your comfort zone varies with your social events, public events, and particularly business relationships. While foreigners may view Americans as cold and distant or aloof, Americans do not appreciate their "comfort zone" being invaded—at least without their consent. Your perceptions of space can impede your ability to communicate internationally if you are not aware of these differences in cultural perceptions of time.

Clothing. A businessperson needs to be knowledgeable about what is considered appropriate dress for men and women in foreign countries. This does not imply that he or she should adopt the native dress of that country but the businessperson should respect customs. For example, female soldiers during the 1991 Gulf War could not wear shorts in Saudi Arabia. The custom there demands that native women be clothed in the traditional black abayas and veils, which is a social more based upon modesty. In some countries, women must be covered from head to toe, with just their eyes showing. While business suits for men and women are appropriate in the United States and most European countries, other attire might be more appropriate in India, Hawaii, or Japan depending on their customs. As another example, Mrs. George Bush, wife of the former President of the United States, appeared on national television wearing Army fatigues while in the Middle East during the Gulf War crisis. While she was not engaging in a business transaction, she was engaging in public relations and observing the dress custom of that country. Before going to any foreign country, you should research the social norms of that country. Some social norms are presented next.

Social norms. The practice of shaking hands or kissing on the cheek as a form of greeting differs from country to country. Italians hug as a form of greeting. Japanese bow. Exchanging business cards is considered essential in China and Japan, and many other countries honor this practice. When presenting your business card, it should have the translation in the host country's language where you will be conducting business and, of course, the English translation on the other side. Presenting your business card with the foreign translation (that side up) is a way of showing respect and concern for successful interaction.

Gift giving. Gift giving is obligatory in some countries, and the status, age, timeliness, and position of the person receiving the gift determines the need as well as the price. For example, giving a gift on the first encounter may be considered undue influence or giving a gift after a deal is made may be considered a payment and therefore insulting.

Many of the gifts that are highly acceptable to another in the United States are inappropriate for other countries due to cultural differences. Flowers are a wonderful gift in American culture, but the color, type, and number of flowers presented to other cultures can cause problems. For example, in Japan, white flowers are for funerals while in Eastern Europe red flowers are used for funerals. In China, giving flowers or any other gift in any multiples of four are representative of death; however, giving an uneven number of white flowers in France would be acceptable. In Germany, flowers other than roses would be an acceptable gift for your host's wife. If you are doing business in some Middle East countries, it is not unusual for the business meeting to be at your host's home. In this case, it would be appropriate to bring an inexpensive gift for his children but not his wife as women have a submissive role.

You should be careful not to give gifts which are considered personal and intimate such as clothing, perfume, or red roses in France. Also, avoid giving liquor as a gift which may be illegal in some countries or giving items that are associated with death such as clocks in China. The best advice is for you to research the social customs of the country you are planning to visit before selecting and presenting a gift.

Body chemistry. Americans tend to neutralize body odors with antiperspirants, cologne, and/or perfume. Americans who have pungent body odors are considered unclean and others would avoid talking to them. However, in the Middle East countries, the more pungent the body odor, the more friendly and concerned the person is assumed to be. He or she truly wants the conversant to feel his or her presence by being overwhelmed with breathing one's breath and aroma.

Directness. Americans tend to be direct, that is, they get to the point so that time is not wasted. Thinking styles differ among genders, male and female, and among countries. American men are more direct than women who use a lot of qualifiers in getting their message across. For example, a male businessperson would say "How much of a price increase is anticipated?" while a female businessperson would say "I'd like to ask how much of a price increase is anticipated?" Although most leaders in the United States are direct, this American style of directness is considered rude in many countries.

Communication patterns—both oral and written—will differ as well. Japanese cultures typically begin conversations with a reference to the season of the year and/or to the weather before they get to the main point; Americans also use this technique to a certain extent.

Management style. Theory X and Theory Y management styles have long been practiced in American firms, but more and more companies are leaning to the participatory management style that involves people from all levels within an organization. Japan has been quite successful in this participatory decision-making style because it helps ensure success of any new business venture with the firm commitment of all individuals involved. For example, the decision to change the size of a computer would not be made by upper management only but the decision would be made by all levels of the organization. Along with management style comes the negotiation style which is directly affected by the way cultures view directness. Americans want to do business first and then develop the relationship later whereas the Japanese spend many hours socializing and getting to know the Americans before they begin business discussions. The Japanese are known for saving face; that is, they do not want either party in a business transaction to be embarrassed or shamed. They believe in the value of peace and harmony. The Japanese are known for using long periods of silence when dealing with the Americans since they know that American executives are uncomfortable with silence. For the American executive, it is best to simply repeat your position after a short period of silence and wait. However, the American executive can look forward to debating with the French to work out agreements and haggling over price with the Mexicans.

American businesspersons need to know that bribery is common and legal in many countries like Italy, Korea, Japan, Germany, the Middle East, Mexico, and some countries in Africa. Many U. S. companies have codes of ethics for decision making, but American business executives are certainly challenged with making difficult ethical decisions when trying to conduct business in the international arena.

Older people are accorded more respect due to their wisdom and experience in Japan, China, Vietnam, and Korea. So the elderly may be a part of the decision making in business transactions. In contrast, the United States, Germany, and Italy admire the energy of youth. Companies sending business executives to these countries to conduct business would do well to match negotiators with those of like status, age, and rank.

Religious customs and laws. In the United States, religion is mostly responsible for the many values, attitudes, and beliefs that Americans use as guides to acceptable behavior, work ethic, and work practices. U. S. business offices are closed on Saturday and Sunday in observance of religious worship; however, in other cultures such as Islam, Friday is the day of worship and business offices are closed on Thursday and Friday.

The Protestant work ethic is practiced for the most part in the United States and Europe; hard work and contribution to society are seen as admirable qualities in workers. Those who are lazy and shiftless are frowned upon which is why American society is experiencing welfare reform. Many Asian countries that follow the teachings of Confucious practice this work ethic. The Japanese practice of this work ethic is called Shinto.

Followers of Hindu and Buddhist religions are to have no desires for material possessions which in turn will cause them not to suffer, but this is quite the contrary to Americans who are motivated by personal achievement and increased salaries.

Religion often dictates what its followers can eat or drink based on cultures. Alcohol is forbidden in Islamic countries and drinking is a punishable offense. Jewish people do not eat pork, and some cultures raise dogs to eat as a delicacy while Hindus consider cows sacred. Research the laws and religion of the country you are visiting to make sure that you are not breaking its laws.

Gender. In many cultures, the male gender dominates while the female gender is submissive. The role of the business man or woman takes on a different perspective in view of this gender difference. In many Middle Eastern countries, women have low status; men do not take orders from women for to do so would make the men appear weak and emotional. In Saudi Arabia, women are forbidden to drive cars or ride bicycles. It would be useless for an American businesswoman to try to conduct business in Saudi Arabia as to do so would be breaking their law and she would not be accorded any respect. Unfortunately, the worth of women in the workplace is not as widely acceptable as it is in the United States. It must also be said that the American businesswoman is still trying to further penetrate the male-dominated upper echelon of management in the United States. Only higher education, training, experience, and equal opportunity will permit the American woman to move into upper management.

Education. The United States is dedicated to educating the masses of people. In general, individuals are usually able to obtain higher education provided they have the aptitude, desire, and the necessary resources. In other countries, such as Japan and the Middle East, only the "cream of the crop" are assured of higher education based upon rigorous, standardized tests. Student performance on these tests can bring either happiness or shame for the student's family. Also, women are not afforded the same opportunity for advanced education in some countries. As already indicated, in some countries the male gender reigns supreme.

National Factors

Two other national factors that you need to know about countries with whom you want to conduct business are the economics and politics of that country. While an indepth study may not be possible before visiting the country, exposure to the customs and the society is of utmost importance.

Standards of living vary from nation to nation, and prices are often controlled by governments or cartels and often a system of favors that other cultures call bribery. Concepts of democracy differ in interpretation; the business person needs an awareness of the politics of the country so as not to flaunt free will to do what he or she wants or to do what is customary in his or her home country. After all, politics has spawned many business relationships.

Nonverbal Communication

Nonverbal communication is sincere since it is unplanned and unconscious. When both verbal and nonverbal cues are present, the receiver will generally believe the nonverbal response. It is impossible not to communicate since we are constantly sending nonverbal messages. Nonverbal communication appears in three distinct forms: sign language, action language, and object language. Nonverbal communication can take the form of a smile, a nod, a hand gesture, a hug or kiss, a color, hand preference and eye contact. Bear in mind that gestures or nonverbal cues such as nodding your head to indicate "yes" or "no" are not universally recognized. Males in Latin America, southern Europe, and the Middle East typically hug and kiss each other on the cheeks as a form of greeting; however, such a greeting is not usually accorded a businessperson in America. In the United States, a long, lingering look is considered as having sexual, sensual overtones.

Arabs disapprove of using their left hand to take food from a serving dish as to do so is considered unclean. What does the left-handed person do in such a situation?

Perceptions influence color preferences. The color "red" in German cultures is associated with death. White is the color for mourning in some Eastern cultures rather than black as in the United States. However, "red" is the color for weddings in China and white is the color for brides in Europe.

People from some cultures maintain profound or piercing eye contact which is normal; however, such intense eye contact can be very uncomfortable to outsiders. Eye contact is necessary in American culture as it indicates believeability. Latin American and Asian cultures avoid direct eye contact to show respect for the person speaking.

Communicating Interculturally and Internationally

In exchanging thoughts and meanings with other cultures, problems arise in the literal translation of English into a foreign language. In some cases, there is no word equivalent in the foreign language. It has been said that foreigners have a better understanding of the English language than the spoken English language. Perhaps, this is because it is easier to learn to "read" the words than to carry on a dialogue. In written communication, American writers follow a standard format—a memo, a letter, or a report. Each of these formats is distinctive. Letters written by writers in the United States tend to be short, personal, direct, and informal. Use of the you-attitude is evident in most written communications. Japanese letters tend to be longer, indirect, formal and flattering; these differences suggest the cultural perceptions of people.

Often in oral communication with other foreign cultures, an interpreter is needed. When using an interpreter, you should use short, simple phrases and sentences, practice verbal communications with the interpreter, and request backtranslation of your oral and written messages.

Telex was once the most common method used to send written communications abroad, but the fax machine is now the predominant method. Approximately 60 percent of the letters coming from foreign countries are written in English, and over 95 percent of 100 companies surveyed engaged in international business reveal their business letters to other countries are written in English.

In reference to the value of culture and its impact on communication, review the following letter written in English, Japanese, Chinese, Korean, and Spanish. What differences are evident? What is your perception of the communication?

Japanese

ＭＧＭＴ３０１の学生の皆さん、

「経済とコミュニケーション」のコースへようこそ。そして、カリフォルニア州立大学にいらっしゃった事をとても感謝しています。

この手紙は、皆さんとの交流と相互理解の土台を築く手掛かりとして、皆さんの母国語で書かせていただきました。

皆さんが、自分の専門分野や個人的な生活においても充分目的を果たしてすばらしい成果を修められるように、どうか、このクラスで最善を尽くして頑張ってください。期待しています。

将来あなたが経済界で成功するためには、話す事と書く事の両方に秀でている事が不可欠です。こうしたコミュニケーションの技術を磨くために、このクラスはもとより、キャンパス内図書館二階に設けられているライティングスキル・センター等を大いに利用してください。勿論、ＭＧＭＴ３０１のインストラクターも、あなたの目的達成のために喜んでお手伝い致します。

この授業が皆さんにとって楽しく、且つ、実り豊かな経験の場となりますように、祈っています。

Marguerite P. Joyce

マルゲリッテ・Ｐ・ジョイス博士

Chinese

亲爱的管理学301 的同学们:

欢迎参加这门商务交流课程，并感谢你选择了加州州立大学洛杉矶分校。

这封信是用你的母语- - 中文写成的，旨在建立良好的关系，以及对文化的尊重和意识。

你在管理学301课程中 应该尽最大的努力，从而实现你的职业和个人目标。杰出的交流技巧，无论是口语还是写作，在未来的商务生涯的成功中都是十分重要的。请利用这门课程和本校园所提供的机会和设施，例如座落在图书馆二楼的写作技巧中心，来帮助你提高交流技巧。你的管理学301指导老师随时愿意帮助你来实现这个目标。

真诚祝愿你在这门商务交流课程中能够获得愉快，成功的经历。

此致敬礼!

Marguerite P. Joyce
Joyce 博士
作者

Korean

MGMT 301 학생께,

저희 Business Communication 코스에 들어오신 것을 환영하며, Cal. State LA를 선택하신 것에 대해서도 감사드립니다.

이 편지를 귀하의 모국어인 한글로 보내는 것은 우호적인 관계와 문화적인 동질성과 의식을 확립하기 위한 것입니다.

MGMT301 수업을 통해 최선을 다하시고, 그리하여 귀하의 직업이나 개인적인 목표들에 보다 전진 하실 수 있기를 바랍니다.

이 과목을 수강하는 동안, 학교 내의 많은 시설물들, 특히, 도서관 2층에 자리한 Writing Center 등을 이용하신다면 여러분의 영어실력을 늘리는데 도움이 될 것입니다. 또한, MGMT 301 강사진이 늘 귀하의 목표를 이루는데 도움을 주고자 합니다.

이 Business Comunication 코스에서 가능한 많은 것들을 얻고 즐기실 수 있길를 기원합니다.

Dr. Marguerite P. Joyce

Author

Spanish

Queridos estudiantes de Management 301

Bienvenidos a este curso de comunicacion de negocios, y gracias por escoger a Cal State LA.

Esta carta esta escrita en su lengua nativa, espanol, para establecer un sentido de relacion, empatia cultural, y conocimiento.

Estas animado para hacer lo mejor en esta clase de Management 301 para que puedas sobresalir en tus metas personales y profesionales.

Excelentes abilidades en comunicacion --oral y escritas--son requeridas para un futuro exitoso en el mundo de negocios.

Toma ventaja de todas las muchas oportunidades disponibles en este curso y en la universidad como en el centro de Writing Skills, localizado en el segundo piso de la libreria, para ayudarte a mejorar tus abilidades de comunicacion. Tu instructor de Management 301 esta disponible para ayudarte en lograr tus metas.

Con los mejores deseos para un divertido y exitosa experiencia en este curso de comunicacion de negocios.

Sinceramente,

Dr. Marguerite P. Joyce
Autora

Dear MGMT 301 Student

Welcome to this Business Communication course, and thank you for choosing Cal State LA.

This letter is written in your native language, English, to establish a sense of relationship, cultural empathy, and awareness.

You are encouraged to do your best in this MGMT 301 class so you may excel in your professional and personal career goals.

Excellent communication skills—both oral and written—are required for your future success in the business world.

Take advantage of the many opportunities available in this course and on campus such as the Writing Skills Center, 2nd Floor of the Library, to help improve your communication skills. Your MGMT 301 instructor is available to help you in achieving your goals.

Best wishes for an enjoyable and successful experience in this Business Communication course.

Sincerely

Marguerite P. Joyce

Dr. Marguerite P. Joyce
Author

Speaking to International Audiences

Dulek and Fielder[8] lists the following guidelines in making presentations:

1. Make a formal presentation (with quality graphic aids). (You want to be professional.)
2. Speak slowly and clearly (apply text across cultures). (You want to adapt your references to the audience.)
3. Interject words and phrases in language of listeners. (You can show you cared enough about your presentation that you learned a few important words in the language of the listeners.)
4. Study nonverbal cues beforehand so as not to misinterpret gestures. (Some cultures may appear to be asleep during your presentation or talk in their native language or look at the floor.)
5. Adapt your presentation to mindset of the listener. (You should make presentation according to expectations; take frequent breaks and slow the sales pitch.)
6. Send information about your company before going to make a formal presentation. (You want to establish trust.)

7. Match rank, age, and gender of presenter to foreign audience. (Some cultures revere age and experience.)
8. Be conscious of your body language and tone of voice. (When foreign audiences are unfamiliar with speaker's language, nonverbal cues take on more importance.)

Writing to International Audiences

When writing to international audiences, you should write in English unless you know the country's language. Remember that the appeals and benefits you use to motivate U. S. audiences may not work on international audiences.

Locker[9] says that business people from Europe and Japan who correspond frequently with North America are beginning to adopt U. S. directness and patterns of organization. Since the Fax is being used widely for messages sent abroad, be sure to use a 12–point type.

Dulek and Fielder (1990) list the following guidelines for writing to international audiences:

1. Determine the culture status of the country, that is, if it is low- or high-context. (It is not necessary to put everything in writing.)
2. Know the hierarchial power structure between you and your readers. (Long letters are interpreted as showing respect.)
3. Adapt your writing style to preferences of the culture. (In low-context culture, more informal written communication takes place.)
4. Use precise wording; avoid cliches and slang.
5. Enclose translation in reader's language when possible. (This shows consideration and smart business sense on your part.)

American companies share written communication most frequently with Japanese, French, English, and Spanish-speaking firms. This is, of course, due to the present trade imports and export agreements permitted among various countries. Have you ever wondered how many people speak English or to what extent the English language is preferred?

Foreign Language Study

Foreigners study English worldwide, but few Americans know more than their own native language. Consider the following facts about the quest to use English which is considered the language of international business as stated by Terpstra and David[10]:

1. Over three hundred million people use English as a primary language.
2. Six hundred and fifty million people use English as a second language.
3. English is spoken, written, and broadcast on every continent.
4. English is the official language in 29 countries.
5. About three-fourths of the world's mail is written in English.
6. One half of the world's newspapers are printed in English.

7. English is the language of three-fifths of the world's radio stations.
8. English is the most widely studied language in the countries in which it is not native.

These statistics were presented to increase your knowledge of how widespread the use of the English language continues to be. Wouldn't it be great if some day similar statistics could be given for French, Mandarin, Spanish, etc.?

Do you know a language other than your own native language? Are you willing to learn a foreign language other than your own? While foreigners are willing to learn the English language, Americans in general are not willing to learn other foreign languages. The number of United States students in elementary or secondary schools who are studying a foreign language has decreased greatly, and the numbers do not appear too great in the colleges and universities either. For example, many elective subjects have been reduced to a minimal; in some instances, a foreign language is not considered essential for admission to many colleges or universities. When foreign languages are offered at the elementary or secondary level, only the gifted students are allowed to take them. Just as members of other cultures are willing to learn the English language, we should at least make an attempt to learn other languages as well.

Preparation for Working Abroad

The sincere businessperson will research all the factors discussed in this chapter to ensure a successful business transaction in the country abroad. Having done your research, you will feel more confident, objective, and accepting of cultural differences.

Learning More about Cultures

CULTURGRAMS offer four-page overviews on each of 102 countries. The CULTURGRAMS are udpated annually. The 1991 price was $40 (U.S.) You can write or call:

Brigham Young University
The David M. Kennedy Center for International Studies
Publication Services
280 HRCB
Provo, UT 84602
801/378–6528

Learning More about International Business

Write or visit the U. S. and Foreign Communication Service. It has offices in 68 cities in the United States as well as international offices in 67 countries. This office offers advice about exports, market research, and sales opportunities.

You may want to write the embassy of a specific country or region you are planning to visit or visit the Web site of various countries.

Some Cross-Cultural Resources

COMMUNICATING WITH CUSTOMERS AROUND THE WORLD, Chan-Herur, ISBN 1–885269–18–8
KISS, BOW, OR SHAKE HANDS, Morrison, et al., ISBN 1–55850–444–3
GOING GLOBAL, Taylor and Webber, ISBN 0–670–86308–4
DOING BUSINESS WITH JAPANESE MEN, Brannen and Wilen, ISBN 1–880656–04–3
MEGATRENDS ASIA, Naisbitt, ISBN 0684–81542–7

References

1. Herta A. Murphy and Herbert W. Hildebrandt, "International and Intercultural Communication," EFFECTIVE BUSINESS COMMUNICATIONS, 6th ed., McGraw-Hill, Inc. 1991.
2. Linda McCallister and Constance S. Bates, "Language as a Proxy for the Study of Culturally based Managerial Value: An Analysis of German and American Expressions," in Proceedings, 51st ABC International Convention (Los Angeles: Association for Business Communication, 1986), p. 68.
3. Retha H. Kilpatrick, "International Business Communication Practices," JOURNAL OF BUSINESS COMMUNICATION, 21, No. 4, (Fall, 1984), p. 33–34.
4. Vern Terpstra and Kenneth David, THE CULTURAL ENVIRONMENT OF INTERNATIONAL BUSINESS, 2nd., South-Western Publishing Company, 1985, p. 32.
5. Deborah C. Andrews and William D. Andrews, TEACHING BUSINESS COMMUNICATION: The International Dimension, 2nd ed., prepared by Linda Beamer, MacMillan Publishing Company, 1992, p. 2.
6. Peter S. Adler, "Beyond Cultural Identity: Reflections on Cultural and Multicultural Man," in International Communications: A Reader, 2nd ed., edited by Larry A. Samovar and Richard E. Porter, (Belmont, CA: Wadsworth, 1976), p. 362.
7. David Victor, 1992.
8. Ronald E. Dulek and John S. Fielden, PRINCIPLES OF BUSINESS COMMUNICATION, MacMillan Publishing Company, New York: 1990, p. 429–437.
9. Kitty O. Locker, BUSINESS AND ADMINISTRATIVE COMMUNICATION, Irwin, 1995.
10. Vern Terpstra and Kenneth David, THE CULTURAL ENVIRONMENT OF INTERNATIONAL BUSINESS, 2nd, South-Western Publishing Company, 1985, p. 32.

Discussion Questions

Intercultural Issues: A Problem-Based Approach

(These cases were presented by Dr. S. Paul Verluyten, Universiteit Antwerpen, Belgium, at the ABC International Convention in November 1991 in Hononlulu, Hawaii.)

1. On the occasion of a visit by a government minister to the Zairese town where your company is located, the mayor requests the use of the company's flagship car, a brand new Mercedes 500 SEL, for two weeks, without compensation. Do you accept this request?

2. Your company stands an excellent chance of getting the contract to build a new hospital in a Middle Eastern counntry, but you know you won't get it if you don't lavishily pay those who are to make the decision; this is obviously illegal in your own country. What will you do?

3. The best negotiator in your American company also speaks very fluent French. He is a vegetarian and never drinks alcohol, wine, or beer. Will you send him to France to negotiate a contract for your firm?

4. You represent a French company which has developed a CAD/CAM system for the production of interior car upholstery. You have sold a similar system to a French car manufacturer. Now you attempt to sell a similar system to the Japanese car manufacturer Mitsubishi.

   Your first contacts with Mitsubishi went smoothly, and now you have been invited to come to Japan and explain the advantages of the system you propose. However, conversations with the 12 Japanese who attend your presentation appear to be stalling. One after another, they fall asleep while you are speaking. All the time, some of them are listening; but others are taking a nap. How do your react after this has been going on for a few days with no apparent progress being made?

   Case #5 submitted by M. Joyce.

5. You manufacture a product that has several side effects. Some of the side effects from consumption of the product are known to cause severe abdominal distress and perhaps even death in infants. Your country will not give you clearance to sell the product; however, you know that in underdeveloped countries the market is wide open. You could sell the product for a modest cost and reap huge profits. How would you proceed?

Questions

1. What are three factors that have made the world appear smaller?
2. Why does international trade take place?
3. Discuss the importance of global awareness as it relates to competition.
4. Who are the leading U.S. trading partners? Is the number of trading partners expected to increase?
5. What recent events have occurred in regard to globalization and international trade?
6. Explain the word "culture."
7. Perceptions are reflective of culture. Give examples of this concept.
8. What is language?
9. Are there cultural differences evident in your workplace? In your classroom?
10. In how many countries is English the official language?
11. Gender roles are evident in some countries. How does this impact communication?
12. Does a difference in a person's makeup indicate that the person is deficient in some aspect?
13. Closeness or crowdedness is evident in what countries? Have you visited any of these countries? How did you feel?
14. Consider the statement: Ethnocentrism can be misguiding. Why or Why not?
15. What is meant by low-context cultures and high-context cultures and give examples.
16. You are told you will be working at a branch office abroad. What will you do to prepare yourself?

APPLICATIONS

1. Write two sentences in English and ask a person of another culture to translate them into his or her native language. Does the translation convey the same meaning?
2. Interview two people from another culture to find out what things you should know BEFORE going to visit their countries.
3. How would you describe an "American" to a person from another country?
4. Ask students from another culture to describe their views of Americans.
5. Research the role of gender, politics, and laws of a country of your choice (India, Saudi Arabia, China, Panama, Japan, or Nigeria) and present your findings in a report to the class. (This could be a group assignment.)
6. Interview a soldier or business person who has spent some time in a foreign country and report his or her experiences to the class.
7. Ask a foreign language instructor how he or she became interested in the language he or she teaches.
8. What kind of international job opportunities exist in your chosen profession?
9. Contrast the management style of the United States versus another foreign country. Present your findings in an oral report to the class.
10. Make a list of benefits and drawbacks based on your gender that you would find if you were going to conduct business in the Middle East or Japan.
11. Write a memo to the instructor in which you list the factors he or she needs to know before visiting your home country if other than the United States.
12. Select five countries other than your own; then list ten words you feel are necessary for communicating and or survival. Include the foreign translation for each English word.

Name ________________________________ Date __________

JEOPARDY QUIZ #3

1. The answer is: The sum total of one's living experiences.

   What is ________________________________?

2. The answer is: Japan, Latin America, and Arabic infer information from the context of the message.

   What are ________________________________?

3. The answer is: Jews, females, Latinos are reflective of this culture.

   Who are ________________________________?

4. The answer is: The latest two countries that now have trade agreements with the United States?

   What are ________________________________?

5. The answer is: I judge people based on my own culture.

   What is ________________________________?

6. The answer is: Employees from all levels are involved in this management style.

   What is ________________________________?

7. The answer is: A country that is dedicated to educating the masses of people.

   What is ________________________________?

8. The answer is: The most predominant method of sending written communication abroad.

   What is ________________________________?

9. The answer is: A language that is spoken, written and broadcast on every continent.

   What is ________________________________?

continued

10. The answer is: Eye contact is necessary in this culture for believeability.

    What is ______________________________?

CHAPTER 4

Dr. Doris Christopher, Professor Computer Information Systems

Communication Technology

Objectives

After reading the chapter and doing the exercises, you should be able to:

1. Trace the methods of how we communicate in a technological environment.
2. Distinguish the difference between the word processor and the microcomputer.
3. State one's perference for workstation equipment and software.
4. Explain the basic software programs a person needs to be able to use in the business arena.
5. Discuss the changes, trends, and issues in software development.
6. Describe the use of telecommunications and its role in business.
7. Explain three types of teleconferencing.
8. Describe the importance of fiber optics and its impact on technology as we approach the 21st century.
9. Discuss the health hazards relative to using technology in the office.
10. Trace the steps involved in the electronic communication process—both orally and in writing.
11. Discuss the difference between LANS and WANS.
12. Describe the purpose of writing analysis software.
13. Discuss the use of outsourcing and its impact on employees.

By its very nature, technology changes the nature of business activities. The advent of the time clock, the telephone, the computer, facsimile, and the Internet have changed the relationship between people and business functions.

Early Communications Methods

In retrospect, let us begin our journey from the traditional office to the office of today. Oral communication was done face-to-face; a message was given to one person to be delivered verbally and physically to another. Or the oral message was given to a runner who ran to the location to deliver the message. With the development of the telephone, oral communication was much easier if not faster. Our written communication developed from writing on stone tablets to the quill pen and paper, talkwriter, and now to the computer screen.

The 1800s saw the development of major technologies emerge such as the telegraph which permitted communication by wire, and the typewriter which certainly improved the quality and speed of written communication. Then came the manual typewriter which certainly improved the quality and speed of written communication. First, there was the manual typewriter, the electric typewriter followed by the electronic typewriter. Electronic typewriters had a memory and could display text before printing. The telephone revolutionized the oral communication process and has had an impact on communication media today.

The early 1900s brought about an acceleration of communication technology, specifically radio and television, dictating machines and duplicating processes—mimeographing, dittoing, and photocopying. The traditional office generally featured an executive assisted by a secretary who used a typewriter. The secretary was skilled in taking dictation, typing, filing, scheduling appointments, screening calls, greeting visitors, handling mail, etc. The secretary in essence typed the correspondence which the executive signed. The original signed letter was sent to the addressee and a copy of the letter was made for the office file; this was virtually a paper shuffling process.

Advent of the Microcomputer

The most important technology which has swept through business, academia, and our personal lives is the personal computer, the microcomputer, notebook/laptop computer, and personal digital assistants. To distinguish between the word processor and the personal computer, let us begin by stating that the word processor is a dedicated machine that permits word processing only. The microcomputer allows performance of a variety of functions—word processing, spreadsheets, graphics, database management, telecommunications, presentation design, desktop publishing, videoconferencing, e-mail, etc.

Technology exists to make our jobs easier; we need to work "smarter." The microcomputer cannot only process words; it can also process data. Microcomputers are small enough to sit on a desk, on your lap (laptop computer), or fit in a briefcase. Because of their versatility and declining cost, they are a major part of today's business communication technology which brings us up to the office of today—the executive work station. The executive work station has a desk, a keyboard, monitor, computer, a fax/copy machine, and a printer; the computer and printer may be linked with other computers in the company or to the company's main computer. The user accesses databases or information for decision making. It has been stated that by the year 2010, the ratio of microcomputers to people will be 3:1—a microcomputer at work, at home, and a laptop computer. Perhaps you have already reached this stage!

Software Advancements

Advancements in software have also contributed to the flexibility and ease of use of the microcomputer. Software programs make it possible to use a microcomputer without having the programming knowledge that was required in the 1960s. In a survey of top management executives, they recommended that students be able to *use word processing, spreadsheet, data base and graphics* software programs *prior* to seeking business employment. (Joyce, 1994) Businesses expect students to be users of technology and software programs in order to increase their productivity. Imagine how much money an entrepreneur can save if he or she were skilled in all these software programs and had a microcomputer with a laser printer?

Popular software programs on the market today are listed in Figure 4.1.

Buying an integrated software program (which has word processing, spreadsheet, graphics, data base, and telecommunications) will reduce costs for the entrepreneur as well. Of special interest is the desktop publishing arena which permits the merging of text and graphics in order to produce professional-looking flyers, documents, or reports at one's desk.

Telecommunication

Telecommunication is the electronic use of communication in which technology is used to signal information long distances through coaxil cables, telephone lines, microwave and/or satellites. Transmission in telecommunication starts with decoding your message,

Word Processing: WordPerfect, Microsoft Word, etc.
Spreadsheet: Lotus 1–2–3, Excel, Quattro Pro, etc.
Graphics: Harvard Graphics, Freelance, Powerpoint, etc.
Data Base Management: Microsoft ACCESS, Foxbase, etc.
Telecommunications: Procomm, Eudora, Netscape, etc.
Desktop Publishing: Quarkbase Xpress, Ventura, Pagemaker, Microsoft Publisher, etc.
Presentation Software: Powerpoint, Draw Perfect, etc.
Web Software: HTLM Editor webpage, Front Page, HotDog Pro, PageMill, etc.
Web Browsers: Internet Browser, Netscape Browser, Internet Explorer, etc.

Figure 4.1. Popular Software Packages

Surprise

Congratulation Party for
Dr. Carol Blaszczynski

Date:
Thursday, May 15,1997

Time:
12:00 p.m. to 2:00 p.m. (lunch will be served at 12:10 p.m.)

Location:
ALMANSOR COURT
700 SOUTH ALMANSOR ST.
ALHAMBRA, CA. 91801

NAME:___________

___ Yes, I plan to attend. Here is my check for $23.50 (which includes a contribution to a gift. Please make check(s) payable to Marguerite P. Joyce)

Entree:
Chicken___________OR
Beef___________

___No, I cannot attend, but I would like to give a contribution of $_____ toward the gift.

Figure 4.2. An Example of a Desktop Published Flyer

transmitting the message, receiving the message, storing the message, retrieving the stored message, and decoding the message.

Telecommunications, of course, may eventually reduce the need or eliminate the need for paper shuffling. Telecommunications software has a number of features, one is electronic mail and another is facsimile (Fax). Electronic mail (e-mail) refers to the sending of messages through a communications network such as by dedicated telephone line, telegraph, radio, or satellite. One can send a message by computer to another computer (locally or distantly). The message can be read on screen at the terminal or printed as a hard copy. Electronic mail provides both speed and accuracy in message transfer.

Facsimile

Facsimile is a machine that scans the printed word, picture, charts, etc., converts the information into electronic impulses, and sends the impulses by telephone to a facsimile receiver. The receiver fax converts the impulses into the original print or graphic form. While faxed documents are fast and relatively inexpensive, the documents are not usually acceptable in a court of law. Also, depending upon the quality of the paper used for the faxed copy, the text or graph may fade over time. Numerous advancements in the refinement of fax equipment have diminished these drawbacks. Business messages are faxed daily. Additionally, food orders are often faxed to restaurants, and faxing one's picture and biography to another is often called computer dating. Still, there are other uses of the fax machine.

Voice-Activated Computer

Another recent development in communication devices is the voice-activated computer, commonly called a talkwriter. Voice-activation refers to having computers respond to one (dependent) or more (independent) human voices. In voice activation, voice sounds are converted into computer signals. With a person "speaking" into a receiver/microphone of the computer and a computer "listening," the communication process occurs.

Speech recognition equipment then changes the voice (sound in the form of airwaves) called analog signals into digital form (stored digital signals). If the computer finds a match between analog and digital signals, it responds by changing digital messages back into analog (voice) signals for screen and/or actual voice reply. Although the voice-activated computer is a technology being refined, its use may rise more as text errors are reduced and the ability to maintain message confidentially is assured. The voice-activated computer has the possibility for eliminating keyboarding skill.

Teleconferencing can be used as a means to conduct meetings with people at distant locations. Three forms of teleconferencing include audioconferencing, computer conferencing, and videoconferencing. Audioconferencing permits a small number of participants to converse by the telephone. Three or more people are connected at one time; all can hear and can talk. Computer conferencing allows participants (who need not be present at the same time) to communicate through their computer terminals and respond at their own convenience. As business travel expense continues to rise, business executives are taking advantage of video

Computing with the power of speech

IBM VoiceType Family

Realizing the power of the spoken word
Since the first non-typist sat at a keyboard to work through a document, people have wished for a computer they could talk to, so they could work as fast as they could think...and think wherever they wanted to work... creating text quickly, naturally, and accurately–just by talking.

With the IBM VoiceType™ family of products, thousands of people around the world are computing with the power of speech. Thanks to IBM's proven, industrial-strength VoiceType technology and today's personal computers, people in a wide variety of occupations are realizing the benefits of affordable, highly accurate speech recognition systems.

IBM VoiceType products have innumerable practical uses in everyday business and professional work. As they evolve, these solutions will continue to offer even more power, control and ease of use. VoiceType can make a real and positive difference in your personal productivity–and the productivity of everyone in your organization–by allowing you to focus on what you need to do, not how you're doing it.

Talk your way to greater productivity
With IBM VoiceType, people who are not proficient at typing or who have never learned to type at all–or those who can't use a keyboard–can get work done quickly and efficiently, simply by talking instead of typing. Even people who are used to typing can minimize repetitive motions–or combine dictation with their keyboard and mouse. IBM VoiceType can benefit just about anyone, in almost every field, including:

- Business and Industry
- Health Care
- Law
- Journalism
- Government and Education

Now, you can work anywhere and anytime you like–after business hours... in the field...at the kitchen table... in your hotel room. All you need is a desktop or portable computer and IBM VoiceType to:

- Dictate reports
- Compose e-mail and other correspondence
- Write documents
- Fill in forms and templates
- Manage routine desktop tasks.

The IBM VoiceType advantage
IBM VoiceType's exclusive speech recognition technology delivers significant and unique advantages. IBM VoiceType actually "listens" and "learns" as you speak. One. Word. At. A. Time. Then, as if by magic, your words appear on your PC screen.

As you speak each word individually and precisely, the system distinguishes your personal speaking style and inflections, enabling it to become more proficient over time. In fact, customers frequently tell us that the system delivers close to 100% accuracy on a regular basis. As VoiceType listens to your speech, it matches your words to the

Figure 4.3. A picture of a person using voice-activated software which works in conjunction with a word processing software program. IBM produces a voice-activated software program.

conferencing which enables the participants to hear and see one another on television monitors. This simulates a real meeting, and videotapes of meetings can be made and kept for record purposes.

Networks

Local and wide area networks are used to e-mail and/or fax a document. More and more communication is transmitted through the computer medium via LANS or WANS.

Networking consists of two or more computers (intelligent devices) linked together to share information as shown in Figure 4.4.

The use of fiber optics, microwaves, and satellites will change the present office. People will be communicating at the speed of light. The workstation will need to produce voice, data, and video applications.

The hardware necessary to transmit this type of information includes:

hard drive (200+ megabytes)
fast processor (32–bit)
CD Rom for accessing stores voice, data and/or video information
sound board
modem modulator-demodulator that converts analog to signals to digital and vice versa
high resolution color monitor to produce on screen graphics and video animation
serial port or network interface
mouse device

The software required for this multimedia environment include:

operating system (DOS, OS/2, UNIX
communication software (for local and wide area network)
device driver software (e.g.) disk drivers, mouse)
graphical user interface (e.g. windows)
applications software packages that your operating system environment can access and process

Communication Revolution

Today's efficient communicators do not use pen and paper to draft a message. They input at the computer, revise, edit, and print out the final copy. It is obvious that people who continue to use pen and paper to write or draft communications are not nearly as productive as those who use technology to their advantage. It is hoped that you have learned or will be taught a word processing software package that will enable you to become a productive writer. As a prospective business executive, your time will be precious; therefore, you will

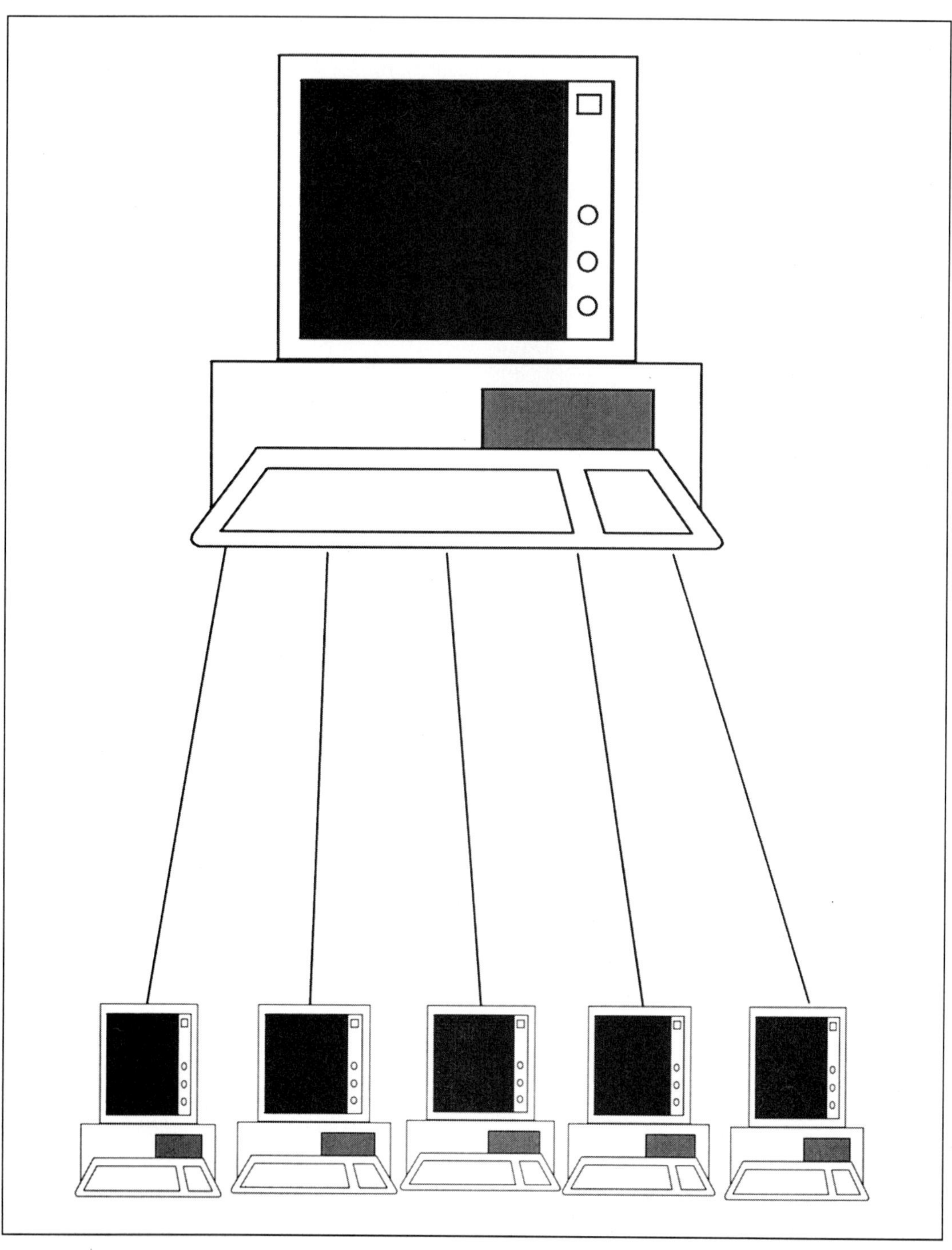

Figure 4.4. An Example of Networked Computers

want to use it wisely and productively. Ideally, as a business writer, you should have a workstation. The information age has ushered in many technological advances. As an end user, you should be aware of the continuous changes evolving, especially with microcomputers.

Workstation Health Problems

Utilizing the microcomputer consistently may cause physical problems if not used correctly. When inputting documents, take frequent breaks to rest the eyes, arms, and body. Extended use of the microcomputer may result in health hazards such as radiation emitted from the back and side of the monitor which may be harmful to pregnant mothers. However, special aprons that retard radiation emission do offer some protection for pregnant mothers who use the microcomputer in the performance of their tasks.

As users of microcomputers, you should consult the Occupational Safety and Health Act (OSHA) guidelines regarding users' entitlements. San Francisco, California, earlier passed the first comprehensive legislation which mandates safety guidelines for users of microcomputers and company responsibility. This legislation has implications for users of microcomputers nationwide.

Types of Documents Produced

Business communication tasks result in some kind of support or document. Any one or all of the following can easily be produced and professional looking using communication technology:

1. a memo or memo to the file
2. a letter
3. a report
4. a printed form
5. a table, chart, or graph
6. a news release, press release, or newsletter
7. a proposal
8. a promotion campaign
9. a brochure
10. a documentation of facts or position

Communication technology has revolutionized the way we create, store, edit, and retrieve information. As companies downsize, layoffs are imminent. Many middle-management positions have been eliminated; thus more and more communication tasks and duties are being assumed and/or thrust upon others. The traditional employees pyramid has now changed to a diamond shape as shown in Figure 4.5. Notice that the clerical and secretarial level has shrunken in size. As can be inferred from Figure 4.5, the need for clerical and secrectarial support staff to do tasks relative to document composing and editing has decreased. Naturally, professional and technical personnel will need to do their own composing and editing.

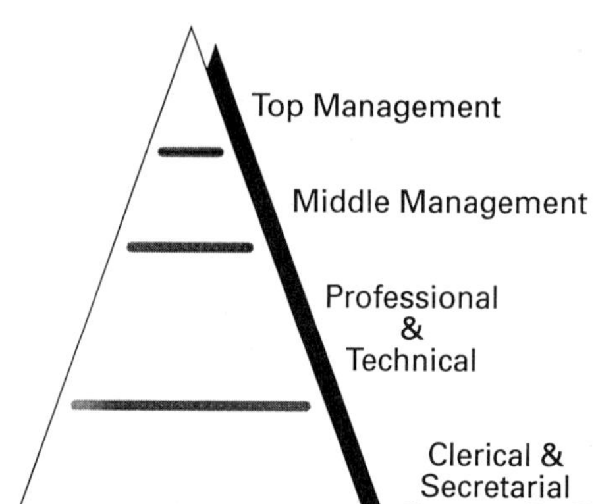

Figure 4.5. Workforce Schema

Document Origination

One method used to transform a composed message into finished form is the typewriter. The manual typewriter is still being used in some schools and companies although most organizations would not want it known. Electric typewriters and electronic typewriters are widely used. The automatic typewriter (MTST and Flexowriter) made its debut earlier in the 1960s, but this typewriter has been replaced with dedicated word processors and microcomputers or computer terminals linked to a network or mainframe. A network called LAN (local area network) or WAN (wide area network) permits the sharing of files, software, and peripherals (fileservers and printers). The network is simply a series of communication devices connected to cables to link computers and transfer information.

The microcomputer or electronic typewriter makes it easier for you to input (compose) messages, to use different highlighting features (bold or underline), or to personalize the document. All of these features can be viewed on the screen or monitor before producing a hard copy.

Document Reproduction

Companies need documentation of communications sent whether it is a memo, a letter, or a report. Carbon paper was used for many years to make one or more copies of documents. Today, carbonless copy sets are readily available. Perhaps you have completed a number of such forms if you have sought a loan, bought a house or car, signed a contract, etc. As a business professional, you will need to provide copies of your communication documents to subordinates or superiors.

The photo copier is used practically in all businesses as the device for reprographics—making multiple copies. Frequently, the print mode can be used for making multiple copies as well.

With desktop publishing software available, some companies are electing to produce their own annual reports, brochures, and newsletters rather than absorb the high printing costs associated with using professional printing companies which use phototypesetting equipment and/or offset printing equipment.

Document Distribution

The writer can hand carry the document or message to the receiver. Interoffice mail can be used to distribute the document if the company is rather large and has a mail room. Naturally, the United States Postal Service, and its competing centers, is the largest and perhaps the best-known physical delivery system. The U. S. Postal Service has issued guidelines for addressing envelopes so that the mail sorters can categorize mail by zip code which is then sorted by optical character readers (OCRs). While the U. S. Postal Service is widely used and the cost for a first-class letter is 32 cents, other competing agencies or message delivery services are available.

These services guarantee fast delivery or lower rates for parcels or bulk packages.

Document Transmission

Messages can be transmitted electronically over telephone wires and satellites. Such devices include teletypewriters, telegrams, mailgrams, electronic mail, and fax. All of these devices are based on the principle of sending documents coded electronically over telephone lines for later conversion to paper format. Document transmission makes it easy for the messenger to send messages at his or her convenience, when transmission channels are less crowded, and when rates are lowest.

Document Storage

Document storage is needed in every organization as documents must be saved for future reference or for later distribution. While the proverbial file cabinet has been used for decades and still is for document storage, the computer revolution has brought about the capability of storing information on magnetic disks, tapes, and cards. Even video recordings and audio recordings of important meetings, telephone conversations, and special events such as weddings are now possible with magnetic and laser technology.

Micrographic equipment is also being used by companies with vast files of information. Pages of documents are reproduced in miniature on microfilm and then viewed using a microfilm viewer. Naturally, using microfilm and magnetic computer disks save space. Concerns have been voiced about the authenticity of documents in this form in court proceedings.

Some companies continue to store paper documents on site as well as offsite in fireproof vaults. While this is for added protection of important documents, this does reflect the desire to have physical copies of documents readily available for self-assurance. This desire negates the earlier proposed concept of the paperless office.

Telecommunication

The telephone has long been used to convey messages. In fact, to reduce the paper explosion, it is sometimes suggested that telephone calls be made when appropriately based on the message content and urgency of the message. Telephone calls speed communication. Telephone technology certainly has improved calling services from rotary dial to push button. Callers can be put on hold while you answer other incoming calls, or you can forward them to another location, signal or alert the called person by an intercom system.

The latest telephone feature includes voice messaging which gives the calling party options for services needed by pressing a number. Of course, the calling party must have a push button phone or the calling party must stay on the line and an operator will answer.

Another feature is the ISDN (integrated services digital network) which flashes the phone number on your computer screen of the incoming call, company, and agent. ISDN is an individual network which allows you to customize the call by saying: "Good morning Mr. Mays; How may I help you?"

Teleconferencing facilities also make use of video equipment; telephones or computers are linked to meeting participants in other locations to allow them to transmit messages and documents electronically.

Electronic Office

Figure 4.6 is representative of what you can expect to see and use in the office of today. The electronic office permits the transmitting of information electronically rather than by paper, but it also represents faster access to data, faster response to customers' needs or complaints, faster reaction to competitors' actions and to recent developments in the field. The electronic office will help you become a productive executive who uses technology to input or access information quickly.

Using a word processing software package allows you to draft, revise, and finalize your documents which can then be printed in hard copy on letter-quality printer for distribution and storage.

Your ability to swiftly input and manipulate numbers of statistical information is needed for using spreadsheet software to maximum advantage. Since reports are needed daily in businesses, your ability to create a cover letter accompanied by a report with graphics is a necessity.

As people tend to remember picture information longer than printed text, presentation graphics are becoming more and more desirable. Also, if you happen to work on the company's annual report, your familiarity with desktop publishing software programs will enable you to merge text with graphics to produce professional looking newsletters, brochures, reports, etc.

Your technological and software sophistication will undoubtedly increase your hiring and job promotion potential. If nothing else, using technology to input or access information will increase your productivity level and allow you more time to assume other duties which shows initiative and makes you more valuable to the company. Whether you use a computer

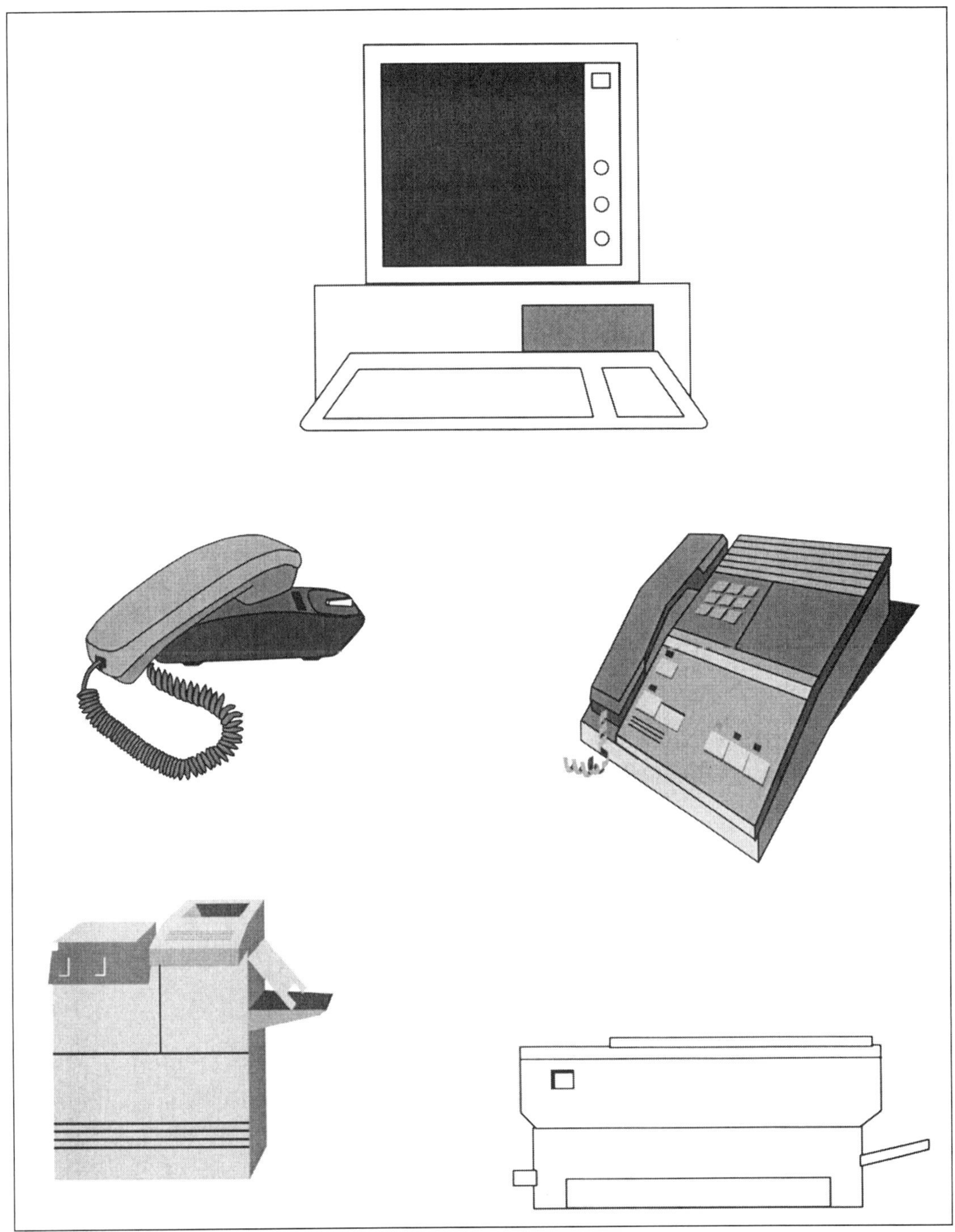

Figure 4.6. An Electronic Office.

terminal or are linked to a LAN, you have communicating capability via telecommunications known as electronic mail or an electronic bulletin board within the organization.

Bulletin Boards

Bulletin boards (electronic) are another device in which to leave messages for later retrieval by the receiver. With telecommunications, one has the ability to consult large data bases or information networks such as The Source and CompuServe.

With the communications links now available, telecommuting is becoming more desirable for employees in certain job classifications. Telecommuting defined means people working at home and keeping in touch with fellow employees, customers, supplies, and superiors, through telephone networks and computer networks. It is estimated that nearly 10,000 Americans working for 300 companies now already telecommute every day; the year 2000 may see 10 million workers telecommuting.

Worker Productivity

Worker productivity is of utmost importance these days with the number of layoffs, downsizing or rightsizing. The microcomputer can be your best helper in document production. The microcomputer with word processing software lets you spell and grammar check your documents. You have a thesaurus available to enhance the readability of your documents. Many word processing software packages offer other features such as outline, graphics abilities, font changes, tables, merge, and templates to create professional documents. Nothing short of clear and error-free documents is acceptable. Your communication reflects you.

Numerous writing analysis software programs are available to critique the readability of your documents; a few are Rightwriter and Grammatik. An example of Rightwriter analysis is shown in Figure 4.7.

Other Technological Innovations

Other innovations to assist in the performance of employee tasks include groupware, digital video, electronic whiteboards, chat lines, the WEB, and personal digital assistants.

Groupware. In today's environment teamwork is not only encouraged but mandatory for an organization to fulfill its mission, goals, and strategic planning necessary to maintain a viable and competitive industry. Groupware provides the tools necessary to support the collaborative process and the activities of team players in the work environment. One of the leading groupware products on the market is Lotus Notes; however, Microsoft's Microsoft Exchange and the Internet can also perform groupware functions.

What is groupware? Groupware includes software for information sharing, electronic meetings, scheduling, and email. Workers can collaborate on and modify various activity work on their own desktop computers simultaneously. An important feature of groupware in-

MEMORANDUM

To: All Employees
From: Donna Bernal, Manager of Accounting Department
Date: October 25, 1994
Subject: Rodent Problem

I have just received notice from our Sanitation Engineer that we have a possible rat problem. Recently, two rats were found<<***_S1.PASSIVE VOICE: were found** *>> in the building.

We can resolve this problem by taking extra caution to keep the office as clean as possible. Please do not bring food to the office. If you bring a lunch, put it in the cafeteria.

To ensure<<***_S13.REPLACE ensure BY SIMPLER be sure?** *>> a clean and rat proof office, we must take preventive action by using utmost care with lunches brought into the building.<<***_G3.SPLIT INTO 2 SENTENCES?** *>> Please do not leave any food overnight. All employees should be alert for signs indicating<<***_S13. REPLACE indicating BY FORM OF SIMPLER show or say?** *>> rodent or insect activity such as droppings, gnawed food, odor, dark rub marks along the wall, ceiling, under door, ventilator as this indicates<<***_S13. REPLACE indicates BY FORM OF SIMPLER show or say?** *>> a runway.<<***_G3. SPLIT INTO 2 SENTENCES?** *>><<***_S3. LONG SENTENCE: 33 WORDS** *>>

If you see any of the above signs please inform the Building Maintenance Office as soon as possible. <<***_P3. INCOMPLETE SENTENCE OR MISSING COMMA** *>>

With your cooperation we can put an end to our rat problem.

<< SUMMARY **>>**

Overall critique for: a:ical.
Output document name: a:\ical.OUT

READABILITY INDEX: 8.59

```
4th      6th      8th      10th      12th      14th
|****|****|****|****|**  |    |    |    |    |    |
SIMPLE        —GOOD—               COMPLEX
```

Readers need a 9th grade level of education.

STRENGTH INDEX: 0.29

```
0.0                 0.5                 1.0
|****|****|****|    |    |    |    |    |    |    |
WEAK                               STRONG
```

The writing can be made more direct by using:

—the active voice
—shorter sentences
—more common words

DESCRIPTIVE INDEX: 0.51

```
0.1            0.5                 0.9       1.1
|****|****|****|****|    |    |    |    |    |    |
TERSE----------NORMAL---------          WORDY
```

The use of adjectives and adverbs is normal.

JARGON INDEX: 0.00

SENTENCE STRUCTURE RECOMMENDATIONS:

15. No Recommendations.

<<WORDS TO REVIEW>>

review this list for negative words (N), jargon (J), colloquial words (C), misused words (M), misspellings (?), or words which your reader may not understand (?).

bernal	(?)	1	ensure	(M)	1
indicates	(M)	1	indicating	(M)	1
not	(N)	2	rodent	(?)	2
utmost	(M)	1	ventilator	(?)	1

<<END OF WORDS TO REVIEW LIST>>

<<Y END OF SUMMARY **>>**

Figure 4.7. Sample of Rightwriter Analysis.

volves groupware writing and commenting. There are now some excellent collaborative group writing software packages on the market which are dedicated to writing and revision.

Groupware can be a beneficial tool in improving the quality of writing that transpires in the work environment. This software if used effectively can lead to improved communication and feedback in the internal and external environments. This technology has been found to be quite effective in facilitating the operations management performs in coordinating and distributing knowledge and information.

Digital video. Television has shaped our society into one of passivity regarding the way we are entertained and taught. The medium of television has impacted the way businesses communicate with the general populace. As a result, visual aids have proliferated in presentations which include eye-catching textual matter, sound, graphics, video, and animation. Audiences are far more receptive to information today which has the power to create a dynamic, eventful sensory experience.

The saying that a picture is worth a thousand words is quite true in the inclusion of digital video in the communication process. Presenters have recognized that the creative use of sound, music, and expressive speaking complement video images more than the pictures themselves. This supports the premise in business communication that audiences will overlook a poor video quality much more readily than poor audio. However, the creative use of music and audio can make or break a presentation. The eyes have a way of forgiving what the ears cannot. There is no effective replacement for a clear, succinct speaking voice which talks with the audience, not at them.

Electronic whiteboards. Electronic whiteboards are the Etch-A- Sketches of the business world (PC World, February 1997). Write on them with a marker and your text or drawings appear on your computer screen, where they can be saved or printed. Whiteboards are especially useful for group meetings. Notes and ancillary information can be saved and printed for later use. This technology is an ideal tool for use in environments which allow creative processing of information and brainstorming to take place.

Personal digital assistants. Personal digital assistants are small, pen-based handheld computers capable of entirely digital communications transmission. The PDAs perform electronic scheduling, calendaring, and faxing and printing capabilities. They can also function as a paging device. Many DPAs come equipped with notepad software and are able to accept handwriting input entered through a special stylus. UPS and JC Penney Company are two companies among many which utilize these small computers. These devices help to maintain inventory and tracking of products and services.

Some digital answering services have unique features which allow the person called to leave their schedule so the "voice activated" personal assistant will know where to reach the individual. Anyone who calls you would get the "voice activated" personal assistant who would ask the caller such questions as "Who are you and why are you calling"? The voice activated would record the caller's responses and place the caller on hold while the digitized assistant tries to reach you. If you are on the other line, the digitized personal assistant would whisper in your ear so only you can hear. If you don't respond, the digitized assistant would tell the caller you are in a meeting and cannot be disturbed. Look at the WEB site for more information on this new technology (http://www.wildfire.com).

The digital assistant can also be programmed to respond differently to different callers based on the caller. According to PC World, February 1997, about one out of five minutes spent on voice mail is lost to fumbling through menus.

The PDA technology is not error-free but these devices hold great promise for the expansion of communication worldwide. Security and privacy will be more difficult to maintain because wireless transmission can be easily intercepted (Laudon, 1997).

Chat lines. Chat lines are similar to standing in the center of a large mall and shouting your personal conversation with a friend to everyone within hearing distance. Messages which transpire in chat discussions are available to all participants to read. Chat messages are placed in the archives to be retrieved for reading months or years later. Few people realize that the use of the chat lines allows online sleuths and backers to develop a complete profile on the net user which can be detrimental to them later on. Communicators often let down barriers when communicating electronically via the Net that they would never forego when talking with strangers via the telephone and other forms of communication mediums.

Information transmitted over the Net is often open to viewing by unauthorized "eyes" which penetrate firewalls by breaking encryption codes to steal information considered confidential. Private information sent via the Net is susceptible to public viewing. The channels by which information is transmitted and used in the technological environment is an issue that does not ensure privacy. Until such time, communicators should take every precaution when sending email, posting messages for a newsgroup, conducting Internet banking and financial matters, and shopping for goods and services.

Users of Internet services can be easily tracked in today's information age. One disparaging fact for Internet users is that little privacy exists in a cyberspace environment. Recently, two people were fired after their "love notes" sent by email were retrieved by a company human resource personnel manager. The supposedly deleted messages were retrieved from the electronic company archives. The two employees conducted their tete-a-tete on company time using company equipment and company software.

A method for accessing information on the Internet is called Gopher. The goal of gopher is to provide an organized method for navigating the Internet. The Gopher is based on menus that move from site to site. One of the fastest growing areas of the Internet is the World Wide Web which provides a rich multimedia environment that includes images, text, sound, and video information. The information on the WEB is provided by web "publishers" in the form of "pages." The initial page is called the home page. The pages are accessed using a special program called a browser. Netscape is a popular web browser. Figure 4.8 is an example of a browser.

Information Overload

We have come a long way since the earliest forms of telecommunications in the world arena. Imagine waking up each morning to 30+ email messages, the home phone ringing off the hook because you forgot to turn on the answering machine, the fax going, the cell phone ringing, the pager beeping. . . . And that's just the beginning of the Information Revolution.

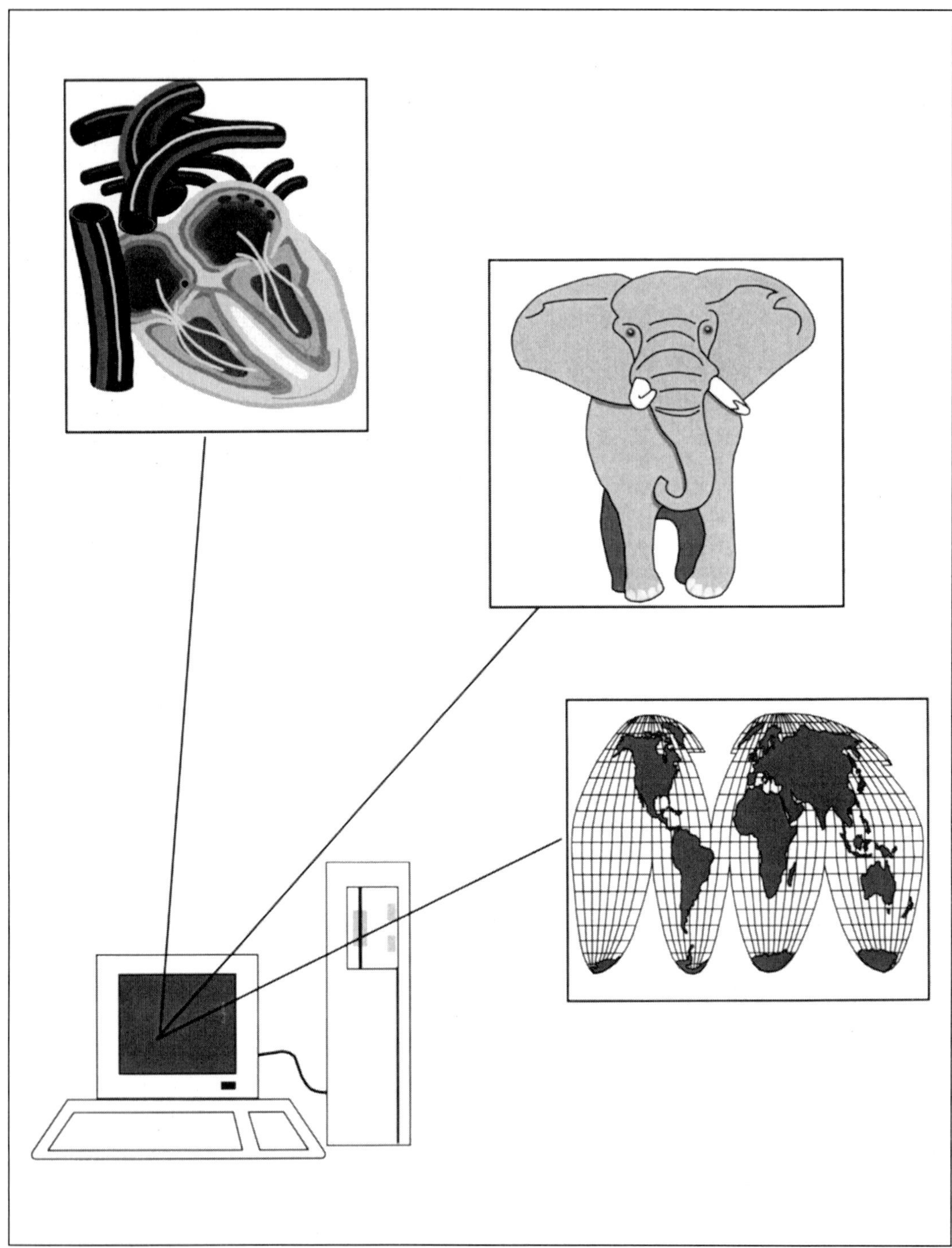

Figure 4.8. Browsing the World Wide Web.

You drag yourself out of bed and head for the computer to retrieve the latest Dow Jones averages on your personal computer while you access your email on your laptop/notebook computer. You look at the clock and realize that some important voice mail messages are probably waiting for you in your office voice mail box. You pick up the vcr/tv remote control and click on the WEB\TV directory listing for the latest news and weather information relating to your latest business trip later that day.

This scenario is played out every day across the world for multitudes of businesspeople. These new and diverse technologies present problems in the communication process for business communicators. Communicators in such an environment are required to make, disseminate, and process the information quickly and efficiently. The more messages and mediums one is bombarded with, the more that miscommunication can occur. Some issues to handling this barrage of communication are as follows: 1) handle problems as they occur, 2) prioritize information—what is important, throwaway?, 3) keep the information flow under control, 4) delegate information to others when possible, 5) make calls at times which require less personal distraction, and 6) learn how to filter information which requires quick, expedient decisions.

Business and the WEB: A New Revolution

A new revolution is looming on the horizon and that new revolution will completely revamp the way we do business in the information age. Today the mere thought of doing business on the WEB is both challenging and horrifying. Businesses view business via the WEB much the same way farmers once viewed using the railroad as a way to transport they products. Will it work? Can it work? Does it work? These questions are on the minds of the most astute business people today. Will the Internet lead to better quality products at a lower price to the greatest number of people? Stories of people revitalizing their business in a matter of hours after entering the WEB business arena are already surfacing.

Large companies players are scrambling to develop WEB sites to inform, sell, and deliver products and services to consumers. The large company players are paying thousands of dollars to reach this new arena of consumers. One large provider of business WEB pages and services stated that the average computer shopper is better educated, professional, and eager to spend excess dollars on products and services provided on the WEB. For example, Living Books, a division of Borderbund Software, has an animated interactive WEB site that introduces potential customers to its line of CD ROM children's stories. Real estate offices have recognized the need to advertise their current listing of home sites to potential customers through WEB pages which link the customer to agents in a particular location.

Suite Software Packages

The latest versions of suite software packages have been reworked to include easy-to-use interface, integrated WEB features such as WEB page design techniques and tools to increase productivity. Communication software such as WEB Phones and CU-SeeMe video conferencing software and SEE-Mail are clearly making in-roads in interacting on a personal level in the technological environment. Clear distinct voice parameters, articulation, enunciation, and breath support as well as direct eye contact will play an important role in the technological medium as it currently plays in the traditional environment when interacting with others.

While all these new innovations are readily available, companies do careful planning and cost analysis before investing in them. In today's environment, companies are trying to operate as lean as possible in an attempt to reduce labor costs. One venture that many companies are resorting to is called outsourcing.

Outsourcing

Outsourcing—the mere mention of "that" word evokes either positive or negative connotation for companies and their employees. Outsourcing in a rapidly changing technological environment can offer a company many benefits if appropriate planning and management controls are put into place before negotiations are entered into with outsourcing agencies.

Overall, companies view outsourcing as a resource-saving mechanism in today's technological age. Many companies have discovered that it is more cost-effective to seek outside skilled labor than to retrain its current workforce. Companies can avoid unnecessary delays and productivity problems by exploring the use of outside temporary outsourcing agencies. Using a temporary agency will provide companies with an up-to-date, skilled workforce when they need it, thus resulting in substantial cost reductions, talent availability, and avoidance of hidden costs.

Outsourcing also frees a company to concentrate on their core activities and issues in a more effective and efficient manner. In this way the company can re-engineer, restructure, and streamline various operations more effectively and efficiently.

Various benefits accrue to companies that manage and plan their outsourcing activities to operate in a cost-effective manner. However, there is also a downside to outsourcing explorations which need to be addressed. Any time a company undertakes a revamping of their corporate structure by using outsourcing will require a careful handling of any legal and personnel issues which may arise.

Outsourcing can upset the delicate corporate culture and climate if management fails to communicate its goals to the staff. Outsourcing can lead to decreased staff morale among the survivors of an organization if outsourcing is used as a tool to downsize the organization. The survivors of the organization may experience increased stress and trauma in the workplace. The survivors may view outsourcing as a threat to them personally and often this may lead to the loss to corporate knowledge and expertise. In other words, if outsourcing is not handled appropriate by human resource personnel, the most talented and skilled personnel will usually be the first to leave an organization. This is exactly the one thing a corporation in its pursuit for skilled labor wants to try and avoid at all cost.

Careful planning is mandatory in seeking outsourcing as a "fix" in the working environment. Companies must realize that outsourcing means relinquishing some or all control of a specific area to the outsourcing agency. Another delicate issue to deal with is in the area of confidentiality. Outsourcing will require the sharing of certain company "secrets" with the outsourcing agency.

Is outsourcing worth the cost in today's technological age? That question is one for all companies to ponder. The answer lies with the needs of each company and its employees and its shareholders. The U. S. in its technological strive for globalization of the work environment has some extremely tough issues to address. What is more beneficial to a company which seeks cost-effective savings in its workforce—to hire a skilled U.S. engineer for $50,000+ a year or an engineer housed in India with 5 years experience earning $5,000?

As technology knowledge and expertise increase in a globalized marketplace, outsourcing may no longer be an option for the workplace but a necessity.

You will need to familiarize yourself with the major types of electronic information available and to whet your appetite to keep using information sources. Innovations in computer and communication technology are changing rapidly. A successful executive is committed to staying abreast of new technologies and how they can improve business operations.

Business Organizational Database

All businesses have what is called an organizational database which is a computer file containing intracompany information such as financial, production data, sales information, etc. Information in databases must be timely, easy to retrieve, and of course accurate.

Many libraries now provide online data bases of their card catalogs and indexed material. You can conduct an electronic search using terminals in the library, in computer labs on campus, and perhaps from your home if your computer has a modem. Two useful electronic business research tools are ABI/Inform and Business Dateline. Using a modem, appropriate communication software, and an assigned password, you can obtain information from around the world by subscribing to the Internet or a commercial online service.

The Internet is a loose collection of millions of computers at thousands of sites around the world (government offices, businesses, and universities) whose users can pass along information and share files. According to Kanter (1994), the Internet is growing phenomenally with about 150,000 new members joining each month.

Other online database searches will be discussed in the section on reports. For now, let us focus on the ethical and legal issues that surface in your business correspondence which will be discussed in Chapter 5.

References

Kanter, E. (1994).

Joyce, M. P. (March 1994). Work force 2000. Implications for Business Education, presentation made at California Business Education Association Conference in Los Angeles, CA.

Laudon, K. (1997). MANAGEMENT INFORMATION SYSTEMS, 2nd edition, Prentice-Hall, New Jersey.

PC World (February 1997). Voice mail.

U.S. Government Printing Office. Occupational Safety and Health Act 1970, Washington, D.C.

QUESTIONS

1. Contrast the evolution of the traditional office to the office of today.
2. Which communication method do you use to input your messages? Why?
3. Discuss the three basic software skills needed today in the work environment.
4. Does using technology increase one's productivity level?
5. What do you want in your executive work Station? Select a picture (from an office management journal or magazine) which portrays it.
6. Are voice mail and electronic mail synonymous? Why or Why not?
7. What software packages do you know and use now?
8. List the six major software packages you should be able to use.
9. Duplicating copies of documents is sometimes refered to as reprographics. What is the common method today for making copies?
10. Documents can be stored on-site or off-site. Which do you recommend? Why?
11. Do you agree with the vision of a "paperless" office?
12. Does the telecommuting concept appeal to you? Why or Why not?

APPLICATIONS

1. Visit a computer store and find out what is the latest in communications technology. Share your information with the class.
2. Read two articles on office technology and prepare an abstract of these articles.
3. Attend an office automation show. What was most interesting or unique at the show?
4. Analyze the differences between using a network and stand alone equipment. Prepare a list comparing the benefits and drawbacks of both.
5. Obtain a copy of the latest issue of Office Automation. Critique the contents of the magazine.
6. Defend the statement: "Using communication technology increases one's productivity."
7. Keep track of the amount of time you spend in handwriting a reply to a letter or memo. Then compose (on the microcomputer) a reply to another letter or memo. Which method was faster? Slower? Which method was easier? With which method do you feel most comfortable? Which method was MORE productive?
8. Interview two professors in your major field of study or two superiors. What office technology do they use in their communication tasks? Share this information with the class or with others majoring in your same field in the class.
9. Draw a picture diagram of the evolution of communication mediums from the earlier days to the present.
10. Describe the use of the telephone in the new automated office.
11. Visit a business using microwave and/or satellite. Describe the satellite/microwave; discuss the company's usage of this transmission as well as future technological needs.
12. Research fiber optics. 1) Will it change the communication needs in the new century? 2) What is the cost to implement fiber optics? 3) Will transmission of information be faster using this technology?
13. Describe the uses of electronic mail in today's office.
14. Explain how voice mail, video conferencing, teleconferencing, electronic bulletin boards, LANS, and WANS, effect communication in today's offices.

Name ______________________________ Date ______________

JEOPARDY QUIZ #4

1. The answer is: Stone tablets and the quill pen.

   What are ______________________________?

2. The answer is: The most important piece of technology that has swept through the business environment.

   What is ______________________________?

3. The answer is: Spreadsheets, word processing, and graphics.

   What are ______________________________?

4. Express Publisher, Ventura, and Pagemaker.

   What are ______________________________?

5. The answer is: The ability to send messages through a communications network such as dedicated telephone line, telegraph, radio, and satellite.

   What is ______________________________?

6. The answer is: A machine that scans printed words, pictures, charts, etc. and converts the information into electronic impulses and send the impulses by telephone to a receiver.

   What is ______________________________?

7. The answer is: Computer conferencing, videoconferencing, and audioconferencing.

   What are ______________________________?

8. The answer is: The ability to speak your message into a microphone and the text appears on the computer screen.

   What is ______________________________?

continued

9. The answer is: The ability to share information and files through a network.

   What is ____?

10. The answer is: The latest form of transmitting signals that can withstand practically any form of interference.

    What is ____?

11. The answer is: The Occupational Health and Safety Act.

    What is ____?

12. The answer is: The ability to merge text and graphics together in a document.

    What is ____?

13. The answer is: The digital system that allows you to customize your answering telephone calls.

    What is ____?

14. The answer is: A service that allows the users to pass along information and share files.

    What is ____?

15. The answer is: Provides a rich multimedia environment that includes images, text, sound, and video information.

    What is ____?

16. The answer is: A popular web browser.

    What is ____?

CHAPTER 5

Ms. Brenda Slesinski, Prudential Preferred Financial Services at Career Fair—Cal State University–LA April 10, 1997

Ethical and Legal Issues in Business Communication

Objectives

After reading the chapter and doing the exercises, you should be able to:

1. Define the term "ethics."
2. Discuss the concept of ethical responsibility and how it has evolved.
3. Explain how unethical decisions affect the company.
4. Critique the legal considerations in company correspondence and your actions towards customers and clients.
5. Explain how unethical decisions affect the customers and clients.
6. Determine your limitations in making a decision that affects the company.
7. Analyze legal and ethical considerations in workplace situations.
8. Distinguish the difference between values and moral obligations.
9. Compare and contrast a company's code of ethics with your ethical beliefs.
10. Cite the Acts that govern information, electronic communication and telecommunication, and computer security.
11. Distinguish between what constitutes slander and libel.
12. Describe defamation of character.

Your Responsibility

The concepts of ethical and legal issues in business communication are discussed next. The purpose is to provide an understanding of the ethical and legal responsibility to yourself, to your company, and to customers and clients. This chapter provides an overview of ethical issues and analysis and considerations in decision making in a workplace setting.

Ethical Propriety of Your Writing

Regardless of the type of business in which you are involved or encounter, you will face ethical and legal questions in the process of communicating orally and in writing. Ethical and legal considerations are important in a business's decision-making process.

Practically every level of authority and profession has been hit by evidences of unethical and illegal actions, from the White House to tobacco companies, and even to the religion entity. As a writer, you should set high standards for yourself and expect those around you to exhibit the same. Never compromise your values; once you do, there is no ending to what you will do.

As a business communicator, you may face three types of legal consierations: defamation, fraud and misrepresentation, and invasion of privacy. Each will be discussed in detail.

Ober (1992, p. 43–44) states that when you have doubts about the ethical propriety of your writing, you should ask yourself these questions:

1. Is the message true?
2. Does it exaggerate?
3. Does it withhold or obscure information that should be communicated?
4. Does it promise something that you or the company cannot deliver?
5. Does it betray a confidence?
6. Does it play unduly on the fears of the reader?
7. Does it reflect the wishes of the organization?

> "Do all the good you can, by all the means you can, in all the ways you can, in all the places you can, at all the times you can, to all the people you can, for as long as you can."
>
> —*John Wesley*

Ethics Defined

In today's complicated world, being ethical in your communication is essential in your personal life and in your business career. To be effective in interpersonal relationships, your choice of what's the right thing to do, the way to behave or the right way to conduct business are essential. So, what is Ethics? The word "ethics" derived from the Greek word ethos, means character or custom. These two meanings convey two basic concepts: (1) individual's character—What does it mean to be a good person; (2) society rules—What rules determine right and wrong. Just what is ethical behavior?

While the definition of Ethics may vary from author to author, they all seem to agree that the concepts of "Right and Wrong" decisions are those which one makes. Schweitzer defines Ethics as "the name we give to our concern for good behavior. (Himstreet & Baty, 1993). Guffey defines ethical behavior as "that type of behavior which is the right thing to do based on the circumstances. She further enumerates four principles—honesty, integrity, fairness and concern for others. (Guffey, 1994) These four principles could be classified, according to Josephson's remarks in "What Price Ethics?' in Entrepreneurial Woman. He says these principles are "like four legs of a stool. "If one leg is missing, the stool wobbles, and if two stools are missing, the stool falls.[1]

It is not enough to pride yourself on your honesty and integrity if you are not fair or caring in making ethical decisions in communicating in business. Therefore, you should consider these factors: Your relations with your employer, your clients, and employees.

Ethical Communication in Business

As a result of business managers and businesses experiencing events during the 1990s and looking to the year 2000, being ethical and making ethical decisions have become a buzzword in companies, corporations, business, schools, politics, and the media. An important consideration when you are communicating is whether it's ethical or unethical to think about your endangering both yourself and/or the organization. Bell (1995)[2] suggests you consider three genres of relationships—*with your employer, employees, and clients*—which in fact could contribute to many law guides affecting one's professional behavior.

Legal and Ethical Implications of Business Correspondence

The written record that you produce when you write a business communication is, in essence, a legal contract. The partners in this contract are you and your business as the "makers" and your communication partner and the business he or she represents as the "receivers."

When you write business messages, consider the following factors:

1. A written communication is acceptable as legal evidence in a court of law. You and your company may be forced to carry out your promises, or you and your company could be sued for breach of contract.
2. Your signature on a letter indicates that you agree with and approve of its contents.
3. You cannot legally change your mind once your written communication reaches the receiver unless you can prove that circumstances have changed enough to legally release you from your previous commitments.

4. If your written statements indicate that a person is unfit to perform his or her job or that a company is unfit to carry on its business, you and your company may be sued for libel.

Libel is the written defamation of a person's character or a company's name.
Slander is the oral defamation of a person's character or a company's name.
The contents of a letter belong to the writer, not the receiver.

Your relations with your employer. You are an employee and an agent of your employer. Therefore, the company becomes responsible for your work-related actions. For example, a business manager cannot execrate another company's constituency or specialty with control. This act transforms both the individual and the company into being sued. It is pertinent that the business manager maintain a degree of care in (e.g. hiring, firing, negotiating policies and contracts), and communicating with governing and regulatory agencies.

Your relations with clients. As an employer of a company, the language you use in communicating with customers about credit and collections is protected by laws passed.[3] If there is a case a manager has to communicate with a client about a credit matter, he should know what to include and not include in writing about the client's worthiness. For example, the client's age, marital status are illegal. The refusal of credit must be written, rather than conveyed verbally and it must be verifiable, according to this law.[4] If a manager has to contact a client regarding an outstanding debt, he should guard against making contact outside business hour time with slanderous language, threats, or false affirmations regarding the courts. This law's implication is that when a debtor can be contacted, what is to be said, what written information, e.g. written response to inquiry in understandable language and accurate records must be provided.

Your relations with employees. Among the many responsibilities you will have as a manager is maintaining in your possession confidential information about your employees. This confidential information could include work history, health conditions, personal references, work performance records, and security clearance. In order for you to preserve and protect this information, *The Federal Privacy Act of 1974—(5 U.S.C.,1982)* clearly defines this law. Its ruling is that you do not uncover to a third party any facts or opinions on an employee's personal record. Two others laws passed in 1972 and 1992 protect the appropriate communication path and content for documents which have to do with the hiring and firing of protected groups in society—namely, women, minorities, the elderly, and the physically challenged.

In all these genres relationships, as a manager, you should combine not only your personal ethical behavior, but you should be throughly knowledgeable of the legal guidelines of laws affecting the communication process. You , too, just might consider the question on how would you avoid unethical communication in your writing and speaking. To avoid possible traps in communicating ethically, the following guidelines in Figure 5.1 are suggested by Bovee & Thill (1995); Guffey (1994).[4]

1 Avoid "saying or writing something when it is clearly illegal."
2 Avoid "stating opinions as facts . . . portray graphic data fairly."
3 Avoid "language that discriminates, manipulates or exaggerates."
4 Don't lie, understate or exaggerate.
5 Don' t plagiarize. Plagiarism is easily avoided if you "give credit for ideas by referring to originators' names within the text; using quotation marks; and, documenting sources with endnotes, footnotes, or internal references.
6 Don't use a vocabulary that the reader does not understand.
7 Don't interpret data before you have first presented all of it objectively.
8 Don't let your prejudice interfere with the content of the message.

Figure 5.1. Ethical Communication Traps.

Ethical Communication Traps

Ethical communication is necessary and should be taken seriously whether you are writing and speaking on a personal level or for a company. If you are in the position to compose a business proposal, a credit or sales letter, a personnel policy, or recruit a candidate for a position, you must make a conscious decision about the phrasing of your writing, the speaking of your language, and how to organize and emphasize specific points. The decisions you make in these deliberations have legal and moral implications for both you and the company. Being ethical in your communication, therefore, is not only essential and the right thing for you to do, it is also contagious. As you experience success in your interpersonal relationships in your business environment, others will sure follow your lead.

Other Interpersonal Communication

In making ethical decisions, it is important for you to be aware of these legal considerations: Defamation of character—libel, slander, and invasion of privacy.

Defamation

Any untrue and spiteful statement that injures the reputation and character of another person constitute *defamation.* To be considered defamation, the statement must be false, made to and communicated to a third person, thereby, causing some injury and scaring that person's good reputation. Under the circumstances, telling Angel Hilbert to her face that she is a liar and cheat is not considered defamation—slander—if a Ignacio Amaya, a third party, does not hear the statement.

You may find that far too often in many organizations management fails to consider what could happen when an employee in significant trust and responsibility is forced to leave. If this happens, the organization can determine if it is left unduly exposed and that the employee has been dealt with in an ethical/sensitive manner and not have violated a labor relations law, duress in the termination process.[5] The issues open for discussion could include: What is the potential of vengeful acts? What is the importance of the notification of co-workers without defamation of character problems? Should the collection of organization property be enforced?

In 1992, exploratory research was conducted to determine the willingness of business firms in the southwestern United States to provide answers to pre-employment reference checks submitted to third-party employers. The assumption of the survey was that the failure to control responses to work reference could increase potentiality for law suits alleging defamation of character. It was concluded that larger firms with more than one hundred employees usually employ human resource managers who strictly control ex-employee reference check information.

On the other hand, small firms usually do not have human resource managers and are more than open to sharing a variety of ex-employee information, thereby, increasing the chance of defamation allegations. Finally, Fenton & Lawrimore (1992) recommends that, whether it be a small or large firm, one individual who is knowledgeable of all employment references about legal risks involving defamation should serve as a *"report person."* [6]

Libel and Slander

Libel. If a statement is either written and widely spread by a source such as radio or television, it is called *libel* . Thus, if defamation is written, it constitutes libel. Generally, truth is the only defense against defamation.

Slander. If a statement is made orally, it is called *slander*. Therefore, if defamation is spoken, it constitutes slander.

Consider the investigations of the bombing at the "Olympic Games on July 27, 1996. The attention was on Richard Jewell, a security guard at Atlanta's Olympics. Mr. Jewell directed the attention to the green knapsack containing a pipe bomb that killed two people and injured three in Atlanta's Centennial Olympic Park. Three days after the explosion, he was named the prime suspect in the Georgia Federal Bureau of Investigation. The next three months, the FBI tested to find solid evidence against him. After eighty-eight days of his suspicion, the FBI sent Mr. Jewell a letter saying he was "no longer a target." On the ninetieth day Mr. Jewell, at a news conference, condemned the FBI, the Atlanta Journal and NBC News and its anchor, Tom Brokaw for "a mad rush"to judgement and that it "almost destroyed me", and sued. A lack of caring and a failure of these agencies to consider thorough circumstances apparently created a wavering ethical position that is difficult to imagine.

Invasion of Privacy

Protection of employees' privacy should be the concern of every employer. Therefore, any purposely intrusion into the private life of any employee or the denial of his/her rights to be left along constitutes an *invasion of privacy*. As an employer, you possess employee personal document information—age, health, employment history, etc. Thus, you may not, without that employee's permission, expose this information. If this is done, you would have been proven wrong for the invasion of privacy of the employee.

As the year 2000 is approximately three years away, more and more do we see employee/employer information manipulated in data banks through the use of microcomputers, electronic mail, and the network, thereby, generating concerns.

Fraud and Misrepresentation

A deliberate misrepresentation of the truth that is made to induce someone to give up something of value is called fraud.

The deliberate concealment of information is often called passive fraud, while the act of deliberately make a false statement is called active fraud.

Misrepresentation is the act of innocently making a false statement with no intent to deceive the other party.

Business Communication and Privacy Act Laws

"Just as the strength of the Internet is chaos, so the strength of our liberty depends upon the chaos and cacophony of the unfettered speech the First Amendment protects."

—Judge Stewart Dalzell
U.S. District Court

The use of computers for the purpose of obtaining information has increased in the last two decades. For the reason of protecting society, Congress has enacted privacy laws which you may find beneficial in the business communicating process.

Privacy Act of 1974. This law protects individuals against unauthorized publication of their letters, photographs and testimonials kept in government files. Also, this law prohibits the disclosure of information which could violate an individual's personal civil right that could result in unfair business advantage or loss of technological advantage.[7]

Freedom of Information Act of 1982. This law provides individuals access to information in governmental files—e.g. Internal Revenue Service. Often times, individuals overburden federal offices by requesting information such as inquires focused on a competitor perhaps applying for an export license. This law was devised in 1986 to include a *fee schedule.* The fee schedule is based on the classification of the requestor—e.g. a commercial user, an educational institution, or a scientific institution.[8]

Computer Security Act of 1987: This law protects the unlawful publication of individual's personal data—e.g. tax records—contained in federal government files. Additionally, this law prohibits unauthorized obtainment and usage of sensitive information contained in government computer systems.[9]

The Electronic Communications Privacy Act of 1986. Under this law, individual's protection is extended to *Electronic Mail, Cellular Telephone Calls, Video Recordings, and Data Transmission.* In addition this law influences both domestic and international business communication—e.g. federal laws, regulations, and stipulations of international conventions influence communication with foreign businesspeople.[10]

The Telecommunication Act of 1996. This new law allows anyone to enter any communications business and to let any communications business compete in any market against any other. Additionally, the potentiality of this law is to change the way we learn, live, and work. Other areas this law affects are our lives, local and long distance telephone services, television cable programming, broadcasting and video services, and those services provided for schools.[11]

Privileged Communication

Oftentimes it appears that the use of unethical business practices is projected as the successful way to operate. A degree of confusion could raise two questions: (1) What is good business? and (2) What is necessary for a business to survive? If the answers to these questions and decisions made appear attractive to a business, then it could become known that the business is in trouble and voracity becomes its driving force. The reverse side of this argument is that standing firm on ethical principles and practices makes it easier to attract clients who want to do business with businesses they trust.

Privileged Ethical and Legal issues to Ponder

Employers are increasingly faced with the need to conduct investigation concerning concerning allegations of discrimination, employment dismissal or sexual harassment. From the first awareness of such a problem, employers can and should take aggressive measures to enclose their investigations from subsequent company litigation. If you are in this situation, you need to be sure that the proper handing of personnel policies, procedures, records and other pertinent information are in order. A question to ponder is: How do you, as a corporate spokesperson, protect yourself and your company if there is an investigation of personnel policies and procedures taking place? Spar, 1996, says that, "Most jurisdictions have grappled with this problem, resulting in an extensive collection of legislation, rules and case law that—if used properly—can protect a corporation from unnecessary disclosure of potentially damaging documents.

If you are faced with such a dilemma, perhaps a short legal course for human resource executives would include a working knowledge of three key privileges—(1) attorney-client privilege, (2) work product doctrine, and the (3) self-critical analysis privilege. If you must gain *attorney-client privilege*, you should consider these required conditions:

- The conditions must be conducted under the directions of the attorney.
- The employee's interview and other components of the investigation must be to provide confidential information to only the attorney.

- All communication must be forwarded directly back to the attorney. Therefore, it is crucial for the employer to involve its attorney before the investigative process is initiated.

If you must engage in work product doctrine in your company, these conditions should be considered:

- The document prepared by the attorney during the litigation or in preparation of the litigation is protected by the work product doctrine. During this process, one attorney cannot gain access to his or her opponent's opinions, legal theories, mental impressions or trial strategies.
- Privileged under the work product doctrine are your interviews of employees and fact witnesses by the attorney. A prevailing fact, however, is that adversaries can obtain a document or documents if substantial needs are required to prepare the case if hardship or an inability in acquiring materials by other means is evident.

If you have the occasion to experience the *self-evaluation privilege or self-critical analysis* for your company, these conditions are suggested for your consideration:

- The underlined premise of this privilege is that an organization *"will not"* be candid in criticizing its' company policies, procedures, and recommended changes if an internal criticism could be used against it or its employees.
- This privilege protect against the disclosure of criticism, opinions, *underlying facts*. If for example, an employer investigates a sexual harassment of an employee after a claim has been received, should it alter its policies and procedures to avoid future claims, its opinions, criticisms, and recommendations for improvement to be exempt? As a result, the underlying fact concerning this investigative charge is that it would be subject to disclosure.

These privileges under existing case law in many jurisdictions can be strong, protective weapons for the confidentiality of company communications. The effectiveness of these requirements—privileges and doctrine—in a company is that of bringing in an attorney to the process as early as possible.[12]

"What do we live for if not to make the world less difficult for each other?"

—*George Eliot*

Ethical Privileged Case to Ponder

The Sullivan & Cromwell's Leak. In 1995, a Wall Street firm, Sullivan & Cromwell blamed a breakdown in communication of the leaks of papers filed under seal by Procter & Gamble in a suit against Bankers Trust by one of their partners, Steven Holley. According to the firm, Holley, was unaware that the papers requested by a Business Week journalist, Linda Himelstein, in New York were filed under seal. The Wall Street firm, Sullivan & Cromwell, maintains that Holley believed the papers to be public documents. A spokesperson for Business Week contends that Holley was telephoned by Himelstein inquiring about whether the papers were sealed. He was assured by Himelstein to continue with these papers for his article and to keep his name for the suit. Later, it was reported Bankers Trust tried to get the article banned from publication saying that the magazine had acted illegally. However, Holley denied that his conversation had ever taken place with Himelstein. Finally, a judge ordered a restraining order be placed on the magazine. This order was nullified by another court, and the papers were made public.

The Sullivan & Cromwell Case concludes by expressing its regrets to Bankers Trust by calling it ". . .'a clear departure' from it's firm procedures." A spokesperson for the company says, 'We have begun an immediate review of the individuals involved to ensure that this type of exceptional breakdown never occurs again.' Bankers Trust, in turn, accepted Sullivan's explanation, followed by a statement, 'We have no dispute with the firm. . . .'"[13]

Whatever informational decision you make to convey, orally, in writing, the key is "ethical choices" or "what's right as to what is wrong" when no question of the law is involved to defend your position.

Chapter 6 will focus on planning, composing, and Revising business messages.

Notes

[1]Guffey, 1994, 74—(Based on Michael Josephson's remarks reported in Alison Bell's "What Price Ethics" *Entrepreneurial Woman*, 68.)
[2]Bell, Arthur H. *Tools For Technical and Professional Communication*, 1995, 14–15
[3]The Fair Credit Billing Act became law in 1974—(15 U.S.C. §1666–1666 (j)
[4]The Fair Debt Collection Practices Act became law in 1977—(15 U.S.C. §§1692–1692 (o).
[5]Bovee, Courtland L., and John Thill. *Business Communication Today*, 4th Ed. 1995, 17, 19; Guffey, Mary Ellen. *Business Communication: Process and Products*, 1994, 73–75.
[6]Wood, C.C., "Duress Terminations and Information Security, *Computer & Security* 1993, 527–535.
[7]Fenton, James W., Lawrimore, Kay, "Employment Reference Checking, Firm Size, and Defamation Liability," *Journal of Small Business Management*, 30(4) 88–85.
[8]Soma, J.T. & Bedient, E.J, 1989, *The Air Force Law Journal*, pp.142–146.
[9]Huff R. L., January, 1989, *The Army Lawyer* 7–15.
[10]Kastenmeier, R. W., 1987, "Communications Privacy," *Communications Lawyer* 5 (1), pgs. 20–25.
[11]http://ftp.fcc.gov/telecom.htm, February 1997.
[12]Source: Spar, Rebecca K. "Keeping Internal Investigations Confidential, *HR Magazine* 41(1):33–36, 1996.
[13]Anonymous Source: "Sullivan & Cromwell's Leak," *International Financial Law Review*, 14(11), 4–5, 1995.

References

Bell, A. H. (1995). TOOLS FOR TECHNICAL AND PROFESSIONAL COMMUNICATION.
Bovee, C. L. and Thill, J. (1995). BUSINESS COMMUNICATION TODAY. 4th Ed.

Fenton, J. W. and Lawumore, K. (1992). "Employment Reference Checking, Firm Size, and Defamation Liability," JOURNAL OF SMALL BUSINESS MANAGEMENT.
Guffey, M. E. (1994). BUSINESS COMMUNICATION: PROCESS AND PRODUCT.
Schweitzer (cities Himstreet and Baty), BUSINESS COMMUNICATION, 1993.
Wood, C. C. (1993). "Duress Terminations and Information Security," COMPUTER SECURITY.
Ober, S. (1992). CONTEMPORARY BUSINESS COMMUNICATION, Houghton Mifflin

Questions

1. What is ethics?
2. How would you define ethics in the workplace? Discuss some ethical standards that you plan to adhere to in your career.
3. Explain why ethics is important in business.
4. Explain how an act could be legal but not ethical.
5. What are some types of unethical behaviors that can be observed in the workplace?
6. How does business communication play a role in such behavior?
7. Should defamation be protected as free speech? Does doing so necessarily prevent liability?
8. What ethical and legal factors of the Richard Jewell case is most disturbing to you? Why?
9. What is the difference between self-evaluation privilege and underlying fact?
10. What is the difference between libel and slander? Cite an example of each.
11. What is your responsibility in business communications that you write?
12. Cite an example of defamation of character.

Applications

1. Find a recent event (business, television, sports, for example) in which ethical or legal standards were violated. Discuss in writing why the violations occurred. What other choices could have been made?
2. Ethics may be described as a difficult topic due to conflicting interests. As a college student, what conflicting interests do you encounter in making ethical decisions. Write two paragraphs discussing your response.
3. Choose two professions and review their Code of Ethics.
4. Find a recent problem in your chosen profession that had or has legal and eithical concerns.
5. Visit a professor in your chosen profession and ask their views on legal and ethical concerns in that profession.
6. Look up your profession and determine if it has a Code of Ethics.
7. Enter OPAC and download list of current books on legal and ethical concerns in business.
8. Enter Lexis/Nexis, etc. and determine 2–3 current articles on ethical and legal concerns in business.
9. If you were faced with compromising your values and ethics, what would be your concerns in decision making?

10. Cite one recent news worthy case (publicized in newspapers, TV, and radio) concerning ethical decision making that unnerved you or you had difficulty accepting.

• • • MINI-CASE SCENARIOS •

Case 1 Group Exercise

Ethical Issue — "The Sullivan & Cromwell's Leak"

Have each group member to read the account of this case in the textbook chapter. As a group, they will need to consult a source such as the World Wide Web or a Law Book to read the entire case. As this case provides insight into ethical issues, each member is to consider these questions?

1. Describe the ethical and legal issues.
2. What conditions created the issue?
3. In your opinion, how did the company handle the ethical situation? How would you have handled the situation?
4. What steps should have been taken to avoid this ethical dilemma?

Case 2

1. Locate on the World Wide Web Fortune 500 companies: AT& T, Chrysler; Texaco, Procter & Gamble; Wal-Mart Stores; J. C. Penney; United Parcel Service, BankAmerica Corporation; Boeing; Coca Cola;Sara Lee; American Express; Eastman Kodak; MCI Communications; Compaq Computer and Albertson's.
2. Summarize four of the Web sites products.
3. What legal or ethical decisions do you see in these web pages? How would you improve them.

Case 3: A Real World Situation—"The Tylenol Crisis"

In 1982 in Chicago, five people died from taking extra-strength Tylenol capsules. The makers of Tylenol, Johnson & Johnson ordered stores nation wide to pull 31 million bottles of Tylenol from their shelves. Additionally, 500,000 doctors and hospitals were notified of the tainted capsules. As a result, consumers were offered to receive free tablets as a replacement for the capsules. As Johnson & Johnson continually received information from around the country, their handling of "The Tylenol Crisis" has been documented as Consumer Confidence continued in its products.

Answer these questions:

1. How do you define Johnson & Johnson's ethical and legal dilemma?
2. What action would you have taken? Explain.
3. What message does this situation send to customers? Is there a cost or lost to the company? If your answer is "Yes," research and summarize your findings.

Name ____________________ Date __________

JEOPARDY QUIZ #5

1. The answer is: The name we give to our concern for good behavior.

   What is ____________________?

2. The answer is: Three genres of relationships that affect one's professional behavior.

   What are ____________________?

3. The answer is: Any untrue and spiteful statement that injures the reputation and character of another person.

   What is ____________________?

4. The answer is: The written defamation of a person or company's character.

   What is ____________________?

5. The answer is: You have spoken derogatory words about a co-worker.

   What is ____________________?

6. The answer is: The purposeful intrusion into the private life of any employee or the denial of his/her rights to be left alone.

   What is ____________________?

7. The answer is: The Act or Law that provides individuals access to information in governmental files.

   What is ____________________?

8. The answer is: The need to conduct investigation concerning allegations of discrimination, employment dismissal or sexual harassement.

   What is ____________________?

continued

9. The Acts or Laws passed in 1972 and 1992 that deal with protected groups in hiring and firing.

   What is ____?

10. The answer is: Protected groups in U.S. society.

    Who are ____?

PART II

COMMUNICATION THROUGH MESSAGES

CHAPTER 6

Planning, Composing, and Revising Business Messages

Objectives

Upon reading this chapter and completing the exercises, you will be able to:

1. Explain what is meant by "frame of reference."
2. Discuss the skills needed to create an effective message.
3. Describe the communication needed to set up a meeting.
4. State the advantages and disadvantages of channels and media of communication.
5. Explain the factors important in determining the medium of communication.
6. Discuss the process of composition.
7. Use transitional words effectively in writing.
8. Explain the term "readability."
9. Calculate the fog index on your writing.
10. Use a popular writing analysis software program.
11. Edit your business messages using proofreaders' marks.
12. Determine when to use a fax message and an e-mail message.

The purpose of this chapter is to help you develop the skills and knowledge to effectively communicate orally or in writing, the art of using language to achieve your intended best effect, and the ability to clearly and accurately inform and explain without coercion or deception. The ability to communicate and to successfully exchange thoughts, messages, or information is a very valuable skill.

Frame of Reference

People receive and perceive information based on their perceptions which are related to their frame of reference. Your frame of reference is influenced by a number of factors including age, gender, family, culture, ethnicity, education, and experience. Your frame of reference determines how you process and retain information. It is "the background against which a thing (message) is perceived," according to the Dictionary of Behavioral Science, and "a system of attitudes and values which provide a standard against which actions, ideas, and results are judged and to some extent controls or directs action and expression." For example, if you come from a family who see little value in higher education, in most cases your view of education would probably be the same.

Your frame of reference is influenced by a number of factors. Figure 6.1 presents the frames of reference for five hypothetical CSLA students to illustrate how various factors can influence our perceptions.

The frames of reference of the hypothetical students listed in Figure 6.1 would be quite dissimilar on the value of higher education or some other topic. The students' opinion would be influenced by their background, culture, ethnicity, etc.

Similarly, your frame of reference determines how you communicate with audiences. Your frame of reference is not better or superior to the frame of reference of another person, group, or organization—just different. For example, in most traditional American companies,

Factor	Student #1	Student #2	Student #3	Student #4	Student #5
Age	18	22	20	24	26
Family	Parents	Single-Parent	Parents	Grand-parents	Single-parent
Gender	female	male	female	male	female
Culture	Taiwanese	Guatemalan	African-American	Middle-Eastern	Anglo-American
Ethnicity	Asian	Hispanic	Africa	Armenian	English-Dutch
Citizen-ship	American	American	American	American	American
Year	Freshman	Sophomore	Junior	Senior	Graduate
Major	Accounting	Special Education	Political Science	Engineering	MBA

Figure 6.1. Frames of Reference.

there is a different frame of reference for management and still a different frame of reference for employees. Management perceives a problem from one perspective and the employees perceive it from another perspective.

Recently, many American companies began adopting the Japanese style of management, and the success of that style is primarily because of procedures that help employees and management view problems from the same perspective—from the same frame of reference. In any organization there are individuals who complain about almost every management decision. Sometimes their complaints are justified, but they might not complain if they understood the criteria management used to make the decision. On the other hand, they might not complain if management *communicated* their frame of reference to employees effectively. Obviously, communication is more difficult if you are trying to communicate with more than one person because you must consider multiple frames of reference.

Tailor Your Message to Your Audience

You should always tailor your communication to match the frame of reference as your audience. A classic example of ineffective communication occurs when a new college graduate applies for a job. Some graduates with good intentions spend hours preparing an exceptional resume, and then send that same resume to ten different companies with job openings. The problem with this approach is that those job openings are all slightly different. Each resume should reflect the best fit between your qualifications and the needs of the company advertising the position. Similarly, your communication should be the best fit for the situation. To become an effective writer requires your honing a number of skills, including decision making.

Skills and Decision Making

As a business writer, you should carefully plan your writing before you begin the writing process. In the planning stage, you have a number of decisions to make before you even begin the writing process. Then, you would gather information, including visual information, you will need to achieve your goal. Now, comes the writing, editing, proofreading, and rewriting stages. Notice in Figure 6.2 the writing and rewriting stages.

Many people struggle with writing because they try to write and edit at the same time. It is very difficult, if not impossible, to wear two hats at the same time. The result is like writing the same sentence or paragraph over and over again. You should focus on one skill at a time. Plan, then gather information, write, edit, proofread, and then rewrite.

Determining Communication Channels and Mediums

The two channels of communication are written and oral. Examples of oral media include: the telephone, a meeting, and the grapevine. Many authorities call these oral media channels.

Skills	Decision Making
1. Planning	What do you want to accomplish with your message? What is the criteria for achieving your goal? What is your audience's frame of reference? What is the appropriate channel(s) and media?
2. Gathering Information	What information is needed? Will you include visual information?
3. Writing	What is the main idea (theme) of your information? How should you organize your information?
4. Editing	What changes can you make to improve the message?
5. Proofreading	What techniques can you use to make sure your message is effective?
6. Rewriting	What final changes are needed to improve your message?

Figure 6.2.

Examples of written media include: memos, letters, E-mail. Each channel and medium has advantages and disadvantages. Oral communication that is face-to-face provides immediate feedback, and opportunities for group problem-solving and decision making. On the other hand a speech at an annual convention does not. Oral communication like meetings or video conferences can easily digress from the goal or purpose; and without accurate minutes there is no follow-up on decisions or action items. Written communication provides a permanent record, and an opportunity to communicate detailed and complex messages. Written communication channels like E-mail and memos may not provide adequate information or details.

You will use both channels and more than one medium to complete routine business tasks. Suppose you want to establish a task force, a temporary group of people and resources to achieve a specific goal. You would write a *memo* to the task force members summarizing the group's *purpose,* and schedule the first meeting. A tentative *agenda* for the meeting would be attached to the memo. A follow-up *telephone* call or *voice-mail* message would be made one or two days before the meeting reminding members about the meeting. At the *meeting* you would ask for revisions to the agenda, and pass out *handouts* as each topic was discussed. At the end of the meeting, you would review the decisions and items that require action for the next meeting, and schedule the next meeting. Within 24 hours after the meeting ends, you would distribute minutes summarizing the discussion, decisions, and list the action items and the people responsible for those items. If you counted correctly, during this process you used three oral media (telephone, voice-mail and meeting) (and four print media (memo, agenda, handouts, and minutes) to achieve your goal.

Selecting the Medium

You should use care in selecting the medium; your decision must be based on the content of the message, the urgency of the message, and the receiver's reaction to the message. An

E-mail would not be a suitable medium for telling an employee that he or she has been fired because it is too casual, impersonal, and the news is unpleasant. While E-mail is supposed to be private, if one wants to access your information, a skilled hacker can access it. A personal visit to the employee first and then a formal letter would be more appropriate because it is more formal and connotes authority.

Time is another determining factor. It takes more time to write and print a letter or memo than it does to write and send an E-mail message. E-mail is not instantaneous, but it is much faster than a memo or letter. A telephone call is even quicker unless the line is busy or the person is away from his or her desk.

Your message may need to be sent simultaneously to many people at different locations, so that may be a concern as well. Always continue to improve your productivity and using the technology available can help you do just that.

Your written communication skills will need to be exhibited more in your entry level position and as you progress up the corporate ladder. Once you reach the upper management level, your interpersonal and presentation skills become more and more important.

Figure 6.3 shows a checklist of questions and decisions needed to help you write messages:

To eliminate unanswered applicable questions that may be of interest or value to your reader, substitute the event, problem, activity, or person you are reporting about for "X" and gather information to answer the following questions:

Planning

For business messages to be effective, they must be well planned, well organized, and of course, well constructed. Routine messages require less planning, but complex messages or

- ✔ Define X? What does X mean?
- ✔ Analyze X? Are there component parts of X?
- ✔ What is the process? How is X made, or done?
- ✔ What is the essential function of X?
- ✔ What are the causes of X?
- ✔ What is the current status of X?
- ✔ What will be the future status of X?
- ✔ What are the facts about X?
- ✔ How did X happen?
- ✔ What kind of person is X?
- ✔ What is the value of X?
- ✔ What case can be made for, or against, X?

Figure 6.3. Checklist to Write Complete Messages

bad-news messages require more planning and take more time to write. Writing is a process; the composition process revolves around three simple categories, namely, planning, composing, and revising.

To effectively create a message you should consider the factors of the Communication Decision Tree: 1) the purpose of your message, 2) to whom you are writing (audiences), 3) the type of communication required, and 4) the writing style. Every business communication or document that you write has a purpose, and if you do not consider that purpose when you communicate, your listener or reader or audience may not understand or respond. The purpose may be simple or complex. Here are some examples:

Purpose	**Main idea**
If you wanted to:	You might write:
Applaud an individual's achievements.	Congratulations on your recent promotion.
Fire an employee.	I am sorry to inform you that effective immediately we will no longer need your services.
Learn the current status of a research project.	Please submit a written report summarizing the progress on your research project.

Composing

In the composing process, you determine the organization of the message—what do you want to say first, then second, third, etc. The content should flow from one thought to another. Do remember that the reader's reaction or expectation determines where the main idea is placed in the communication.

You will also need to include information to support your main idea. For example, if the reader wants to know when the order will be mailed, that is what should appear in the first paragraph, not in the last paragraph. Or if you have been asked to give a recommendation about a problem in the organization, your recommendation should come first in the document —not given after various amounts of supportive information. In most cases, the person is already familiar with the supporting information; naturally, you will want to give your recommendation first and the reader can read the supporting details after reading your recommendation.

After your message is organized using an established format, you will have to write *transitions* linking sentences and paragraphs. Writing *transitions*, which help the reader move from one subject to another, is one of the most *important* writing skills. It is *important* because transitions keep readers involved in your message. Each sentence or paragraph is an extension of the previous sentence or paragraph. *Transitions* are like bridges; if *they* are not properly established, your readers or listeners may fall right out of your message.

Sentences are linked using pronouns, repeated key words, transitional expressions, or parallel structure to create unified paragraphs. *Paragraphs* are primarily linked using key words or transitional expressions. You can also use a short paragraph as a link between longer paragraphs. The key word "paragraphs" link this paragraph to the first paragraph in this section. Consider the expressions and examples shows in Figure 6.4.

An example of a paragraph illustrating transitional expressions appears next:

> Today's customers are astute buyers; they do comparison shopping and want the best product for the best price. These buyers are willing to shop around and spend an extra ten to fifteen minutes just to save a few dollars. Moreover, these buyers want satisfaction for their money.

Revising

At this stage, you will want to reflect on the Communication Decision Tree elements and the content of the entire communication. Ask yourself if the content reflects the needs of your audience. Have you used the correct format—a memo or letter or report? Does the communication have a purpose? Is the content arranged correctly or organized correctly? If you can answer "yes" to all these questions, then you are now ready for the last stage in the writing process; that is, the revising stage. When you revise, you do the following:

1. Edit the printed draft message which you inputted
2. Make changes on the draft and input the changes
3. Print out another draft of the message
4. Proofread the message
5. Correct any errors
6. Print out the final copy of the message

Transitional Expressions	Examples
Pronouns	their, they
Key Words	transitions, linked sentences
Transitional Words	Moreover, but, here, similarly, to this end, therefore, in brief, meanwhile
Parallel Structure	repeated sentence pattern or structure

Figure 6.4. Transitional Expressions and Examples.

As a business writer, you will need to know how readable is your writing. Various journals, books, magazines, and newspapers are written on a certain reading level so that the readers who subscribe to these literatures can understand the content.

Readability (Fog Index)

Formulas to measure readability have been available since the early 1930s. Two best known formulas are Robert Gunning's Fog Index and Rudolph Flesch's Reading Ease Formula. The Fog Index measures the average sentence length and the number of words with more than two syllables. Generally, readability formulas are based on the idea that it is easier to read and understand short words and short sentences. Long sentences, with a series of thoughts packed into one sentence, make the content difficult to comprehend and retain.

Calculating the Fog Index

To calculate the fog index on a piece of writing, select a paragraph of 100 plus words. A word is anything with a space on either side of it. A sentence consists of a subject, verb, and object, or two complete sentences joined by a conjunction or a semicolon. Then, count the number of words and the number of sentences. Determine the average sentence length and the percent of difficult words. Add the sum of the average sentence length and the percent of difficult words together and then multiply by 0.4. The answer is the number of years of education needed to understand the writing. Compute by hand the fog index on the following paragraph.

> People work in *organizations* to achieve their own goals as well as the goals of the *organization*. An *organization* can be defined as an *entity* of people working *together* to achieve common goals. An *organization* cannot exist without people. These people are *essentially* the *employees* of the *organization*. *Employees* need *information* to perform their tasks; they need feedback regarding their *performance*. *Employees* need to be kept abreast of the *organization's* goals and its *performance relative* to goal *achievement*. *Communication* plays an *important* role in the *organization*, whether it is an *employee* talking to a *customer* or client, an *employee* talking to a *supervisor*, *employees* talking to each other, or a *supervisor* talking to an *employee*.

This paragraph has: 115 words
27 difficult words
6 sentences

Average sentence length 115/6	= 19
Percent of difficult words 27/115	= 23
Total	= 42
Multiply by 0.4	= 16.8

Readability level is 16.8; a person with 17 years of schooling is able to comprehend this paragraph.

Some Tips for Readable Writing follow:

How Readable Is Your Message?

Score	Level	Average Words per Sentence	Syllables per 100 Words	Publication	Grade Equivalent
90–100	Very Easy	8	123	Comics	5
80–89	Easy	11	131	Pulp	6
70–79	Fairly Easy	14	139	Fiction	7
60–69	Standard	17	147	Reader's Digest or Newspaper	8–9
50–59	Fairly Difficult	21	155	Literary Journal	10–12
30–49	Difficult	25	167	Scholarly Journal	13–16
0–29	Very Difficult	29	192	Professional Journal	College Graduate

Writing Mechanics

Your communication is most effective if it is understandable in a single reading or hearing. When you write your business messages, you should aim at a level that your readers can understand. Generally speaking, you should gauge your business writing at the 12th grade level. However, if you are a business person who is asked to speak to a fourth-grade class, you would, of course, tailor your message to that audience.

Do you want to know if your writing is interesting? Count the number of personal words and sentences your message contains, and estimate its human interest value using an adapted interest index formula.

Personal Words Include

1. Personal Pronouns — you, we, our, they, us (people)
2. Nouns with Gender — woman, man, boy, girl, aunt, uncle (do not include common gender like teacher, doctor, or employee)
3. Name of People — Oscar, Doris, Mrs. Frise (one word)
4. Special Words — folks, people (count as personal words)

Find the percent of personal words by dividing the number of personal words by the number of words in your message.

Personal Sentences Include

1. Spoken Sentences	He said, "She snores so loud the walls vibrate."
2. Exclamations	What a creative way to write a message!
3. Questions	Did you read the "Soloist?"
4. Directions & Requests	Proof your message after you rewrite it.
5. Incomplete Sentences	She learns because she rewrites, and rewrites, and . . .

Convert the number of personal sentences to a percent by dividing the number of personal sentences by the number of sentences in your message.

How Interesting Is Your Message?

Human Interest	Level of Interest	% of Personal Words	% of Personal Words	Typical Magazine
60–100	Dramatic	17	58	Fiction
40–59	Very Dramatic	10	43	New Yorker
20–39	Interesting	7	15	Reader's Digest
10–19	Mildly Interesting	4	5	Trade
6–0	Dull	2 or less	0	Scientific

Editing the first printed draft. With your first draft of the communication task, you should review it for format. Although you asked yourself the following questions in the composing stage, review the draft again and check if it is in correct memo or letter style? Are the memo parts placed correctly? Are the letter parts placed correctly? Does the communication contain a routine, good-news, bad-news, or persuasive message? Once you have determined this, then review carefully where the main idea is placed in your communication.

Use Positive Tone

Being adept at communicating will require your ability to use positive tone as much as possible. Tone is the way a statement sounds. Some writing situations will necessitate the need for a tactful tone. Consider the examples that follow; which statement is more positive?

State ideas using positive language.

Remember to mail your ballot by Friday.
Don't forget to mail your ballot by Friday.
We cannot ship your sweater until you send us your size.

You will receive your sweater as soon as you send us your size.
As an author, I could help you edit your newsletter.
I would be glad to help you edit your newsletter.

Use Active Voice and Action Verbs

Using active voice and verbs makes your writing more alive. In active voice, the subject does the acting. In passive voice, the subject is the receiver of the action; this voice is better when you have to present unpleasant or negative information.

Active voice. Jose completed the job ahead of schedule.

Passive voice. The job was completed ahead of schedule by Jose.

Active voice. The manager called the meeting to order.

Passive voice. The meeting was called to order by the manager.

Action verbs. The costs skyrocketed. The market plummeted. Enrollment decreased by 20 percent. Profits jumped to 12 percent over last year's.

Make changes. Using the following list of proofreaders' marks in Figure 6.5, indicate changes directly on the draft; then make the changes on the computer.

Use Bias-Free Language

In today's competitive workplace, a business writer or speaker cannot afford the risk of sending an insensitive message or communication. Additionally, managers cannot afford to alienate employees and/or customers. As a business writer, try to carefully select words to eliminate any trace of insensitivity regarding race or ethnic group, religion, age, gender, or disability.

For instance, avoid using the pronoun "he" when referring to a group of people that may include women.

Example:

When your insurance agent comes, he is to make the offer.
Upon arrival, the insurance agent is to make the offer.

Try to use gender-free language.

Standard Proofreaders' Marks

Capitalize ≡	George Taylor, public relations director, Academic Technology Support, will direct the press conference.
Close up	Weekly staff meetings begin at 8 a. m.
Delete	Word-processing software available today is capable of interfacing with voice recognition software.
Insert ^	This system can accommodate a networked printer. new
Insert space #	Senior managers address this problem everyday.
Insert comma	Clear concise messages save much time and money.
Insert period	The agenda is included in the minutes
Insert apostrophe	The Dean perspective is opposite. 's
Insert hyphen	The toy comes with easy to follow instructions.
Move copy as indicated	Today your August payment was received.
Change copy as indicated	Employees will be able to share in the profits.
Lowercase /	Dennie Christopher is Self-Employed.
Paragraph ¶	This textbook was a collaborative effort.
Align type vertically	DATE: May 28, 1997. SUBJECT: Internships Available
Transpose	Americans beleive in truth and fairness.
Stet (keep original thought)	We plan an intercultural event in May. STET
Move down; lower	April 27, 1997
Move up; raise	November 13, 1997
Move to left	1. Begin the date on Line 12.
Move to right	Indent paragraphs within double spaced text.
Single space	Miss Taylor Shane SS Vice President
Double space	Reverend Wayne C. Cooper DS Senior Pastor

Figure 6.5.

Example:

The supervisor (not foreman) is attending the meeting.
The manager (not businesswoman) is going to make the presentation.
The working parent (not working mother) is on leave of absence.
The host (not hostess) is such a wonderful person.

Avoid insensitive wording.

Examples:

The black mayor of San Francisco is up for re-election.
Instead, use this wording:
The mayor of San Francisco is up for re-election.
The Jewish representative has an offer to make.
Instead, use this wording:
This representative has an offer to make.

Avoid words with negative or judgmental connotations such as handicap, unfortunate, afflicted, culturally-disadvantaged.

Example:

Blind employees will be telephoned.
Instead, use this wording:
Employees with vision impairments will be telephoned.
This elevator is for handicapped individuals.
Instead, use this wording:
Employees with disabilities will use this elevator.

Print out another draft. Review this second draft carefully. Now you want to check the communication for completeness, coherence and clarity. Have you answered the reader's questions or concerns? Does every sentence make sense? Are your thoughts clear and concise? Have you reviewed every sentence to see if you can cross out any unnecessary words?

Many word processing software programs are available on the market so you can check readability statistics using any of them. Most word processing software packages have a writing analysis feature that can display the number of words, characters, paragraphs, and sentences, the average number of sentences per paragraph, words per sentence, and characters per word, and other readability indexes for the document or message you are reviewing. Readability levels are based on word choice, sentence length, and sentence structure. A key point to remember is that readability level is a measure of the complexity of your writing, not the content.

Hopefully, you will be composing your messages at a computer. Many of the mechanical and grammatical problems such as subject-verb agreement errors, tense errors, misspelled words, sentence types, readability, and incomplete sentences are flagged as problem areas, but YOU have to correct those errors. Spell checkers, grammar checkers, and writing analysis programs only highlight probable errors; it takes the human mind to correct communication for content or meaning. Popular writing analysis software programs are Rightwriter and Grammatik; many word processing software programs have grammar checker and spell check features. Although grammar, spelling, punctuation, and typographic errors may appear trivial to some people, your readers will view your attention to specific detail as a measure of your professionalism. Remember that a spelling error or typo is just like a very noticeable stain on a suit or dress—it detracts from the purpose of your message. At this stage, you may want to use a writing analysis package to give you more feedback on your writing ability.

Correct errors. If you have answered "no" to any of the questions asked above, then you need to make those corrections now. If the writing analysis gives you suggestions and you agree, then make those corrections. Or, you may need to review the Communication Decision Tree components or writing styles.

Proofread. This is a critical stage, so be extra careful to proofread the entire document. Your communication reflects you, the company, and its products and services. You want your communications to be free of errors. How do you proofread? Well, you can read your communication aloud to yourself; you can ask someone else who is proficient in English mechanics to read it for you; you can read the communication backwards starting from the bottom line; you can look at the writing analysis list of words for review or check for spelling, or you can set the communication aside for a while and read it again in a quiet place. Then, you correct any errors you find.

Print out the final copy. Lastly, you are now ready to print out the final copy of the communication. Proofread it again carefully and slowly BEFORE you sign it.

Format and Arrangement of Short, Informal Messages

Memos and letters are considered short, informal messages. Memos have unique arrangement, and letters have different letter parts. You choose writing styles based upon the reader's reaction. When the reader will be pleased, you use the direct or deductive writing style where the main idea is in the first paragraph. When the reader will be displeased, you use the indirect or inductive writing style where the main idea or bottom line is placed in the third paragraph. When you have to persuade the reader to do as you have asked, then the main idea is

Writer's Checklist

Ask yourself the following questions to ensure your message is clear, understandable, and effective:

Topic	Test
Communication	Is the message simple, clear and understandable ? (Coherence) Did you choose the correct and appropriate words? (Diction) Did you use the correct punctuation to communicate your meaning?
Organization	Is the thesis or primary theme adequately explained and developed? (Emphasis)
Visual Aids	Did you use graphics to increase readership and improve understanding?
Completeness	Does the message contain all the information of interest or value to your audience?
Accuracy	Is the message complete?
Readability	Are the transitions smooth and flowing? Have unfamiliar words or statements been defined, clarified or replaced?
Tone	Is the tone appropriate to the theme and purpose of the message?
Legality	Does the message contain words or statements that might damage an individual's reputation? (Defamation) Does the message contain embarrassing facts about an individual without just cause or good reason? (Invasion of Privacy)
Channel & Media	Did you use the right channel and medium or media to deliver your message?

placed in the last paragraph which calls for action on the reader's part. The AIDA approach is a four step plan which is key to paragraph development in letters of persuasion. The "A" stands for Attention; the "I" stands for Interest; the "D" stands for Desire, and the "A" stands for Action. The AIDA plan relates to the elements of persuasion which are discussed in detail in Chapter 10.

Composing Business and Personal Messages

Information presented in this textbook focuses on composing business messages that you will write for a business purpose. Just as you will have to write routine, good-news, bad-news, and persuasive messages in a business organization, you can use the same techniques in writing personal messages. The audiences will be different, so you will need to tailor your messages to fit the occasion. Additionally, you will soon be writing employment communication to secure a full-time position. You will use these same techniques in those messages. Your business messages will be printed on company letterhead and put in company envelopes while your personal messages will be printed on personal stationery or plain paper and put in personal or plain envelopes. More will be discussed on Career Preparation in Chapter 17 and Letters of Application and the Interview Process in Chapter 18.

The importance of writing error-free business messages cannot be over emphasized. You should use correct English mechanics and never offend any reader or listener. A brief review of English is presented in this chapter rather than an appendix to emphasize its importance in the writing process. Meaning is conveyed through word choice, punctuation, mechanics, and vocabulary. Some fundamentals of grammar and usage are presented next.

Punctuation

When you are driving, you see signs to tell you when to slow down or stop, turn, or merge; likewise punctuation helps your readers grasp the meaning of your message.

Periods. Use a period to end a sentence that is not a question, with abbreviations, and between dollars and cents in money amounts.

Examples:

Thank you for your assistance.
The U. S. is the land of opportunity. I received a check for $2,500.83 to repair my car.
Will you send us a check today.

Question Marks. Use a question mark after a direct question that requests an answer.

Example:

Are you planning a graduation party?

Exclamation Point. Use an exclamation point after highly emotional language; in reality most business writing is not emotional.

Example:

Congratulations on your promotion!

Semicolons. Use a semicolon to separate two closely related independent clauses, when the items in a series already have commas within them, and before conjunctive adverbs.

Examples:

A final revised table of contents is due Friday; the complete report is due within two weeks.
The test dates are February 9, 1998; June 6, 1998; and December 28, 1998.
I was hired; however, I do not know my starting date.

Colons. Use a colon after a saluation in mixed letter style punctuation and at the end of a sentence or phrase introducing a list or idea:

Examples:

Dear Mrs. Cardella Powers:

Her test score was high in three areas: aptitude, situational ethics, and integrity.

The categories are as follows:

hybrid
natural
dominant

Commas. Use a comma to separate items in a series and introductory clauses; a comma is used after an introductory phrase, to surround parenthetical phrases or words, between compound adjectives, before family generation names, incorporated companies, before and after the year when writing month, day, and year, to separate a quotation from the rest of the sentence, and whenever necessary to avoid confusion.

Examples:

Please order paper, pens, and disks.
Leslie addressed the Special Education parents, and I addressed the Honor students.
Because of your skepticism, the event was cancelled.
Yes, we are in agreement.
The new homeowners, the Fowlers, are pleased with the services they received.
He is scheduled for a long, difficult surgery.
George Foreman, I, George Foreman, II, and George Foreman, III are all sons of the boxer, George Foreman.
Shane, Incorporated which is owned by Jeffrey Shane, a Ph.D., is a relatively new company.
The dinner meeting will be December 15, 1997, in New York.
The subpoena reads, "You are to appear in Superior Court on Friday, March 5, 1997."
Ever since, they scrutinize all written contracts.

Dash. A dash is used to indicate a sudden change of thought, to emphasize a parenthetical word or phrase, or to set off a phrase that contains commas. (A dash is indicated by two hyphens with no spacing before, between, or after.

Examples:

This year's profits — well over $1 million — are still down.
ABC membership — now $50 and rising — is well worth it.
All our newest offices — San Francisco, Los Angeles, and Chicago — have opened.

Hyphens. Use a hyphen to separate the parts of compound words beginning with prefixes as self, ex, quasi, and all, with prefixes before a proper noun or vowel at the end of the prefix when the first letter of the root word is the same, with compound adjectives that come before the noun, and to divide words at the end of a typed line. Use a dictionary or grammar checker.

Examples:

The ex-football player is a guitarist.
The anti-American was attacked.
This is an 8 percent interest-bearing account.

Apostrophes. Use an apostrophe to form a possessive noun or to indicate a contraction.

Examples:

On her desk was a reply to Connie Chung's letter regarding the missing printer.
We'll call you tomorrow; however, I don't think the result will be positive.

Quotation marks. Use quotation marks to surround words that are repeated exactly as they were said or written, to set off the title of a newspaper story or magazine article, and to indicate special treatment for words or phrases. (Be sure to include both sets of quotation marks; periods and commas go inside the quotation marks; colons and semicolons go outside them. A question mark goes inside the quotation marks only if the quotation is a question. If the quotation is an entire sentence, the question mark goes outside.)

Examples:

The last statement said, "Pay by February 15 or return the merchandise."
You must read "The Chalkboard Kitchen" in the Today's Journal.
Our Strategic Planning "team" does more complaining than solving problems.
During the strike, we wondered, "Is the board with us?"
What did Pat mean by "You haven't heard the end of this"?

Parentheses. Use parentheses to surround comments that are incidental or figures in arabic numerals that follow the same amount in words in legal documents.

Examples:

I sent the money (although I hated to waste $15) by Western Union.
The sum is One Thousand ($1,000).

Underscores and italics. Use an underscore to indicate the title of a book, newspaper, or magazine or to provide emphasis.

Example:

Business Communication for the 21st Century has a 1997 copyright date.
The net profit is higher than expected.

Capitals. Capitalize the first word that begins a sentence, days of the week, proper nouns, places, and things, titles within families, governments, or companies, the first word of the salutation and complimentary close of a letter.

Examples:

These are writing mechanics exercises.
The Deacons' meeting is on Tuesdays, and the Deaconnesses' meeting is on Saturdays.
Mrs. Mays has been informed that her interview is today.
Macy's is opening a new store in the West, near Flagstaff.
The Pentagon building in Washington, D. C. is an architect's delight.
My Aunt Bea was very close to my mother.
Dear Mr. Randle and Sincerely yours are typed correctly.

Numbers and money. Spell out all numbers from one to ten and use arabic numerals for the rest. However, do not begin a sentence with a numeral. Use numerals for consistency in a list of numbers, for percentages, time of day (except with o'clock), dates, and dollar amounts. Use a comma in four digit numbers, and a decimal point only if cents are included or for consistency in a list.

Examples:

Twenty people who came to the meeting purchased 400 shares of stock within the first 30 minutes.
Our weekly sales quote rose from 7 to 14 to 39. Our School is responsible for raising 10 percent of its operating budget.
The Task Force meeting is scheduled for 8:30 a.m. on May 27.
Please add $5 for postage and handling costs.
Our enrollment target is 3,856 students for the next academic year.
I received two checks, one for $768 and one for $2,500.
I think $489.02 is sufficient.

English Writing Mechanics

The following exercises are presented as a brief review of the mechanics of writing. How many of the exercises can you complete correctly? Your instructor will review them with you.

Spelling Checkup

If a word is spelled correctly, write "C" in the space provided; if it is misspelled, write the correct spelling of the word(s). Test your own knowledge before using the dictionary.

1. supercede ______________________________
2. accomodate ______________________________
3. recieve ______________________________
4. discribe ______________________________
5. priviledge ______________________________
6. seperate ______________________________
7. buisness ______________________________
8. benefitted ______________________________
9. accompaning ______________________________
10. desirable ______________________________
11. judgment ______________________________
12. questionaire ______________________________
13. congradulations ______________________________
14. embarassing ______________________________
15. indespensable ______________________________
16. Saleable ______________________________
17. sincerly ______________________________
18. vacillate ______________________________

19. lableing ______________________________

20. omission ______________________________

21. desperate ______________________________

22. begining ______________________________

23. elligible ______________________________

24. convenient ______________________________

25. personel ______________________________

Passive/Active Voice

Rewrite the following sentences so that they are in active voice.

1. The award was given by Dr. Carol Choi.

   ____

2. The check was received by the Accounting Department.

   ____

3. Mrs. Mimi Young moved to Atchison, Kansas.

   ____

4. The trio was questioned by the agent.

   ____

5. Estimates for supplies will be prepared by Mattie Madison.

   ____

6. Praise from the manager was often given to the employees.

   ____

7. The statement was presented by the witness.

   ____

8. The flowers were delivered by Conroy's.

   ____

9. Mary Lynne made the statement.

____

10. A request for vacation should be submitted by each worker.

____

11. Last week's meeting of the Student Affairs Committee was not attended by Ms. Zaitz.

____

12. Accreditation was received by the School of Business and Economics.

____

13. The contract has been scrutinized by her attorney.

____

14. The structure was designed by Frank Lloyd Wright.

____

15. ____

(Write in your own sentence written in active voice on the line above.)

Writing Mechanics Checkup

1. Change the following sentences to active voice where needed.

An award was given to Colin Powell by the President.

____

The student was asked several questions by the instructor.

____

The chairperson called the meeting to order at 9 a.m.

____

The Metropolitan Water District's College Fair was attended by representatives from 18 different colleges in southern California.

____

____

____

A gift was presented to me by the staff members.

____

2. Indicate the type of sentence, put in the corect punctuation, and give the rule.
Only Liz and I went to the college fair

____

After you decide please give me the courtesy of sharing the information with the staff first

____

We started with eight staff members but we now have only five.

____

If I had known I would be working at the counter I would not have accepted the position however I am glad I took the job now

____

Areceli is leaving the office she has accepted another position across campus

____

3. Make essential changes in word usage, spelling, and punctuation as needed.
After you search Lexis/Nexis you should look at newspaper indices for aditional buisness articals.
I look forward to you corporation in this new venture.
Since I recieved your payment late I have no choice but to notify the credit burrow.
The mechanixs of English is essential mispelled words are unexceptable.
One of the many things we are confronted with are personnel problems.
4. Edit the following sentences for grammar correctness:
Walking, bicycling, and going to jog are my favorite hobbies.
Mari did not know where she is staying at.
There is the kitchen that still needs to be carpeted.
When a small girl, by brother taught me to ride the bike.

Mediums of communication and an in depth discussion of routine, good-news, bad-news, and persuasive messages will be presented in Chapters 7, 8, 9, and 10.

Questions

1. What is the impact of people having different frames of reference?
2. Which of the skills needed to create effective messages is more important?

3. What are the steps involved in the composition process?
4. How are transitional words used?
5. Which medium and channel is used more?
6. When should you use a faxed message?
7. When should you use an E-mail message?
8. What are the steps involved in revising your message?
9. What is meant by "organizing" your message?
10. Give examples of factors that affect a person's frame of reference.
11. Are there privacy issues in the use of faxed or E-mail messages?

Applications

1. Which medium and channel would you use in the following situations?
   a) You have to lay off a staff member who has been with your department for over ten years.
   b) Your assistant does not proofread documents you have asked him to prepare for your signature.
   c) You have an employee who is an agitator—likes to stir up emotions in people.
   d) a Japanese official who is in town is planning to speak to your organization. He wants to know the length of time for his speech.
2. Using the checklist to write Complete Messages, Figure 6.3, use the writing skills of students in the School of Business and Economics as the event. Print out your analysis.
3. Using the Communication Decision Tree's element of purpose, craft a sentence for each main idea.
   a) Send a back-order message about a fax machine.
   b) Cut dental benefits.
   c) Approve a personal holiday for Taylor Shane.
   d) Deny Winston's request for a higher course grade.
4. Analyze the different frames of reference that might surface when a course section is cancelled.
5. Tie the following thoughts together using transitional words:
   a) Doris wants a raise. Pat wants to be transferred to another department. Clifton has asked for one week of vacation.
   b) Mary has been promoted to Senior Accountant. Carol has finished the revisions for her dissertation.
   c) The interest rate rose in 1992 and again in 1995. The present interest rate is stable.
6. Input a memo (100 word or more) giving your impressions of the Business Communication class thus far. Compute the fog Index on it.
7. Input a memo (100 words or more) to your professor in which you share with her or him some technical aspect of your major field of study.
8. Correct the following paragraphs using Proofreaders' marks:
   An artical appear inthe LA times regarding the poor writing skill of rescind graduates. It seems that business is more and more concerned about how new hires are able to communicate in writting and in speaking.

The year 2000 will be challenging especialy for those who has not chosen to farther there education. The jobs aas they exists today will not be avaiable. All workers should try to farther they're education or at least took some courses to get more informations.

9. Key in the paragraphs (#8 above) according to the proofreaders' marks you made.
10. Punctuate the following sentences:
    a) I want to order a large walnut desk
    b) Larry do you want me to order your lunch
    c) Marguerite is an articulate dedicated administrator
    d) If you cannot keep the appointment please cancel it
    e) Mr. Hines who has often spoken to our group is now a licensed broker
    f) Our profits have declined this year therefore we are offering a small dividend
    g) Many of the employee work nearby and they often walk to work
    h) My sister who lives in Lone Star Texas is now a home owner
    i) The colors of the American flag are red white and blue
    j) In fact Terry Shane is an executive with John Deere in Des Moines Iowa
11. Critique the following sentences. Indicate the error(s).
    a) Please send me more informations on this subject.
    b) The staffs is ready for the press conference.
    c) She got job after graduation.
    d) He said she is ready for the verdict.
12. To help increase your vocabulary, look up the meaning of the following words and then write a sentence using the word.

articulate	dissuade	novice	defamation
caveat	neophyte	attributes	predicated
eschew	egress		

Name ______________________________ Date ____________

JEOPARDY QUIZ #6

1. The answer is: The background against which a thing (message) is perceived?

   What is ______________________________?

2. The answer is: Planning, gathering information, writing, editing, proofreading, and rewriting.

   What are ______________________________?

3. The answer is: In addition, On the other hand, Similarly, and However.

   What are ______________________________?

4. The answer is: A measure of the writer's writing level.

   What is ______________________________?

5. The answer is: Insert, Paragraph, and Delete.

   What are ______________________________?

6. The answer is: Oral and written communication.

   What are ______________________________?

7. The answer is: A software program that critiques your writing.

   What is ______________________________?

8. The answer is: The telephone, a meeting, and the grapevine.

   What are ______________________________?

9. The answer is: The best method(s) for telling someone he or she has been fired.

   What is (are)______________________________?

continued

10. The answer is: To whom you are writing, the kind of document required, the writing style, and the purpose of your communication.

    What are ____?

CHAPTER 7

Career Day at
California State University, Los Angeles

Written Business Communication Mediums

Objectives

Upon reading the chapter and doing the exercises, you should be able to:

1. Discuss the various realms or audiences with whom you will communicate.
2. Describe the internal communications used in organizations.
3. Describe the external communications that take place within an organization.
4. Discuss the informal type of communication within an organization.
5. Explain what is meant by "customer service."
6. Distinguish between the types of channels and mediums.
7. Input a memo using correct headings.
8. Analyze why memos are so widely used in organizations.
9. Input a letter using standard letter parts as well as special letter parts.
10. Explain the letter punctuation styles.
11. Fold a personal letter to go in a personal size envelope.
12. Fold a business letter to go in a business size envelope.

You will be communicating with various realms or audiences within the organization and outside the organization. You should always keep in mind that you are a company spokesman, and your every conversation and letter should reflect the company's goodwill. The types of audiences include the company's internal audiences which consists of its owners and its employees. The external audiences will include customers and/or clients, vendors, the general public, and other businesses and government officials. Your communications will be formal communication which are approved by the management tier of the organization.

Internal Communications

In internal communications, you will be communicating back and forth with supervisors, co-workers, and others whom you may supervise. Internal communication is important to ensure the smooth flow of work processes, coordinate performance among many departments, keep employees informed of company performance, and to detect problem areas. Internal communication also helps to set policies and to influence decision making. Internal communication can include such mediums or documents as memos, reports, meetings, person-to-person conversations, telephone conversations, oral presentations, and speeches. Each company must be committed to improving its internal communication system. At California State University at Los Angeles, faculty, staff, and department chairs work closely with administration to provide its customers, you the students, with correct, up-to-date information regarding University policies and procedures.

The informal communication network in organizations is the grapevine. Much of the interchange of ideas and information that occurs along this network seems to have no specific or definite purpose relative to formal purposes of an organization. The informal chats that occur among people in organizations fits into this area as well.

In addition to the internal mediums mentioned earlier, electronic mail and surveys are frequently used to better internal communication.

External Communications

External communication permits the organization to secure a foothold in the marketplace and serve to enhance smooth company operations. Communicating with the public is needed to influence customer decision making. For example, sales letters are written to prospective audiences to get them to buy your products and/or services. Advertising your products and/or services creates an image of the organization, differentiating your products and/or services from other similar products and/or services of the market. Your external communication may include making a sales presentation, handling complaints about products and/or services, and order fulfillment. In addition, you may communicate with your customers and/or clients in a meeting, telephone call, face-to-face conversation, and oral presentation, or a through a written proposal. *Customer service* is the act of ensuring that customers feel valued, that their needs are met, and that you stand behind your products and/or services.

A company may need to purchase some goods or services from other companies in order to produce its own products or services. These transactions are opportunities to nurture relationships and to promote your company's best interests. These communications may be in the form of letters, oral presentations, meetings, telephone calls, written proposals and informal conversations.

Business sales contracts, federal, state and local laws dealing with organizations, and business requests for information about government laws and regulations such as taxes, unemployment compensation, social security issues, etc. are examples of business-to-government communication.

Communication Mediums

While communication needs can take a variety of mediums, the predominant ones are memos, letters, reports, facsimile, and electronic mail. Each of these mediums will be discussed in detail. Your writing should be positive and reflect the goodwill of the company. Where appropriate you should also write using the you-attitude; that is, write with the reader in mind. Information contained in your documents should be carefully monitored so as to be read by only the intended readers. The wording and privacy issues are extremely important.

Your *memorandums* should establish and maintain favorable relationships with your readers. Memos are usually one page documents which stay within the company and have a specific format. They are sent from one employee or supervisor or to another employee, group of people, or a supervisor. Memos usually deal with day-to-day operations of the organization or personnel matters. They are used to coordinate worker performance and to foster in-house communication as well as to help ensure smooth company operations. The body of memos is single spaced with double spacing between paragraphs. The paragraphs can be blocked or indented five spaces from the left margin. The heading of memos always includes the word "Memorandum" and has four side headings—To, From, Date, and Subject. Practically all business organizations have their own preprinted Memorandum stationery. Figures 7.1, 7.2, 7.3, and 7.4 feature traditional but different formats for memos. When you are asked to input a memo, be sure to follow the guidelines of the company for which you are working as each company may use a style peculiar to it.

Memos are the most widely used type of written communication that is sent to members within the organization; often times they are also sent to readers outside the organization. The memo is a medium for various kinds of messages including requesting action, transmitting information, and building goodwill. Moreover, memorandums are necessary for a written record of communication and to document actions and decisions.

When you write *letters*, keep in mind that the readers are forming a mental image of you, the company, and its products and services. You want to establish, nurture, and maintain relationships with your customers and/or clients and stakeholders, as well as others outside the organization.

You want the readers of your letters to focus on the content rather than on mechanical errors such as poor arrangement, misspelled words, punctuation errors, grammatical errors, etc. Letters to those outside the company are written on the company's letterhead or preprinted

MEMORANDUM

Date:	**February 21, 1997**
To:	**All Employees**
From:	**Payroll Department**
Subject:	**Signature Required for Pay Slips**

Effective immediately, you must sign your signature on the face of the pay slip.

Due to recent record keeping changes, signatures are mow required on the pay slip along with any other required bus inspection reports.

Thank you for your cooperation.

Figure 7.1. Memo Format.

MEMORANDUM

To:	**All Employees**	**Date:**	**February 21, 1997**
From:	**Payroll Department**	**Subject:**	**Signature Required on Pay Slip**

Effective immediately, you must sign your signature on the face of the pay slip.

Due to recent record keeping changes, signatures are now required on the pay slip along with any other required bus inspection reports.

Thank you for your cooperation.

Figure 7.2. Memo Format.

quality bond paper. Letters can be written in either indirect, inductive or direct, deductive writing style.

The body of letters is single spaced with double spacing between paragraphs and letter parts. The paragraphs are blocked or indented depending on the letter style. The body of the letter should be attractively arranged on the paper; the letter style conveys different impressions of the writer and/or the company.

Letter punctuation styles are called mixed or open. The open letter punctuation style is shown in Figure 7.5 and the mixed letter punctuation style is shown in Figure 7.6 In the open letter punctuation, there is no punctuation after the salutation nor the complimentary close. In the mixed letter punctuation style, a colon is placed after the salutation and a comma is placed after the complimentary close.

MEMORANDUM

To:	**All Employees**
From:	**Payroll Department**
Date:	**February 21, 1997**
Subject:	**Signature Required on Pay Slip**

Effective immediately, you must sign your signature on the face of the pay slip.

Due to recent record keeping changes, signatures are now required on the pay slip along with any other required bus inspection reports.

Thank you for your cooperation.

Figure 7.3. Memo Format.

MEMORANDUM

All Employees
Payroll Department
February 21, 1997
Signature Required on Pay Slip

Effective immediately, you must sign your signature on the face of the pay slip.

Due to recent record keeping changes, signatures are now required on the pay slip along with any other required bus inspection reports.

Thank you for your cooperation.

Figure 7.4. Simplified Memo Format.

Open Letter Style Punctuation:

Dear Mr. Rodiquez	or	Dear Mrs. Shane
Sincerely	or	Very truly yours

Mixed Letter Style Punctuation:

Dear Mr. Ogawa:	or	Dear Mr. Cheng:
Yours sincerely,	or	Yours truly,

June 6, 1997

Mrs. Andretta Jones
Pasadena High School
Pasadena, CA 91103

Dear Mrs. Jones

Thank you for your invitation to speak to your Algebra class. Yes, I will be happy to come on July 10 for the Career Day Fair.

I will bring brochures for all options in the School of Business and Economics. I also have some momentos for the students as well. I have a 15 minute video I would like to show to give the students some exposure to the campus.

Please send me a parking permit for that day.

I look forward to seeing you on July 10.

Sincerely

Dr. Marguerite P. Joyce, Director
Student Academic Services

Figure 7.5. Letter with Open Letter Style Punctuation.

June 6, 1997

Mrs. Andretta Jones
Pasadena High School
Pasadena, CA 91103

Dear Mrs. Jones:

Thank you for your invitation to speak to your Algebra class. Yes, I will be happy to come on July 10 for the Career Day Fair.

I will bring brochures for all options in the School of Business and Economics. I also have some momentos for the students as well. I have a 15 minute video I would like to show to give the students some exposure to the campus.

Please send me a parking permit for that day.

I look forward to seeing you on July 10.

Sincerely,

Dr. Marguerite P. Joyce, Director
Student Academic Services

Figure 7.6. Letter with Mixed Letter Style Punctuation.

The three traditional letter styles include full block, modified block with or without paragraph indention, and simplified. For example, in full block form, all lines begin flush at the left margin; no lines are indented as pictured in Figure 7.7. This arrangement is fast and easy and widely used in the United States but not in all other countries. Paragraphs are blocked and the body is single spaced with double spacing between paragraphs.

In the modified block arrangement, certain letter parts are indented or not indented depending on the style. For example, in the modified block with paragraph indention format, the paragraphs are indented five spaces, and the date and complimentary closing begin at the centering point as shown in Figure 7.8.

In the modified block without paragraph indention format, the paragraphs are blocked and the date and complimentary closing begin at the centering point. Figure 7.9 is an example of this format. If you are using special letter parts, then the letter style will determine where to place these parts, which will be discussed later in this chapter.

The simplified letter style as shown omits two letter parts—the salutation and the complimentary close as shown in Figure 7.10. In this style, a triple space always comes before the subject (written in all capital letters) and after the subject. Readers will usually expect the traditional letter parts but using this style, which is not widely accepted, will cause some distraction on the reader's part.

Letter Parts

Business letters will almost always contain the following standard letter parts:

letterhead
date
inside address
salutation
body of letter (content)
complimentary closing
signature and title of the writer
reference initials (of the typist)

Other special letter parts are the following:

attention line
subject line
company name
enclosure notation
copy notation
blind copy notation
postscript

June 6, 1997

Mrs. Andretta Jones
Pasadena High School
Pasadena, CA 91103

Dear Mrs. Jones:

Thank you for your invitation to speak to your Algebra class. Yes, I will be happy to come on July 10 for the Career Day Fair.

I will bring brochures for all options in the School of Business and Economics. I also have some momentos for the students as well. I have a 15 minute video I would like to show to give the students some exposure to the campus.

Please send me a parking permit for that day.

I look forward to seeing you on July 10.

Sincerely,

Marguerite P. Joyce

Dr. Marguerite P. Joyce, Director
Student Academic Services

Figure 7.7. Letter in Full Block Format.

June 6, 1997

Mrs. Andretta Jones
Pasadena High School
Pasadena, CA 91103

Dear Mrs. Jones:

Thank you for your invitation to speak to your Algebra class. Yes, I will be happy to come on July 10 for the Career Day Fair.

I will bring brochures for all options in the School of Business and Economics. I also have some momentos for the students as well. I have a 15 minute video I would like to show to give the students some exposure to the campus.

Please send me a parking permit for that day.

I look forward to seeing you on July 10.

Sincerely,

Dr. Marguerite P. Joyce, Director
Student Academic Services

Figure 7.8. Letter in Modified Block Format with Paragraph Indentation.

June 6, 1997

Mrs. Andretta Jones
Pasadena High School
Pasadena, CA 91103

Dear Mrs. Jones

Thank you for your invitation to speak to your Algebra class. Yes, I will be happy to come on July 10 for the Career Day Fair.

I will bring brochures for all options in the School of Business and Economics. I also have some momentos for the students as well. I have a 15 minute video I would like to show to give the students some exposure to the campus.

Please send me a parking permit for that day.

I look forward to seeing you on July 10.

Sincerely

Dr. Marguerite P. Joyce, Director
Student Academic Services

Figure 7.9. Letter in Modified Block Format with No Paragraph Indention.

June 6, 1997

Mrs. Andretta Jones
Pasadena High School
Pasadena, CA 91103

JULY 10 PRESENTATION

Thank you for your invitation to speak to your Algebra class. Yes, I will be happy to come on July 10 for the Career Day Fair.

I will bring brochures for all options in the School of Business and Economics. I also have some momentos for the students as well. I have a 15 minute video I would like to show to give the students some exposure to the campus.

Please send me a parking permit for that day.

I look forward to seeing you on July 10.

Dr. Marguerite P. Joyce, Director
Student Academic Services

Figure 7.10. Letter in Simplified Format.

Letterhead

Letters you write to readers outside the organization that pertain to company matters should be printed on the company's letterhead stationery. Preprinted letterhead stationery is usually printed on quality bond or high grade paper. The letterhead contains the company's name, address, and telephone number, fax number, worldwide web address, and e-mail address. All of this information is usually printed within the top two inches of the stationery. If you were writing a personal letter, your home address is your return address which is similar to the letterhead. With most graphics software programs on the market today, you can design your own personal letterhead. The word processing software in the computer labs at CSULA allow you to design yur own letterhead.

Date

The date is usually typed a double space below the bottom of the letterhead. The date should be spelled out such as:

January 30, 1997 or 30 January 1997

If you are inputting a personal letter and using plain paper to print, leave a one-inch top margin and start the date on line 8 or 9 (single spacing) as shown below:

6580 Bralorne Court
Stone Mountain, GA 30083
June 6, 1997

Mr. Dejavan Shane
Shane Property Management
616 South 16 Street
St. Joseph, MO 64501

Dear Mr. Shane

The Inside Address

The inside address refers to the address of the person to whom you are writing. This address consists of the person's name, title or position (if writing to a company), street address, city, state, and zip code. Examples of inside addresses, which are to be single spaced as is the body of the letter are presented below:

Ms. Mari Baldwin
Baldwin Fabrics
5002 Stevens Street
Lone Star, TX 75963

Dr. Carol Blaszczynski
Department of Management
School of Business and Economics
California State University,
Los Angeles
D3072 King Hall
5151 State University Drive
Los Angeles, CA 90032

Mrs. Gloria Mays
2519 Messanie Street
St. Joseph, MO 64501

Mr. David Chang
Computers R Us
100 Any Street
Stone Mountain, GA 30083

Salutation

The salutation is the greeting to the person to whom you are writing. The salutation can be personal (use the person's first name if you know him or her personally) or in a business letter you would use the person's title and last name as shown below:

Dear Dr. Blaszczynski
Dear Mr. Chang

Dear Mari
Dear Mrs. Mays

If you are writing to a business and you do not know the name of the particular person, the salutation which is double spaced after the inside address should be as follows:

Grey Manufacturing Corporation
1100 Dobson Road
Houston, TX 74532

Ladies and Gentlemen

Body of the Letter

The content of the letter is arranged in indirect, inductive or direct, deductive order. The content usually contains information, a decision or action, supporting details, and ends on a courteous, friendly note. Remember the body of the letter, the content, is always single spaced with double spacing between the paragraphs. Letters are usually short, containing 3 to 6 paragraphs although sales letters are typically longer. An in depth discussion of different types of letters is included in Chapters 8, 9, and 10.

Complimentary Close

Use of a salutation in a letter necessitates the need for a complimentary close. The complimentary close consists of one to three words which express your consideration for the reader. Some traditional wordings for complimentary closes in business letters are as follows:

Sincerely
Yours truly

Sincerely yours
Yours very truly

Some personal wordings for complimentary closes might include:

Cordially　　　　Cordially yours
Fondly

The complimentary closing "Respectfully" is usually used when writing to someone in high authority, such as a President or Congressperson.

Signer's Name and Title

The typewritten name and title of the person who signs the letter are placed below the complimentary close. An example is shown below:

Sincerely		Yours truly,
Robert Cephus Mays President	or	Freida Gorman Director

It is not necessary to use the courtesy title of "Mr." before a man's name, but include a courtesy title before a woman's name such as "Mrs., Miss, or Ms." so the reader will know how to address her.

Reference Initials

The reference initials are those of the person who actually typed the letter. They are placed at the left margin a double space below the name and title of the signer of the letter. No reference initials are needed if the signer is the same person who inputted the letter. See the examples below:

Sincerely

Lionel Joyce, Vice President

LJ:mj

or

Yours truly,
Wayne C. Cooper, Pastor

wcc/mpj

Enclosure/Attachment Notation

The word enclosure or attachment is used in each letter in which you include something. This notation is placed a doublespace below the reference initials. If you are enclosing something of value, such as a check or a stock premium, be sure to state the check number or premium number as follows:

Enclosure Check #4567—$500
Enc. Stock Certificate #103745
Attachment: Proposal

Copy Notation

Sometimes it is necessary to send a copy of the letter you are writing to someone other than the addressee; in this case a notation is placed a double space below the enclosure notation. The notation may be "pc" for photo copy or "cc" which traditionally meant carbon copy but now means "computer copy." The format for copy notation is show below:

Copy to Mrs. Roberta Warren
pc: Mrs. Judy Haynes
Copies to: Aletha Wilson, Zachary Mays, and Clifton Gorman

Blind Copy Notation

When you want to send copies of the message to other people without telling the reader, you use the blind copy notation. Blind copies are not mentioned on the original; they are listed on the copy saved for the file with the "bc" notation.

Postscript

A postscript is used to emphasize statement(s) made in the body of the letter, not for including inadvertently omitted material. The postscript is the last item on the letter.

For example, you would type:
P. S. The Harve Benard long jumper is fully lined and will be a top selling item.

Special Letter Parts

Three special letter parts are the *attention line*, the *subject line*, and the company line or company name. The *attention line* is placed a double space below the last line in the inside address in a letter or it may appear as the second line on the envelope address. You do not use an attention line if you are writing to a specific person in the company. The *subject line* describes specifically the important contents of the letter. The subject line is placed a double-space below the salutation and follows the letter style arrangement. The subject line usually consists of one to five key words; it is never a complete sentence. The *company line* or company name is typically used by legal persons representing the company or top level management.

It is typed a doublespace below the complimentary close and is typed in all capital letters. Examples of all three special letter parts are illustrated below:

Ortega Printing Company
3 Sutherland Road
Montclair, NJ 07042

* Attention: Credit Manager

Ladies and Gentlemen

****

Mr. Shu Chin Lee Flowers R Us 945 Alosta Avenue Azusa, CA 91702 Dear Mr. Lee	or	(Simplified) Joyce Designers 5207 Penfield Road Houston, TX 77042
* Subject: Red Rose Buds		BILL BLASS SUITS

****

Sincerely

* YUNG'S CONSTRUCTION CORPORATION

Cheryl Cruz, Attorney At Law

The United States Postal Service recommends the use of two-letter abbreviations for states. The list of abbreviations used in the United States, Guam, Puerto Rico, Virgin Island, District of Columbia, and Canadian Provinces is presented below:

Two-Letter Abbreviations for Canadian Provinces

Alberta	AB	Northwest Territories	NT
British Columbia	BC	Nova Scotia	NS
Labrador	LB	Ontario	ON
Manitoba	MB	Prince Edward Island	PE
New Brunswick	NB	Quebec	PQ
Newfoundland	NF	Yukon Territory	YT

Two-Letter Abbreviations for States (and Guam, Puerto Rico, U.S. Virgin Islands, and District of Columbia)

Alabama	AL	Montana	MT
Alaska	AK	Nebraska	NE
Arizona	AZ	Nevada	NV
Arkansas	AR	New Hampshire	NH
California	CA	New Jersey	NJ
Colorado	CO	New Mexico	NM
Connecticut	CT	New York	NY
Delaware	DE	North Carolina	NC
District of Columbia	DC	North Dakota	ND
Florida	FL	Ohio	OH
Georgia	GA	Oklahoma	OK
Guam	GU	Oregon	OR
Hawaii	HI	Pennsylvania	PA
Idaho	ID	Puerto Rico	PR
Illinois	IL	Rhode Island	RI
Indiana	IN	South Carolina	SC
Iowa	IA	South Dakota	SD
Kansas	KS	Tennessee	TN
Kentucky	KY	Texas	TX
Louisiana	LA	Utah	UT
Maine	ME	Vermont	VT
Maryland	MD	Virginia	VA
Massachusetts	MA	Virgin Islands	VI
Michigan	MI	Washington	WA
Minnesota	MN	West Virginia	WV
Mississippi	MS	Wisconsin	WI
Missouri	MO	Wyoming	WY

Figure 7.11 shows the placement of all letter parts although a letter would not contain every special letter part. The examples of letter styles are presented to help you visualize how to set up letters and to arrange the content. The appearance of your letter or other business message does affect the reader's reception. Your letter can be attractive if you use good quality bond paper for your letterhead and neatly arrange the contents of the letter. With word processing software on the market today, all have default margins that you can change to meet the needs of your letter or document arrangement. For short letters, use wider side margins; for medium letters, use less wider margins, and for long letters (two or more pages), use the default margins.

Other Considerations

If your letter is more than one page, you should be careful to use the right heading for the second and subsequent pages.For example, the heading takes on the format of the letter style.

Letterhead

(The letterhead should require no more than two inches, or twelve vertical spaces)

April 11, 19—(date on line 14 or 15 from top of sheet)

Smith Manufacturing Company (three to eight lines below date)
2081 Hickory Ridge Road
Macon, GA 30567

ATTENTION SALES MANAGER

Ladies and Gentlemen:

SUBJECT: REQUEST FOR ADJUSTMENT, INVOICE NO. 1239

(First line of first paragraph. All paragraphs are single spaced, with a double space between paragraphs.)

(Second paragraph)

(Third paragraph)

(Last paragraph. No rule can be given for the number of paragraphs a letter should contain. Paragraphs should be fairly short for easy reading.)

Sincerely yours, (a double space below last paragraph)

THE NOBLE CORPORATION (company name in all capitals)
(Three or more lines for signature)

Vicki Woo, President (could also be on two lines)

rt

Enclosures: Check and contract (not always specified)

Copy to Robert Wilson, CPA, Wilson Associates

P.S. The enclosed brochure contains a special offer that will increase your equipment sales.

Figure 7.11. Letter with Standard and Special Letter Parts.

Full Block
Christopher Kim
Page 2
January 19, 1997

Modified Block
Mrs. Marilyn Brigham -2- January 19, 1997

Your envelopes should match the letterhead in quality, weight, color, and printing. Practically all business letter envelopes are the Large Size No. 10, and the address on the envelope is typed just like it is in the inside address as shown below:

Mrs. Constance Cooper
1037 Bell Street
Pasadena, CA 91101

The United States Postal Service advocates using the computerized form below which seems simpler and faster:

MRS CONSTANCE COOPER
1037 BELL STREET
PASADENA CA 91101-1234

OR

ABC NETWORK
ATTN TOM BROKAW
10010 AVENUE OF THE AMERICAS
NEW YORK NEW YORK 10010-1456

Finally, when putting a letter into a business envelope (No. 10 size or a personal size envelope (size 6¾), it is important to fold it correctly as shown below:

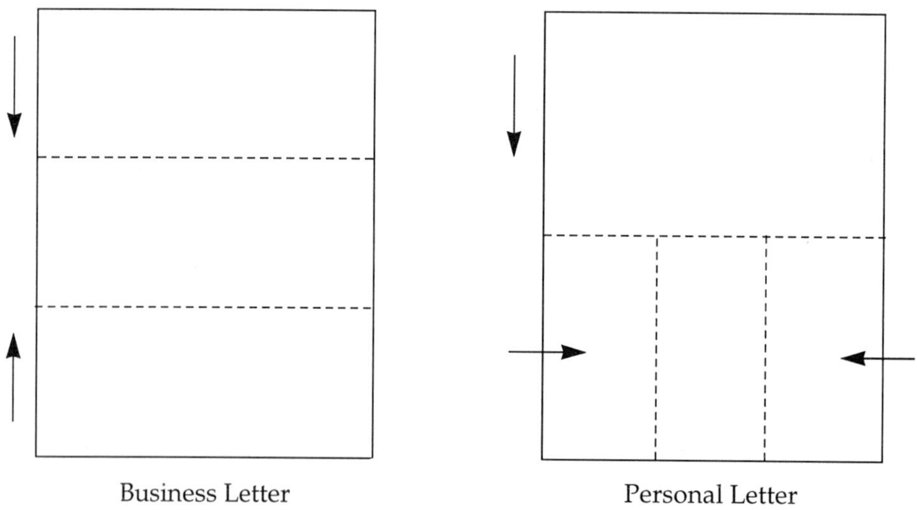

For a business letter, fold the $8\frac{1}{2} \times 11$ into thirds, starting from the top $8\frac{1}{2}$ inch side; fold the top third down and the bottom third up. You are ready to put it in the No. 10 size envelope.

Fold the personal letter in half, starting from the top $8\frac{1}{2}$ inch side. Then fold the half into thirds; fold the left third toward the right and the right third toward the left. You are ready to put it in the No. $6\frac{3}{4}$ size envelope.

If you have to send reports such as the annual report to someone, be sure to use a 9×12 large envelope and type the person's address on a label and affix it to the envelope. Handwritten addresses on envelopes should be reserved for personal correspondence.

Reports

From time to time, you will be called upon to write a report or to be a part of a team to write a report. While most reports may need to be in typewritten format, some reports consist of spoken words, columns of figures, computer printouts, or perhaps a combination of these. Reports are a management tool, and they are ordinarily assigned. Reports convey information to be used in the decision making process. Reports can be short or long, can be form reports, or they can be in manuscript format, meaning double spaced. When you are asked to write a report, you must make sure you know what is expected in the report. Chapter 11 will present more information about reports.

Electronic Communication Mediums

Facsimile

Fax, which is the short term for facsimile transmission, offers the advantage of transmitting information to other FAX machines anywhere in the world of exact copies of written materials, drawings, charts, pictures, etc. This transmission is completed in only a few seconds and is sent over regular telephone lines or by satellite. Facsimile transmission is the chosen medium now widely used in international communication. Messages can be faxed from one machine to another within the company or outside the company or in distant locations, as long as the receiving party has a fax machine or access to one. Many printing companies and Mail Boxes, etc. have fax services available for customers. The courts are still out on the issue of the authenticity of a faxed copy. Be careful about the information you fax and who will see it, particularly if it is confidential and time is of the essence.

Electronic Mail

Electronic mail in its specific sense is the ability to send messages from computers to computers by linked networks (used for internal mail). Messages can be sent thousands of miles away without regard to time zones or just up the hall or to others on the top floor. An e-mail message is sent from one computer screen to another "mailbox" to be retrieved by the receiver at his or her convenience. E-mail messages can be read on the screen or printed out if necessary. As a business person, you will need to determine when it is appropriate to use e-mail messages in light of the fact that a major disadvantage of E-mail is the lack of privacy. Any message sent by E-mail can become public knowledge. E-mail is fast and informal so care is needed in wording e-mail messages. Once the message is sent, it is usually difficult to retrieve it before the receiver reads it.

For good-news messages, you use direct writing style. For bad-news messages, you use indirect writing style. For persuasive messages, you use the elements of persuasion (AIDA). Routine, good-news messages are discussed in Chapter 8.

QUESTIONS

1. With what audiences will a typical business communicate?
2. What are the types of internal communications in an organization?
3. What are the types of external communications in an organization?
4. Is the "grapevine" a good source of information? Why or why not?
5. What is the most widely used type of communication in an organization?
6. Cite two examples each of a channel and a medium.
7. How can letter punctuation styles be determined?
8. What are the letter styles used? Which is the fastest letter style?
9. What is meant by the letterhead?
10. What are the two letter state abbreviations for California and Guam?

APPLICATIONS

1. You are the Director of Student Academic Services at CSULA. With what audiences or realms will you be communicating?
2. You have just secured a full-time job as a (fill your major). With what audience(s) will you communicate?
3. How would you define customer/client service as it relates to your chosen profession?
4. Use your critical thinking skills and argue for or against the statement: "Your writing should be positive and reflect the goodwill of the company."
5. Using the word processing software in the lab (C362 SH, design your own memo stationery. Be sure to include the standard headings.
6. Compose a business letter to your instructor attesting to the need or no need for this Business Communication course. Include 8 of the letter parts (including special letter parts).
7. Lionel L. Joyce needs letterhead for his new company Joyce Enterprises, 42 Grand Avenue, Glendora, CA 91725; this company sells personal services such as arranging family gathering, family reunions, Xmas shopping, special holiday shopping, tracing family genealogy, and hosting entertainment parties. Design the company letterhead and logo for him (Use your own imagination and color scheme.)
8. Input a personal letter to a family member thanking him/her/them for something they have done for you.
9. Input a memo to another student in this class in which you introduce yourself to him or her.
10. Input a memo to your professor telling him/her what you have learned from this chapter.

Name ______________________________ Date ____________

JEOPARDY QUIZ #7

1. The answer is: Stakeholders, customers or clients, vendors, and the general public.

   What are ______________________________?

2. The answer is: An informal communication network is all organizations.

   What is ______________________________?

3. The answer is: The act of ensuring that customers or clients feel valued, their needs are met, and you stand behind your products and/or services.

   What is ______________________________?

4. The answer is: Government laws and regulations, taxes, social security issues, and unemployment compensation.

   What are ______________________________?

5. The answer is: The most widely used type of communication used in organizations.

   What is ______________________________?

6. The answer is: The body is single spaced with double spacing between paragraphs.

   What are ______________________________?

7. The answer is: Mixed and open styles.

   What are ______________________________?

8. The answer is: Full block, modified block, and simplified.

   What are ______________________________?

9. The answer is: Copy notation, postscript, and company name.

   What are ______________________________?

continued

10. The answer is: Sincerely, Cordially, Yours truly, and Yours very truly.

    What are ____?

CHAPTER 8

Career Day
at
California State University, Los Angeles

Writing Routine, Good-News Messages

Objectives

After reading this chapter and doing the applications, you should be able to:

1. Determine how messages are characterized.
2. Decide what writing style should be used.
3. Explain the difference between the two basic writing styles.
4. Examine the writing styles of various letters.
5. Write routine or good news messages.
6. Describe three main characteristics of effective writing.
7. Discuss various techniques for effective writing.
8. Write an example of four different sentence types.

The types of messages written can be characterized by the anticipated reader's response to the message and the writer's purpose. Routine, good-news messages are perhaps easier to write, and in reality, the majority of the messages you will write will be routine, good-news. Companies focus on providing customers or clients the best products and services possible as a company's profits are directly linked to customer service.

Determining Writing Style

If you are just conveying information—telling employees about company policies—you would expect the reader to be neutral. If you are granting a customer's request for a credit card, the reader is going to be pleased with your message. If you are sending out routine information on a weekly basis, this type of message also requires the direct writing style. The content of your message, either neutral or routine or good-news, requires the direct or deductive writing style.

As the reader is just as anxious to get your message as you are to state the main idea or bottom line, you should present the information as quickly as possible. As the writer, you should always strive to maintain the good will of the reader since this helps to foster good business relationships.

Arrangement of Content

As stated before, the direct or deductive writing style puts the main idea or bottom line usually in the first paragraph of the message, followed by supporting details, and ending on a positive note. The three-step plan is shown in the Direct/Deductive Writing Shell:

State the main idea/bottom line
Present supporting details or explanation
End on a courteous note

The reader will either be pleased or neutral at receiving the message. You should structure the message to make it as clear and concise as possible. The direct/deductive writing style can be used in presenting good news and routine messages in either memos or letters and is the preferred business writing style except for bad-news messages.

Types of Routine, Good-News Messages

Types of routine, good-news messages which will be discussed in detail later in this chapter include the following:

Inquiry messages
Direct request
Order letter
Routine reply

Credit request
Routine Claim/Adjustment Letter

Types of Special Messages

From time to time, you will want to write special messages to customers, clients, and subordinates or superiors to convey your goodwill. These messages, which also should be written in direct/deductive writing style, include:

Congratulatory
Appreciation
Greeting (welcome/seasonal)
Condolence

Techniques for Writing Effective Routine and Good News Messages

Your messages must be coherent, logical, and concise. You will find that writing coherently requires the need for you to revise messages so that your thought patterns are clear and understandable. Use a logical chain of thoughts. Messages should only contain the necessary information, but you should not forsake completeness for brevity. For example, read the letter in Figure 8.1 and determine if the content meets the tests of coherent, logical, and concise.

Word choice. Your choice of words influences the clarity and effectiveness of your routine and good news messages. As a writer, you should use simple words, concrete words, and first-, second, or third-person voices. Wayne and Dauwalder[1] state that you should write with sensitivity to your readers and their backgrounds, and consider what information they need to know. Write to express, not to impress. If you were an economist, and you were writing to other economists, you would use such terms as elasticity, recession, inflation, etc. If you were writing to the general public, then you should present the terms in language the non-economist can understand. Or if you were a loan officer helping a person to buy a home, you would certainly explain the term "negative amortization." While you do not want to offend your readers by making your writing too simplistic, you also want to avoid using terms that are too complex.

Mr. Complex Word List

For example, Mr. Complex is unfurling a list of king-size words that have been compressed. Do you see any of your favorites in the list?

King-size Word	*Small-size word*
acquaint	inform
ameliorate	improve

January 30, 1997

Mr. Clifton Mays
616 South 16 Street
St. Joseph, MO 64501

Dear Mr. Mays

It has come to my attention that you are delinquent on your taxes for your home. You owe back taxes for the years of 1995 and 1996 for a total amount of $3,200.

We telephoned you on Thursday, January 21, but got no answer. We also telephoned you on Monday, January 25, but we still got no answer. We even telephoned you today and still got no answer. If you do not call us by February 5, 1997, your name will appear in the newspaper as a delinquent taxpayer.

Please be informed that your home can be sold for the taxes due. I would like to take this opportunity to encourage you to pay your taxes. The Star-News is the newspaper.

Sincerely

Sid Cherry

Sid Cherry, County Tax
Supervisor

Figure 8.1.

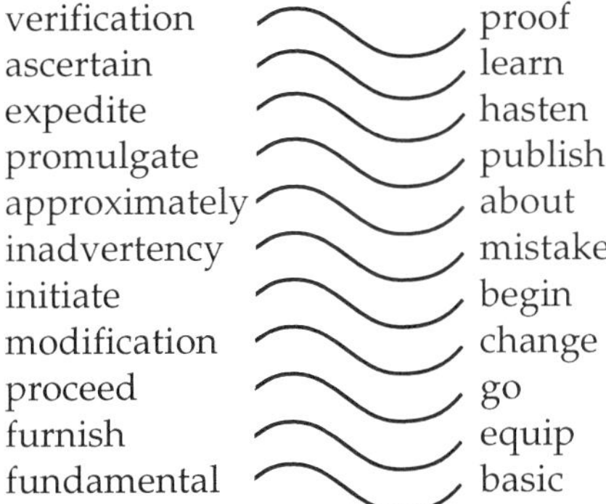

Concrete words. Your use of concrete words eliminates the need for the reader to interpret abstract words and or generalizations. You want the reader to understand your point or bottom line and to act or accept the message. Concrete or specific wording emphasizes key ideas and makes them easier to grasp. If you want to de-emphasize certain points, then abstract wording is useful for ideas not essential to the main message.

Verbs. Use of active verbs helps the reader to visualize the action more readily. Your use of active verbs in routine and good news messages makes the thoughts come alive and increases comprehension. As a writer, you will need to use the passive verbs to de-emphasize thoughts, particularly in bad-news messages.

Your attitude. The you-attitude is used mainly in informal messages; this "second-person" approach makes your writing more reader-centered. The you-attitude personalizes the message and helps to convey empathy with your readers. It also helps to ensure that your readers will read carefully the whole message.

Use of pronouns. In English, pronouns rename or take the place of nouns referring to people or things. The First Person pronouns are "I" and "we;" the Third Person pronouns are "he," "she," "they," and "it." Just like the use of "you" focuses on the reader, the use of "I" focuses on you the writer and may be useful when emphasizing your experiences for instance in a letter of application. However, overuse of the word "I" in a personal or business letter makes the message writer-centered.

When you want to de-emphasize points not central to your main idea, you use the third-person. When you need to present both good news and bad news in the same message, your use of the you-attitude where appropriate and the use of the third person work quite well. Consider the following example which illustrates the use of both second person and third person pronouns:

EXAMPLE

Your manuscript was well written, but the editor chose not to publish it.

Writing Effective Sentences

As a writer, try to vary your sentence types. To communicate effectively in routine and good news messages, use short sentences to emphasize ideas and use longer sentences to de-emphasize or subordinate ideas.

The four sentence types include: simple, compound, complex, and compound-complex. Examples of each are presented in the discussion that follows:

A *simple* sentence emphasizes one idea and is one independent clause. The simple sentence contains a subject and a verb.

EXAMPLE

I saw the Super Bowl game.

A *compound* sentence emphasizes two ideas and a conjunction joins these two ideas together. The compound sentence contains two subjects, two verbs, and a conjunction. A comma is used to separate the two ideas.

EXAMPLE

Bob watched the game, and Pat worked at her computer.

A *complex* sentence emphasizes one idea and subordinates another idea although both ideas convey a relationship. The complex sentence has one subject and one verb referred to as the independent clause and a dependent clause which has no subject nor verb. A comma is used to separate the dependent clause from the independent clause.

EXAMPLE

Although the surgery was a success, I felt overwhelmed by the cost.

A *compound-complex* sentence contains two or more independent clauses, one or more dependent clauses, a conjunction or adverb to link ideas together, a comma to separate the dependent clause from the independent clause, and a semicolon to separate the two independent clauses. Compound-complex sentences are longer, but in some instances, can be very useful.

EXAMPLE

"Although the survey was a success, I felt overwhelmed by the cost; but I paid my share of the cost within two months."

Varying your sentence types will help to make your writing interesting and effective. You will need to practice writing and using each one of these types of sentences in messages.

Achieving emphasis. In business writing, you want to be concise and to filter your messages to only the pertinent details. You can use paragraphs to emphasize main ideas. The shorter the paragraph, the more impact it has. It is perfectly acceptable to use one sentence paragraphs in business writing which is contrary to the expository writing you probably did in English classes. Longer paragraphs tend to swallow up the main idea and the reader has to dig for the main points. However, long paragraphs are useful for embedding negative information.

Other techniques to include emphasis are: providing a subject line, underlining key words, using capital letters, using asterisks (*), and bullets (•), indenting paragraphs or lists, or using the dash—. All of these techniques can be effective in routine and good news messages, but do not use too many in any one message or else the reader will be confused about what are the main points.

Achieving Logic and Conciseness in Writing

Logic. Your thoughts should flow from one to another to enhance the reader's comprehension. Group all thoughts centering around the same idea together and then move on to the next idea and group those thoughts together. When you group all ideas and or questions in a logical and easy-to-read pattern, you help the reader comprehend your points and the underlying details more easily as well as get the answers you are seeking.

Conciseness. Many writers tend to equate quantity with quality. However, quantity does not indicate they are more knowledgeable or more productive. Businesspeople face many time constraints, so it is critical that writers filter down their communication to only the most pertinent. Wordiness camoflauges your main points; therefore, you should choose appropriate vocabulary and sentence structure that make your point directly. Use as few words as possible; first drafts are often wordy. So it is important to revise a document with conciseness as one of your main goals. Consider the following examples:

EXAMPLE

Wordy: A substantial number of employees are in disagreement over the Performance Salary Step Increase policy, and the employees are hopeful that the problems can be resolved by the Union.

EXAMPLE

Concise: Many employees disagree with the Performance Salary Step Increase policy and are hopeful the Union can resolve the problems.

Examples of Routine and Good News Messages

You will have occasion to write many good news messages such as a memo or letter of inquiry, a direct request, an order letter, a request for credit, a routine claim or ask for an adjustment.

Most companies have preprinted purchase requisitions on which to place orders, but you personally may have a need to write such a letter.

In each of the examples that follow, apply the decision tree guidelines and the direct/deductive writing shell. The good news messages are presented in both memo and letter formats:

EXAMPLE 1A: AN INFORMATIONAL MESSAGE IN MEMO FORMAT

Scenario: In order to better allocate the human resources, one office was merged with another and the office enlarged to accommodate both divisions. The name was changed as well to keep in line with the other office names. The services will remain the same. Write an informational memo to the students informing them of the changes.

MEMORANDUM

To: **All Undergraduate and Graduate Business Students**
From: **Dr. Marguerite P. Joyce, Director**
Date: **January 28, 1997**
Subject: **Renaming of Office**

Effective January 1, 1997, the Undergraduate Programs Office, which was expanded to house the Graduate Programs Office in the School of Business and Economics, will be called the School of Business and Economics Advisement Center.

This name change is in line with the names of the other four advisement centers. The Center will continue to provide undergraduate students and graduate students with the best service possible.

Thank you for your assistance in publicizing the name change.

Example 1B: A Routine Reply in Letter Format

Scenario: Bill Madison has written you requesting information about health care coverage for his family. He did not give you specific information, but he wants prompt information. You will have an agent call him, but the agent needs more information to custom-tailor his health care coverage. Write Bill a letter alerting him of the upcoming phone call to him. His address is 1164 Rockwell Place, New Rochelle, NY 00714

January 28, 1997

Mr. Bill Madison
1164 Rockwell Place
New Rochelle, NY 00714

Dear Mr. Madison

I have received your inquiry regarding your health care coverage. One of our agents will be contacting you by phone shortly.

In order to handle your needs promptly, please provide him information on your other health care coverage plans. We offer two specific health care coverage packages for dependents.

We look forward to serving your needs.

Sincerely

Samuel Mays
Samuel Mays

Example 2A: A Good-News Message in Memo Format

Scenario: Two professors wrote a lottery fund proposal requesting money and release time to set up an information kiosk and web server for the School of Business and Economics (SBE). The SBE Lottery Committee recommended it for funding, the Dean of SBE concurred, but the President had final authority to grant or not grant the funding. You have now learned that the President did fund their proposal. Write a memo telling them of the great news!

MEMORANDUM

To: **Dr. David Liu, Computer Information Systems**
From: **Dr. Hugh Warren, Acting Associate Dean**
Date: **January 15, 1997**
Subject: **Lottery Fund Grant**

Congratulations! You and Dr. Joyce have received funding by the President to develop the The Information Kiosk and Web Server for the School of Business and Economics.

Please work out your release time with your Department Chair to begin work on this project.

I wish you both the best in completing your project this Winter quarter.

Example 2B: Good News Message in Letter format

Scenario: Faculty now have to compete based on their outstanding performance in teaching, scholarly activities, and university/community service to receive Performance Salary Step Increases (PSSI). Each person must now apply for a PSSI and include documentation to support the application. More applications are turned in than money is available to award to all of them. A school-based committee reviews the applications and makes recommendations to the Dean and President who has the final say. He has approved a salary increase for Dr. Cruz as well as others. Write a good news letter to Dr. Cruz.

January 6, 1997

Professor Cheryl Cruz
1123 Avenue 60
Los Angeles, CA 90032

Dear Professor Cruz:

It is with a great deal of pleasure that I award you one performance salary step, retroactive to July 1, 1996. This is based on your outstanding performance at Cal State L.A. during the review period.

I have every expectation that you will continue to perform in this manner.

Congratulations on your achievements!

Sincerely,

James M. Rosser

James M. Rosser, President

JMR:mm

cc: Provost
Dean, School of Business and Economics
Department Division Chair

Example 3A: Routine Claim in Memo format

Scenario: You gave a farewell party for your assistant who has been employed in your office for over ten years; she left for a promotion and higher-paying job. You had planned to absorb the cost yourself, but people are calling to tell you they want to come and say good bye to your assistant. You are sure your Supervisor will reimburse you; he came to the affair. Write a memo to him asking for reimbursement. Your expenses were: $15 for the cake; $38 for the Kentucky Fried Chicken; and $24.67 for the trimmings. Your receipts are attached.

MEMORANDUM

To: **Jonas MacCord, Supervisor**
From: **Judy Haynes, Secretary**
Date: **November 14, 1997**
Subject: **Reimbursement for Farewell Party Expenses**

I am requesting reimbursement of $77.67 for the expenses incurred for the Farewell Party for my assistant on October 14, 1997.

A breakdown of my expenses is as follows:

$15	for the cake
$38	for the Kentucky Fried Chicken
$24.67	for the trimmings
$77.67	Total

My receipts are attached.

Thank you for your presence and your assistance.

Example 3B: Routine Claim Letter or Adjustment

Scenario: You recently bought a Sony CD disk player, model number #1576. You have been listening to music as you go walking as well as when you ride the rapid Metrolink to work. Now the disk player, which you have had for only one month, seems to be playing music which sounds garbled. Write to the company CALTRONICS, Inc., 124 Flower Street, Los Angeles, CA 91445, requesting a replacement disk player which costs $135.89. You really want a replacement disk player, but you will settle for a credit adjustment.

April 21, 1997

CALTRONICS, Inc.
124 Flower Street
Los Angeles, CA 91445

Ladies and Gentlemen

Subject: Request for Sony Disk Player Replacement

I am requesting a replacement Sony Disk Player, Model #1576, for the one I bought from you a month ago.

This disk player is now defective as it seems to be playing music that sounds garbled.

I listen to music as I ride the train so I would like a prompt replacement. If this model is no longer in stock, I would accept a credit adjustment.

Thank you for your assistance in this matter.

Sincerely

Matthew DuFrene

Example 4A: Printed Purchase Requisition for Joyce Company

Scenario: You work for Joyce Company, and you want to order two dozen Sip Master Filtering Straws at $10.95 each from Market America Products. The address is 3113 South Center Street, Santa Ana, CA 92704.

April 30, 1997

Chadwick, Ltd.
P. O. Box 4500
Boston, MA
Attention: Order Department

Ladies and Gentlemen

I would like to order two dozen Sip Master Filtering Straws at $10.95 each.

Please send the Straws by United Parcel Service within two weeks. I plan to give them as gifts to my employees. Please call me at 818/963-9598 to let me know the cost, and I will mail you a check.

Thank you for your assistance.

Sincerely

Zach X. Mays

Zach X. Mays

Example 4B: Personal Order Letter

Scenario: You are getting married, and you want to order three Mother of Pearl Tie Tacks at $59 each and three Mother of Pearl Necklaces at $80 each which you saw in the Chadwick, Ltd. catalog. You do not know the model number, but you feel the Company will know the item. You plan to give these as gifts to the bridesmaids and groomsmen in your wedding party. Write an order letter requesting the merchandise and enclosing a check for $456.36 which includes the tax and shipping costs. The address is Chadwick, Ltd., P. O. Box 4500, Boston, Massachusetts. Include your phone number.

February 2, 1997

Market America Products
3113 South Center Street
Santa Ana, CA 92704
Attention: Order Department

Ladies and Gentlemen

This is an order for the following merchandise to be shipped to the address above as soon as possible:

Quantity	Number	Item	Cost
3		M. of Pearl Necklaces @ $80	$240.00
3		M. of Pearl Tie Tacks @ $59	177.00
		Tax/Shipping Cost	39.96
		TOTAL	$456.36

EXAMPLE 5A: A DIRECT REQUEST IN MEMO FORMAT

Scenario: As Supervisor of the Information Systems Department, you know that employees will be scheduling their vacations for the summer. Since your Company has a union, you know that the senior employees should have first preference to vacation time. Write a memo to your employees asking them to submit a request for vacation time and to give their first, second, and third preferences for vacation time. You may need to stagger vacations as the work of the Department must still be done.

MEMORANDUM

To: Information Systems Employees
From: Winston Robert Mays
Date: March 13, 1997
Subject: Vacation Request

Please submit to me by April 30, 1997, your request for vacation time.

Since I will need to stagger vacations, please give me your first, second, and third choices for vacation time. We will need to have three to four employees working each of the three shifts.

Thank you for your assistance.

EXAMPLE 5B: A DIRECT REQUEST IN LETTER FORMAT

Scenario: You have been asked to select a hotel from among many in the Redondo Beach, Long Beach, and Marina del Ray area for the Western Regional Association of Business Communication. You anticipate 50 to 70 people attending the Conference. You would like the hotel rate to be no more than $95 for a single or double. The Conference will be held in April 1998. Write a letter to the Holiday Inn Crowne Plaza requesting information about the hotel and its accommodations. You also would like free lodging for one night so that you can check out the hotel and sample food items from its restaurant menu. The address is: 1840 Lake Shore Drive, Redondo Beach, CA

May 2, 1997

Holiday Inn Crowne Plaza
1840 Lake Shore Drive
Redondo Beach, CA 91922

Ladies and Gentlemen:

Subject: Hotel Site for Convention Headquarters

I have selected your Hotel as one of four to tour and seek complimentary lodging for one night in order to make a choice of a hotel for the Western Regional Association of Business Communication Conference.

The Conference will be held in April 1998, and we would like hotel accommodations for $95 or less per day for single or double rooms. We anticipate 50 to 70 people will be attending the Conference.

Please send me your Hotel brochures and any other information you have available regarding your accommodations for this Conference.

Thank you for your prompt assistance.

Sincerely,

Mari Baldwin

Mari Baldwin
Conference Coordinator

Example 6A: An Inquiry Message in Memo Format

Scenario: You need to know how many employees are planning to attend the Company picnic in May at Disneyland. Write a memo to your employees requesting the number of people in their families who will be coming. This is an annual affair which is free for all employees and their families. Prepare a response card for the employees.

MEMORANDUM

To: **Marketing Employees**
From: **Taylor Shane**
Date: **June 6, 1997**
Subject: **Annual Company Picnic at Disneyland**

Our annual Company Picnic at Disneyland is rapidly approaching. Are you and your family planning to come?

We are excited about the opportunity for all employees and their families to have an afternoon of fun and good food. So that we can prepare for our picnic, please complete the response card and indicate the number of people in your family who will be coming. Send your response card via interoffice mail by June 15, 1997.

I look forward to seeing you all at the picnic!

Attachment

- -

Company Picnic at Disneyland
July 4, 1997

Name ______________________________ Department ______________________

Number in Family ____________________ Adults ____________ Children ____________

Example 6B: A Credit Request in Letter Format

Scenario: You want a credit card from Bloomingdale's, the newest upscale department store that has opened in Century City. You were told that they do not take telephone requests for a credit card application and you do not know when you will be able to get there. So now you want to write a letter to request a credit limit of $5,000. The address is:

Century City, CA.
700 Orchard Loop
Azusa, CA 91720

August 6, 1997

Bloomingdale's
Century City, CA
Attention: Credit Manager

Ladies and Gentlemen:

I am requesting credit privileges at Bloomingdale's in the amount of $5,000.

I have an excellent credit rating, and I will continue to maintain such a rating as a credit card customer of yours.

I would like to shop in the ambience of Bloomingdale's, which is known for its superb products.

Thank you for your assistance in this matter.

Sincerely,

Damicia Shane

Damicia Shane

Special Messages

From time to time, you will have customers and/or clients who have shown their loyalty to your products and services over the years. As a gesture of good faith and thankfulness, you may want to send them a letter of appreciation and/or a seasonal greeting. For example, an insurance company may want to send its long-time clients a calendar for the new year.

Similarly, you may want to congratulate an employee or friend who has received a promotion or you may want to express your sympathy to a family who has lost a loved one.

Figures 8.2, 8.3, 8.4, and 8.5 are examples of these four special messages:

MEMORANDUM

To: **Elizabeth Strother**
From: **Marguerite Joyce, Director**
School of Business and Economics Advisement Center
Date: **November 10, 1996**
Subject: **Your Promotion**

Congratulations, Liz, on your promotion!

You served the Undergraduate Programs Office extremely well during your tenure here.

The students keep asking for you, which is a testimony to the kind and caring attitude you showed to them.

You are sorely missed, and I wish you the very best.

Figure 8.2. Memo of Congratulations.

July 9, 1997

Mr. Alfred Walker
Walker Printing Company
2401 South 21 Street
Niles, Michigan

Dear Mr. Walker:

You have been a customer of ours for the past 20 years, and we are saying "thank you" for your loyalty.

We feel that our paper products are the best on the market, so you will always be able to fulfill your printing orders using our top-of-the-line products.

We wish you continued, successful years in your business, and we look forward to our future business relationship.

Sincerely,
Naomi Nelson
Naomi Nelson

Figure 8.3. Letter of Appreciation.

Bankers' Bank

January 8, 1997

Mr. Louis Olson
155 Doe Deer Run
MaComb, IL 661955

Dear Mr. Olson

Welcome to the community!

We extend sincere wishes for your happiness in our community.

As a small token of our service to you, please accept this new 1997 calendar which lists all of our services we can provide you.

We offer one-stop service from your car or phone.

Best wishes for your continued prosperity this year!

Sincerely

Alan Ware

Alan Ware
President

Figure 8.4. Letter of Welcome.

December 30, 1996

Mrs. Leslie Fowler
465 East Fairview Avenue
Arcadia, CA 91007

Dear Mrs. Fowler

We extend to you our heartfelt sympathy on the loss of your husband, George.

Although we knew George for just a short period of time, his loving spirit and caring attitude will forever linger in our minds.

Let your loving memories of him be of comfort to you and the girls.

Sincerely

Marguerite Joyce

Marguerite Joyce

Figure 8.5. Letter of Condolence.

QUESTIONS

1. What determines the writing style in a memo or letter?
2. What is the general purpose of every message you write?
3. How can a writer achieve emphasis in a message?
4. Explain the statement " A writer should never forsake completeness for brevity."
5. What is the best approach for writing a routine message?
6. How would you expect a reader to react to a neutral message?
7. Should you emphasize yourself or the reader in a good news message?
8. What are some examples of routine messages?
9. What are some examples of special messages?
10. As a writer, should you write to impress or write to express?

APPLICATIONS

Routine Messages

1. Due to security precautions, you have just been told that all employees must begin wearing a photo ID badge starting September 1, 1997. You know that most senior employees, those who have been working for the company longer than 10 years, do not have a photo ID badge. The cost of a photo badge is free, but each employee must schedule his or her own appointment. Stan, the photographer, will take the pictures and make a badge; this procedures will take about 10 minutes in the Benefits Office. Write a memo to the employees telling them of this new security precaution.
2. Due to recent changes in staffing in your Office, you need to have regular Staff meetings at least twice a month. You have decided to have a Staff meeting the second and fourth Wednesday of each month; if no items are pressing, you will not have a meeting. All staff will be notified if a meeting date is cancelled. Please ask the staff to mark off the second and fourth Wednesdays of each month for this Staff meeting. If the employees have questions or concerns, they are to come prepared to share them at this staff meeting. The meeting time is 8:30 a.m.

Order Letters

1. Find a J.C. Penney, Sears, or other catalog. Choose an item(s) you want to buy and fill out their order form. Bring the order form to class to discuss.
2. Your boss asks you to order four dozen jogging socks ($19.95 a dozen) to give as Xmas gifts. The socks can be initiated with the beginning letter of the last name ($2 per initial). The advertisement was in Chadwick, Ltd. magazine. The socks come in white or black with a contrasting initial color. Since the company now has an exercise room, this gift is ideal. The shipping costs is $6.95 and the tax is 8.4 percent. You are to enclose a check for the amount. Your boss asks for initials as follows: 3-P; 24-J; (the first initial of the company name); 3-E; 3-M; 3-L; 3-C; 3-K; 3-B; and 3-H.

3. You need to order a keyboard for your home Dell computer. The "keyboard error" light message keeps coming on the screen, but the keyboard is plugged in to the monitor. Order it from the Price Club, Foothill Boulevard, Azusa, CA 91702. The cost is $75, and you need it quickly. Shipping and tax is $5.95.

Inquiry Messages

4. Input a letter to Office Depot inquiring when they will have their Office Automation Show. You want several of your staff members to attend as you found it most informative in terms of the latest technology. You need to know the price per person to attend and the dates and times of the Shows and if advance reservations are needed. Their address is: 377 Huntington Drive, Monrovia, CA 91770.
5. Input a memo to Michelle Villaneau regarding her interest in the full-time Clerical Assistant III position in your office. She once worked in your office but left to take her current position which pays more money and is a promotion. She called you recently to tell you she is unhappy in her present position and wants to come back to your office. At first you could only get funding for six months for the position so you suggested she stay where she is; however, now you have received funding for the full-time yearly position. She would receive the same salary she had before she left.

Direct Request

6. Several cases of AIDS have been confirmed at your organization. As these AIDS-infected employees will at some time need reduced workloads due to their impaired health, you now need to get as much information as possible to share with your employees. You want to avert any hysteria. Input a letter to the National Foundation for AIDS Research, 1002 Avenue of the Americas, New York 10070 asking for information, pamphlets, and guidelines dealing with AIDS in the Workplace.
7. Input a memo to Facilities Operations in which you ask that the clocks be put back on the wall. The painter who took them down to paint assured you he would replace them. You saw him (Jeff) across campus and he promised to replace them that day. It has been two months since the clocks were taken down, and you want them put back on the wall quickly. You don't know who is responsible as Jeff is a hired contractor; you just want the clocks put back up.

Routine Claim

8. You ordered 25 black and white ties (#5) for the Male Chorus at your church. These are new ties to complement the black suits the men have. However, you received 25 brown and white ties. Input a letter requesting the correct #5 style ties and that they be mailed by United Parcel Service as the Male Chorus has a singing engagement in two weeks. Tell the company you will return the other ties once you receive the correct ones; of course, you want to be reimbursed for the shipping costs. The invoice number is 468925. The address is: Cervantes Neckwear, Inc. 2431 South Main Street, Los Angeles, CA 90044.

9. You bought a Sony combination Color TV and VCR on March 21. It has been playing good for the last month; however, the sound tends to get louder when commercials are aired. You have to keep adjusting the volume. The floor models you were shown prior to buying the Sony showed no evidence of the volume fluctuation. Input a letter requesting a new Sony Color TV and VCR as you suspect that this set may be defective. The address is: Sony Products, Unlimited, 3600 Boardway Place, Los Angeles, CA 90007.
10. Input a letter to a retailer or manufacturer regarding a product or service you recently bought with which you are not completely satisfied.

Credit Request

11. As Mrs. Karen Cook, input a letter asking for a $20,000 line of credit at Nordstrom. Mrs. Cook is opening up an upscale clothing boutique in Burbank, CA. Her customers tend to be in the middle-class income bracket. Her merchandise includes ladies' clothing, leather shoes and handbags. Your store specializes in one of a kind merchandise; thus your shoppers are not likely to see someone else with the same clothing.

Credit Approval

12. Input a letter to Mrs. Cook (#11 above) granting her request. Her references and financial reserves appear excellent. The interest rate is 18.5 percent and payments are due on the first of the month. Tell her about any upcoming sale you are having.

Special Letters

13. Input a condolence letter to your former boss's family. Your former boss recently died of cancer. He was your boss for two years. You really liked his/her style of management.
14. Write a congratulations letter to Dr. Anthony Graceson; he was recently appointed Acting Dean of the School of Business Administration at Jonesboro University. He was a former department chairperson of the Management Department and has been at this University for 18 years. Jonesboro University is located in Columbia, South Carolina.
15. Input a goodwill letter to thank Mr. and Mrs. Sim J. Kim for patronizing your business for over 15 years. You are sending them a crystal clock as a token of your appreciation. Their address is 4102 San Juan Drive, LaCanada, CA 91785.

Name ______________________________ Date ____________

JEOPARDY QUIZ #8

1. The answer is: The writing style is based on this technique.

   What is ______________________________?

2. The answer is: A three-step writing style plan for good-news and routine messages.

   What is ______________________________?

3. The answer is: Inquiry, direct request, order letter, and credit request.

   What are ______________________________?

4. The answer is: A four-step writing style plan for bad-news or persuasive messages.

   What is ______________________________?

5. The answer is: A technique used to personalize the message and help to convey empathy with your readers.

   What is ______________________________?

6. The answer is: Simple, Compound, Complex, and Compound-Complex.

   What are ______________________________?

7. The answer is: Contains an independent clause and a dependent clause.

   What is ______________________________?

8. The answer is: Used to help your thoughts flow from one to another.

   What is ______________________________?

9. The answer is: The ability to write using as few words as possible.

   What is ______________________________?

continued

10. The answer is: A type of verb used to help the reader to visualize the action more readily.

    What is ____?

CHAPTER 9

Career Day
at
California State University, Los Angeles

Writing Bad-News Messages

Objectives

After reading this chapter and doing the exercises, you should be able to:

1. Defend the rationale for using the indirect writing plan for conveying bad-news messages.
2. Write with the reader's reaction in mind in bad-news messages.
3. Organize the arrangement of information in bad-news messages.
4. Explain the steps in the indirect writing style.
5. Analyze the type of message required in writing bad-news messages.
6. Filter out only the essential information to include in conveying bad-news messages.
7. Apply the decision tree to each writing task for bad-news messages.
8. Discuss how research is involved in decision making in reply to bad-news messages.
9. Explain the differences between reasons that lead up to a decision and the decision itself.
10. Write examples of refusal statements in the dependent clause of a complex sentence.
11. Describe the role of a "buffer" in the indirect writing style.
12. Write a variety of bad-news messages.
13. Explain laws that relate to ethical issues concerning credit.
14. Convey information about people in recommendation letters objectively.
15. Analyze the need for conveying crisis information.
16. Determine the best way for handling crisis situations.

From time to time, you have to convey information or a message that is negative; naturally, we expect the reader to be unhappy or displeased with the content. Your task in writing these messages includes stating the bad news, having the reader read the entire message and accept the message, while trying to maintain as much goodwill as possible. Negative messages take more care because you want to present a good image of you, the company, and its products and services. Negative messages include saying "no" to a request, refusing to do something, imparting unpleasant information about cuts in employee benefits, or increasing employee costs for benefits, recall of products, etc. Other unpleasant messages include writing negative employee performance appraisals and giving disciplinary notices.

Determining Writing Style

Just as you determined the writing style for the good-news and routine messages based on the reader's reaction to the message, you would use the same reasoning here. You need to ask yourself, "Will the reader be unhappy, displeased with this message?" If so, you will need to take the reader step by step through how you arrived at your decision while at the same time trying not to increase the reader's disappointment.

Do companies write bad-news messages using direct writing style? Yes, but the preferred style is the indirect writing style. Recipients of bad-news messages written in direct writing style are more likely to read the first paragraph with the refusal in it and put the letter in the trash can. They may even be angry at this point. What you really want to do is to soften the bad-news and get the reader to read the entire message with the intent that he or she will understand and perhaps agree with your rationale. Bad-news messages require a different format.

Locker (1) says that some messages which at first appear to be negative can be structured to create a positive feeling. You as a writer should strive to help the reader understand that you have deliberated seriously over the situation and that your decision is firm, fair, reasonable, and perhaps the same decision that the reader would likely make.

Arrangement of Content

Bad-news messages are written using the inductive or indirect writing style. If you know the reader is going to be unhappy or displeased with your message, then use the following pattern as discussed earlier to help you deliver the bad-news yet maintain the reader's goodwill:

1. Use a buffer
2. State the reasons that lead up to your decision or bottom line
3. State the negative information or refusal, and offer an alternative (if appropriate), and
4. End with a courteous, positive statement

When you apply the communication decision tree discussed earlier, you would do the following: 1) determine the type of message format required or asked for, 2) find out to whom you are writing, 3) determine the purpose of your message, and 4) select the writing style.

Now, let us focus on organizing the content of bad-news messages. A bad-news message must first start with a *buffer* which is a neutral or positive statement which is relative to the reason for the message. This buffer gives no clues to the decision. The buffer can be one to two statements as an opening paragraph.

All decisions in businesses are based upon some kind of research whether it is reviewing past sales reports, comparing past performance levels, or projecting future sales forecasts. This research becomes the basis of your reasoning or critical thinking in finally arriving at a decision. So the next step in delivering the bad-news is to *present the reasoning that led up to the decision.*

The third step in bad-news messages is to *state the decision explicitly* so that it is not necessary to say "no" a second time. When you have to write or impart bad-news, you only want to do it just once. Therefore, implying a "no" only makes the reader think you did not say "no" exactly. So implying a "no" will only cause you to have to say "no" explicitly this second time.

Occasionally, you may be able to offer an alternative, discount, or compromise to help the reader meet his or her need. When any one of these methods is available, you will want to phrase the refusal in the dependent clause of a complex sentence so that the alternative, discount, or compromise gets more emphasis.

The final step in the arrangement of bad-news messages is to *end on a pleasant, courteous note or statement.* The last sentence in a bad-news message should not focus on the negative but offer hope for future business relationships and mutual goodwill.

Types of Bad-News Messages

Review Figures 9.1 and 9.2 for the arrangement of content in bad-news messages. Refer to the scenario below.

EXAMPLE

Scenario: Let us consider for example, you were asked to submit a report today to the Human Resource Management Department regarding which of your staff members would like to switch to the new dental plan. However, you have not yet requested this information as you have been so busy with other things.

You will experience having to write a variety of bad-news messages. Most of them will deal with responding to unclear orders for your products or services, back orders for merchandise not yet received, claim refusals, adjustment refusals, and credit refusals. As a writer, you should keep in mind that whatever your decision is you must state it clearly and convincingly. Do not use the fact that the company policy does not permit you to do something. There may be times that you will enforce policies that you did not write or make announcements that you do not relish but do not criticize others. Write with the reader in mind and try to convince him or her of the soundness of your reasoning.

Since many bad-news messages are written to your customers or clients, the examples shown will be in letter format.

MEMORANDUM

To: Zack Mays, Human Resource Management
From: Gilda Irvin, Accounting
Date: January 8, 1997
Subject: Report on Number of Employees Selecting the New Dental Plan

Our new Delta dental plan benefits appear to be more comprehensive than our old policy.

Of the numerous tasks that I am required to perform, none has been more time consuming than the audit report. We have had a number of auditors present who need various ledgers, records, etc. on a daily basis.

Although my duties have keep me so busy that I could not get the report to you today, you will have it within two days.

I am sure you will have overwhelming support for this new Delta dental coverage.

Figure 9.1. Bad-news Message in a Memo.

Ethical Issues Concerning Credit

Many state laws and federal laws specify the responsibilities of businesses in issuing credit and collecting debts. Issues in collecting debts will be discussed in Chapter 10, but here are some laws that are applicable to businesses:

Credit must be equally available to all creditworthy customers, and the content of credit applications and any oral questioning of credit applicants must not include references to race, color, religion, or national origin. Credit decisions cannot be based on age, marital status or future personal plans. The Equal Credit Opportunity Act requires that all credit refusals be in writing.

The Fair Credit Billing Act protects credit card users against false charges made to their accounts and specifies procedures that creditors and consumers must follow in resolving problems.

Requirement for full disclosure of credit terms to consumers is stated in the Federal Truth-in-Lending Act. Lenders must disclose clearly service charges, finance charges, and the effective annual percentage rate. The Act also specifies that a borrower has the right to cancel an agreement within three business days after signing the contract.

Communicating Bad-News Messages

About people. The Privacy Act gives employees access to information about themselves. For example, it is important when serving as a reference that you respond only to specific requests that have been approved by the employee. Also your comments can only relate to the employee's job performance; the comments must be objective, given without malice, and in

November 13, 1997

Mr. Peter Mays
440 North 12 Street
Augusta, GA 30097

Dear Mr. Mays

Recently we wrote you about becoming one of a select few holders of the Platinum Card; this offer was in effect until November 1, 1997.

Today we got a phone call from you about accepting our offer which gives holders an unlimited balance for large, major purchases once a year.

Although we cannot extend our offer again to you at this time, we will make a notation in your file regarding your interest. The next time Gold card holders are reviewed for Platinum Card membership, we will extend the offer to you again. Since this a unique membership, accounts are reviewed only every five years.

We appreciate your patronage and would like to see you eventually become a Platinum Card holder.

Sincerely

Robert Cephus

Robert Cephus, President

Figure 9.2. Bad-News Message in Letter format.

March 30,1997

Advisement Center
School of Business and Economics
California State University, Los Angeles
256B Salazar Hall
Los Angeles, CA 90032

Ladies and Gentlemen

Your recent order for office supplies and calendars is very much appreciated.

We are able to fill your office supplies order, and you will receive it on April 5, 1997, by UPS.

The Solar Eagle calendars have been a huge seller, and presently we are out of stock. However, we will ship your five calendars to you on April 10, 1997.

Best wishes for another successful academic year.

Sincerely

Alfred Huang

Alfred Huang
Owner

Figure 9.3. Example of Unclear/Back Order Bad-News Message.

February 12, 1997

Mrs. Kurt Merrill
6440 Rosemead Boulevard
Pasadena, CA 91105

Dear Mrs. Merrill

We appreciate your having bought our latest model of the Jenn Air Range. Your Jenn Air Range will give you many years of enjoyment and will be a topic of conservation.

We buy in bulk so that we can pass the savings on to you. In addition, we do not have a large overhead as we do not showcase our merchandise. Therefore, we can offer you top of the line merchandise at reduced cost.

While we cannot repair the Range free of charge, the repair that your Jenn Air Range needs can be easily done by having one of our service persons come to your home. The initial inspection cost is $35 with a maximum charge of $89 for appliance repair within one year of purchase.

Best wishes for many happy hours of cooking enjoyment on your Jenn Air Range.

Sincerely

Herb Haynes

Herb Haynes
Owner, Haynes Appliances

Figure 9.4. Example of an Adjustment Refusal.

April 15, 1997

Mr. Robert Hines
12 Riverboat Walk
New Orleans, LA 70159

Dear Mr. Hines

Thank you for your letter regarding reimbursement for your hotel costs in Centerville, Tennessee.

Our auto club plan provides a variety of services to its members, and we are delighted you have taken advantage of a few of them. The auto club plan covers all costs associated with repair of automobiles.

Although we cannot reimburse you $159.86 for your hotel costs while your automobile was being repaired, we can offer you a $50 discount on your next family trip out of state. This discount is good at all Auto Club restaurants.

Best wishes for a great vacation next summer.

Sincerely

John Powers

John Powers

Figure 9.5. Example of a Claims Refusal Message.

May 6, 1997

Mrs. Cardella Randle
Joyce-Powers Landholders
4302 Paris Avenue
New Orleans, LA 70122

Dear Mrs. Randle

The Air Travel Credit Card can indeed make your trips interstate and intrastate more enjoyable.

The Air Travel Credit Card is for business executives whose companies have Corporate credit accounts with us for their employees. The minimum corporate credit account available with us is $50,000.

In reviewing your request for an Air Travel Credit Card, I noticed that you do not have sufficient financial reserves for a corporate credit account. While I cannot open a corporate credit account for you at this time, I would be glad to review your application again once your financial reserves meet the minimum required.

Thank you for your interest in Air Travel Credit Card Company.

Sincerely

Gwen Liggins

Gwen Liggins
Corporate Credit Manager

Figure 9.6. Example of a Credit Refusal Message.

May 30, 1997

Mr. Averrial Thomas, Manager
Chateau Restaurant
129 Chef Menteur Highway
Westbank, LA 70115

Dear Mr. Thomas

Subject: Recommendation for Mr. Jesse Pollard

I am responding to your request for information on Mr. Pollard for the Chef's position you have available at your restaurant. Mr. Pollard was an employee at the Chez Restaurant for 10 years; he worked his way up from dishwasher to head cook. He knows the restaurant business and manages his time well in the preparation of the many dishes.

When he took on the head cook position, he was then put in a supervisory position without having the people skills needed. Often times, he was impatient with the other cooks. With more training in people skills, he would do well in assuming a Chef's position.

I wish Mr. Pollard well in his search for a Chef's position, and I ask that this information be used for the purpose it was intended.

Sincerely

Larry Mays

Larry Mays
Owner, The Charthouse

Figure 9.7. Example of Bad-News/Good News Message about a Person.

February 9, 1997

Mr. Ronnie Clifhaven
1012 Chevron Court
Pasadena, CA 91103

Dear Mr. Clifhaven

We thank you for your service to and patronage of our Company for the last 15 years.

We have enjoyed many profitable years on this corner. The larger department chains are moving in, which is squeezing out the smaller stores. We have had to rethink our market share as of lately.

A decision has been made to close this store by the end of the year. You will receive a severance check or the opportunity to compete for a position in any of the other four stores in the Montclair area. While this decision was a tough one to make, we feel confident that it was the best one under the circumstances.

We feel sure that your talents could be used at one of the other stores. Please stop by my office if you have any immediate questions.

I plan to call a storewide meeting on February 15 to answer any questions you may have.

Sincerely

Xavier Gorman

Xavier Gorman

Figure 9.8. Example of a Bad-News Message about a Company.

good faith. If you have to give some negative comments, they should be tempered with positive comments. As a writer, you should weigh carefully your decision to write letters of recommendation. If you cannot in all sincerity write a positive letter of recommendation for someone, it is better for you not to write one at all.

About the Company. With many companies facing difficult decisions regarding employee layoffs, relocation, product recalls, merging, etc., you will be faced with having to write unpleasant messages or bad-news messages about the company to employees or preparing press releases to the public. In a crisis situation, the best advice is to admit the mistake, apologize, and state what is being done to make sure the event does not happen again. The greatest advice is to be proactive—set up procedures beforehand to handle emergency situations. For example in crisis communication, Jack in the Box was applauded by some for the quick steps it took in dealing with the situation regarding the deaths of two children and their link to contaminated hamburger meat. On the other hand, Jack in the Box was criticized for its handling of the situation by saying that in-house people cannot be completely objective and that it excluded outsiders on its crisis team. The company did report a $29.3 million lost the second quarter but it has rebounded. (Bovee and Thill, 1995 p. 14)

Persuasive messages are discussed in Chapter 10.

QUESTIONS

1. Discuss the need for writing bad-news messages.
2. Which is the preferred writing style for writing bad-news messages?
3. What are the two main reasons to keep in mind when writing bad-news messages?
4. Should you write a recommendation letter for a person when you know you cannot write a positive one?
5. What steps are involved in arriving at a decision to put in a bad-news message?
6. Should a refusal be implied or stated explicitly? Why?
7. Explain what is a "buffer."
8. What should be the ending statement in a bad-news message?
9. Explain the steps involved in writing bad-news messages.
10. Should terms relating to credit be implied? Why?
11. What is meant by crisis communication?
12. Give an example of a company which recently had to face handling crisis communication. How effective was the communication?
13. Concerning credit requests, should credit be made available to everyone?

APPLICATIONS

Unfavorable Message about Product or Service

1. You and several other professors are concerned about the writing skills of your business students as most of them use English as a second language. These students have been told

to go to the Writing Skills Center on the second floor in the Library for help. Some students just do not want to improve their writing skills; however, some of them do go, but they say that the tutor checked their papers and found them to be okay. You disagree as you check the same papers and find numerous errors in English mechanics. What should be done in this case? Who is at fault? Is there a solution to the problem? The students feel the professors should be lenient and not grade their papers so harshly. The other students feel they should be held to the same standards as they are. Many students (for which English was not their first language) have earned As and Bs in these courses. Input a letter to your instructor expressing your opinion.

2. You recently flew on Northwest Airlines to Atlanta, Georgia. You had just suffered a broken wrist which was in a cast. As you boarded the plane, the stewardesses were standing in front of you as you tried to juggle your carry-on luggage. None of them even offered to help you, and they could see you were struggling. You are disappointed with the Airline and its customer service. Input a letter to Northwest Airlines President expressing your dissatisfaction. You refuse to fly this airline again.

Credit Refusal

1. Mr. Junior Perry, a carpenter, has applied for credit at your store. His references are impressive, but he has been delinquent on three different accounts by 60, 90, and 120 days respectively. You fear he may be a poor credit risk. Input a letter refusing his request for credit and suggesting that you would prefer to do business with him on a cash-only basis for now.
2. You are the owner of a church furniture company. Mt. Pisgah Baptist Church, a small store-front church, has applied for credit to buy 34 new church pews for their new church. This church has done business with you in the past, but you had to keep sending them notice to make their payments. They only owe $575 now, but you do not want to go through this all over again. You want them to pay off the $575 before you extend credit again. Input a letter to the Chairman of the Trustee Board, Mr. Larry Gorman, 1701 East Oakland Avenue, Bloomington, IL 61701.

Refused Request

3. You have been asked to be the keynote speaker at the Association of Business Communication Convention in Washington, D.C. in November 1997. You have another engagement for which you have committed. Input a letter declining the invitation to Dr. John Myers, Executive Director Association of Business Communication, Baruch College, New York, NY 10011.
4. Several staff members have asked that the nonsmoking policy be changed to permit them to smoke in a designated restroom. You do not condone smoking, and you must consider the health safety of all employees. Input a memo to these staff members informing them of the no smoking policy and that smoking is NOT permitted anywhere in the building. No restroom can be designated as a smoking area.

5. Input a memo to all Advisement Center Employees refusing to close the office from 12 to 1 for lunch. The Center needs to be open from 9 to 6 to accommodate the students. The 12 to 1 hour is for some students the only time they can come to campus. While some staff members end up having to take late lunch breaks or do not get to lunch at all, the Center must service the heavy student traffic during the 9 to 6 work day. You may suggest another solution such as staggered lunch hours.

Claim Refusal

6. You are the Customer Service Manager at Symes Cadillac Company on Auto Row in Pasadena, CA 91103. A customer brought her car in for transmission repair at a cost of $468.47. The customer picked up her car one morning and brought it back within one hour. It seems that the tire rim was bent. The customer claims it happened during the time it was in your service center. While it is possible the service person could have damaged the tire rim, you really have no proof. Input a letter refusing her claim to have Symes accept responsibility and repair the bent tire rim free of charge.

Claim Refusal

7. Input a letter to Clifford Fang who states he returned merchandise to Price Club on August 6 by United Parcel Service and now wants a credit to his account. Unfortunately, the Price Club has not yet received the merchandise from Mr. Fang. You cannot credit his account until you receive the merchandise. Write to Mr. Fang telling him that perhaps he should file a claim with United Parcel Service. Once Mr. Fang presents a receipt of delivery and merchandise stock or item numbers, you will be glad to credit his account. His address is: 740 Innes Street, San Francisco, CA 94544.

Job Denial

1. You are the Human Resources Director in a large manufacturing company. You are seeking to hire two persons to fill the positions in your Management Department. Four current employees have applied for these positions; two of whom have college degrees. The two without college degrees will not be considered for the positions, but they are doing a good job in their present positions at the company. Write a form letter to go to these two candidates. You want to maintain their goodwill and motivation to continue to do a good job.

Name ______________________________ Date ______________

JEOPARDY QUIZ #9

1. The answer is: A neutral statement at the beginning of a bad-news message.

   What is ______________________________?

2. The answer is: Letters of refusal, negative messages, or having to say "no" to someone.

   What are ______________________________?

3. The answer is: Although you do not meet our requirements at the present time, we will be glad to review your application later.

   What is ______________________________?

4. The answer is: Buffer, rationale, decision, and positive closing.

   What are ______________________________?

5. The answer is: The law that gives individuals access to information about them.

   What is ______________________________?

6. The answer is: Be proactive; admit mistake, apologize, and state what will be done to prevent situation from happening again.

   What is ______________________________?

7. The answer is: Letters that require more care in the wording of the content and the reader's reaction.

   What are ______________________________?

8. The answer is: Indirect or Inductive writing style.

   What is ______________________________?

9. The answer is: I am sorry to inform you that I cannot grant your request.

   What is ______________________________?

continued

10. The answer is: Although I cannot repair the damage free of charge, I can offer you a 20 percent discount.

    What is ____?

CHAPTER 10

Mr. Aki Mihara
California State University, Los Angeles
Career Fair—April 10, 1997

Writing Persuasive Messages

Objectives

Upon reading and doing the chapter exercises, you should be able to:

1. Write effective persuasive messages.
2. Determine the writing style for persuasive messages.
3. Accept the principle that all persuasive messages are designed to sell something.
4. Use correct arrangement of content for persuasive messages.
5. Use the AIDA approach in writing persuasive messages.
6. Discuss the two types of persuasive messages.
7. Distinguish between ethical and nonethical behavior in business practices.
8. Use various techniques for persuasive writing.
9. Explain the differences in the letters written in the series of collection letters.
10. Determine the central point in sales letters.
11. Explain the rationale for using the indirect writing style in persuasive messages.
12. Analyze today's consumers in terms of their needs, perceptions, and astuteness in buying products and services.

As a business executive, you will have occasion to persuade others to do something for you, to take some specific action, or to seek support for a decision you or other top executives have made. Examples might include persuading prospective customers or clients to buy your product or service, seeking donations for a particular non-profit agency, asking for employees' support for unpopular decisions such as a nonsmoking policy or higher cost of benefits, or supporting persons in the hiring process.

Three basic types of persuasive messages include the sales letter, persuasive requests, and the collection letter series. The sales letter can be a form letter that is personalized using mailmerge features of word processing software. Other sales messages may include a sales presentation, a sales brochure, a newspaper advertisement, or an oral message regarding a sales item.

Persuasive messages are useful when it is believed that the readers or receivers of your communication will be resistant to your request. Writing persuasive messages is important in the world of work for it is through cooperative effort among people and with people that company goals are accomplished. It is people working together in organizations who help produce the desired products and services that consumers want based on their needs.

Convincing someone else to do something requires skill in the art of persuasion. In other words, your ability to use effective techniques in persuasive communication hinges upon how convincing you can be. In this chapter you will write letters to persuade someone to buy a product or service or take some desired action or persuade someone to pay an outstanding debt.

Determining Writing Style

If you are trying to convince someone to do something for you, you cannot tell them directly and expect to be persuasive. You must use a psychological appeal to help the reader understand how you have arrived at your request.

In writing persuasive messages, you use the indirect writing style. Think about what persuades you. When you go shopping, what do you look for? Do you want people telling you what is the best buy? Why it is the best buy? Or do you just make your own decision? Surely, something that the salesperson had said may have influenced you to buy a particular product or service.

The AIDA approach is helpful for writing persuasive messages using the indirect or inductive writing style. AIDA is the acronym for Action, Interest, Desire, and Action. The AIDA approach includes the elements of persuasion. This approach is widely used and accepted in marketing and advertising as well.

Elements of Persuasion

The AIDA approach moves the reader through four stages of the persuasion process:

1. You must gain the *attention* (A) of the reader. Your first sentence should make the reader think about what you are saying.

Which sentence grabs your attention?

Did you enjoy preparing your own tax documents this year?
I have a tax preparation service I would like you to consider.

2. You must arouse the reader's *interest* (I) in your product, service, or idea.

   Which sentence arouses your interest?

   You will have endless hours of fun on your new sailboat.
   Our sailboat will help you enjoy your free time.

3. Next you must create a *desire* (D) in the reader to want your produce, service, or idea, and

   Which sentence builds your desire for the product?

   Your purchase of this new computer comes with six different software programs already installed and ready for your use.
   This computer comes with six different software programs pre-installed.

4. Lastly, you must request the reader's *action* (A) and make the action easy to take. You want to persuade the reader to take the action right away while the reader is still interested and convinced.

   Which sentence makes you want to act?

   Your call today to order this appliance gets you a free additional one-year warranty.
   This appliance if bought today allows an additional one-year warranty free.

Before trying to sell any product or service, you must know the product very well or you must know the service you provide very well. Today's consumers are very astute; they do comparison shopping, and they want the best product or service for their money. Remember the readers will not automatically be receptive to your message, so you will have to really "sell" your product or service. The main idea of your persuasive message is to get the reader to act now—your request for *action.*

Occasionally you may get letters soliciting information about your company's products and/or services. In this case, you can use the direct writing style since the reader has already expressed an interest in your products and/or service. At all other times, you should use the indirect writing style for sending unsolicited letters.

Before selling a particular product or service, it is best to know in advance the background of your prospective clients or customers. Knowing their demographics—educational level, salary range, gender, social background, culture, recreational interests, and spending habits helps you tailor the sales message. For example, it would be pointless to try to sell a computer to a welfare recipient; it would be more appropriate to try to sell a Mercedes to an upper-income customer.

		Self-Actualization		
Creativity	Wisdom	Self-Realization	Vocation Fulfillment	
		Esteem and Status		
Self-Worth	Uniqueness	Respect	Recognition of Community	
		Social		
	Affection	Friendship	Ties to Group	
		Safety and Security		
Personal Confidence		Stability	Protection from Enemies	
		Physiological		
Air	Food	Water	Shelter	Sleep

Figure 10.1. Maslow's Hierarchy of Needs.

Today's consumers have different desires and needs. Of course, we all are concerned about our daily food, shelter, affection, family members, and financial security. Once people have the basics of life, they are motivated by different things.

Numerous books present a variety of methods of motivating people to buy. These methods include emotional appeals, rational appeals, and credibility. Abraham Maslow's hierarchy of needs lists the needs based on lower level needs to the higher level needs. Once people have secured the lower level needs which are basic needs will they venture to reaching the higher level needs. Maslow's Hierarchy of Needs is presented in Figure 10.1.

For example, once a person has achieved self-esteem, he or she may want to pursue a Ph. D. degree if that is what will make him or her feel fulfilled.

People are motivated to buy products and services by how closely that product or service matches their level of needs. So an important step in choosing a selling point is matching the needs levels of potential customers to the features of the product or service you are selling.

The best persuasive messages aim to influence audiences who are likely to resist. Once you have analyzed the needs of your audiences, you can craft a message that perhaps will motivate them to buy. Because everyone's needs are different, people respond differently to any given persuasive message. For example, once an executive has reached the fifth level, self-actualization, it is possible that he or she may want to reward himself or herself with a Rolex watch. Or a teenager may only be interested in being able to socialize with friends; these friends probably have a designer purse such as a Dooney and Burke, or a Louis Vuton. Naturally, this teenager will want what his or her friends have to give him or her ties to the group.

Crafting Persuasive Messages

As a writer, you want to be careful when constructing emotional appeals. Your emotional appeal should be subtle. You can use certain words that reflect emotion. Words such as success, free, value, and comfort exhibit strong feelings and may put the reader in a frame of mind to accept your message. For example, you could say that buying a particular product is the best value on the market. Or you could say that buying this product gives the buyer the comfort he or she deserves. Emotional appeals work well for products and/or services that can or affect people personally.

You can also use a rational appeal where you emphasize logic. Logical appeals call for human reason and work well in business-to-business selling. For example, if you buy a computer, naturally you will want to buy the peripherals necessary for the application you plan to use it for. Also, if there is a maintenance agreement plan for your computer, you may want to buy it although some situations do not warrant it. Using both an emotional and a rational or logic appeal in a persuasive message can achieve the best results.

In using appeals, you should note that appealing to emotions is different from manipulating emotions. When you manipulate emotions, you put the reader on a guilt trip by relating how not buying the product or service lowers his or her self-esteem.

Another appeal is credibility. Can you be believed? Are you reliable? Do others have confidence in you? The best way to support your credibility in a persuasive message is to support your message with facts. These facts can be stated in the form of testimonials, research evidence, statistics, product or service guarantees, and description. Consider the various ads on television and the radio. Do they portray testimonials from celebrities regarding various products? What about the ads in the newspapers? Some of them do have testimonials from prominent people who have used the products and services they are promoting. The credibility appeal in your persuasive message can be very effective. The old adage says "You cannot truly sell that which you have not used." Do you agree? While you must know the your products' selling points, you must talk about the benefits to customers and/or clients.

Selling Tactics

Consumers are protected by law from deceptive sales and advertising practices. Fine print in a document or contract can be construed as an intent to conceal under certain circumstances. Also, technical terms not likely to be understood by the average consumer may also be interpreted as an attempt to conceal. Various states have passed "plain" language laws that require writing to be understood by the average reader. Fraud is a deliberate misrepresentation of facts in order to deceive, but this misrepresentation need not be confined to spoken or written words but can also consist of omission or concealment of information.

Types of Sales Contacts

Selling can be done by sending sales letters to a list of prospective clients or customers. Or companies can buy mailing lists from other companies. For example, you order something from a mail-order catalog. You paid and received the item; now you are receiving catalogs from other companies that you did not request. Companies do sell their mailing lists; these mailing lists are rather expensive and they become outdated in no time. Some companies use a statistical method that enables the direct marketing experts to "predict" a response rate. Buying mailing lists can be productive in some instances, but more often than not the potential customers are not likely to be prospects. Now with telemarketing, some success has been garnered using mailing lists. Telemarketing is the use of the telephone to sell products and/or services. Also, many products and services are sold on home shopping channels as well as on the Internet. The yellow pages lists companies that prepare specific mailing lists by state, zip code, or other factors; for a directory of companies that make, sell, and rent mailing lists, you can contact the U. S. Department of Commerce.

Choosing a Central Selling Point

All products and or services have unique features. Even the best product on the market has to be "sold." A prospective customer must see value in the product and perceive that it will meet his or her needs before deciding to purchase. The central selling point should be chosen on the basis of the interests of the buyer. You should emphasize the reader-centered strategy. Try to get a mental picture of the buyer (or reader) and choose the central selling point based on an analysis of the buyer. The central selling point can be the durability of the product, the price of the product, the fine, detailed quality of the product, the unique features of the product, or the benefits or performance of the product.

Structuring Sales Messages

Sales messages should be carefully structured so as not to cause legal hassles for the company. Always get permission BEFORE using a person's name, photograph, or other identity in a sales letter. You should never include any private or personal information about a person without his or her consent. In writing sales messages, you must use the highest standards of business ethics and make every attempt to persuade without manipulation. Use the "you attitude or you approach" and write truthful facts about your products and/or services.

The sales letter is usually accompanied by a brochure, an order blank and postage paid return envelope. Sometimes a small sample size of the product or trial coupon offer and other incentives are included to persuade the customer and/or client to buy. Most persuasive messages are usually longer, and the sales letter is no exception. Some sales letters, using all the fancy features of word processing, can be two to three pages long. Frequently, the addressee's name is highlighted in red if black is the main color of print. According to Bovee and Thill, "the overriding purpose of a sales letter is to get the reader to do something."[1] What you want is for the reader or customer to take action right away. As an incentive, you can offer a discount for orders placed within 48 hours or free trial of the product for three weeks or any other similar inducements.

Writing sales messages allows you to use a variety of mechanical means of emphasis. You could use a dash —, bullets •, ♦, colors, arrows → ←, lists, indentations, underlines, graphics, pictures, diagrams, ALL CAPITALS, and even white space to set off ideas.

Types of Sales Messages

Figures 10.2 to 10.4 provide examples of sales letters and an analysis of each letter based on information presented regarding writing effective sales messages.

July 9, 1997

Mrs. Marilyn Brigham
2228 Pennsylvania Avenue
Fairfield, CA 94333

Dear Mrs. Brigham

Summer time is approaching; picnics will be numerous. Did you have a fun time on your last picnic?

You can have even more fun when you set up your mesh patio tent! This tent will allow you to seat 10 people comfortably around rectangular tables and yet you can feel the cool breeze of the summer day. The pesty flies and insects will not bother you as you savor the aroma of barbeque!

The Patio Tent is made of durable metal and heavy textured mesh which will not tear. It is easy to assemble and folds away neatly. This tent can be yours for a low cost of $79.95 with a money back guarantee.

Why not order your Patio Tent today for your next picnic? Your family and friends will certainly enjoy it as well. A sample brochure and order blank are enclosed for your convenience.

Sincerely

Cephus Mays

Cephus Mays

Enclosure

Figure 10.2. Sales Letter.

March 27, 1997

Mrs. Rennie Theophile
4302 Paris Avenue
New Orleans, LA 70122

Dear Mrs. Theophile

A family reunion is an exciting time to get together!

Maybe you have wanted to have a reunion for some time but just did not have the time to devote to planning it. Well, we have the answer for you. We offer a professional service that will do all of the planning, mail out the letters to family members, and make all of the arrangements for meals and hotel reservations.

You can sit back and enjoy meeting all of your loved ones without the hassle. Just give us a list of family members and their addresses, tell us your dates for the reunion, and the types of meals you want, and we will do the rest. Can you imagine having someone else do all the work for you for a modest price of $250?

We recently arranged the reunions for the Mays family, the Cooper family, and the Gorman family. You may contact any of them for a reference should you chose; they voluntarily gave their permission for us to use them as references. I am sure they would welcome your call.

If you have not had a family reunion for some time, you can have one now. We are just a phone call away at 213/348–1040.

We are ready to serve YOUR needs.

Sincerely

Pat Gorman

Pat Gorman

Figure 10.3. Sales Letter.

August 11, 1997

Ms. Gwendolyn Brooks
200 Avenue C
Lake Charles, LA 70601

Dear Ms. Brooks:

Have the years treated you well body wise? Do you look as young now as you did ten years ago?

Age lines, excess skin, and sagging skin can easily be removed using our latest technology called Laser Trim. This Laser Trim gets rid of the excess skin in just a few minutes, and the healing time is reduced in half.

You can be the young, beautiful person you want to be with Laser Trim! Your personal consultation can be arranged at your convenience, and your Laser Trim healing time will require only a couple of days recuperation.

Your calling 213/267–8000 today to arrange a consultation is just the beginning of a younger looking YOU! Payment plans are available.

Let Laser Trim beautify you today.

Sincerely,

Charles Luddie

Charles Luddie, M. D.
Plastic Surgery Specialist

L U D D I E F A C I A L S , I N C .
Frazier Building, Suite 706
Lake Charles, LA 70605

Figure 10.4. Sales Letter.

Frequently persuasive requests are written to solicit funds, information, action, cooperation, or favors. In an organization, you may have occasion to persuade employees to cooperate with an unpopular decision, to persuade management to promote an employee, or to persuade top management to buy new equipment or to change procedures and/or policies. All of these situations are internal persuasive messages.

External persuasive messages are usually more difficult to write because readers are bombarded with competing requests for donations, have no time to take on new commitments, and many requests offer them nothing tangible in return. People will only respond to persuasive requests when they feel confident about the request and that they will gain something in return. When writing a persuasive request, you should take special care in including the benefits, both direct and indirect, to the reader.

Examples of persuasive requests for action appear in Figure 10.5 to 10.6.

In writing a persuasive claim, your goal is to persuade someone to grant your request. Perhaps you were not satisfied with a product or service or what you got was not what you had expected. Maybe the product was defective or a part was missing.

MEMORANDUM

To: **Dr. Hugh Wang**
From: **Dr. Marguerite P. Joyce, Director**
Student Academic Services
Date: **February 26, 1997**
Subject: **Request to Buy Two Memory Typewriters**

I am requesting we buy two memory typewriters rather than repair the memory typewriters we have.

We could save $150 in service call cost which would almost pay for one new memory typewriter; this is the second time in less than one year that the typewriters have needed repair. The $75 service call cost does not include parts. We can buy two new memory typewriters at a cost of $275 each; salvage value on the two memory typewriters we have would amount to $100. We would realize a repair cost savings and payback within two years.

We need memory typewriters so we can put in memory the various courses required for the option specialty rather than type in each course for the 15 or so options we offer.

Should you concur with my analysis, please let me have your decision as soon as possible.

Thank your for your assistance.

Figure 10.5. Persuasive Request.

September 8, 1997

Mr. and Mrs. John Chan
2445 Bristol Drive
San Marino, CA 91770

Dear Mr. and Mrs. Chan

As parents of college graduates, we know you care about the future of America.

Many of our young students do not have parents to encourage them nor the funding to realize a college education. That is why Jack and Jill of America stepped in to help bring about a better educated future generation. Jack and Jill offers scholarships and a supporting environment for these young people.

Your children will be able to give something back to the community, and we would like for those children who are less fortunate to have the same opportunity to give something back to the community. For a small donation of $100 we can offer modest scholarships to dedicated students. Our goal is to get 1,000 people to contribute $100 each. We thought you would want to be included in this 1,000 goal.

Can we count on your participation? A call from you today to 213/447–7000 to accept being a part of this goal will permit us to help another less fortunate but dedicated student realize a college education.

Sincerely

Jason Fernandez

Jason Fernandez

Figure 10.6. Persuasive Request for a Donation.

Ethical Issues in Sales Messages

In business writing, the term "persuasion" is used. However, the more applicable term probably is "to convince." Treece stated that "products and services are sold because buyers believe that it will be to their advantage to buy, not because the seller by eloquent perusasion or hard-sell tactics caused them to buy. Your persuasive messages should be convincing, not manipulative. To be manipulative or to exhibit pushy sales tactics are types of unethical conduct.

Ethical Issues in Collection Procedures

Writing collection letters is a sensitive issue which is monitored by federal and state laws. You are concerned with the amount of money owed, the time elapsed, the credit agreement and the creditor's attitude. However, laws were passed to protect people from unreasonable persecution and harassment by debt collectors. These laws state how many times you may contact a debtor, how many times you may call them, and what information you must provide to the debtor. The Fair Debt Collection Practices Act of 1978 prohibits the following:

1. Falsely implying that a lawsuit has been filed
2. Contacting the debtor's employer or relatives about the debt
3. Communicating to other persons that the person is in debt
4. Harassing the debtor (although definitions of harrassment vary)
5. Using abusive or obscene language
6. Using defamatory language (such as calling the person a deadbeat or a crook)
7. Intentionally causing mental distress
8. Threatening violence
9. Communicating by postcard (not confidential enough)
10. Sending anonymous C.O.D. communications
11. Misrepresenting the legal status of the debt
12. Communicating in such a way as to make the receiver physically ill
13. Giving false impressions, such as labeling the envelope "Tax Information"
14. Misrepresenting the message as a government or court document

Some credit worthy customers become embarrassed about the situation and pay up; others do not care and may consciously or unconsciously blame you for their problems. You will need to write positively and to accentuate the benefits of complying with your request for payment.

Collection Letter Series

From time to time, it is necessary for a company to write customers and/or clients asking them to pay their bills. Many customers and/or clients truly do try to honor their obligations to pay their bills. However, some customers and/or clients over extend their credit worthiness; on the other hand they are sometimes delinquent in paying their bills because of unforeseen circumstances such as natural disasters, loss of jobs, costly medical bills, or sudden death of the main provider in the family.

Companies have their own stages of sending messages regarding collecting payments for past due accounts. Naturally, the number of messages in each stage differs from company to company. It also differs in the length of time from the beginning of the collection letters series until the ultimatum. Generally, the total time of the collection letter series is longer for good credit risks than for poor credit risks.

Credit is extended to customers and/or clients based on their credit worthiness. The four C's of credit used by practically all credit managers are: Character, Capacity, Capital, and Credit. Of these four, the one most important is character. A customer could have a lot of money and just not like to pay his or her bills. A customer could have great credit and something unusual happens to damage it. Or a customer could have great capacity at the time to honor obligations but somehow over extends himself or herself later. However, character is a personal trait that focuses on moral and ethical quality as well as integrity.

The series of collection letters or messages range as follows:

1. First-Notice Collection
2. Second-Notice Collection
3. Follow-up Collection
4. Last-Resort Collection

OR

1. Early-Stage Collection
2. Middle-Stage Collection
3. Late-Stage Collection

OR

1. Reminder-Stage Collection
2. Appeal-Stage Collection
3. Ultimatum-Stage Collection

Each stage in this array of collection letter series is designed to be progressively more persuasive, and each stage has several steps within it. The main two points of collection letter series are to get the customer to pay and to maintain goodwill. The Reminder, Appeal, and Ultimatum stages best reflect the increasing seriousness of the collection letter series.

The *Reminder* stage is for customers who intend to pay but just need a reminder. Usually sending a second or third direct request for payment or a duplicate bill is all that is needed. Messages in this stage are courteous and failure to pay is assumed to be just an oversight on the customer's part. Should the customer fail to pay on perhaps the third request for payment, then you would move to the next stage.

The *Appeal* stage is stronger because the customer has not paid or heeded the reminder messages. At this stage, you need to review the customer's paying habits. You will have to select the type of appeal that will get the customer to pay. You can appeal to the customer's pride, credit rating, reputation, character, or morality. The appeal collection letter is positive and courteous. The customer may have experienced a situation beyond his or her control; so you want to write to the customer to find out what is the problem. Sometimes customers are unhappy with a product that needs to be repaired, so they withhold payment until the repair is done. Of course, this situation may be out of your control as a credit manager, but you still must appeal to them to make their payments on time or to pay their bill. The persuasive appeal letter uses the AIDA principles. Letters at this stage are usually signed by someone in upper management. If the customer still does not pay, then you move to the last stage which is the ultimatum.

The *Ultimatum* stage is the final attempt to collect what is due you or the company. When you reach this stage, your only interest is in collecting the amount past due. At this stage, this is the last chance for the customer to pay an account before it is transferred to a collection agency, a negative rating is entered on the customer's credit report, or the account is turned over to an attorney. Neither the appeal letter nor the ultimatum should convey anger; you should not state you are turning the account to a collection agency or an attorney unless you fully intend to do so. Use the direct writing arrangement in the ultimatum collection letter.

Figures 10.7 to 10.9 show examples of the Reminder, Appeal, and Ultimatum collection messages.

References

Bovee, C. L. and Thill, J. V. (1995) BUSINESS COMMUNICATION TODAY, 4th edition, Mc-Graw-Hill, Inc., p. 322.

Maslow, A. H. (1954). MOTIVAATION AND PERSONALITY, Harper and Row, New York, 1, 19.

Treece, M. (1994). SUCCESSFUL BUSINESS COMMUNICATION FOR BUSINESS AND THE PROFESSIONS, 6th edition, Allyn and Bacon, Needham Hts, MA.

Questions

1. What is a persuasive message?
2. What determines the writing style for a persuasive message?
3. What is the desired writing style for a persuasive message?
4. Discuss what is meant by the AIDA approach.
5. What are the basic types of persuasive messages?
6. What are the ethical issues in sales messages?
7. What are the purposes of writing collection letters?
8. How would you classify today's consumers?
9. What are some techniques to use in sales messages?
10. Why are persuasive messages ineffective at times?
11. What are the laws protecting consumers in regard to debt collection?
12. What is the main idea in a sales message? In a persuasive message?

October 23, 1997

Mr. Keyong Lu
1234 Bane Street
Los Angeles, CA 90065

Dear Mr. Lu

It is that time again—the first of the month when your payment on your carpeting is due.

We know this was an oversight on your part and that you will be sending your payment as soon as you get this reminder.

We are sure you are enjoying your new living quarters now that you have new carpeting.

We appreciate your business.

Sincerely

Ghandi Khrusrow

Ghandi Khrusrow, Credit Manager

Figure 10.7. Reminder Collection Letter.

November 13, 1997

Miss Lin Tai
3614 Belle Chase Drive
Covina, CA 91773

Dear Miss Tai

Aren't you enjoying your new home? Has anything happened that we should know about?

We have sent you two notices about the past due payments on your home mortgage. You were a good credit risk when we made you the loan, and we know you want to maintain that standing.

We are just a phone call away; please let us know when you can make your past due payments. We do have various plans to help you catch up on your mortage payments; we just need to hear from you as soon as possible.

Should you need any other information, please call me. We are here to help you.

Sincerely

Gin Bordinski

Gin Bordinski, Credit Manager

Figure 10.8. Appeal Collection Letter.

December 28, 1997

Mr. David Lau
10219 Valley Boulevard
El Monte, CA 91664

Dear Mr. Lau

Your payment for $450 must be in our office by January 10, or we will turn your account over to a collection agency.

We have attempted to contact you numerous times, but you have not responded. We asked that you put forth a good faith effort as we did toward you.

If we do not receive the payment by January 10, the Joyce Assets Company will be contacting you. At that point, a negative rating will be placed on your credit report.

We thank you for the opportunity to be of service to you.

Sincerely

Yue Mak
Collections Manager

Figure 10.9. Ultimatum Collection Letter.

APPLICATIONS

Persuasive Request

1. As Ms. Judy Asazawa, Director of Development for the School of Business and Economics, compose a fund raising letter to be sent to all members of the Alumni Association at CSULA. The funds will be used for annual scholarships for deserving students. Try to get the members to give something back to the University in the way of scholarship funds.
2. Your son is one of six students going to Boston, Massachusetts for a Speech Contest. He needs sponsors to help pay his way; the cost is $450. Write a persuasive letter to be sent to friends and family members to get them to contribute $25 to $50 each to help send your son to Boston.

Persuasive Claim

3. Northwest Airlines baggage personnel damaged your Gorgio black leather bag—the left handle was ripped off. The Baggage Claim Manager gave you two $25 travel vouchers as payment for the damaged bag. This bag has traveled to Germany and France without a tear or rip in the leather. You do not feel the $50 is adequate payment as you paid $90 plus tax for the bag about four years ago. You do not plan to fly Northwest Airlines again. Input a letter requesting the full amount to cover the cost to buy a new Gorgio bag.
4. As Ms. Lisset Mays, input a letter to Dooney and Burke to replace your $195 cream and brown leather handgage. The snap on the shoulder strap came off a while ago, but you have been so busy you just forgot, but now you want to get the bag fixed so you can carry it again. You had the ID registration number, but now it is misplaced. You want them to replace the bag or repair your bag. Choose a solution.

Sales Letters

5. You have just started a pre-burial funeral business. You cater to the middle-class who perhaps have a better understanding of what pre-burial plans can do for family survival. Most low income families are trying just to survive. You know that pre-planning is the best route and can bring peace of mind to the surviving loved ones. Input a form sales letter to be sent to a select group of middle-class people.
6. You are the owner of a Financial Planning Service. You have been trying to sell your service to a professor who seems interested but seems to think of things that may come up that may require her to use the money. The professor is worried that if she commits a certain amount each month, she will perhaps need it later on. It is obvious that she has not been able to save much because as soon as she does, one of her children calls for financial help and there goes her money. Input a letter to Dr. Pat Dickey-Olson, 600 South Cottage Avenue, Normal, IL 61761, convincing her of the need to start planning for her retirement. Her tax sheltered savings is not subject to taxes now so she will realize some extra savings in income tax withholding in her paycheck.

Sales Letters

7. You own a travel agency, and you are trying to get people to one of the newest vacation spots—Aruba. Travelers will fly from Miami and have five days and four nights for $825 per person. This includes round-trip air fare from Miami, hotel accommodations at the Aruba Resort and Casino, airport and hotel shuttles, and a $25 coupon for use in the Casino. Input a form sales letter to go to a select group of people.

Collection Letters

8. Input a form reminder letter to get car owners to pay their accounts which are two months' past due as of today.
9. Ms. Mari Baldwin has not paid her furniture in two months. You have sent her several notices; she has always made her payments on time so you feel something is wrong. Input an appeal letter to see what is wrong and to get her to make a payment on her account. Her address: 5002 Stevens Street, Lone Star, TX 75455.
10. Mr. Jack Sang wrote to tell you that he is unable to make a payment on his account due to the fact that he lost his job last Monday. However, he has not made a payment in six months so the fact that he just lost his job does not excuse the other months he did not make a payment. He was a poor credit risk to begin with, but you wanted to give him another chance. Input an ultimatum letter to him. He lives at 407 East Duarte Road, Arcadia, CA 91107.

Name ______________________________ Date ____________

JEOPARDY QUIZ #10

1. The answer is: Sales letters and collection letter series.

   What are ______________________________?

2. The answer is: Requires the indirect writing style arrangement.

   What is ______________________________?

3. The answer is: Attention, Interest, Desire, and Action.

   What are ______________________________?

4. The answer is: Credit, Character, Capacity, and Capital.

   What are ______________________________?

5. The answer is: Early stage messages, middle stage messages, and late stage messages.

   What are ______________________________?

6. The answer is: Psychological, Safety and Security, Social, Esteem and Status, and Self-Actualization.

   What are ______________________________?

7. The answer is: Emotional and Rational appeals used in messages.

   What are ______________________________?

8. The answer is: Requires that writing be understood by the average reader.

   What is ______________________________?

9. The answer is: Types of letters that are longer and require convincing the reader.

   What are ______________________________?

continued

10. The answer is: Written to maintain goodwill and to collect the money owed.

    What are ____________________________________?

PART III

COMMUNICATION THROUGH REPORTS

CHAPTER 11

Dan Frise, Lecturer
Department
of Management

Proposals and Reports

Objectives

After reading this chapter, and doing the applications you will be able to:

1. Define a business report.
2. Identify major types of business reports.
3. Contrast primary and secondary research.
4. Cite major sources of secondary research sources.
5. Name major primary research methods.
6. Describe data organizational techniques.
7. Develop a problem statement.
8. Analyze the different purposes among various types of reports.
9. Explain the basic contents of a Request for Proposal.
10. Search the Internet, OPAC, and Lexis Nexis for report topic information.
11. Select information to be included and excluded from available research information.

Through your years of school, you have become accustomed to writing reports for various reasons. In most courses, your goal is to exhibit your expertise to an authority, usually a teacher. Just as you prepare verbal and written reports for your course work, business reports play a vital role in today's business environment.

Unlike school reports, however, business reports are written to provide valuable information for making decisions in the business environment. All business decisions are based on some type of research, whether it is looking through past sales reports, comparing year end profits, or analyzing company performance. In this case, you are the authority on the subject. As the report writer or presenter, you are displaying the results of your research, education, and background search to the reader or readers charged with the decision making task. You are charged with the task of including pertinent information, while omitting unnecessary material.

The business report writer and presenter bear certain responsibilities in consideration of the audience, subject material, and the report purpose. First, business writers must present factual information, without bias, to the reader. Secondly, the report information must be presented in a clear and concise manner, so that it is usable to the reader. Finally, the writer must include information necessary for decision making.

Business reports are not limited to providing in-depth, detailed, lengthy, and somewhat boring accounts of business activities. Written reports provide a historical record for a business, which may be written in a memo, letter, or manuscript format, meaning double spaced text.

Reports are typically generated to answer questions. For example, suppose you could not enroll in a class you needed. You would wonder why this is so and conjure up responses, which are likely answers, including:

1. Is the class full?
2. Do I have the prerequisites for the class?
3. Why aren't more sections being offered?

Likewise, suppose your department has a high turnover ratio. You probably would want to know the answers to the following questions:

4. What is the reason(s) for the high turnover?
5. How does the turnover compare to last year?
6. Are there communication or personality problems?
7. What are the jobs involved?

Pondering the possible answers to these questions begins the process of analyzing the problem and could become areas of discovery and investigation. This questioning process is known as the critical thinking process. Reports may be written in either the direct or indirect order. The reader's reception of the report will usually determine the presentation order of the information. The direct order, which presents the conclusions and recommendations first, saves the reader's time since the main ideas are presented at the report's outset. This order is particularly useful for readers who are already familiar with the problem. If the reader may be skeptical or is unfamiliar with the situation or problem, using the indirect report order is better. Here you present introductory information first, then the findings, followed by the conclusions and recommendations. This arrangement enables the readers to follow step-by-step analysis of how you arrived at your decision.

Probably, many of you, at your job sites, have either created some type of business report or provided direct report information. Common business reports include attendance records, supply inventories, cash balances, and activity reports. Can you think of at least one instance that you were involved with a business report either verbally or in writing?

Proposals and How They Are Used

Similar to reports, you may have probably made a proposal in one form or another, either verbally or non-verbally. Whether it be suggestion to go to a movie or a restaurant, you are constantly making proposals that are either initiated by the invitation of others or self prompted.

Likewise, proposals are used in businesses for the collection of ideas, information or services. Proposals that are requested are called solicited proposals. Proposals that are not requested are called unsolicited proposals. Both are widely used in the business environment.

Requested proposals are solicited by clients who are in need of certain services or goods. The submission of a proposal to meet the client's needs or services is called a Request for Proposal, also known as RFP. Companies or individuals responding to RFPs communicate their ability to provide the requested goods or services to meet the needs of the solicitor.

When companies receive a Request for Proposal, careful consideration must be given as to whether they are able to fulfill the requirements for the goods or services being requested. This entails careful analysis of the scope, requirements, and procedures of the projected job.

Content of proposals. The organization of proposals generally follow the same format. If the format is stated in the RFP, you must follow the instructions with extreme care. If the Request for Proposal does not include a format, the following format is generally included:

1. The Introduction:

   A. States the purpose of the proposal
   B. Defines the scope of the project
   C. Presents background information
   D. Sets limitations on the job or service.

2. The Body:

   A. Describes and stipulates the costs, personal, facilitates, equipment, and methods of complying with the contract.

3. The final Section:

   A. Summarizes the final points of the proposal.
   B. Requests a response or a decision.

Unsolicited proposals, on the other hand, are initiated by the supplier of goods or services. These proposals generally include the same information as solicited proposals. Since however, these are uninvited proposals, the receiver must be convinced of the need for the particular goods or services being offered. Usually, more space is devoted to explaining the rationale behind the need for the goods or services than that in the solicited proposal. A business plan, submitted to a financial institution for the purpose of funding, is an example of an unsolicited proposal.

Proposals for obtaining funds in exchange for goods or services are known as Sales Proposals. Again, these proposals may be either solicited or unsolicited. The details contained in sale proposals demand careful attention because they are both legally binding and are generally subject to competition from other firms participating in the bidding.

Reports and How They Are Used

Reports serve the main function of communicating information in the business environment. Surely, from your own work experience and course work, you realize that a huge diversity of tasks are required in today's workplace. Similarly, the types of business reports vary with the functions they perform.

Reports may be considered a managerial tool. They assist personnel, charged with decision making activities, by providing current and up-to-date information upon which decisions are based. In this Information Age, can you appreciate how having the correct information, at the right time and place, can lead to a competitive advantage?

Managers do not have access to all information all the time. Like everyone else, they rely on other people, both internally and externally to the business, for decision-making information. One of the main objectives for generating a report is to provide correct and timely information that is easily accessible.

Like other types of business communication, reports generally follow the chain of command. Just as lower managers compile information for eventual use at higher management levels, some reports, generated initially at lower management levels, may eventually filter to the upper managerial ranks.

Report characteristics. In deciding the format, organization, and style of a report, it is helpful to consider the following report characteristics:

1. Was the report authorized, requested, or volunteered?

   If the report is volunteered, more detail must be given to the background of the report than a report that was authorized or requested.

2. What is the report's topic?

   Generally, the subject of the report will also affect its presentation and vocabulary. A legal topic, for example, requires legal terminology, which, in turn, may require defining and a special report format.

3. How often is the report prepared?

   The timing of a report will indicate whether it is a routine report, being created on a regular time cycle (such as weekly or monthly) as opposed to a special, nonrecurring report that is made only once.

4. Who will be the recipient of the report?

   Informal reports are generally prepared for an internal audience within an organization. Often these internal informal reports tend to be shorter than formal reports and may even appear in a memo format. Formal reports are usually created for an external audience and follow strict formatting guidelines.

5. What is the reason for the report preparation?

   If the report is to present information, the report is called an informational report. These reports are generally organized around the report's sub-topics. If the report is to analyze, conclude, and recommend action, then it is labeled an analytical report. Analytical reports are generally organized around logical arguments. Report classifications will be discussed in a later section in this chapter.

6. What is the reader's anticipated reaction to the report?

   Just like other business communication writing, the reader's anticipated reaction to the report can assist the writer in determining the report's organization. If the reader is familiar with the subject or if the reader's probable reaction is agreement, then the direct order, conclusions, recommendations, followed by details) may be utilized in the report's format. Similarly, if the reader's reaction will be reserved, or not accepting, then the indirect format (details, followed by conclusions and recommendations) is utilized. Report organization will be presented in greater detail in the next section.

Informative and Analytical Reports

As previously mentioned, reports can either be informative or analytical. Depending on the probable audience reaction, a report's structure may follow the direct or indirect organization. These report classifications and organizations are examined a little more closely below.

The goal of informative reports is to report information clearly, conveniently, and particularly to the reader. These reports are used by all businesses to control and monitor business functions, state policies and procedures, comply with regulatory agencies, and justify business decisions.

It is important to realize the range of existing informational report formats, since literally hundreds of different occasions for using these types of reports exist. Many informational reports, including those for use within a company or for regulatory compliance, are prepared on pre-printed forms. A preprinted format, usually prepared by the users of the information, simplifies the report preparation in addition to easing the task of extracting information.

Because of their frequency in business use, different types of informational reports demand attention. These include periodic reports, personal activity reports, feasibility reports, justification reports, progress reports, and credit reports. The periodic report is generated to describe activities occurring during a specific time, such as a week, month, or fiscal quarter. These reoccurring reports inform managers and others about activities so that they will remain up-to-date, make informed decisions, and take corrective action if a situation warrants.

A second type of informative report is the personal activity report. These reports describe the undertakings of individuals, including attendance at conferences, meetings, and other work-related activities. Personal activity reports are generally written in memo format and are usually organized chronologically. If the reader is interested in the report's subject content, a report organized around topics is advisable, due to simplifying its comprehension.

Feasibility reports weigh the chances of one option's success over another. This type of informational report focuses on two or more solutions to a problem or situation, and determines the best alternative. The conclusion would state the best alternative, while the recommendations would suggest its implementation.

Justification reports, also known as recommendation reports, are informational reports written by personnel who want to make suggestions to a business organization. Justification reports are a formal alternative to suggestion boxes. These reports are generally written in the direct format so that readers will know the writer's conclusions and recommendations without having to take time to read the entire report at once.

Progress reports are another type of informational report that tells other business personnel how a long term project is developing. Items generally included in progress reports include the project's scheduling information, problem occurrences, and plans for completion. Usually, this type of report discusses the project's background history or description, followed by details of work already completed, then details about work progress completed within the last period, and finally an anticipated time and work schedule for the project's completion.

Credit reports, the last type of informational report conveys credit information in a clear and standardized format. Since the purpose of a credit report is always the same, no background or introductory information is usually included. Unlike other types of reports, credit reports only tell credit facts relating to individuals or companies; they do not include conclusions or recommendations.

Since the purpose of the analytical report differs from the informative report, its organization is also structured differently. While information reports serve to educate their readers, analytical reports are prepared to help readers accept certain conclusions and recommendations. What is essential in creating a sound analytical report is to show readers how your sound thinking and data analysis leads to the report's conclusions and recommendations.

Report Organization

Just as with other types of reports, analytical and informative reports may be prepared using either a direct or an indirect organization. If the anticipated report's audience is expected to be receptive toward its conclusions or recommendations, then the direct organization will be suitable. Since the report's acceptance is anticipated, the direct organization positions the report's information around its conclusions and recommendations. This format stresses what should be done, rather than why certain conclusions or recommendations were made.

The indirect format is used if the anticipated audience reaction will be skeptical, or less than accepting of the report's conclusions or recommendations. Logical arguments for the conclusions or recommendations are necessary to convince readers why they should accept them. This organizational format places the report's information around the logical arguments, which in turn, leads to the report's conclusions and recommendations. The use of subheadings are useful for organizing the report structure, and enabling easier readability. Additionally, subheadings offer a greater sense of factual presentation.

Justification, trouble-shooting, and research reports can be classified as analytical in nature. You may recall that justification reports were already presented as informative reports. However, a justification report may also be analytical if its main purpose is to persuade an audience, rather than to inform.

Trouble-shooting reports are created to offer suggestions or alternatives to a situation occurring in the business environment. Often this task is not an easy one, given the possible negative ramifications of a decision. Approaching a trouble shooting report as analytical provides a sense of factual and non-biased thought, thus ending with a logical follow through of conclusions and recommendations. Readers, negatively impacted by a report's recommendations, will be in a better state to comprehend factors that lead to an adverse decision.

Research reports, as the name connotes, are reports based on researched facts and data. An examination of the various ways to collect data for creating a report is presented next.

Methods of Data Collection

Data collection can be classified by how it is obtained. There are two fundamental ways to gather data, either through secondary or primary sources. As with other types of business communication, the purpose and needs of the report will dictate which data sources are required.

Many reports are based on secondary data sources alone. These reports concentrate on extracting data that is already published, that is, secondary to the report writer. Some of sources of secondary data, readily assessable to both students and business writers, include general and specialized libraries, government repositories and local agencies, business records, and computerized databases and Internet connections. The following is a partial listing of the many secondary research materials available for business use:

Periodicals:
Business Week
Business Horizons
Harvard Business Review
Times
U.S. News and World Report

Journals:
Advertising Age
American Economic Review
Business Economics
Business Forum
Computer Information System Journal
CPA Journal

Newspapers:
Los Angeles Times
New York Times
Wall Street Journal
Washington Post

Indexes:
Baron's Index
Business Periodicals Index
Los Angeles Times Index
Washington Post Index

Journals:
Financial Management
Financial World
Forbes
Journal of Business Communication
Journal of Business Ethics
Journal of Systems Management
Journal of Small Business Management
Journal of Accountancy
Journal of Consumer Affairs
Journal of Economics and Business
Journal of Marketing
Journal of Consumer Research
Management Review
Sales and Marketing Management
Supervision

Selecting secondary research resources. Secondary data for business reports may be found in a variety of sources, including magazines, newspapers, journals, government publications and financial records. Computerized sources include CD-ROMS and Internet connections to databases. Although various secondary data sources exist, it is essential that the user of this information be selective in determining which source to use. It is also imperative to avoid biased or opinionated material, this will result in the inaccurate reporting of facts. Additionally, it is important to consider the credibility of the author and data, sometimes warranting a background investigation.

Timeliness and relevance. The timeliness and relevance of the data must be also be considered. In this Information Age, data is constantly being updated at a very fast pace. It is important that the report's data reflect the most current information available that will ultimately become the basis for conclusions and recommendations. The data must also reflect the needs and purpose of the report. Data that is suitable to the report content should be included, while unrelated data should be discarded.

The Internet. The Internet is quickly becoming the medium of choice for business researchers. This computer tool, sometimes referred to as the "information superhighway" allows users to quickly access a wide range of information by browsing through an interconnection of networks. Again, as with any source of information, care must be taken to determine the relevancy, timeliness, credibility, and the objectivity of the data. In fact, Internet users should exercise extreme care, Internet users and data are not necessarily screened for credibility.

Accessing the Internet is not difficult, even for first time users. The required Internet equipment consists of a computer, preferably a 486 or Pentium, with a large hard drive and an abundant amount of RAM, a high speed modem, to accelerate the research process, and browsing software called browsers to find specific online information. Nearly all Internet information is stored on web pages that are inter-linked so that users may "drill down" through topics, called hypertext, to find additional related information.

The Netscape Navigator is a popular Internet navigational suite. Among various tools, this suite offers a graphical Web browser, which assists researchers in finding information. As a standard, the World Wide Web, a term referring to the global linkage of information, uses Hypertext Transfer Protocol shortened to "http," for the transmission of hypertext.

Netscape includes various search engines that allow researchers to key in descriptive words to locate information on the Web. Yahoo, Magellan, Lycos, Excite, Infoseek, and Alta Vista are popular search engines available with Netscape, each providing the users with particular strengths and weaknesses. If using one search engine does not locate needed information, then you should try another. Generally, search engines allow users to access information by either selecting from a list of general topics, or by specifying keywords related to the research topic. After a researcher locates relevant information, a search engine can be utilized to further expand or limit the available information.

Another option available to Internet users is to directly access a Web page, which will contain pertinent research information. To directly access a Web page, type in the desired location in only lower case letters. Although their are hundreds of Web pages available, the following is a partial list of web pages relating to the business field:

1. **The Commercial Sites Index:** provides a list of businesses who have set up Web Pages.

   Location: http://www.directory.net/

2. **Interesting Business Sites on the Web:** lists a small number of business Web Sites.

   Location: http://www.owi.com/netvalue/index.html

3. **Internet Business Connection:** allows users to browse for products and services.

   Location: http://www.charm.net/~ibc/

4. **PR NEWSWIRE:** lists the best and important business Web sites.

   Location: http://www.prenewswire.com

5. **The 25 Best Business Web Sites:** lists sophisticated business Web pages.

   Location: http://techweb.cmp.com:2090/techweb/ia/13issue/13topsites.html

6. **Thomas HO's Favorite Business Sites:** displays the best of business and economic sites.

   Location: http://engr.iupui.edu/~ho/interests/commmenu.html

7. **NewsPage:** a good source of daily business news.

Location: www.newspage.com/

8. **Wall Street Journal:** displays business news.

   Location: http:www.wsj.com/

9. **Fidelity Investment:** provides investment information.

   Location: http://www.fid-inv.com/

10. **Bank of America:** lists banking, finance, and capital market information.

    Location: http://www.bankamerica.com/

11. **Internet Business Library:** displays domestic and international reports on business topics

    Location: http://www.bschool.ukans.edu/intbuslib/virtual.htm

12. **The Los Angeles Times:** displays general and financial news items.

    Location: http://www.latimes.com

13. **United States Department of Commerce**

    Location: http://www.doc.gov/

14. **United States Department of Labor**

    Location: http://www.dol.gov

15. **United States Department of the Treasury**

    Location: http://www.ustreas.gov

16. **United States Federal Trade Commission**

    Location: http://www.ftc.gov./Welcome.html

Related literature versus literature review. When preparing to write a report dealing with primary or secondary research, it is essential to first conduct a primary literature review. A primary literature review includes finding and reading sources from both internal sources, meaning from within a company's records, and external sources, from outside the company. This literature review serves many purposes. First, it helps the writer to become fully knowledgeable on the various aspects of the report topic. This will provide many benefits, including avoiding potential embarrassment, by identifying and addressing all issues surrounding a research topic. Secondly, a literature review may uncover data that would either enhance, or even render primary data collection unnecessary. Finally, a literature review assists report writers in the organizational aspects of the report process by viewing how others have approached the subject.

Not to be confused with a literature review is the review of related literature section of a report. The intent of this separate report chapter is to provide more than just a summary of literature related to the report topic. This report section identifies important research already accumulated on the report topic, compares and contrasts opposing research findings, and establishes how your report ties into previously conducted studies. The review of related literature will be discussed in depth in the chapter on report writing.

Documentation of report sources. Documentation of secondary report sources is an important element in any report. Report writers are required to give credit to authors of direct quotes, that is, when an author's exact words are used. Direct quotations should be used sparingly in report writing, that is, only if the quoted text would add a greater substance to the report, as opposed to an author's paraphrase. Passive research is a term for the use of secondary sources in a report.

Many people are unaware, however, that even using the ideas of another author requires documentation as well. An easy rule of thumb is to remember to give credit where credit is due, even when it comes to ideas and concepts. Paraphrasing someone else's ideas, that is, rewording an author's text, still requires full documentation, just the same as direct quotes.

Legal aspects surrounding documentation focus on plagiarism, that is, copying someone else's ideas. Plagiarism is a serious legal offense and is enforced under a variety of laws. Aside from the legal aspects, it is also considered unethical to steal somebody's ideas. Finally, documentation adds credibility to a report, by including strong documentation from experts in the business field, national and global leaders, or from other prominent sources.

Two types of documentation styles are in wide spread use today, the Modern Language Association (MLA) style and the American Psychological Approach (APA style). It is essential, that once you have chosen a documentation style for a particular report, to remain consistent by using it throughout the entire report.

There are many good guidebooks illustrating the use of the MLA or the APA documentation formats. One such publication is titled *Form and Style* by Campbell, Ballou, and Slade. This guidebook is constantly being updated to reflect changes that occur in report writing and contains many suggestions for citing works from other publications.

In the body of a report, the MLA style of documentation concentrates on citations including the author's last name and page number. The bibliography entry focuses on the details of the publication. The following examples will illustrate common types of MLA documentation:

Text Citation	There are several benefits to using computers (Smith 67). *(Author, Pg)*
	"There are several benefits to using computers" (Smith 67). *(Direct Quote) (Author, Pg)*
	According to Smith, there are several benefits to using computers (67). *(Author is named in text)*

Bibliography Citation	Smith, James. *Computers in the Business Environment.* Boston: Houghton, 1996. *(Indent all second lines 5 spaces)*
Text Citation	Computers are changing the workplace (Smith, Jones, Ann 104) *(Three or less authors)*
Bibliography Citation	Smith, John, Jones, Andrew, and Ann, Mary. *Computers.* Los Angeles: Educational Press, 1997. *(Author, Book, Publisher, Date)*
Text Citation	There are machines for all computational purposes ("Computer Technology" A8). *(Source without an author)*
Bibliography Citation	"Computer Technology Claims Jobs." *Los Angeles Times,* 10 Jan. 1997, A8+. *(Article, Newspaper, Date, Page)*
Text Citation	The GNP is higher than last quarter at this time (Clooney 198).
Bibliography Citation	Clooney, Thomas. "The Mystery Behind the GNP." *U.S. and World Report,* 7 March 1997, 198. *(Author, Article, Magazine, Page)*

The APA or the American Psychological Approach focuses on the authors and dates of publication. Again, the citation is given in the report's text and in its bibliography. The following examples show common forms of APA documentation:

Text Citation	There are benefits to using computers (Smith, 1996). *(Author, date)*
	"There are benefits to using computers" (Smith, 1996). *(Direct Quote)*
	According to Smith, there are several benefits to using computers (1996). *(Author is named in text)*
	According to Smith (1996), there are several benefits to using computers. *(Author and Date is in text)*
Bibliography Citation	Smith, James. (1996). *Computers in the business environment.* Boston: Houghton. *(Indent all second lines 5 spaces)*
Text Citation	Computers are changing the workplace (Smith, Jones, Ann, 1997). *(Three or less authors)*
Bibliography Citation	Smith, John, Jones, Andrew, and Ann, Mary. (1997) *Computers.* Los Angeles: Educational Press. *(Author, Date ,Book, Publisher)*
Text Citation	There are machines for all computational purposes ("Computer Technology," 1997). *(Source without an author)*
Bibliography Citation	Computer technology claims jobs. (1997, 10 Jan.). *Los Angeles Times,* pp. A8+. *(Article, Date, Newspaper, Page)*
Text Citation	The GNP is higher than last quarter at this time (Clooney, 1997).

Bibliography Citation Clooney, Thomas. (1997, 7 March). The mystery behind the GNP. *U.S. and World Report, p.198. (Author, Date, Article, Magazine, Pg)*

Internet MLA

Text Citation Computers will see rapid hardware advancement during the next decade. (Smith). *(Author's name only)*

Bibliography Citation Smith, Thomas. <tsmith@csula.edu> "Tomorrow's Technology" 19 April 1997. Base article. <http://www.msnbc.com/get/news/html> (20 Feb. 1997).

Text Citation "Hardware development will undergo extensive technological changes in the next ten years" (Smith).

Bibliography Citation Smith, Thomas. <tsmith@csula.edu> "Tomorrow's Technology" 19 April 1997. Base article. <http://www.msnbc.com/get/news/html> (20 Feb. 1997).

Internet APA

Text Citation Computers will see rapid hardware advancement during the next decade (Smith, 1997).

Bibliography Citation Smith, T. (20 Feb. 1997). "Tomorrow's technology." <http://www.msnbc.com/ get/news/html>

As you can see, the differences between the MLA and the APA styles are slight; however, attention to detail is important in report writing. In comparing the MLA and APA styles, note the different order of citation information, punctuation differences, and the use of upper and lower case letters. As a final note, it is vital to include both the full biographical entries in the report's bibliography to match the parenthetical citations in the report's text.

Primary Research

You may be probably thinking by now, what if the report information and data is not available through secondary research sources? At these times, researchers must go out and gather their own information. Primary research is the collection and interpretation of data by a researcher. This is called first-hand or active research. Thus, the information becomes primary to the use of the report. The process of collecting primary information can be a challenging, yet a personally rewarding exercise.

Types of primary research. There are four fundamental means to conduct primary research. Documents, observations, surveys, and experiments all provide a means of extracting meaningful and relevant report data. The four primary research instruments are discussed next.

As you already realize, the purpose of *business documents* is to relay pertinent data to the users of such information. Just as valuable, however, is the data that these documents can bring in a research environment.

Consider the value of an attendance report from an accounting department. This information, from a periodic report, becomes the basis of issuing pay checks and qualifies personnel for benefits, including vacation and sick leaves. After they are used by the payroll department, the attendance reports are stored for future reference. If these reports are used again, for similar purposes, they are considered secondary research sources.

Now consider that this company wants to determine the optimal number of accounting employees needed to complete a special assignment. Among other variables, the researcher must determine the number of hours accountants spend per week to maintain the company's records. The attendance reports for an entire year are collected and analyzed for information purposes. The researcher is now converting the attendance record information into new data for the purpose of the report. Thus, the year's worth of attendance reports become a primary research tool for the report.

Observation. Observation is a second vehicle for collecting primary research. All of us use our five senses to observe our environment. Consider being late for a final exam and speeding on a freeway. Suddenly, you observe the cars in front of you slowing down quickly, for no obvious reason. Through previous observation experiences, you may assume that either an accident or a police person is ahead. Consequently, you slow your vehicle down.

Similarly, these types of informal observations have their place in business. As you already know, part of the communication process demands informal observation of the receiver of your message. Formal observation is a valuable research tool and is often required in collecting primary data.

The process of formal observation requires adherence to guidelines to ensure the collected data is without bias and other adulteration. The following guidelines apply to the creation of the observation form:

1. Create an observation form that contains all possible observable behaviors in a clear and organized manner. Group like behaviors together for easier data recording.
2. Be sure to include clear and thorough instructions for carrying out the observation.
3. Record observations immediately after they occur; do not rely on your memory.
4. Ensure that your observation form is complete. Performing a "trial run" of the form is one way of accomplishing this task.

When making the actual observations, it is also necessary to follow guidelines to ensure the accuracy and completeness of data. The following guidelines are helpful:

1. Make certain that the conditions under observation allow for the representativeness of data needed.
2. Complete enough observations to create data credibility.
3. Train all observers so that consistency in observation is established.

Surveys. Surveys are another means of collecting primary data for reports. Surveys may be either written, as on a survey form, or verbal, as in an interview. Just like the observation process, certain guidelines are established to ensure the integrity of the data collection instrument.

1. Limit questions to only pertinent information needed for the research report.
2. Word questions to obtain the information needed. Open-ended questions provide researchers with the respondent's own answers, usually resulting in various types of responses. Close-ended questions limit responses to choosing among provided answers. Close-ended questions are much easier to tally or summarize than open-ended questions, by either ranking or rating them.
3. Arrange the questions in a logical and, if written, in a visually appealing manner. Group similar questions together, with more interesting questions first. This will help to generate interest in the survey or interview process and may evoke more responses.
4. Clearly and consistently phrase the instrument's questions and directions. This will result in receiving useful and pertinent information for use in a report. Additionally, if respondents may feel uneasy about answering certain questions, promise and adhere to strict anonymity.

Experiments. Experiments are the last primary research technique. A true experiment consists of a variable factor, which changes, and fixed variables which remain the stable. In classic experiments, mice run through a maze after a piece of cheese. Fixed variables may include room temperature, lighting, maze shape, noise, and the type of cheese used. The variable factor may include injections of different memory altering chemicals. After a series of maze runs, with fixed variables being held constant, and memory altering chemicals being changed, it may be possible to determine which chemical has more effectiveness on increasing the memory of mice.

Similarly, businesses are often engaged in experiments. In a business experiment, two groups are used, a control group and an experimental group. Control groups hold fixed variables constant and while a variable factor is injected into an experimental group. Any difference that occurs between the two groups can be perceived as a result of the injection of the variable factor into the experimental group. Test marketing products can yield valuable presales data about a product, its price, and its consumers. Although this is considered an experiment, keep in mind that this is not a true experiment in the laboratory sense. In the real world, all fixed factors cannot be held constant, just as the change of the variable factor cannot be completely credited with any end experimental result. Therefore, the experimentation process in the business environment must be carefully constructed and reviewed periodically to prevent the formation of invalid experimental conclusions which may otherwise appear. Similarly, the use of experiments is not applicable to all business situations.

Factors Considered in Selecting Types of Primary Research Needed

The decision to use a primary research instrument is often a challenging and critical decision in the report creation process. The use of a testing instrument that does not provide necessary report information constitutes a waste of time, money, and effort. To avoid this type of error, consider the following factors:

1. What is the research problem? Defining the precise problem statement will lead to credible clues as to which research instrument should be used. Does the report problem demand gathering information that can be extracted from documents, observations, surveys, or experiments?

2. What was revealed in the literature review? Perhaps other researchers have already gathered pertinent information on a similar research topic using a particular research tool. Decide whether the same tool will work in your research investigation. If a suitable primary research tool has already been developed, use it.

Data Organization

Once the secondary and primary information is collected, it is time to formulate a plan for the presentation of the acquired information. Just like other written business communication, it is essential that data is presented clearly, accurately, and concisely.

Organizing data requires shifting through the primary and secondary data and applying logical thought to develop a sound structure. Often, the nature of the research will lend itself to natural organization. Some of these organization structures include:

1. A chronological order in which a time sequence establishes a certain order. This is often the structure of reports that are historical or procedural in nature.
2. A compare and contrast order serves to show similarities and differences among people, places, and things. This organizational structure is effective when distinguishing one entity from another.
3. A spatial structure lends itself to those items that are physically or geographically definable. This structure is particularly useful in businesses that convert materials into end-products, or operate in a geographical diverse locations.
4. A cause and effect structure emphasizes events or circumstances that force or create other events or circumstances. This structure works particularly well in using experimental primary research, although, as previously mentioned, true experimentation in the business environment is extremely difficult to achieve. This report structure should address and explain as many variables in the research as possible.
5. An analysis structure breaks a report topic down into its components and discusses each component in turn. Analysis can be defined as defining and creating the subdivisions of a topic.

Another way of viewing data organization is to follow a series of steps:

1. Divide the report subject using two or more alternative methods.
2. Select the most logical and effective method of report division from step 1. This will become the report's main divisions.
3. List the report's subdivisions, using parallel construction, under the report's main divisions created in step 2. These will become the report's sub-headers.

Sample of Reports

Data analysis and interpretation of report information will be discussed in Chapter 12.

A Proposal Excerpt Example

A PROPOSAL TO ESTABLISH A BUSINESS LIBRARY
AT CALIFORNIA STATE UNIVERSITY, LOS ANGELES

INTRODUCTION

The business communication students of California State University, Los Angeles are pleased to have this opportunity to submit this proposal to establish a business library held within the School of Business and Economics. This bid, in response to RFP CA-93534, will establish a business library that will satisfy the research and learning needs of students, staff, and faculty members.

BACKGROUND

California State University, Los Angeles is a major source of qualified business graduates in the Los Angeles area. Undergraduate options within the School of Business and Economics include marketing, economics, accounting, finance, computer information science, and management. As a priority within the school, students are educated in their respective areas of study with the latest available technology and learning materials.

Faculty and staff members, who provide direct assistance to business students, also require direct access to these learning mediums. In this Age of Information, it is essential to maintain an accurate and current knowledge base.

The ideal of securing these information sources, however, is directly contrary to the amount of public funds available to establish a business library.

An Example of a Personal Activity Report

ORION MANUFACTURING
WEEKLY ATTENDANCE REPORT

Name: JOHN SMITH
Department: GROUNDS MAINTENANCE

Days	Monday	Tuesday	Wednesday	Thursday	TOTAL
Date	2–24–97	2–25–97	2–26–97	2–27–97	
Hours Worked	10	10	0	10	30
Sick Hours	0	0	10	0	10
Vacation Hrs	0	0	0	0	0

Employee Signature: ______________________________

Supervisor Signature: ______________________________

Justification Report Sample

To: John Smith, Dean of Business and Economics
From: Mary Jackson, Professor
Date: August 25, 1997
Subject: Development of an Advanced Multimedia Course

As you requested at the August 15, 1997 staff meeting, I have prepared this written proposal to initiate a new, advanced, multimedia course in the Fall Quarter, 1997. This course proposal will detail the course requirements, student learning benefits, and the required materials for this class. Additionally, teaching methodologies and strategies will be discussed.

PREPARING STUDENTS FOR SUCCESS IN THE BUSINESS ENVIRONMENT

Businesses in the greater Los Angeles area are constantly recruiting qualified business students to work in their firms. Among the many changing technological factors in the business environment is the effective and efficient communication in a presentation setting. Newly evolved technologies have greatly enhanced the presentation process; however, specialized training is required for an employee's optimal success.

CIS 382: ADVANCED MULTIMEDIA TECHNIQUES

Computer Information Science, Course 382, will enable students, desiring to advance their presentation skills, to gain proficiency in the latest technological areas surrounding multimedia creation and presentation.

An Excerpt of a Feasibility Report

RECOMMENDATION FOR REPLACING WINDOWS 3.1
WITH WINDOWS 95 IN THE ADVANCED COMPUTING LAB

The Purpose and Scope of the Study

The purpose of this study is to determine whether the computers in the Advanced Computing Lab should be converted over to the Windows 95 operating system from the Windows 3.1 operating environment. Monetary factors included in this report include hardware and software costs, personnel training costs, and on-going technical support costs. Direct benefits discussed in this report include updated technical skills of both students and faculty members and its impact on the Los Angeles business community.

Factors not addressed in this report include securing funding sources, changing course content, and obtaining compatible application software. The following research , obtained from surveying one thousand Los Angeles businesses, indicate the need to expand campus technologies. Additionally, cost and time constraints are also discussed.

Findings

Survey results of the use of the Windows 95 operating system by 1000 Los Angeles businesses indicate the following:

1. Currently, in the Los Angeles area, two hundred and fifty businesses, or 25 percent, of the total, have successfully converted their entire computer operations to the Windows 95 environment.
2. Of the remaining seven hundred and fifty companies, 50 percent indicated they will switch operating systems within six months.
3. Three hundred and seventy-five companies indicated that, although no firm decision has been made yet, it is probable that they will convert their systems over to Windows 95 within two years.

References

Bovee, C. L. & Thill, J. V. (1986). *Business communication today*. New York: McGraw-Hill.
Campbell, W. G., Ballou, S. V. & Slade, C. (1990). *Form and style*. Boston: Houghton Mifflin Company.
Sapre, P. M. (Ed.). (1991). *Research methods in business education*. Delta Pi Epsilon.
Treece, M. (1991). *Successful communication for business and the professions*. Boston: Allyn and Bacon.
Wayne, F. S. & Dauwalder, D. P. (1994). *Communicating in business*. Boston: Irwin.

Questions

1. Compare and contrast the APA and MLA styles of documentation.
2. Distinguish primary research from secondary research.
3. Discuss the ethical considerations of report writing.
4. Explain the difficulties of conducting experiments in the business environment.
5. Differentiate between a solicited and an unsolicited proposal.
6. List seven types of informational reports and their respective use in the business environment.
7. Explain the importance of the timeliness and relevance factors in the collection of data.
8. Discuss the pros and cons of using the Internet as a source of information.
9. Distinguish observation methods from experimentation methods in obtaining primary research.

Applications

1. Describe ten different business situations that would require a report. Define which report type would satisfy each situation.
2. Compare and contrast the following terms:

   A. Primary and Secondary Research
   B. The Review of Related Literature and a Literature Review
   C. The MLA and APA style of documentation
   D. A direct quote and a paraphrase
   E. Informative and Analytical Reports.
   F. The direct and indirect report writing styles.

3. Discuss the types of primary research instruments you would use to accomplish the following?

   A. The average height of students enrolled in your business communication class.
   B. The proportion of Accounting, Management, and Finance majors in your business communication class.
   C. The opinions of students in your business communication class regrading affirmative action in the hiring process.

4. Create an observation form to obtain data related to student's using proper keyboarding techniques.
5. List different ways that you would find secondary sources related to a report on "The Dangers of Using a Microcomputer." Include in the list all indexes and computerized databases that would be usable in your search.
6. Prepare a bibliography with the sources related to "The Dangers of Using a Microcomputer" found in Application 5.
7. List several alternative methods for structuring a report on "The Dangers of Using a Microcomputer." Select the best method and list the subheaders using parallel construction.
8. Prepare a report on the environmental impact of smoking cigarettes in the workplace. What are some ethical issues you may face in creating this report?
9. Search the Internet for information on "The Impact of Stress in the Workplace."
10. Create an observation form to elicit information about the types of drinks that students purchase.

Name ______________________________________ Date ____________

JEOPARDY QUIZ #11

1. The answer is: Attendance records, supply inventory, cash balances, and activity reports.

   What are ______________________________________?

2. The answer is: A RFP.

   What is ______________________________________?

3. The answer is: Periodic reports, progress reports, feasibility reports, and credit reports.

   What are ______________________________________?

4. The answer is: Smith, 1996.

   What is ______________________________________?

5. The answer is: Contains conclusions and recommendations.

   What is ______________________________________?

6. The answer is: The manner in which the collection of data is classified.

   What is ______________________________________?

7. The answer is: Considerations when establishing the credibility of research sources.

   What are ______________________________________?

8. The answer is: The collection and interpretation of data by a researcher.

   What is ______________________________________?

9. The answer is: Documents, observations, surveys, and experiments.

   What are ______________________________________?

continued

10. The answer is: Variable factors and fixed factors.

    What are ____?

CHAPTER 12

Career Day at
California State University, Los Angeles

Data Analysis and Interpretation

Objectives

After reading this chapter, and doing the applications you will be able to:

1. Define instrument reliability and validity.
2. Extract a sample population.
3. Apply the concept of systematic and stratified randomness to a population.
4. Use the Measures of Central Tendency.
5. Understand the meaning of correlation and trend analysis.
6. Apply rating and ranking tools to interpret data.
7. Understand the use and apply statistical software.
8. Develop awareness of common interpretive errors.

Once you have collected the primary data, it is time to perform analysis. Researchers, applying their critical thinking skills, review the facts and establish meaning from the collected data. By approaching the data from different angles, researchers find evidence to answer the questions raised by the report's topic. This can be a fun and personally rewarding part of the research process.

Data Analysis Process

To ensure that the proper interpretation of data is gathered from the analysis phase of report writing, researchers must be concerned with the treatment of data. This section discusses some of the many methods of data interpretation and analysis.

Instrument Reliability and Validity

Reliability and validity are two important elements to consider when designing a data gathering instrument, such as a survey or an observation form. To ensure that the instrument will gather the correct data in a consistent manner is of paramount importance prior to using the instrument for obtaining research data. Imagine conducting primary research using a thousand surveys, only to find the needed information is not obtainable or is not consistent, despite your hard work and efforts.

Usually, the process of determining the validity and reliability of a testing instrument is accomplished after its written, but prior to its actual use in gathering data. In effect, this phase is equivalent to test driving a prototype car before it is actually mass-produced for the general public.

The term validity refers to an instrument's ability to gather research data that is necessary for the report. Actually, the instrument is not considered valid, rather the inferences that the researcher can make from the instrument are considered valid. Thus, the instrument's data must be related to the research topic and serve the needs of the researcher. This information will, in turn, become the basis for the report's conclusions and recommendations.

Validity has several implications. First, the concept of instrument validity is dependent on who is using the instrument and how is the instrument being used. One instrument given to one group, for instance, may offer valuable data. Another group, however, using the same instrument, could give completely invalid data, based upon their interpretation or perceived use of the survey.

Validity also infers the instrument provides meaningful, appropriate, and useful research data. Meaningful data implies that the data has some type of significance in light of the research topic. What good is collecting data if it does not mean anything? Appropriate data infers that the data derived from the instrument is directly related to the research problem. Finally, useful data is data that is directly usable in the research project, leading to conclusions.

Reliability is another term used in conjunction with validity. The term, reliability, refers to the consistency of the scores or answers the instrument would produce if it was given a number of times to the same person or group of people. Certainly, it would be doubtful if a person, or a group of people, filling out a survey form would answer all questions exactly the same given two survey administrations, but the scores should be relatively close.

All researchers, using primary data, should perform a validation exercise on the testing instrument before it is implemented for a research project. The validation process checks an instrument for reliability and validity so the researcher can determine whether the data collected is both accurate and consistent.

An instrument's validity may be established by cross-checking data it produces with the research problem to ensure the inclusion of all necessary data and the omission of all irrelevant data. This step can be accomplished by enlisting the help of others who can actually complete and critique a data collection instrument before it is administered.

The validation step of establishing reliability may be accomplished by retesting and comparing the scores of groups taking the same instrument over time. Actually, re-testing only representative samples of groups is necessary to establish that the instrument will produce similar results if re-administered.

Sample Populations

The term "population" in research refers to the entire universe. This would include all people, things, or entities that comprises the topic of a research project. Not all populations are easy to define. For example, listing all "Fortune 500 Companies" would be a relatively straight forward task, but not all populations are so easy to define. Consider the task of listing all companies who are incorporating advanced technology in producing goods or services. How would you define advanced technology in the midst of rapidly changing technologies?

Sampling provides a way for researchers to limit the data collection process and yet obtain a true representation of the entire population. This is based on the assumption that a population contains a range of similarities that can be captured by sampling, that is, by taking a part of the whole.

The only true way to draw a representative sample from a population is by using random drawing. Random refers to entities having an equal chance of being selected out of a population This means, over the long run, a certain characteristic of a population will be countered by another characteristic, given both characteristics have an equal chance of being selected.

Simple random sampling infers placing all the names included in a population into a container and drawing a sample by drawing names. For example, imagine a class section that can accommodate three additional students, but ten students want to add the course. A professor could place the names of the students in a bag and draw three names of students who will be permitted to add the section. Although simple randomization may work under certain circumstances, randomization is often not possible or practical to use all the time. For instance, imagine if ninety nine students desired to add a class section. It may be impractical, due to time constraints, to collect all ninety-nine names. Therefore, other randomization techniques, including systematic and stratified sampling have been developed.

Systematic sampling consists of taking every "nth" value from data in a list or other format. For example, to select three names from ninety nine students wanting to add a course section, one could visually select each thirty-third person standing in a line, with thirty-three becoming the "nth"value. The "first" student, however, would be selected randomly. This would be accomplished by labeling numbers one to a hundred, and randomly selecting one, by drawing a number from a bag. This number would indicate which student standing in line will become the "first"in the counting process. Thus, each student would have an equal chance of being selected.

Stratified sampling entails the extraction of random selections from existing subgroups. For example, if a researcher wants to survey courses within the School of Business, logical subgroup divisions could include the finance, accounting, computer information systems, management, marketing and economics and statistics options. Then, depending on the percentage of student enrollment in each option, which compromises the whole, a researcher could determine the number of people in each option to include in the study. For example, let's assume that the following percentages of students comprise the School of Business in a study requiring a survey of sixty students:

Major Options Available in the School of Business and Economics	Percentage of Students in Each Option	Number of Students Selected for the Study
Finance	15%	9
Accounting	35%	21
Computer Information Systems	25%	15
Marketing	18%	11
Economics and Statistics	7%	4
Total	**100%**	**60**

As the chart indicates, having demographic knowledge of the population is essential in properly executing the stratified sampling technique.

Data Interpretation

By now you are aware of the importance of developing a reliable and valid testing instrument and how to establish random sample from a population. From here, the next step is to gather the data, then, to interpret the data.

Interpreting the data means that the researcher looks at the bits and pieces of data obtained from the testing instruments and attempts to determine meaning from them. By examining data from different perspectives, researchers obtain unique interpretive meanings. As the data pieces fall into place, tentative research conclusions are constructed, which may be later accepted or rejected.

Rating and ranking are two methods for transforming collected data into meaningful information. Ranking involves placing an estimated value on each factor under study. For example, suppose a study is underway to determine how students view the parking, food service, and security of their campus as factors for determining the best college campus to attend. The researcher would list each factor and with assigned weights to indicate their particular importance.

For example, in this study, it is determined that parking would receive a forty percent weight, food service would receive a fifty percent weight, and security would receive a ten percent weight. Notice that the sum of all weights must equal 100%. Additionally, the researcher would assign values to the quality of each factor, number 1 to signify excellent, 2 to indicate adequate, and 3 to connote poor quality of each factor. The following table illustrates the data results of a survey given to students at each campus:

Campus One			
Factors	Quality Ranking	Assigned Weight	Total
Parking	1.2	.40	0.48
Food Service	2.34	.50	1.17
Security	2.76	.10	0.276
		Total	**1.926**

Campus Two			
Parking	2.14	.40	0.856
Food Service	2.96	.50	1.48
Security	.98	.10	0.098
		Total	**2.434**

The table indicates that, since campus one received a 1.926 rating, this would be the best campus to attend.

Rating involves taking a more quantified approach to transform research data. The researcher assigns a scale to measure the various factors under study. For example, a researcher could assign the following scale to the campus study:

Scale:	**1**	**2**	3
Parking	1000+ spaces	500-599 spaces	under 500 spaces
Food Service	150+ menu items	100-149 menu items	under 100 food items
Security	200+ guards	100-199 guards	under 100 guards

Again, weights may be assigned, according to the importance of each factor under study. Assuming the same weighting scale, a visit to each campus determines the data for each factor as follows:

Campus One			
Factors	Scale	Weights	Rating
Parking	1	0.4	0.4
Food Service	3	.50	1.5
Security	2	.10	0.2
		Total	**2.1**

Campus Two			
Factors	Scale	Weights	Rating
Parking	3	.40	1.2
Food Service	1	.50	0.5
Security	2	.10	0.2
		Total	**1.9**

Using the above rating system, Campus Two is the best campus, since it received an overall rating of 1.9.

The Measures of Central Tendency are often applied in the data interpretation phase of research. These measurements include the mean, median, and mode of the collected data. These tools, if properly applied, can lend credible insight into the meaning of data; however, if these tools are misused, they can also result in misrepresentation.

Determining the mean value of a data set is the same as finding the arithmetic average. Suppose that the income levels of four students enrolled in Business Communication courses are as follows:

$ 3, 000, 5, 000, 7, 000, 8, 000, 10, 000

The mean is computed by adding the values of the data together and dividing by the number of data sets observed:

3000 + 5000 + 7000 + 8000 + 10000= 33000   33000 / 5 = 6600

The mean income of our sample is $6,600. Consider, however, the following sets of numbers:

$4, 000, 5, 000, 6, 000, 7, 000, 24, 000

The mean is computed as:

4000 + 5000 + 6000 + 7000 + 24000 = 39000   46000 / 5 = 9200

The mean income of the second set, $9,200, is clearly not representative of the income of the surveyed students. The mean is overstated due to the large range of numbers in the data set, namely 24 000–4 000 or 20 000. The range of the first set of data, 7,000 (10000–3000), is more representative of the sample. In short, the mean value can become exaggerated if the range of data, the difference between the highest and lowest data point, is large.

The median can be defined as the midpoint in a series. Taking the data obtained in the first example of student income, 3000, 5000, 7000, 8000, 10000 the number at the midpoint, or third in a series of five, is 7000.

If the number in a series is an even number, determining the median employs two extra steps. First, add the two center numbers together, then divide by two. For example, if our data set is 3000, 5000, 7000, 8000, add 5000 and 7000 together, then divide by two. The answer is:

5 000 + 7000 = 12 000   12 000 / 2 = 6 000

The median value in this set is equal to 6 000.

The mode value represents the most frequently occurring value in a data series. It is possible that one data set contains more than one mode. For example, the income of students in a Business Communication section are as follows:

$ 3 000
3 000
4 000
5 000
7 000
7 000
8 000
10 000

The mode values of the data set would be 3 000 and 7 000.

It is interesting to note that the mean and the median values are considered useful in analyzing data. Generally, the mean reflects the total values of an entire sample, since each sample unit is utilized in determining the mean. The median value, on the other hand, is considered a typical score of the sample, since it is merely the midpoint of a series.

This section would be incomplete without a mention of other statistical tools used to analyze primary data. Although it is not within the scope of this chapter to offer an in depth exclamation, an introduction to correlation and trend analysis is given below.

Correlation analysis is a valuable statistical tool when the researcher wants to determine whether the data is related to two or more variables. It is important to note from the start, that correlations do not necessarily determine that a variable is a cause of another variable, but rather there is simply a relationship that exists.

For example, suppose in a Business Communication class, a midterm examination is given. The professor finds, through correlation, that students who took the exam near the windows scored higher than those who sat next to the door. The following table illustrates these findings:

Breakdown of Midterm Grades in Relation to Seating Arrangement

Student SID	Window Seat Score	Student SID	Door Seat Score
5678	78%	5841	67%
1234	89%	5642	72%
4563	99%	7841	81%
4657	93%	9637	56%
6327	88%	5895	54%
5678	79%	2598	66%
Mean Score	**0.87666666667**	**Mean Score**	**0.66**

The data in the table indicates that those students taking the midterm near the window scored an average grade of 87 percent, while those students seating near the door scored an average grade of 66 percent. Logic would dictate that a window would not increase a student's ability to score a higher midterm grade than a student sitting near a door. Likewise, it would be an error to state that a window seat caused the effect of a higher grade, and a door seat caused the effect of a lower grade. The users of statistical measurements must be careful in the interpretation of their analysis.

Trend analysis seeks to examine the change of data over time. Businesses often seek this type of analysis, especially when product sales are seasonal, such as sun screen lotion. The table below illustrates the sales of sun screen throughout a year interval:

Sun Screen Sales by Month, 1997

Month	Units (100's)	Sell Price	Revenue	% Revenue
January	1,256	$7.89	$ 9,910	2.2217898144
February	1,354	$7.89	$10,683	2.3951460261
March	2,365	$7.89	$18,660	4.1835453114
April	3,654	$7.89	$28,830	6.4637101767
May	4,548	$7.89	$35,884	8.0451433727
June	5,568	$7.89	$43,932	9.8494631264
July	6,892	$7.89	$54,378	12.191540924
August	7,854	$7.89	$61,968	13.893262104
September	8,892	$7.89	$70,158	15.729422795
October	7,235	$7.89	$57,084	12.798287665
November	4,561	$7.89	$35,986	8.0681396048
December	2,352	$7.89	$18,557	4.1605490793
Total	**56,531.00**		**446029.5**	**100%**

Viewing the results of trend analysis through graphics is particulary helpful in determining the relationship of time to units. In this case, the months of the year and the units sold are illustrated below:

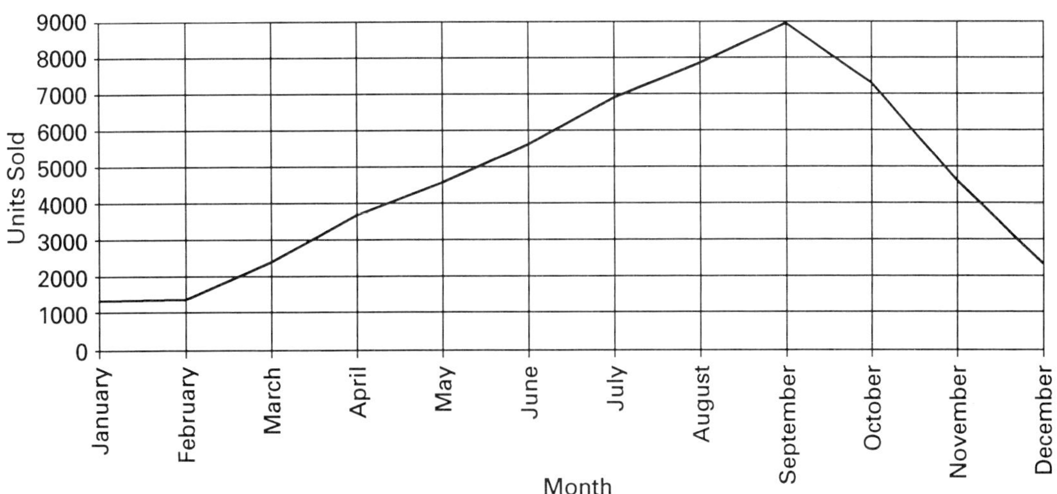

The above graph illustrates the sales trend of sun screen over the months over the year. The chart clearly shows a fluctuation of product sales over the months of the year, and can assist production personnel in determining demand forecasts, and sales personnel in determining consumer demand.

Statistical Software

A researcher's ability to perform data analysis has been enhanced by the development of new software. Specialized software packages have been developed to assist researchers with statistical requirements. However, it is still necessary for the researcher to know what the data needs to reflect in order to choose the proper statistical tool. One well known and used software package is SPSS or the Statistical Package for the Social Sciences. This powerful program is capable of deriving numerous statistical measurements from business research data.

Other sources of statistical data include the recent release of Excel version 7, and its older counterpart, Excel version 5. This spreadsheet program, and others, including Lotus 1–2–3 version 5, are ideal not only for sorting, displaying, and charting research data but also for determining invaluable statistical values.

To use the statistical capabilities in Excel version 5, it is vital to precisely input data in a systematic and orderly fashion. Suppose, for example, we need to analyze the following sets of data, using the Measures of Central Tendency, pertaining to the volume of case orders received by a local soft drink manufacturer:

345, 468, 523, 789, 345, 784, 123, 566, 789, and 923.

The first step is to set up a spreadsheet, with emphasis on accuracy and on organization. An example of this spreadsheet could be as follows:

Row #	Column A	Column B
1	Unified Soft Drink Company	
2	Order Quantity for June 15, 1997	
3		
4	Customer	Case Order
5		
6	Mo's Liquor Store	345
7	Derick's Office Supply	468
8	P and K Pharmacy	523
9	Linda's General Store	789
10	The Corner Store	345
11	Corn Dogs, Incorporated	784
12	The Pizza Place	123
13	The Way Things Were	566
14	Big Volume Discounts	789
15	Big and Cheap	923
16		
17	Mean	
18	Median	
19	Mode	

Computer users have many available options to perform statistical analysis on this data set. One way is directly entering a specific equation into the correct cell. The general format for entering most equations in spreadsheets, including Excel, is as follows:

=*FUNCTION* (*Beginning Cell* : *Ending Cell*)

The mean is computed with the following equation inputted into cell B17:

=AVERAGE(B6:B15) *Note: no spaces between characters!*

Note that columns, which extend vertically, are labeled with letters, while rows, extending horizontally are labeled with numbers. A cell's address is designated by the Column Letter and Row Number. The colon between the cell addresses refers to the range of cells, beginning with the first cell and ending with the final cell.

The median value is determined with the following equation in cell B18:

=median(B6:B15)

Note that the same formula structure is used when inputting these equations.

Finally, the mode value is inputted into cell B19, following the same technique:

=mode(B6:B15)

The equations in the spreadsheet appear as follows:

Mean	=AVERAGE(B7:B16)
Median	=MEDIAN(B7:B16)
Mode	=MODE(B7:B16)

The final spreadsheet yields the data and statistical data required for analysis:

UNIFIED SOFT DRINK COMPANY

Order Quantity for June 15, 1997	
Customer	Case Order
Mo's Liquor Store	345
Derick's Office Supply	468
P and K Pharmacy	523
Linda's General Store	789
The Corner Store	345
Corn Dogs, Incorporated	784
The Pizza Place	123
The Way Things Were	566
Big Volume Discounts	789
Big and Cheap	923
Mean	565.5
Median	544.5
Mode	345

Other statistical values are obtainable from the most widely used spreadsheets, including Excel, Lotus, and Quarto Pro. The following is a partial listing of common statistical measurements:

AVERAGE	Returns the average of a set of data
COUNT	Counts how many numbers are in a set of data
MAX	Returns the maximum value of a set of data
MEDIAN	Returns the median value of a set of data
MIN	Returns the minimum value in a set of data

A discussion of spreadsheets would be incomplete without reference to obtaining statistical functions beyond the Measures of Central Tendency. In Excel, version 5 and 7, many statistical functions are readily available to the user. Before using a built-in statistical function, select the cell that should contain the solution. Then, follow these steps:

1. To access these functions, simply left click on the Function Wizard button on the standard toolbar, which is labeled as "fx."
2. Select the main function category you wish to use, for example, the statistical category by left clicking on the appropriate selection.
3. Scroll down the right side of the Function Wizard dialog box, and select the statistical function you wish to apply to your data.
4. Left click on the "Next>" button.
5. Move the Function Wizard dialog box so that the data is visible by pointing to its title bar (the top colored area) and dragging the box to a new location.
6. Highlight the data to be analyzed by dragging through the data entries you wish to include in your analysis.
7. Drag the Function Wizard Dialog box back into view.
8. Left click on the "Finish" button and the answer will appear in the selected cell.

To learn how to use other spreadsheet programs for determining statistical measurements, select the "Help" pull down menu and choose either the "Topic" or the "Content" option. By indicating which assistance is required, the Help option will give you detailed instructions for completing almost any required task.

Common Interpretation Errors

Through years of experience, researchers have determined the importance of anticipating how particular errors may occur throughout the course of a study and lead to adverse findings. To avoid such errors, it is important for researchers to acknowledge and consider the following factors and their consequences while planning and implementing a study:

1. Selection bias refers to the selection of the study's subjects that possess certain a trait or traits which may impose unintended research results. If not controlled, subject traits, such as, a person's age, gender, and religious beliefs, may adversely impact the study's data integrity.

Suppose, for example, a study is undertaken to determine if showing classic movies during the evening at the Student Center is a practical idea for generating money for a campus organization. A survey form is developed to elicit information and is given to students attending night classes. The survey results indicate that there is no interest in attending this activity. Perhaps the reason for this lack of interest is that these polled students know that they will be attending class during the evening hours.

2. Mortality refers to the loss of subjects through the course of a study. For various reasons, including death and illness, people or subjects may need to withdraw their participation from a study. The loss of subjects could introduce biases to a research project if those, who dropped out, would have generated different study results.

For example, suppose a researcher wants to determine if a student's major has an impact on their participation in social activities over a year interval. At the study's conception, two hundred and fifty students, representing all majors, are chosen to participate in this study. However, after six months, the university slashes course sections due to budget constraints, resulting in a campus wide fifteen percent enrollment decline. Subsequently, the next survey indicates a substantial increase in attendance to social events, and a dramatic decrease in course units. This data, in turn, has a large impact on the study's findings.

3. Locations of where data is gathered may also affect a study's results. Whether data from a survey or an interview is drawn from a participant's home or work environment may affect the outcome of the data. Similarly, the location may supply a distinct benefit or a drawback to an entity that could also affect a study's outcome.

For example, assume a study is conducted to survey student's satisfaction towards the content in a finance course. The professor requires students taking the course to do all in class financial computations using a calculator, while homework assignments may be accomplished using a computer. Suppose most students find using the computer a distinct benefit to finishing the homework assignments and the calculator a distinct disadvantage. A survey or interview completed in the classroom may indicate a lower sense of subject content dissatisfaction than if taken at students' homework site.

4. A testing instrument itself may result in inaccuracy. This can result if the instrument, including the scoring of information, changes in some way throughout a study. Likewise, personnel who use a testing instrument may unintentionally inflect a bias through factors including fatigue or lack of training in computing scores.

For example, suppose a group of five marketing students want to determine the most common types of meals, meaning either breakfast, lunch or dinner, that are ordered at the campus cafeteria. Each student will observe the cafeteria's patrons for an entire day using the following observation form:

Date	Breakfast	Lunch	Dinner
Monday			
Tuesday			
Wednesday			
Thursday			
Friday			
Saturday			

Two students make the assumption that all meals purchased between 7 a.m. and 11:30 a.m. are considered breakfast, meals bought between 11:31 a.m. and 2 p.m. are lunch, and the remaining meals are dinner. The remaining three students observe the type of food purchased and make meal assumptions based on the typical types of food eaten for each meal. The differences in the students' observation methods will cause the inaccuracy of collected data.

5. Data collectors themselves are also possible sources of testing errors. Factors including the age, nationality, gender, and language patterns of a test administrator, can distort the outcome of a study's data. If any of these variables are somehow related to the study's data collector, distortion of data is likely to occur.

For example, a study is undertaken to determine the effectiveness of two different professors' teaching methods in a Business Communication course. One professor utilizes a large amount of visual displays, while the other mainly lectures. Students are given a survey forms to gauge their attitudes towards the course. Suppose further, that each professor is asked to administer and collect the survey forms. The survey results indicate high course satisfaction levels in both classes, despite different teaching methods employed in each section. Quite possibly, the survey results may be biased because of the survey's administration, rather than the teaching styles of the professor.

6. Data collector bias is another source of error in the data collection process. Data collectors, either consciously or unconsciously, may impose a bias or biases that will ultimately invalidate a study's data. Examples of this include the data collector asking leading questions, allowing more subject response time, observing events differently, and favoring one entity over another.

For example, a student develops a survey form to determine the greatest concerns of night students. A section of the developed survey form contains the following questions:

A. Are you aware of the vicious crimes that are taking place on campus during night classes.
B. Are you concerned about your personal safety while attending night classes on campus?

Not surprisingly, because of the leading questions, the survey results indicate that night students are very concerned about their personal safety. In fact, students indicated that they are much more concerned about their safety than what was indicated in previous studies. The nature of the leading question leads to instrument bias by those who were surveyed.

7. The testing process itself could also result in errors that result in inaccurate study data. If, for example, the subjects know the testing content, it is probable that they will perform better than others who didn't have that information. Additionally, if the subjects are able to figure out the "correct" responses on attitude or perception tests, then they may answer those questions accordingly. These factors, in turn, will result in the inaccuracy of the data obtained.

For example, a professor of a Business Communication Course, gives a test at the beginning of a course to determine students' ability to use proper grammar and punctuation while writing. The students are told they will retake the same test after completing the course. The professor discovers that students preform much better on the second test administration than on the first. The professor, however, cannot assume that students' performance boost is solely based on the course content since the students are aware of the test's questions and format. Perhaps they "crammed" for a grammar and punctuation test the night before.

Chapter 13 presents information and guidelines for using graphic aids and multimedia in reports.

References

Bovee, C. L. & Thill, J. V. (1986). *Business communication today*. New York: McCraw-Hill.
Sapre, P. M. (Ed.). (1991). *Research methods in business education*. Delta Pi Epsilon.
Wayne, F. S. & Dauwalder, D. P. (1994). *Communicating in business*. Boston: Irwin.

Questions

1. Compare and contrast the terms validity and reliability.
2. Compare and contrast the terms population and sampling.
3. Discuss when you would use either a rating and ranking method.
4. Explain the extent to which correlation studies explain the cause and effect of research variables.
5. Cite instances where correlation and trend analysis would provide useful information in the business setting.
6. Explain how you would find additional information about statistical functions in spreadsheet programs.
7. List and give examples of seven different types of common errors in data interpretation.

••• APPLICATIONS •••

1. Develop and validate a survey instrument that will determine the following aspects about your business communication class:
   A. The average height of students.
   B. The proportion of Accounting, Management, and Finance majors.
   C. The opinions of students regrading affirmative action in the hiring process.
2. Using the measures of central tendency, determine the following data on:
   A. The average height of students in your business communication class.
   B. The opinions of students regrading affirmative action in the hiring process in your business communication class.
3. Using the stratified sampling technique, determine how Accounting, Management, and Finance majors feel about affirmative action in the hiring process.
4. Create and validate an observation form to obtain data related to student's using proper keyboarding techniques in computer labs.
5. Using statistical software or a spreadsheet, determine the measures of central tendency for the number of hours students in your class are employed per week.
6. List the possible interpretative errors that could arise in determining the opinions of students regrading affirmative action in the hiring process in your business communication class.
7. Using a newspaper as a source of data, prepare a trend analysis chart depicting three different stocks and their daily values for a two week period of time.
8. Randomly select students from your Business Communication class using systematic and simple random sampling techniques.

Name ______________________________ Date ____________

JEOPARDY QUIZ #12

1. The answer is: The process used to check an instrument for reliability.

   What is ______________________________?

2. The answer is: Systematic and stratified sampling.

   What are ______________________________?

3. The answer is: The midpoint in a series.

   What is ______________________________?

4. The answer is: A visual that shows the change of data over time.

   What is ______________________________?

5. The answer is: Factors to consider while planning and implementing a study.

   What are ______________________________?

6. The answer is: Excel and Lotus 1–2–3.

   What are ______________________________?

7. The answer is: Ranking and rating.

   What are ______________________________?

8. The answer is: The sampling process in which everyone in the total population has an equal chance of being selected.

   What is ______________________________?

9. The answer is: The mean, median, and mode.

   What are ______________________________?

continued

10. The answer is: The extraction of random selections from existing subgroups.

    What is ____?

CHAPTER 13

Career Day at
California State University, Los Angeles

Using Graphic Aids and Multimedia

Objectives

After reading the chapter and doing the applications, you should be able to:

1. Explain the purpose of using graphic aids in reports.
2. State the guidelines for including a graphic aid in reports.
3. Describe the procedures for inserting a graphic aid in reports.
4. Name some popular graphic aids software programs on the market today.
5. Discuss the merits of interpreting with graphic aids.
6. Distinguish between a table and a figure.
7. Compose some simple graphic aids by hand or with graphic aids software.
8. Input a short paragraph on interpreting data in a visual aid.
9. Analyze why photographs are better in annual reports than diagrams.
10. Select one to two different visual aids to use in your research report.

Assuming that you determined before hand what you wanted the data to tell you and that you used a systematic method for collecting, recording, evaluating, and analyzing your data, you are now ready to interpret the data and present the data in a meaningful way for your readers. Once the data has been collected, you essentially have what is called raw data. The raw data mean nothing until it has been interpreted and analyzed.

Sometimes the writer has a preconceived idea of just how the data will come out. Then as the writer begins to interpret the data, the analysis is just the opposite of what was expected. The tendency for some writers is to use bias in writing the report to make the data come out a certain way. However, you do not want to fall into this snare. You, as the writer, should interpret the data and present it objectively. Your main goal in interpretation and analysis is to be honest and objective.

Purpose of Graphic Aids

Graphic aids are helpful in presenting report data. Graphic aids serve to supplement the text. The statement "A picture is worth a thousand words" is just as appropriate today as it was in earlier times. Because today's readers are busy reading large amounts of material, anything that can help the reader absorb report information is essential. Research has shown that people respond better and are able to visualize better with icons or graphic aids than text. If fact, one of the reasons why business people are so swamped with reading large volumes of mail is that the writer does not use graphic aids as much as he or she should. Wayne and Dauwalder (1994) p. 359 state that most people think visually better than they do verbally. They state further that visual images are usually a better representation of concrete reality than words, which are abstract.

Graphic aids can help the reader to retain the report information as well as to reduce reading time, both of which contribute to positively enhancing your reader's perception about your report. Lastly, by making the report information easier to read, understand, and absorb by using graphic aids, you encourage the reader to take action on your report information.

You should read the report carefully and determine where you would include a graphic aid(s). Essentially, you will need to look at the type of information that can support a graphic aid. For example, if you wanted to include the number of females and males who completed your survey, you could put that information in a sentence rather than a graphic aid. On the other hand, if you wanted to illustrate the number of females and males who were juniors and seniors and had received a scholarship, then a graphic aid would support that variety of data.

Guidelines for Inserting Graphic Aids in Reports

Graphic aids should be included in reports only if a need exists to help clarify or supplement the information. The graphic aid should be understandable just by looking at it.

First, alert the reader that you intend to include a graphic aid and then place the graphic aid as close to where it is mentioned as possible. Do not refer to a graphic aid by stating that it is shown below. Always give the graphic aid a number and title. For example, you would state: Table 1 contains the Awardees of Scholarships for Winter 1997. Or you would state that Figure 4 lists the names of Alumni Certificate Honorees in the School of Business and Economics by Departments.

Graphic aids may be placed within the body of the report or in an appendix. In inserting the graphic aid in the text, be sure to leave three lines above and below the graphic aid to separate it from the text so that the graphic aid stands out. Each graphic aid must have a title; placement of the title depends of the type of graphic aid. In discussing a graphic aid, you only discuss the significant information. No need exists to discuss everything in the graphic aid; to do so is really a waste of the reader's time. If the graphic aid is not closely related to the material being discussed, it should be placed in an appendix. Frequently, the information in a graphic aid is relevant but not needed for that portion of data being discussed. A brochure which is relevant to the topic can also be placed in an appendix.

Using Graphic Aids Software

Graphic aids can also be called visual aids. People respond better to visuals than text. The software for creating business visuals is classified into two types—*graphics software* and *presentation software*. Graphics software can create diagrams, pictures, and flowcharts. You can create the pictures using clip art or you can scan in photos or drawings in your text document. Presentation software enables you to create visuals for meetings as well as overhead transparencies.

Visual aids also attract people's attention as well as help them retain the information. For example, with Microsoft Word, you can see, visualize, the options by looking at the icons on the Toolbar.

For professional-looking visuals, you have a variety of graphics programs available such as Harvard Graphics, CorelDRAW, Aldus Freehand, MacPaint, and Lotus-1–2–3 or Excel. Harvard Graphics is a dedicated graphics program, and CorelDRAW can be used to create logos. Lotus 1–2–3 and Excel are spreadsheet programs which help you calculate, sort and then display numbers in a graphic format. Visuals can be created and then imported into your text document. To create computer graphics, you need a microcomputer with large memory, a color monitor, a color printer, a graphics card, and an input device such as a mouse.

Interpreting with Graphic Aids

Graphic or visual aids are useful in written reports to emphasize written material or interpret written material. They are also useful to emphasize information in an oral presentation as well as to interpret information in an oral presentation. One crucial factor to keep in mind is that the visual aid must be clear and understandable.

Visual aids must be well constructed so as not to distort facts and figures. Visual aids can be used to show trends and relationships, but they must be accurate and clear. Steer clear of inappropriately sized grids, uncomparable dimension sizes, and beginning the quantitative axis somewhere other than zero. Examples of construction errors in visual aids are illustrated in Figures 13.1, 13.2, and 13.3. Errors in the construction of visual aids impede understanding of the visual aids. Interpret information in a meaningful way, document the source of visuals constructed by others in the literature, and give a title, legend, and other explanatory information to help describe the data in each visual aid. Clip Art is perhaps the most well-known and probably most-used piece of graphic information. It can consist of home-made flyers to professional looking graphic aids.

Types of Graphic Aids

Various kinds of graphic aids can be used to emphasize significant points and to show trends and relationships. The two types of graphic aids that can be included in reports, both written and oral, are *tables* and *figures*.

Tables. A table is an arrangement of exact, detailed information, both numerical and/or alphabetical, in columns and rows. Tables can be in unruled, ruled, or boxed format. A table has a title and column headings. Figures 13.4, 13.5, and 13.6 are illustrations of tables.

Figures. The category of charts consisting of line charts, bar charts, and pie charts are called *figures*. Each is used to show certain information. *Line charts* are especially useful for analytical purposes. They illustrate trends over time or plot the relationship between two variables. A line chart should contain no more than three lines on any given chart, particularly when the lines cross. To include more than three lines would make the analysis difficult to comprehend. In constructing a line chart showing trends, the vertical axis shows the amount,

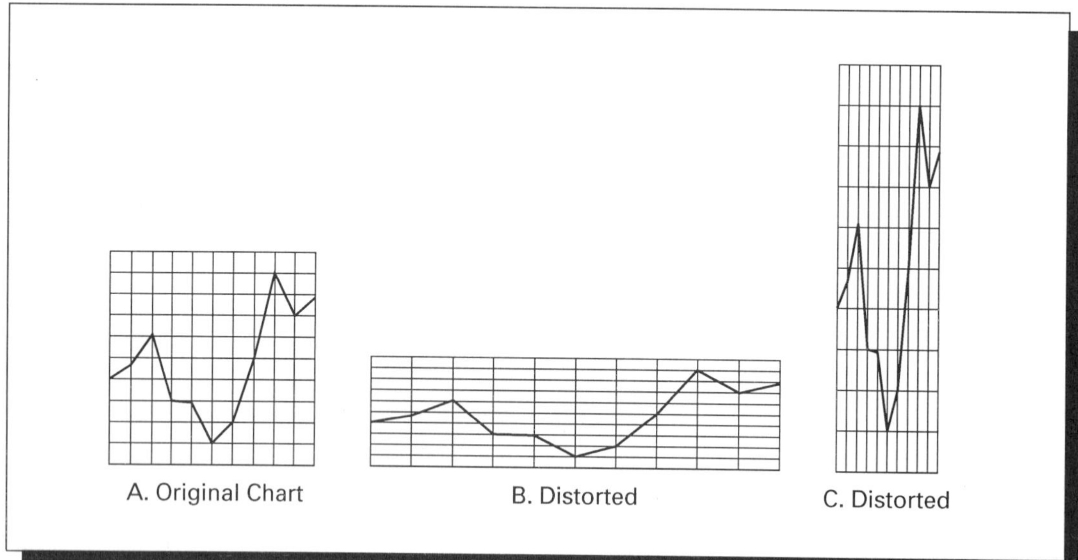

Figure 13.1. An Example of a Distorted Grid. *Source*: Adapted from Mary Eleanor Spear, Practical Charting Techniques (New York: McGraw-Hill, 1969, p. 56–59).

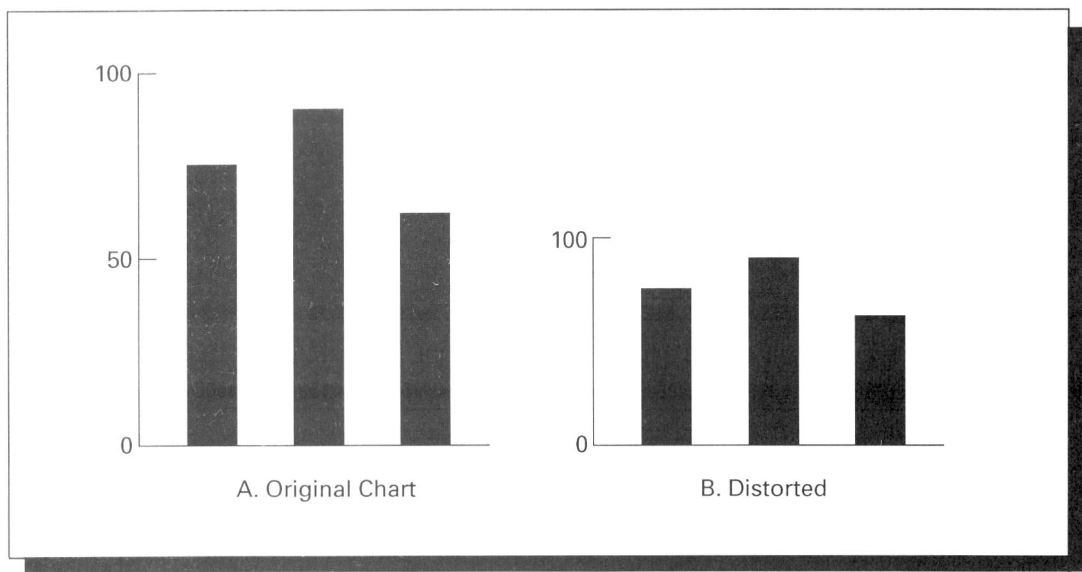

Figure 13.2. An Example of Missing Intervals. *Source*: Adapted from Mary Eleanor Spear, Practical Charting Techniques (New York: McGraw-Hill, 1969, p. 56–59).

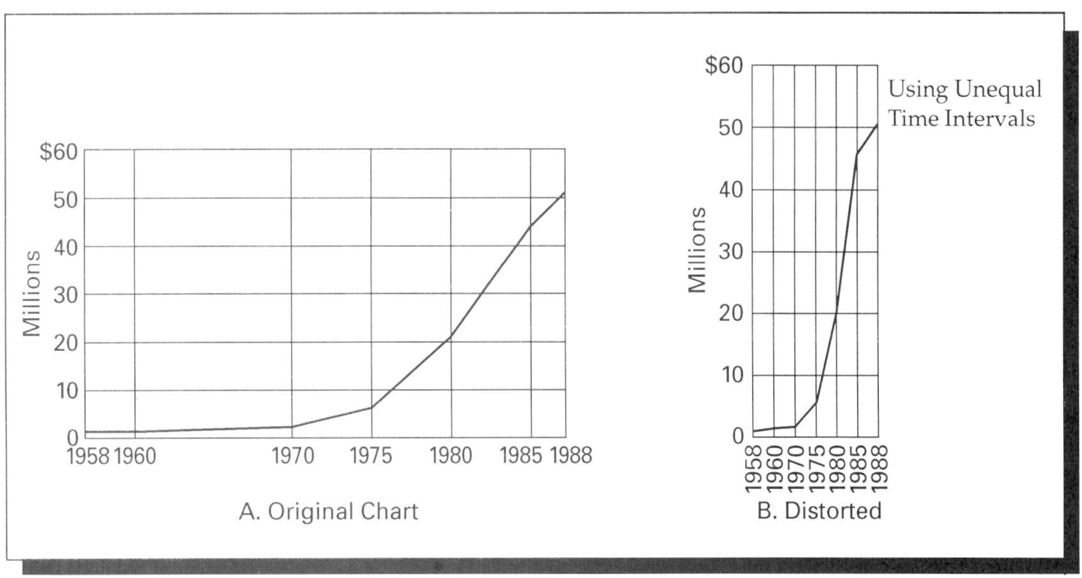

Figure 13.3. An Example of Uncomparable Time Dimension Sizes. *Source*: Adapted from Mary Eleanor Spear, Practical Charting Techniques (New York: McGraw-Hill, 1969, p. 56–59).

California State University, Los Angeles

HEADCOUNT BY CLASS LEVEL

	Number	Percent
Freshmen	3,143	16.7%
Sophomores	1,774	9.4%
Juniors	2,964	15.7%
Seniors	6,114	32.4%
Graduate/post-baccalaureats	4,854	25.8%

Figure 13.4. A sample of an unruled table.

California State University, Los Angeles

HEADCOUNT BY CLASS LEVEL

	Number	Percent
Freshmen	3,143	16.7%
Sophomores	1,774	9.4%
Juniors	2,964	15.7%
Seniors	6,114	32.4%
Graduate/post-baccalaureats	4,854	25.8%

Figure 13.5. A sample of a ruled table.

and the horizontal axis shows the time or factor and the quality being measured. Both scales should begin at zero ordinarily; however, the vertical axis which shows the amount can be broken to show that some of the data increments have been omitted. When you have data that are far above zero, this option is acceptable as long as you alert the reader of this fact. Figures 13.7 and 13.8 are examples of line charts.

Bar charts are useful for comparison purposes. The amounts are visually portrayed by the height of the vertical bars or by the width of the horizontal bars. Bar charts, both horizontal and vertical, are used to compare quantities. In constructing bar charts, remember that all bars should be of the same rectangle width. Points are plotted on the rectangle bars and a line

California State University, Los Angeles

HEADCOUNT BY CLASS LEVEL

	Number	Percent
Freshmen	3,143	16.7%
Sophomores	1,774	9.4%
Juniors	2,964	15.7%
Seniors	6,114	32.4%
Graduate/post-baccalaureats	4,854	25.8%

Figure 13.6. A sample of a boxed table.

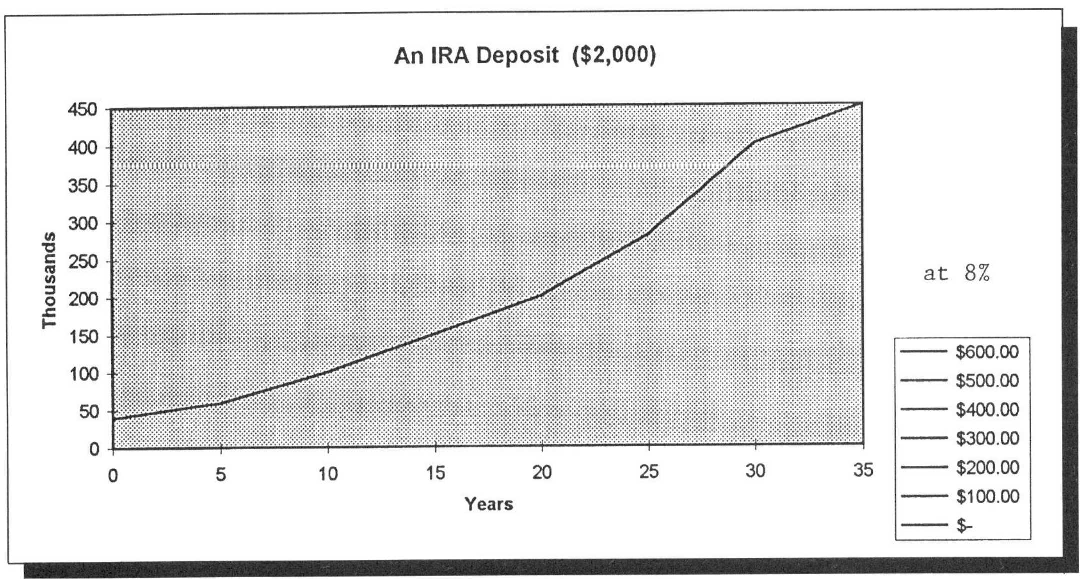

Figure 13.7. An Example of a Line Chart.

drawn to connect the points together. Bar charts can be used to show changes in one item over time periods, compare the size of several items at one time, and show the size of component parts of a whole. Bar charts can be bilateral, containing negative quantities, or subdivided with each bar representing 100 percent of a whole and each bar containing various percentages to make up the whole. Figures 13.9 and 13.10 are examples of the bilateral bar chart and the subdivided bar chart.

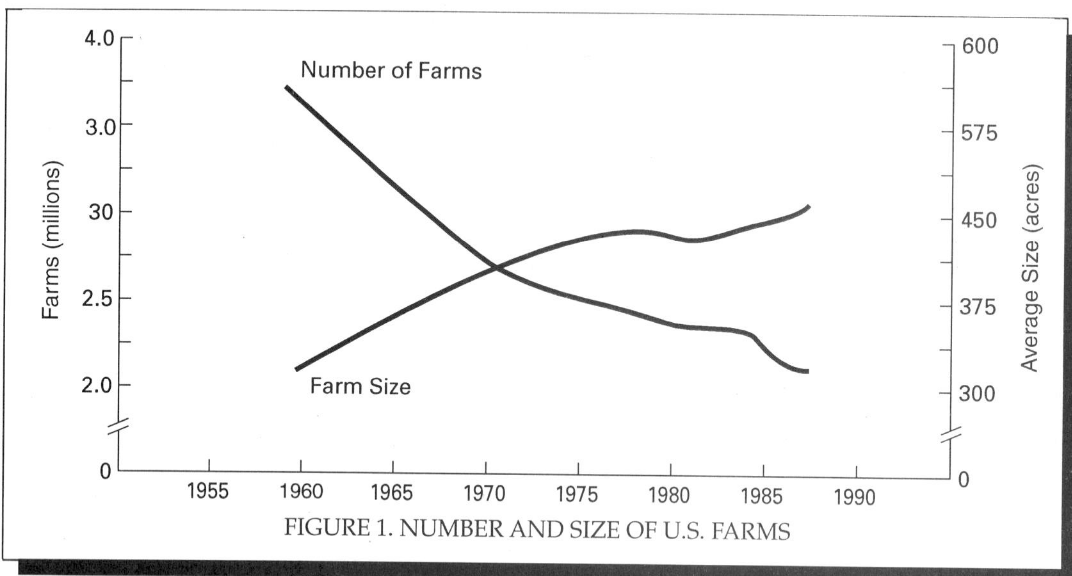

Figure 13.8. Simple Line Chart. *Source*: Department of Labor, *Occupational Outlook Handbook, 1988–89 ed.*, (Washington, DC: Government Printing Office, 1989), p. 332.

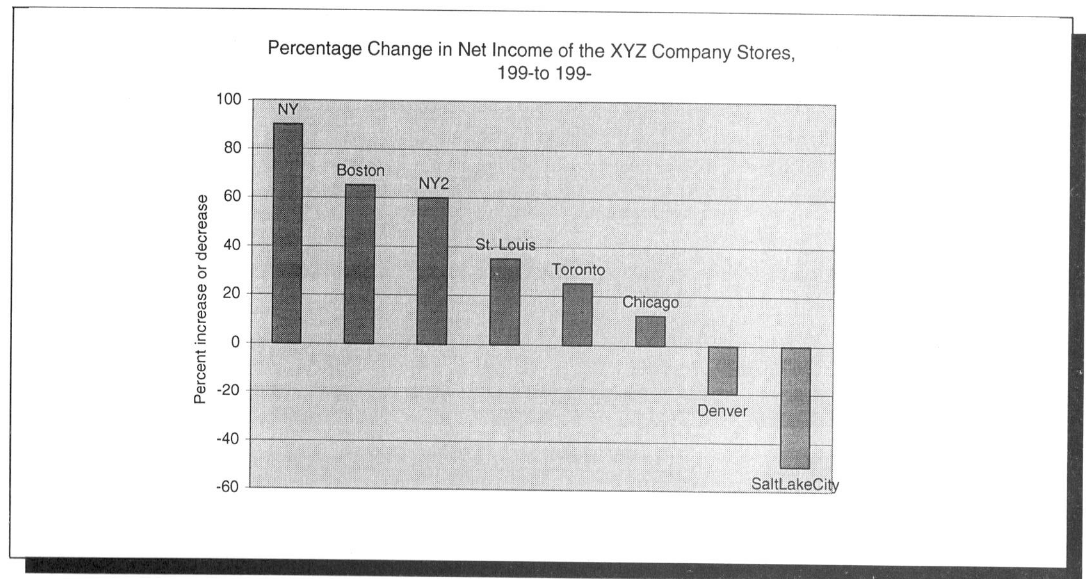

Figure 13.9. A Sample of a Bilateral Bar Chart.

Pie charts some times referred to as circle graphs or circle charts are used to show 100 percent of a whole. The percentages are represented as slices in a pie. A pie chart is useful to

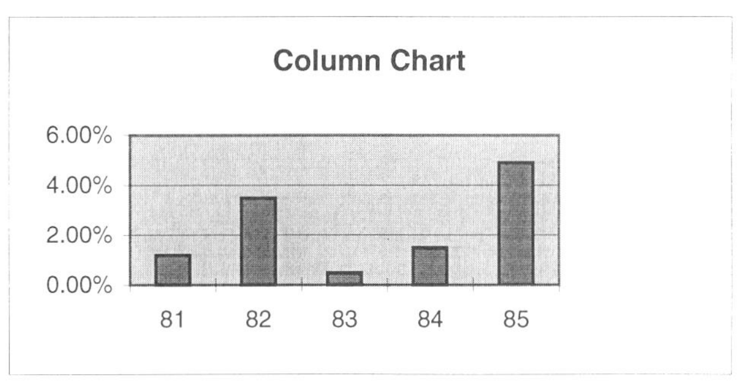

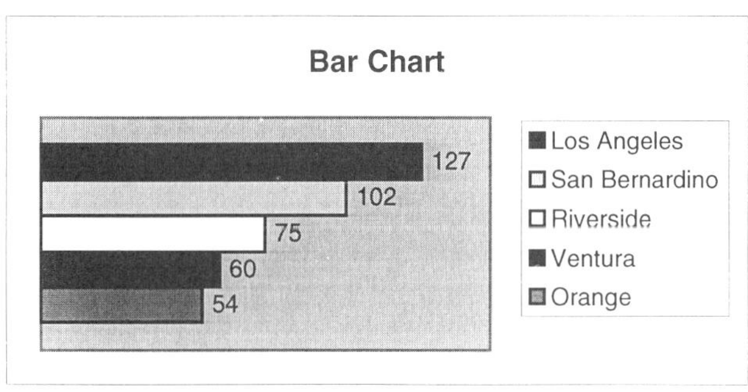

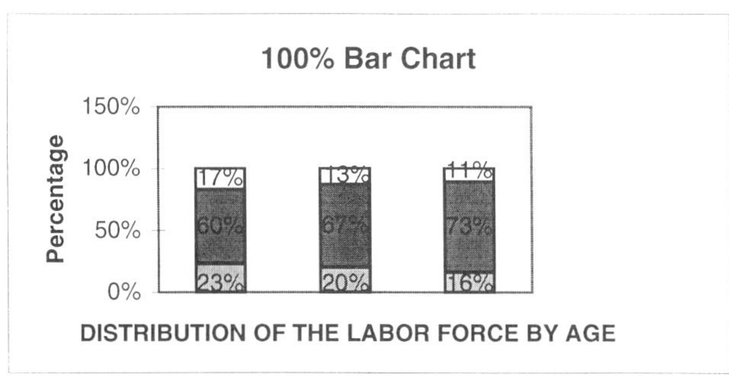

Figure 13.10. The above are samples of bar charts—vertical and horizontal and a subdivided bar

show exactly how each slice relates to the whole. When composing a pie chart, use no more than seven slices so that the chart is not cluttered. The slices should be arranged in descending order of magnitude, starting with the largest percentage at the 12 o'clock position and the other percentages follow clockwise in descending order of magnitude. The slices of the pie need to be labeled, add up to 100, and distinguished by color to show the most important slice. Figure 13.11 illustrates a pie chart.

Miscellaneous visual aids include flow charts or organizational charts, gantt charts, pictogram, maps, drawings, diagrams, and photographs. Figures 13.12, 13.13, 13.14, 13,15, 13.16, 13.17, and 13.18 are examples of the miscellaneous visual aids.

A flow chart is used to show a sequence of events from beginning to end and how each part relates. The Gantt chart is useful when the need exists to track or show the amount of time needed to complete a project. You should use different colored blocks to indicate items completed, items yet needed to be completed, and where the project is on any given date.

A pictogram converts the bars into a line of symbols such as dollar signs ($) or some other items other than words or numbers.

The drawbacks to using symbols are the inability to show exact amounts and the preparation needed to compose the symbols.

Maps are useful to show concentration of items or something by geographical area

Drawing and diagrams are often used to show how something looks or operates.

Photographs are most useful in annual reports or newsletters for they can demonstrate the exact appearance of phenomenon.

Multimedia

A thorough discussion on communications technology was presented in Chapter 4; now, the use of multimedia is becoming more of a choice. For example, companies use multimedia —video, text, sound, and animation—in a variety of ways.

Bovee and Thill (1995) cite Deutsch's article on Corticorp's multimedia benefits kit. Citicorp gave each employee a printout of their benefits, a computer disk, an extensive workbook, brochures, special face-to-face training meetings, a take-home video and access to a hot line. With this multimedia approach, the employee could chose the media with which he or she felt most comfortable. Such an approach is likely to become more popular as work forces grow more and more culturally diverse.

Once you have determined what types of visual aids to include in a report, you can now begin to concentrate on the report format and arrangement which will be discussed in Chapter 14.

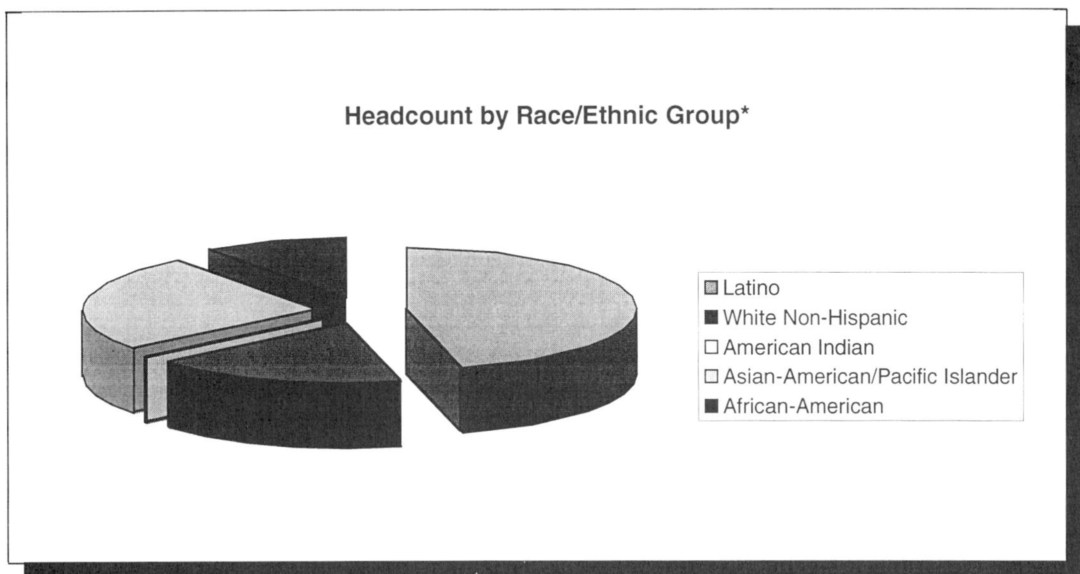

Figure 13.11. A Sample of a Pie Chart.

Regenerative Life Support System.

In a controlled ecological life support system, as diagrammed here, biological and physico-chemical subsystems would produce plants for food and process wastes for reuse in the system. A bioprocessing unit, in which bacteria oxidize and catalyze the extraction of metals from their lunar or asteroidal ores, could be incorporated into this system. The bioprocessing unit would contribute to the gas and nutrient recycling, the biomass inventory, and the waste processing of the life support system.

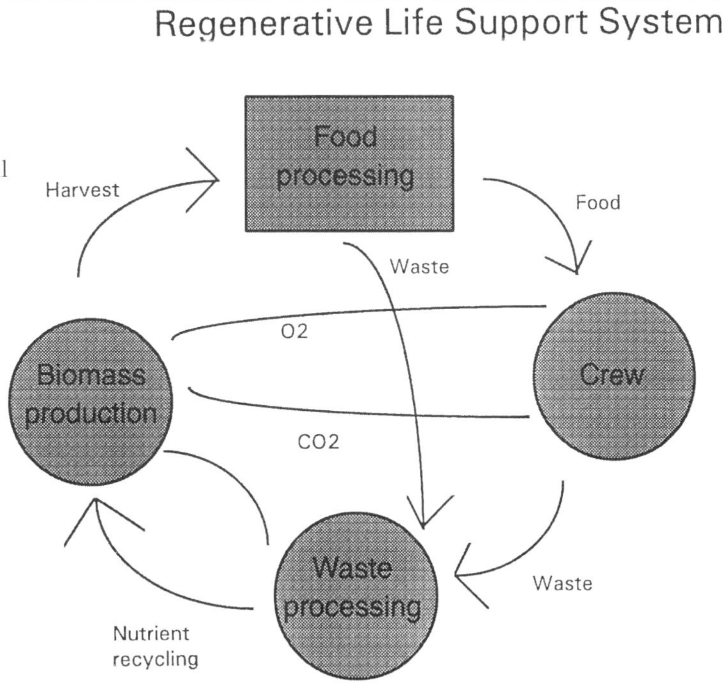

Regenerative Life Support System

Food processing
Harvest
Food
Waste
O2
Biomass production
Crew
CO2
Waste processing
Waste
Nutrient recycling

Figure 13.12. An example of a Flow Chart. *Source*: McKay, McKay, and Duke, 1992, p. 236.

Setting Up an Advisement Kiosk System for the School of Business and Economics						
Activity	**Week 1**	**Week 2**	**Week 3**	**Week 4**	**Week 5**	**Week 6**
Decide on Information Needed	X					
List the Types of Information	X					
Gather the Forms Needed		X				
Key in the Instructions Relating to the Forms		X	Today			
Prepare a List of Advisers and Office Hours			X			
Develop a program for information				O		
Configure the system				O		
Pilot test the system					O	O
X—Completed Tasks			O—Tasks to be Completed			

Figure 13.13. An Example of a Gantt Chart.

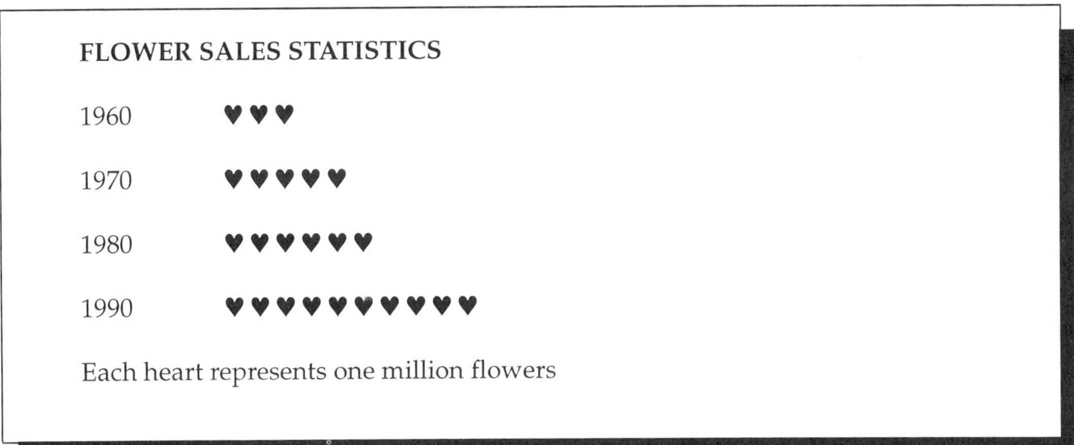

Figure 13.14. A sample of a Pictogram.

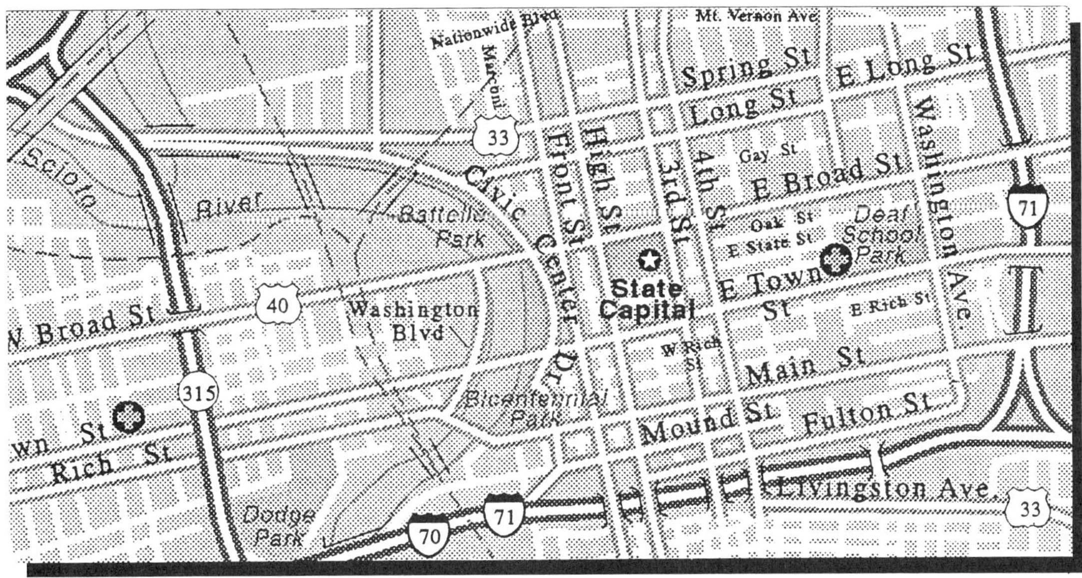

Figure 13.15. A sample of a Map.

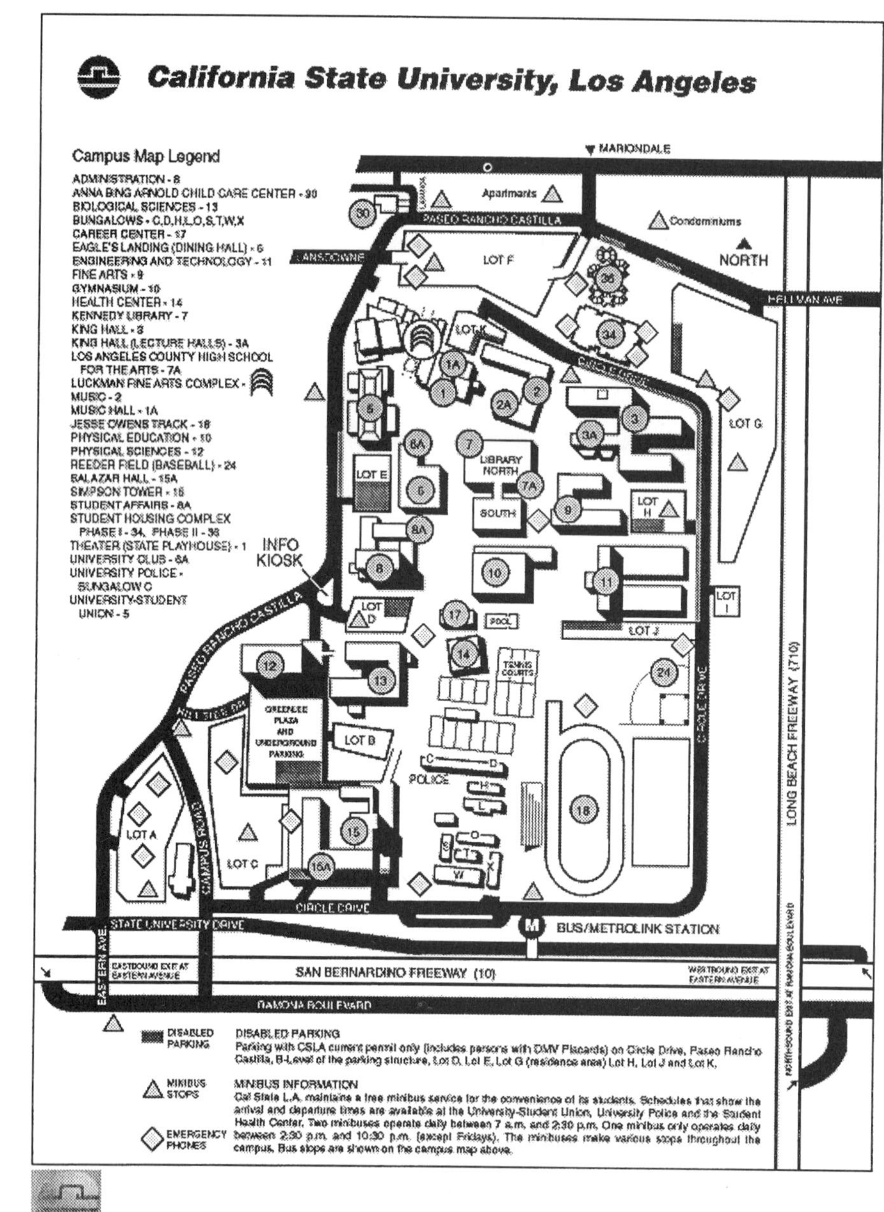

Return to CSLA Home Page

25-Aug-1995
WebMaster@calstatela.edu

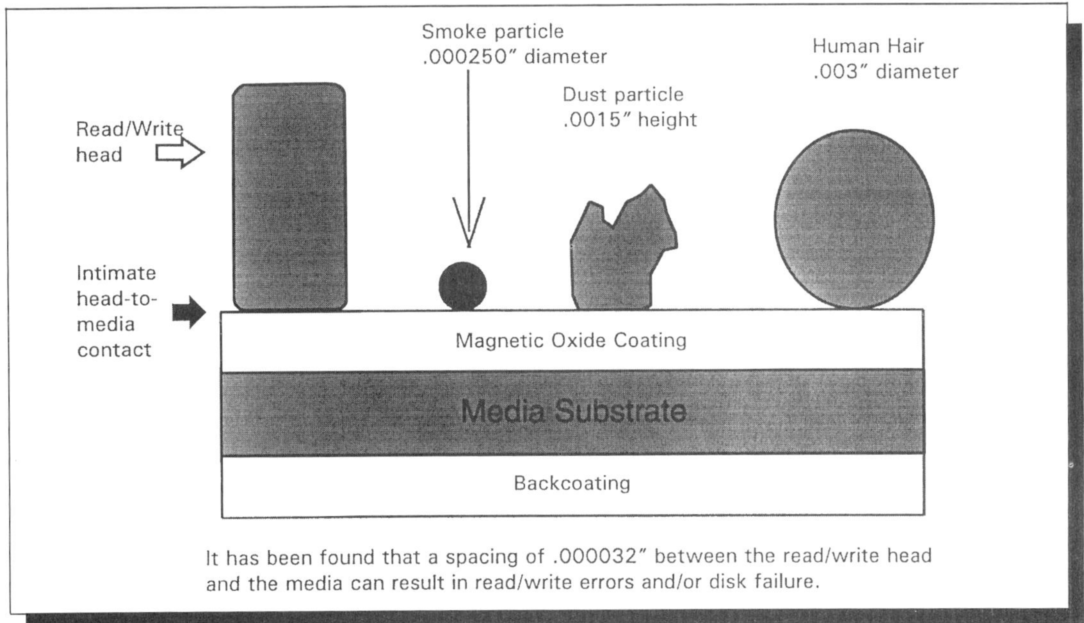

Figure 13.16. A Sample of a Drawing.

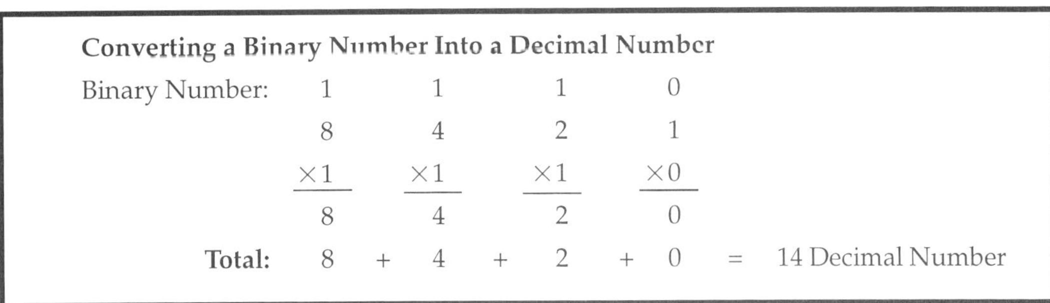

Converting a Binary Number Into a Decimal Number

Binary Number:	1		1		1		0		
	8		4		2		1		
	×1		×1		×1		×0		
	8		4		2		0		
Total:	8	+	4	+	2	+	0	=	14 Decimal Number

Figure 13.17. An Example of a Diagram. A Diagram Used to Clarify a Difficult Concept. *Source:* TECHNICAL COMMUNICATIONS: SITUATIONS AND STRATEGIES by Mike Markel, 4th edition, 1996, p. 300.

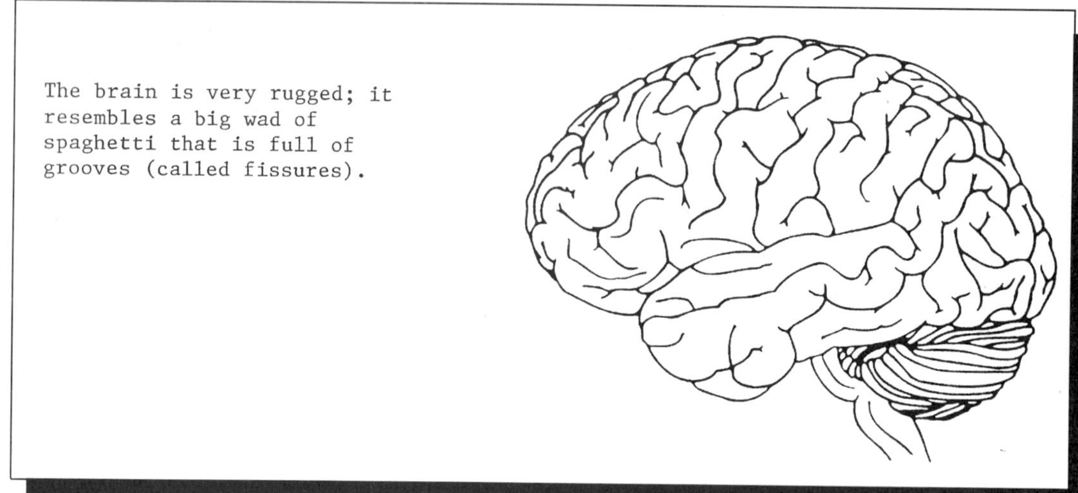

Figure 13.18. A Picture of the Human Brain.

References

Bovee, C. L. and Thill, J. V. (1995). BUSINESS COMMUNICATION TODAY, 4TH edition, McGraw-Hill.

Cal State L. A. Facts #19, California State University, Los Angeles, December 1996.

Markel, M. (1996). TECHNICAL COMMUNICATION: Situations and Strategies, 4th ed., St. Martin's, p. 294, 300, 307.

OCCUPATIONAL OUTLOOK HANDBOOK, Department of Labor, 1988–89 ed., Washington, D. C. Government Printing Office, 1989, p. 9.

Spear, Mary Eleanor (1969). PRACTICAL CHARTING TECHNIQUES, New York: McGraw-Hill, p. 56–59.

Wayne, S. and Dauwalder, D. (1994). COMMUNICATING IN BUSINESS: An Action-Oriented Approach, Austen Press, Irwin.

Questions

1. Why would you include a graphic aid in a report?
2. When would a graphic aid be placed in an appendix?
3. What are the most frequently used types of charts?
4. What kind of information is displayed in a line chart?
5. What kind of information is displayed in a bar chart?
6. Which type of chart would you use if you wanted to show numerous figures?

7. What is the purpose for using a subdivided bar chart?
8. What phenomenon surfaces in visual charts when symbols are not equally parallel?
9. How do you determine when to use a table or a figure?
10. What are the pieces or wedges called in a pie chart?

Applications

1. Survey students in your business communication classroom and do a tally of how many are seniors or juniors, males, and females, and their majors. Find out from the data if there are any trends. Then prepare a graphic aid and input a short paragraph of your analysis.
2. Describe an appropriate graphic aid for the following information:
   a. Your activities to relax
   b. Student satisfaction with CSLA
   c. The average amount paid by companies for employee training
   d. The kinds of faculty interaction you would like
   e. The types of companies offering employee educational assistance programs
   f. The number of companies that have employee fitness centers in house
3. Choose three companies in your profession and view their annual reports. Critique the types of visuals used and who are portrayed in the visuals.
4. Locate a current CSLA Fact Sheet (PUblic Affairs OFfice) and input a paragraph that summarizes the graphic aids.
5. Visit one of the computer labs on campus and go through a tutorial on Harvard Graphics. Create a line chart, a bar chart, and a pie chart.
6. Diagram how you got from your home to campus or from your home to your first class of a particular day.
7. Go to a Powerpoint presentation and develop a three picture slide presentation.
8. Find a set of data and incorporate it in a bar chart and a pie chart.
9. List and rank the top five cars (include price) you would like to own some day. Put in a table format.
10. Locate today's paper (LA TIMES) and list the communication skills required for a job in your major; then create a graphic aid.
11. Choose an existing graphic aid and critique it for clarity and effectiveness.
12. Develop a flow chart for adding or dropping a class after the add/drop deadline.
13. Visit a professor in your field and determine the changes in skills needed five years ago, skills needed today, and skills needed 5 years from now. Create an effective graphic aid.

Name ______________________________ Date ____________

JEOPARDY QUIZ #13

1. The answer is: Used to supplement the information in a report.

   What are ______________________________?

2. The answer is: A visual aid that shows numerical and/or alphabetic information.

   What is ______________________________?

3. The answer is: Two basic types of visual aids.

   What are ______________________________?

4. The answer is: Harvard, CorelDRAW, and Aldus Freehand.

   What are ______________________________?

5. The answer is: A systematic arrangement of data in columns and rows.

   What is ______________________________?

6. The answer is: Uses slices to show 100 percent of a whole.

   What is ______________________________?

7. The answer is: A type of chart that is useful for comparison purposes.

   What is ______________________________?

8. The answer is: Uses two axis to show relationships of variables over time.

   What is ______________________________?

9. The answer is: A type of chart that is useful to show communication channels of the positions, divisions, or functions of the organization.

   What is ______________________________?

continued

10. The answer is: A type of visual aid that demonstrates exact phenomenon of something.

    What is ____?

CHAPTER 14

Dr. Carol Blaszczynski, Assistant Professor
Department of Management

Report Format and Arrangement

Objectives

Upon reading the chapter and doing the exercises, you should be able to:

1. Distinguish the difference between the need for prefatory and supplementary parts in a report.
2. Describe the prefatory parts of a report.
3. Determine where to place a graphic aid or visual in a report.
4. Explain what is meant by blind reviewed reports.
5. Discuss the difference between personal and impersonal writing in a report.
6. Cite an example of the need to use a road map in a report.
7. Determine the time perspective for reporting data, events, and information in a report.
8. List the parts included in the text of a report.
9. Explain the difference among a summary, conclusions, and recommendations.
10. Write an effective, clear and complete formal research paper.

The purpose of this chapter is to solidify all of your research efforts into producing a final, polished report. The report that you have been or may be asked to do may be short and informal or complete and formal. Reports are usually requested by upper management. Typically, a short report does not contain the preliminary or supplementary parts. However, a long, formal report does contain the preliminary and supplementary parts. These parts are needed to tie the report together because of its length.

Letter reports, memorandum reports, progress reports, and justification or recommendation reports can be classified as formal reports. Letter reports and memorandum reports are typically longer than a regular memo or letter and follow the same conventions of single spacing and double spacing between paragraphs. Figures 14.1, 14.2, 14.3, and 14.4 are illustrations of these reports.

Reports can be presented in manuscript format as shown in Figure 14.5. For example, research projects done by scholars are inputted in manuscript format, usually double spaced, to permit ease of reading for reviewers. One measurement of a professor's commitment to staying abreast of his or her field of study is to conduct research that is applicable to the improvement of teaching ability or subject knowledge enhancement. The results of solicited or unsolicited research projects are submitted as manuscripts to add to or verify existing information in the field. Manuscripts written by scholars or professors are submitted to journals, preferably refereed, for blind review; that is, the names of the authors are removed from the research study and it is then sent to experts in the field for critique and publishability in that journal. Figure 14.6 is a good example of a scholarly researched report written by two well-known business educators which was published in THE DELTA PI EPSILON JOURNAL, which is the premiere journal in the field of business education.

Writing Style and Arrangement

If you know your readers and your report is likely to meet with their approval, you can adopt a more informal tone. For example, you can refer to yourself as "I" and to your readers as "you." This style is used in a memorandum report or a letter report, although there are exceptions based on individual situations.

Long reports, those that may be controversial or perhaps complex, usually take the formal approach. You can achieve a formal tone by using the impersonal style which involves eliminating all references to I, we, us, you, and our. This formal style allows you to remain unemotional, objective, and businesslike. On the other hand, you can often tell what tone is appropriate for your organization by looking at other reports of similar type in your company. Once determining the writing style, you might want to adopt that writing style for the reports you are asked to prepare.

In summary, the writing style is more than knowing when to use personal pronouns; it really depends not only on your relationship with your readers but also with your company's expectations. The nature and purpose of the report are also factors to be considered.

Physical Arrangement of the Report

As the report writer, you must keep in mind that your readers do not know how the various parts of your formal report fit together, so you will need to present a road map so they

Salcedo, Inc.

Bridge Crossing

Elwood, Kansas

January 8, 1986

Mr. Robert Ming
President

Dear Mr. Ming

Subject: Reducing Clerical Turnover

Here is the letter report you requested on reducing the high turnover of office help.

Reasons For and Nature of Report

Due to the salesperson's rush to complete sales of spas, a number of problems have surfaced. Inaccurate or insufficient credit information regarding prospective buyers has caused delays in completing credit checks and much wasted time on the telephone. Also, the work day is not planned efficiently for clerks to be the most productive.

Summary of Findings

The five salemen canvass prospective buyers from 9 a.m. to 2:00 p.m.; they return to the office to write up the completed contracts. The clerks then do credit checks and type up the contracts before the salemen leave at 4 p.m. Sometimes the clerks do not leave the office until 7:30 p.m. The long hours of overtime and the rush to work after a day of waiting has resulted in a 100 percent turnover of the clerks in the past ten months.

Development of Report

This high turnover of clerks is costing extra money in training expense. The salesmen should be more accurate in recording contract information. Although there are numerous ways to reduce the high turnover of clerks, I recommend these solutions:

1. Provide personal digital assistants for the salesmen to record accurate information on contracts *at the time they are with the customer*.
2. Mail prepared contracts within 24 hours.
3. Check accuracy of customer's Social Security Numbers and address for credit checks.

Conclusion

I recommend that Salcedo, Inc. provide the salesmen a personal digital assistant to record information which can be sent to the Office and that contracts should be mailed within 24 hours. Following a combination of these solutions will result in productive and content clerks.

Sincerely

Affany Soekodanu

Affany Soekodanu
Assistant Manager

Figure 14.1. A Sample of a Letter Report.

MEMORANDUM

To: Jeffrey N. Shane
Head of Operations Management

From: Nancy L. Mays
Director, Human Resources Management

Date: September 5, 1997

As you requested, I have received information on the fees charged for employment recruitment from five employment agencies in this area.

Practically all of the employment agencies use the same basis for their fees. A 10 percent charge based on the annual salary is the going rate.

I have determined that the Emplyment One Agency is the one we should consider. Based on my conversation with the President, they have a team of people who will be involved in this recruitment process. Our wishes are their command. They can either handle all of the recruitment process or we can be involved if we so choose.

Since we are rather short on personnel and really do not have the time to do the intense recruiting needed, we might want to consider going to an outside agency such as Employment One to recruit for the upper level management jobs we have open.

The Employment One Agency's fee schedule is as follows:

Salary	Fee
$50,000 - $59,999	$5,000 - $5,999
$60,000 - $69,999	$6,000 - $6,999
$70,000 - $79,999	$7,000 - $7,999
$80,000 - $89,999	$8,000 - $8,999

Please let me know your decision on whether we should use the Employment One Agency. We have a time span of four months to hire three new managers.

Should you have any other questions, please call me at X2800.

Figure 14.2. A Sample of a Memorandum Report.

Gorman Enterprises
River Crossing
Atchison, KS

MEMORANDUM

July 9, 1997

To: Mr. Samuel T. Kang
Director of Southern California Sales

From: Mr. Joseph A. Phoung
San Gabriel Sales District

Subject: Quarterly Report for San Gabriel Sales District

SUMMARY HIGHLIGHTS

After nearly four months of operation in San Gabriel, I have leased office space in the Arcadia downtown area, have trained three salespeople, and have nurtured and cultivated thirty of the fifty customers in this district. Since our operations are rather new, we have not shown a profit as yet; but we expect to show one in another two months. Prospects in the San Gabriel area are exceptionally bright.

OFFICE OPERATION

The Board of Directors authorized me to open this San Gabriel office on April 25. I looked at three different locations in the San Gabriel area before settling on the Arcadia location. The office suite selected rents for $1575 per month; it has six executive offices, each in close proximity to a three-person secretarial office. I have anticipated an increase in office personnel which is why I decided to lease this office suite in order to eliminate having to move to larger quarters at a later time.

PERSONNEL

I hired an Executive Secretary, Mrs. Mimi Young, who has excellent skills and experience. She has proved to be very efficient and effective; she will supervise the other two Secretaries whom we will hire at a later time. In addition, I have hired and trained three salespeople—Mr. Jay Nakamoto, Ms. Cathy Nguyen, and Mr. Jensen Chao. All three hirees have excellent credentials and over thirty years of sales experience among them. I feel our staff is adequate for the present time.

PERFORMANCE

After a two-week training session, which I conducted personally, the salespeople were assigned to specific territories in the San Gabriel area. Within three weeks of their calling on their sales list contacts sent to me by Mr. John Gonzalez, I am happy to report the following monthly sales:

Mr. Jay Nakamoto	$17,890
Ms. Cathy Nguyen	$21,230
Mr. Jensen Chao	$15,975
Total	$55,095

While the total sales are below our target, I do believe with more concentrated effort on the salespeoples' part, their sales will match our break-even point for the next month of $65,050. The prospects appear very promising, and the potential for increased sales is good.

Figure 14.3. A Sample of a Progress Report.

MEMORANDUM

To:	Ms. Nancy Phu	Subject:	How Mechanical Pencils Would Save Money for Murphy Company
From:	Dennis Christopher	Date:	January 12, 1997

Purpose: To save the Murphy Company's Accounting Department $15 in pencil expense each year, I recommend that we purchase mechanical pencils instead of wooden ones for use by our thirty accountants.

Cost and Savings: A year's supply of mechanical pencils and refills would cost about $39 as compared with more than $54 for wooden pencils, resulting in a yearly saving of $15+.

Procedure: Continental Office Supply in Covina, California, would supply our yearly need of approximately 70 pencils with the Murphy Company name on them at a price of forty-two cents each. I would distribute them and maintain records for our control.

Conclusions: The Murphy Company would enjoy four advantages by using mechanical pencils rather than wooden ones:

1. We would save at least $15+ a year.
2. I would have fewer pencils to store and issue.
3. Accountants would be more careful not to misplace them.
4. Mechanical pencils provide sharp, clear writing with little loss of time.

Discussion of Conclusions:

1. Yearly Average Pencil Costs are as follows:

	1996
Wooden Pencils (5 for $1.80 x 30 =	$54.00
Pencil Costs (2 each @ 42 cents + 45 cents for lead refills = $1.29 x 30 Accountants) =	$38.70
Saving	$15.30

2. I would only have to store approximately 70 mechanical pencils compared to over 150 wooden pencils, thus taking less space.
3. Murphy Mechanical pencils are more valuable and more conspicuous; accountants would exhibit more care in using them and keeping them at the office. Of course, any mechanical pencils misplaced would be at least worth the cost as advertising.
4. Mechanical pencils would reduce down time; accountants would only need to replace the lead and continue working.

Figure 14.4. A Sample Recommendation Report.

Expert Systems: Panacea or Pandemonium?

Excerpt of an Article

Abstract

Artificial Intelligence (AI) is one of the most exciting and promising developments of the computer age. One of the main categories of AI is expert systems, also known as knowledge systems, which capture in computer programs the reasoning and decision-making processes of human experts, providing, in effect, computerized consultants. While this development is promising, it opens issues and concerns such as how do we choose this expert, how do we define "expertise,: of what value is the system, what are the risks, and what is the impact of expert systems on the organization?

An Expert System is a computer program that incorporates the knowledge of an expert of group as experts on a particular subject and enables the program user to systematically ask questions related to that knowledge (Regan and O'Connor, 1989). A definition of intelligence is not easy as even the psychologists still debate its meaning. However, Webster defines "intelligence" as the ability to "cope with demands created by novel situations and new problems, to apply what is learned from experience, and to use the power of reasoning and inference effectively as a guide to behavior." Kupsh and Rhodes (1989) state: "artificial intelligence is really machine intelligence—an imitation of something natural.

The goal of an expert system, ideally, is to emulate the reasoning of highly trained and experiences human experts. An expert system mimics human reasoning by using facts, rules and a user interface (Regan & O'Connor, 1989).

Figure 14.5. An Example of an Excerpt from an Article.

Keyboarding Instruction at NABTE Institutions:

Are We Teaching Techniques to Reduce CTD Incidence?

by

Dr. Carol Blaszczynski

and

Dr. Marguerite Shane Joyce

California State University, Los Angeles

Funding for this study was provided by the National Delta Pi Epsilon Research Foundation.
(Reprinted with Permission from Delta Pi Epsilon)

Figure 14.6. Formal Resarch Report

continued

Abstract

Each of the 193 NABTE representatives was surveyed in Fall 1994 to determine their familiarity with Cumulative Trauma Disorders and to ascertain the teaching techniques used in their keyboarding classes. Over three quarters of those sampled responded. A panel of ten keyboarding experts was consulted about their familiarity with CTDs and perceptions of correct techniques used to combat CTD incidence. Multiple regression analysis revealed that 59 percent of the variation of those who teach and those who do not teach preventative techniques could be explained by the department in which the course is taught, familiarity with CTDs, the use of wrist rests.

The goal of this study was to determine the techniques employed in keyboarding classes taught at National Association of Business Teacher Education a (NABTE) institutions in the United States. Such information would be helpful in determining if business educators at these institutions are teaching techniques to reduce the incidence of Cumulative Trauma Disorders (CTDs) and Carpal Tunnel Syndrome (CTS).

Need for the Study

While this study dealt with NABTE institutions and keyboarding/typewriting experts and their awareness and perceptions of teaching techniques to reduce the incidence of CTDs and CTS, this area has wide ramifications. Any subject taught that requires the use of a computer, whether during class in an electronic classroom or outside of class, can be fertile field for a potential lawsuit. All instructors, business educators, information professionals, computer science instructors, and trainers have potential liability for not preparing informed and well-trained users of computer technology.

Review of the Literature

Wentling (1992, p. 30) defines keyboarding as "...the act of placing information into the computer through the use of a typewriter-like keyboard, involving the placement of fingers on designated keys on the middle "home" row of the keyboard and moving fingers as needed to depress other keys."

Keyboarding has been described as a tool for literacy in today's information economy. Use of a keyboard to input, edit, and obtain information from a computer still remains the primary means of human-machine interaction despite the development of voice input/recognition technologies. In fact, voice input may not be the panacea for CTDs as office personnel should be warned that the use of their voices for more than 30 minutes without a break raises the risk of injury of the vocal cords (Pascarelli & Quilter, 1994).

In a survey of business professionals (former business graduate), Wentling (1992) found that 74 percent of the respondents use the computer greater than 15 percent of a typical work day. The computer is used 16 to 30 percent of an average work day by 28 percent of the professionals. In addition, she found that 67 percent felt that keyboarding skills contributed substantially to their productivity.

In a study of office support personnel, Evans (1994) found that over 50 percent of those surveyed experienced pain or discomfort when keyboarding. In addition, she found that most of the office support personnel do not perform stretches or exercises for their hands, arms, or backs at the worksite.

continued

In 1982, according to the Bureau of Labor Statistics, repetitive strain injuries (RSIs) amounted to 21 percent of illnesses related to occupations. This percentage increased to 56 percent by the year 1990. "The National Institute for Occupational Safety (NIOSH) has stated that by the next decade half of all workers will have jobs with the potential for repetitive-motion injury" (Perkins, 1992, p. 29).

In 1994 Compaq announced that it would print RSI warnings on the keyboards it manufactures (Elmer-Dewitt, October 1994). The Compaq Presario 9546 has this warning printed on the keyboard: "Warning: To reduced risk of serious injury to hands, wrists, or other joints read Safety and Comfort Guide." The IBM Aptiva has a tutorial that is bundled with the machine that details Ergonomic Tips. Employees with RSI have filed over 2,000 lawsuits against manufacturers of computers (Cone, 1994).

Workers now and in the year 2000 will be using computers to input, retrieve, and access information. Approximately 70 million Americans spend a portion of each work day at a keyboard. This figure includes an increasing number of schoolchildren (Elmer-Dewitt, October 1994). Workers will spend more than half of their work day at computer stations. This prolonged period at workstations will cause these workers to experience higher rates of health problems.

Carpal Tunnel Syndrome is also known as Cumulative Trauma Disorder, Repetitive Motion Injury, and Occupational Neuritis. Compression of the median nerve with inflammation and swelling can lead to symptoms that are collectively known as CTS (Crouch & Madden, 1992).

Sensory symptoms of CTS include: coldness; stiff, swollen joints; tingling; burning; and numbness, especially at night. Motor symptoms of CTS are aching, clumsiness, weakness of the thumb, smaller thumb muscles, and loss of hand strength (Crouch & Madden, 1992). CTS is recognized as a costly drain on the human and financial resources of businesses and is estimated to result in medical costs of about $2,000 per wrist (Perkins, 1992).

Claims from workers compensation and other RSI injury expenses may amount to as much as $20 billion annually in costs to employers (Gallen, et al, 1992). According to Marvin Dainoff, Miami University's Director of the Center for Ergonomic Research (1992), a single case of RSI may cost an employer $80,000, including lost work time, surgery, and retraining.

Almost half of all recorded workplace injuries are CTDs. Repetitive motion syndrome affects 5 million Americans each year at a cost to a business of about $27 billion (Zeloznicki, 1992). The use of mice as a computer input device also can contribute to RSIs (Elmer-Dewitt, October, 1994). CTDs are predicted to be the greatest workplace hazard of the 1990s (Huntley, 1990).

OSHA stipulates that employers must maintain safe and healthy work environment recognized hazards (Title 29, USCA, Labor, Sec. 654(a)(1)). This is known as the general duty clause. Carpal tunnel syndrome might be interpreted as a hazard under OSHA's general duty requirement clause (DuFrene & Wilmeth, Fall 1991). The National Institute for Occupational Safety and Health has been developing ergonomic regulations (Franchi & Fleck, March-April 1994). However, business resistance to such efforts is strong.

According to Dainoff (1992), RSI can be attributed to four risk factors, which act in combination:

1. awkward posture
2. high repetition rates
3. lack of adequate rest and subsequent recovery
4. excessive force on the keys

continued

To prevent computer-related CTDs, Zeloznicki (1992) suggest changing the force and speed of keystrokes. Is this a challenge for business educators and for keyboarding and computer information systems instructors, in particular?

Much of the literature centers on knowledge and attitudes of employees in the workplace, but little of the literature has emphasized the techniques used by keyboarding instructors in their keyboarding classes. This is particularly crucial as university level keyboarding instructors at NABTE institutions may be the ones instructing methods classes, which prepare future high school and community college keyboarding instructors.

Research Questions

This study addresses the following research questions:

1. What is the level of familiarity with carpal tunnel syndrome and other maladies of keyboarding instructors at NABTE institutions?
2. Are these instructors teaching to reduce the incidence of CTD among their students?
3. Do the experiences and perceptions of a panel of ten keyboarding experts parallel those of the NABTE keyboarding instructors?

Method

Materials

A 16-item questionnaire was pilot-tested among business educators who are members of a local Delta Pi Epsilon Chapter. These educators had experience teaching keyboarding methods classes. The questionnaire was revised based upon the feedback received from the instructors.

Procedures

In October 1994, questionnaires were mailed to 193 NABTE representatives as listed in the December 1993 issue of the Business Education Forum, along with a postage-paid, stamped envelope. A total of 157 questionnaires were returned, representing a return rate of approximately 81 percent. Although respondents were not instructed to discontinue completing the questionnaire if keyboarding was not taught at their institution, seven persons returned blank questionnaires with the comment, "Keyboarding is no longer taught at this institution." Thus, 150 questionnaires were usable, representing a 77.7 percent return rate.

Participants

The second part of the study involves a panel of ten experts comprised of the leading keyboarding researchers/writers in business education. Selected experts were those who had published most frequently in the are of keyboarding/typewriting as revealed by citations in the last ten issues of the Business Education Index (from 1984 to 1993). These ten experts were contacted by phone initially and then by letter for their consent to participate in this study. An Informed Consent Form, along with a copy of the interview questions, was mailed to them with a return envelope to better prepare the experts for the telephone interview. Once written permission was secured from the experts, phone calls were made to the individuals.

Data were analyzed using SPSS for Windows.

Results

As Table 1 indicates, over two thirds of the respondents have 20 or more years of teaching experience. The mean number of years of teaching experience is 23.79. It is interesting to note that one

continued

Table 1
Number of Years of Teaching Experience

Years	NABTE Institutions Number	NABTE Institutions Percent	Experts Number	Experts Percent
Over 40	1	0.95	—	—
35–40	19	14.29	1	10.0
30–34	35	23.81	3	30.0
25–29	20	10.48	2	20.0
20–24	31	18.10	3	30.0
15–19	18	12.38	1	10.0
10–14	13	9.52	—	—
5–9	7	3.81	—	—
Under 5	5	5.71	—	—
No Response	1	0.95	—	—

third of the respondents have taught for at least 30 years. The experts have taught an average of 27.3 years, slightly longer than the NABTE respondents. These descriptive statistics are reflective of the business education professorate as a whole, as it has a more experienced (and aging) faculty.

Over 65 percent of the respondents hold a doctoral degree, about a third hold a master's degree, and three percent hold a bachelor's degree as their highest degree as depicted in Table 2. Comparatively, 90 percent of the experts hold the doctorate.

As shown in Table 3, keyboarding is currently taught in over 75 percent of the institutions for both groups. Of that number, almost 50 percent of the NABTE institutions require the keyboarding course, while keyboarding is required at three-quarters of the expert's institutions.

Keyboarding is taught in the Office Systems/Business Education Department at almost 70 percent of the responding NABTE institutions, compared to three-quarters of the experts' institutions. At over 10 percent of the responding NABTE institutions, the CIS Department teaches keyboarding compared to a quarter of the experts' institutions, while at 20 percent of the NABTE institutions keyboarding is taught by another department in the business schools as revealed in Table 5. The exodus of keyboarding class from its traditional home is probably due to the merging of office systems and business education departments into others, a trend across the nation.

At most NABTE institutions and all institutions of the experts, keyboarding is taught on a computer. As shown in Table 6, 7 percent of the NABTE institutions do not teach keyboarding on a computer. At those institutions, it is taught on electronic typewriters.

About 80 percent of the NABTE respondents were familiar with Cumulative Trauma Disorder or Carpal Tunnel Syndrome, while all of the experts indicated familiarity as revealed in Table 7.

The major sources of Cumulative Trauma Disorder awareness were reading the literature and talking with others; 95 (and all ten experts) and 93 NABTE respondents, respectively, checked off those items. Responses were not converted to percentages as respondents could check as many categories as applied. The next most frequently listed sources of CTD awareness, illustrated in Table 8, were a presentation and other. Most who responded to the other category listed a friend, colleague, or family member having the affliction as their source of awareness.

continued

Table 2
Highest Degree

Degree	NABTE Institutions Number	NABTE Institutions Percent	Experts Number	Experts Percent
Doctorate	98	65.35	9	90.00
Master's	48	32.0	1	10.00
Bachelor's	4	2.7	—	—

Table 3
Keyboarding Currently Taught

Taught	NABTE Institutions Number	NABTE Institutions Percent	Experts Number	Experts Percent
Yes	113	75.3	8	80.00
No	37	24.7	2	20.00

Table 4
Is the Keyboarding Course Required?

Required	NABTE Institutions Number	NABTE Institutions Percent	Experts Number	Experts Percent
Yes	74	49.3	6	75.0
No	54	36.0	2	25.0
No Response	22	14.7	—	—

Table 5
Department Teaching Keyboarding

Department	NABTE Institutions Number	NABTE Institutions Percent	Experts Number	Experts Percent
Office Systems/Bus. Ed.	78	69.0	6	75.0
CIS	12	10.6	2	25.0
Other	23	20.4	—	—

At a little over a third of the responding NABTE institutions, students exhibited concern about Cumulative Trauma Disorders compared to 40 percent of the experts' institutions as portrayed in Table 9.

As Table 10 depicts, only 22 percent of the NABTE respondents and 40 percent of the experts themselves have exhibited symptoms of Cumulative Trauma Disorder such as numbness and tingling of ht fingers.

continued

Table 6
Keyboarding Taught on A Computer

Computers	Experts NABTE Institutions Number	Percent	Number	Percent
Yes	109	72.7	8	100.0
No	23	15.3	—	—
No Response	18	12.0	—	—

Table 7
Familiar with CTD/CTS

Familiar	NABTE Number	NABTE Percent	Experts Number	Experts Percent
Yes	118	78.7	10	100.0
No	29	19.3	—	—
No Response	3	2.0	—	—

Table 8
Sources of CTD Awareness

Source	NABTE Experts Number	Percent
Reading the literature	95	10
Talking with others	93	7
Presentation	40	5
Personal experience	28	3
Other	40	1

Table 9
Students Exhibit Concern About CTDs

Concerned	NABTE Number	NABTE Percent	Experts Number	Experts Percent
Yes	53	35.3	4	40.0
No	84	56.0	6	60.0
No Response	13	8.7	—	—

continued

Table 11 reveals the equipment most often requested for an ergonomically designed classroom. Wrist rests were mentioned by almost half of the NABTE respondents, a protective screen by over a third of the respondents, and aprons by one sixth of the respondents. The experts' responses were comparable. The other category, checked by 45 of the NABTE respondents, was a potpourri category which was dominated by chairs and lighting.

Although wrist rests would be requested at about half the institutions, only 13 percent of the NABTE institutions and 20 percent of the experts' institutions currently have keyboarding classrooms equipped with wrist rests as shown in Table 12. A little over a third of the NABTE respondents and 50 percent of the experts currently have classrooms equipped with ergonomic furniture as revealed in Table 13.

Table 10
Have Respondents Exhibited CTD Symptoms?

	NABTE		Experts	
Symptoms	**Number**	**Percent**	**Number**	**Percent**
Yes	34	22.7	4	40.0
No	111	74.0	6	60.0
No Response	5	3.3	—	—

Table 11
Equipment Most Often Requested For An Ergonomically Designed Classroom

Equipment	**NABTE Number**	**Experts Number**
Wrist rests	72	4
Protective Screen	60	5
Aprons	24	0
Other	3	1

Table 12
Classrooms Equipped with Wrist Rests

	NABTE		Experts	
Wrist Rests	**Number**	**Percent**	**Number**	**Percent**
Yes	20	13.3	2	20.0
No	109	72.7	8	80.0
Will Be	3	2.0	—	—
No Response	18	12.0	—	—

continued

As Table 14 illustrates, 53 percent of the NABTE respondents and half of the experts indicated that they teach techniques to reduce the incidence of Cumulative Trauma Disorder. Twenty percent of the NABTE respondents indicated that they do no know whether or not they teach techniques to reduce the incidence of CTDs, 43 provided specific techniques they used. Of these, 31 respondents mentioned techniques relating to posture, the wrist and the hand, and workstation setup.

Open-Ended Question

In the last item on the questionnaire, respondents were asked to provide any additional comments they may have. About a third of the respondents did provide comments. These comments are presented in Appendix C. Three comments, which are typical of those made, follow:

"It is my (scientifically unfounded!) opinion that posture and keying technique are major contributors to the problem—did we really find this such a problem when far harder keystroking was required on manual typewriters!"

"This is a real concern to me."

"I would like to do anything I could in order to reduce the health risks of my students."

Six of the ten experts responded to the open-ended question. Two comments follow.

"The development of speed, accuracy, decision making, and creativity at the keyboard need to be revitalized. We did better 30 years ago on manual typewriters than we are going on computers today."

"Most students are not aware of CTS."

Table 13
Classrooms Equipped with Ergonomic Furniture

	NABTE		Experts	
Furniture	**Number**	**Percent**	**Number**	**Percent**
Yes	57	38.0	5	50
No	67	44.7	4	40
Will Be	7	4.7	—	—
No Response	19	12.7	1	10

Table 14
Teach Techniques To Reduce CTD Incidence

	NABTE		Experts	
Teach	**Number**	**Percent**	**Number**	**Percent**
Yes	80	53.3	5	50
No	28	18.7	4	40
Will Be	30	20.0	—	—
No Response	12	8.0	1	10

continued

Experts

Experts were asked if the textbooks they have used for keyboarding provided adequate coverage of proper techniques for avoiding CTD. As Table 15 indicates, 90 percent of the experts queried found the textbooks inadequate. One author admitted that he is revising his book and does plan to cover techniques for CTD avoidance.

Experts were also asked about the likelihood that business educators who teach keyboarding may be held liable for the contraction of CTDs by students and former students. Of the ten respondents, as indicated in Table 16, half were uncertain. Only one respondent felt it was likely. Curiously enough, this respondent had contracted CTS.

Regressions

Multicollinearity and Missing Data. Provisions were made to protect against multicollinearity. The tolerance level was set at .30. Mean substitution was used for missing data.

To identify characteristics of those keyboarding instructors at NABTE institutions who teach techniques to reduce the incidence of Carpal Tunnel Syndrome/Cumulative Trauma Disorders, eight independent variable were employed in a stepwise regression. Those variable included: years of teaching experience, highest degree, concern with CTD, use of computers, department in which the course is taught, familiarity with CTD, wrist rests are used, and wrist rests would be used.

The results are presented in Table 17. Note that 59 percent of the variation of those who teach and those who do not teach preventative techniques could be explained by an optimal linear weighting of the four variables entering the equation: department in which the course is taught, familiarity with CTD, use of wrist rests, and wrist rests would be used.

Table 15
Keyboarding Textbooks Provide Adequate Coverage

Response	**Number**	**Percent**
Yes	1	10.0
No	9	90.0
Will Be	7	4.7
No Response	19	12.7

Table 16
Likelihood of Liability for Contraction CTS by Students and Former Students

Likelihood	**Number**	**Percent**
Very likely	0	0.0
Likely	1	10.0
Not Likely	0	0.0
Not very likely	4	40.0
Don't know	5	50.0

continued

Obviously, to be able to teach good preventative keyboarding techniques, one needs to be aware of what those techniques are. Unfortunately, at this time, there is quite a bit of controversy about what constitutes "proper" techniques. As 20 percent of the NABTE group is unsure of proper techniques, this is an area that lends itself to further research, training, and education.

Discriminant Function Analysis

A discriminant function analysis was run on the variable "teaches techniques to reduce CTD incidence." The three groups were recoded to two by lumping those responding no and do not know into the second group. Prior probabilities for these two groups are listed in Table 18.

One discriminant, the maximum number possible, was significant at the <.05 level with an Eigenvalue of .1859. The strongest weights for the discriminant are associated with CTD familiarity and computers. A complete listing of structure coefficients appears in Table 19.

The classification table from SPSS is reproduced in Table 20. Note that 69 percent of the cases were correctly classified, while on a chance basis, approximately 50 percent of the cases would have been correctly classified. The proportional reduction in error was 38 percent (.68-.50)/.50 = 38 percent, which exceeds the 20 percent benchmark used as the minimum level of desirability.

This discriminant performed well in identifying members of Group 1, but incorrectly identified Group 2 members as Group 1 members more often than not.

Discussion

More and more workers now and in the year 2000 will be using computers to input, retrieve, and access information. These workers will be spending a large proportion of their workday at the

Table 17
Predictors of Those Keyboarding Instructors Teaching Techniques to Reduce CTD Incidence

Variable	**Beta**	**t**	**Significance of T**
Department Taught	.32	3.76	<.01
CTD Familiarity	.20	3.71	<.01
Wrist Rests Used	.29	3.22	<.01
Would Use Wrist Rests	.22	3.59	<.01

Note: R = .77
R^2 = .59
Adjusted R^2 = .58
N = 150

Table 18
Prior Probabilities
Teach Techniques to Reduce CTD Incidence

Group	**Prior**	**Label**
1	.50	Yes
2	.50	No

continued

Table 19
Structure Coefficients

Variable	Structure Coefficient
CTD Familiarity	.77195
Computers	.45899
Highest Degree	.34666
Taught on a Computer	.32739
Personal Experience	.32008

Table 20
Classification Table—Predicted Group Membership

Actual Group	Cases	Group 1	Group 2
1	77	68	9
		88.3%	11.7%
2	56	32	24
		57.1%	42.9%

computer with the increased potential of experiencing greater rates of health problems. Uninformed keyboarding/computer technology instructors add to this burden. Unless instructors and their students are well trained in proper keyboarding techniques, the resulting impact on business (and its employees), manufacturers of technology, and the legal system will take the form of increased costs and diminished productivity, exclusive of human suffering.

Greater awareness by keyboarding/computer information systems instructors of the proper techniques for reducing CTD/CTS incidence is warranted. Instructors of these subjects have an obligation to provide students with up-to-date information about these afflictions. This is particularly critical concerning the two following developments:

1. Because of losing a lawsuit, McDonald's now prints the words, "Caution: Contents Hot" on its Styrofoam coffee cups. Similarly, other fast food chains have following McDonald's lead.
2. A high school student in Pennsylvania, who had developed carpal tunnel syndrome, sued a keyboarding instructor and won the suit.

The issue of potential liability on the part of keyboarding/computer information systems/computer science instructors rears its ugly head. Not only do instructors wish to prevent disabilities in their students, they are wise to avoid potential lawsuits. Therefore, instructors should encourage the use of good keyboarding techniques including, but not limited to, the following:

1. Avoiding the resting of wrists on a wrist rest or keyboard
2. Pressing keys, instead of striking them with great force
3. Taking a 10-minute break every hour

The publication of instructional materials for keyboarding such as textbooks, software programs, and videotapes that incorporate good techniques might help to prevent some disabilities.

continued

As many of the keyboarding courses that were formerly taught at the university level have moved to the two-year colleges, a survey of community college institutions might prove useful. If time and financial resources were plentiful, a survey of the high school and elementary levels would prove interesting. As many students now begin their formal keyboarding training at the elementary level, knowledge of the techniques used at this critical time in skill development would be beneficial.

In addition, in a society where litigation is easily begun, it would behoove instructors of keyboarding/computer information systems to carry malpractice insurance as a professional and personal safeguard.

References

Cone, E. (1994, June 27). Keyboarding injuries: Who should pay? *Information Week*, 30–33, 36.

Crouch, T. & Madden, M. (1992). *Carpal Tunnel Syndrome and Overuse Injuries: Prevention, Treatment, and Recovery*. Berkeley: North Atlantic Books.

Dainoff, M.J. (April 13, 1992). The illness of the decade. *Computerworld*, 27.

DuFresne, D. & Wilmeth, N.J. (Fall 1991). The Occupational Safety and Health Law as Applied to the Office Environment. *Office Systems Research Journal*, 10, 22–29.

Elmer-Dewitt, P. (1994, October 24). A royal pain in the hand. *Time, 144,*. 60–62

Evans, C. (1994). Are office support personnel aware of the ergonomical issues associated with computer keyboarding? *Proceedings of the 1994 National Research Conference*, Little Rock: Delta Pi Epsilon, 3–6.

Franchi, K. & Fleck, R.A. Jr. (March/April 1994). Ergonomic improvements in the office environment. *Business Horizons, 37*, 75–79.

Galen, M., Mallory, M., Siwolop, S., & Garland, S. (July 13, 1992). Repetitive stress: The pain has just begun. *Business Week*, 142–144.

Huntley, D. (June 1990). Key injuries hurt companies. *HRMagazine, 35*, 72–75.

Pascarelli, E. & Quilter, D. (1994). *Repetitive Strain Injury: A Computer User's Guide*. New York: John Wiley & Sons, Inc.

Perkins, W.E. (December 1992). Keyboarding hazards—new areas of technique emphasis. *Business Education Forum, 47*, 29–32.

United States Code Annotated (USCA), Title 29, Labor (1985). St. Paul, MN, West Publishing Co.

Wentling, R.M. (February 1992). Business professionals and keyboarding skills. *Business Education Forum, 46*, 30–32.

Zeloznicki, S. (September 1992). Make the office work for you. *HRMagazine, 37*, 65–67.

Authors' Note

The authors gratefully acknowledge: Carol Mitzner, Beta Pi Chapter member of Delta Pi Epsilon, for suggesting the initial research area; members of Beta Pi involved in pilot testing the instrument used in this study; Daniel Frise and Atsuko Ogawa, research assistants, for their fine work; and Dineen Chiocon for superb clerical assistance.

can see how the parts relate to one another. To give the readers a sense of the overall structure, you first have to inform them that your formal report consists of three major divisions: preliminary information, the report body (text or report proper), and supplementary parts. You can help keep your readers focused by using an opening, headings, correct tense (time perspective), transitional words, and endings.

The opening. The opening consists of the introduction, which introduces the subject of the report, states why the subject is important, and previews the main ideas and the order in which they will be presented.

Headings. Headings are brief titles at the beginning of each subdivision within the report that gives a clue about the content of the section that follows.

Time perspective. In writing up the data information and analysis, be sure to present the information is its correct time sequence. For example, if you are describing history events, then start at the beginning and cover each order of occurrence. If you are explaining steps involved in production of a product, then present each step in proper sequence. If you are reporting how people responded to survey questions, then report the responses in the past tense. For example, if thirty people filled out the questionnaire survey, you would state: "Thirty people completed (past tense) the survey."

Transitional words. Transitional words such as additionally, similarly, in addition to, on the other hand, naturally, moreover, besides, furthermore, therefore, consequently, accordingly, likewise, still, conversely, however, but, nevertheless, if, although, for instance, in this case, formerly, after, meanwhile, in fact, indeed, in brief, in short, that is, in other words, all can be used to achieve emphasis. Transitional words can be used to provide additional detail, establish a casual relationship, compare or contrast, state a condition, give an illustration, specify a time sequence, or summarize.

The ending. The ending is the section that leaves a lasting impression. If your report is written in direct order, you may want to restate your conclusions and recommendations again; remember, they come first in direct order. If your report is written in indirect order or is an analytical report, present your conclusions and recommendations last. The conclusions are based on the findings of your research, and the recommendations suggest solutions based on the conclusions.

In writing formal business reports, the following parts usually are included as shown in Figure 14.7.

Prefatory Parts.

Cover. The cover, usually of a heavier paper and imprinted with the company's name and logo, is used to hold the report together and to make the report neat and attractive. Be sure an informative title is placed on the cover; the writer's name may be optional but a date is needed.

Prefatory Parts	Text of Report	Supplementary Parts
Cover	Introduction	Appendices
Title Fly	Body	Bibliography or References
Title Page	Summary	
Letter of Authorization & Letter of Acceptance	Conclusions	
Letter of Transmittal	Recommendations	
Table of Contents		
List of Illustrations		
Synopsis, Abstract, or Executive Summary		
List of Definitions		

Figure 14.7. Parts in a Business Report.

Title Fly. The title fly is a sheet of paper which contains only the title of the report. This prefatory part is typically optional.

Title Page. This is an important page which lists the following information:

1. The title of the report
2. The name, title, and address of the person, group, or organization that authorized the report
3. The name, title, and address of the person, group, or organization that prepared the report
4. The date on which the report was submitted

The Letter of Authorization. The letter of authorization conveys permission to you to do the report. This authorization may be in the form or a memo, a letter, or an oral command. When you receive a written authorization, you should include it in your report. Most letters of authorization specify the problem, scope, time and money restrictions, due date, and any special instructions.

The Letter of Acceptance. This letter is written by the researcher or writer; its purpose is to acknowledge acceptance of doing the report. The letter of acceptance can be written in memorandum or letter format, but a letter would be more businesslike.

The Letter of Transmittal. The letter of transmittal written by the writer conveys the report to your audience. The contents include what you have done, some significant findings, suggestions for followup studies, and may express appreciation at having been asked to conduct the research report. This letter follows the direct writing plan for a good-news or routine message and is placed just before the Table of Contents.

The Table of Contents. The tentative outline you made to research the problem becomes the table of contents in its finished form with the addition of page numbers. The table of contents is prepared after the entire report is finished. The headings and subheadings should be worded exactly as they are in the text of the report. The table of contents helps keep the reader focused on the the major points. If you have only a few visual aids to include in the report, you can list them in the Table of Contents.

List of Illustrations. The list of illustrations gives their titles and page numbers. You can list the tables separately as well as the figures separately.

Synopsis, Abstract, or Executive Summary. A synopsis is a brief overview (one page or less) of a report's most important points. An Executive Summary is used to give the executive enough information so that he or she can make a decision without reading the entire report. The introduction, conclusions, and recommendations arranged in direct order must be included in a synopsis. In long informational reports that deal with professional, technical, or academic subjects, the synopsis may be called an abstract. At professional conferences, usually abstracts are passed out, and after hearing the presenter, the interested person can then ask for a copy of the entire report.

Body or Text of the Report.

This section of the report begins with the major sections—introduction and continues through to the conclusions and recommendations. The Introduction, Body or Findings, Conclusions, and Recommendations can be called the "meat" of the report. Each of these major sections will be discussed next.

The *Introduction* clarifies why the report was written, in other words—who authorized the report, the purpose of the report, previews the content and organization of the report, and establishes the relationship between the writer and the readers. In essence, you tell the readers what you are going to tell them in this major section. The introduction may include the following side headings:

Authorization

(This authorization is omitted if you use a letter of authorization.) The content of this section contains who authorized the report, who is to write the report, any special details of the report, and the due date.

Problem or Purpose

The need for the report is emphasized in this section as well as what is to be accomplished as a result of the report.

Background

This part previews the history relating to the problem or purpose of the report and what is the status of the problem up to this point.

Scope

The reader needs to know the complexity of the report, namely, what is and what is not covered in the report. For instance, if you were writing a report on the rise of violence, you could narrow it by limiting the scope to workplace violence.

Sources and Methods

The types of sources used such as secondary sources and primary sources of information are included in this section. Your purpose here is to convince the reader that the methods and sources you chose are the best ones to ensure a creditable report.

Limitations

As the writer of the report, you do have the ability to state the factors that are beyond your control in this part. You want the reader to know that you did the best you could within the limitations such as inadequate time frame, lack of monetary sources to do a thorough job, and unavailability of data.

Definitions

A list of definitions (only if needed) may be included in the report. This is a list of specialized terms defined operationally; in other words, how they are used in the report. According to the previous example, if your report is on workplace violence, then you would need to define what you mean by violence—a person(s) being injured or killed or physical abuse inflicted by one employee upon another employee.

Report Preview

This section of the report is very helpful to the reader. It tells them what is covered, in what order, and is the roap map for helping the reader understand the flow of information in the report.

The *BODY OR FINDINGS* consists of another major section, sometimes called chapter(s), that present the information, analyze and interpret the findings from your investigation. As the writer, you must include enough detailed information to support the conclusions and recommendations you make. Your readers will expect you to do nothing less. Naturally, you tell them what you found or collected in your research study. You will naturally be doing a review of the literature, that is, the articles that have already been published on your topic, or you will be critiquing articles that can be related to your research topic. Do not forget to document where you got your information.

At this point, you should know how many and what types of graphic aids to include in the body of the report. Also, consideration should be given to your audience needs; that is, do they need the introductory information before presenting your conclusions and recommendations which would require the indirect writing arrangement or will you use the direct writing arrangement if the audience is already familiar with the problem?

The *SUMMARY, CONCLUSIONS, AND RECOMMENDATIONS* is the final major section of the report. In this section you tell the readers what you told them. Whether you put the summary, conclusions, and recommendations in separate sections depends on the length of your report and your readers' familiarity with the situation or problem.

To help you understand the differences among a summary, conclusion, and recommendation, note the terms as defined.

A summary is a paraphrased presentation of the key findings stated in the order presented in your report.
A conclusion is the answer to the questions raised that led up to the report.
A recommendation is your sound reasoning about a proposed course of action or solution to the situation or problem.

Conclusions and recommendations must be made only on the findings presented in earlier sections of the report; no new information should be presented in the concluding sections of the report. These conclusions and recommendations can be shown in in paragraph form, but the better way is to present them in an objective way and in numerical format as shown in the examples below:

Conclusions

Conclusions based upon the findings from the research study are presented next:

1. Workplace violence has increased thirty percent in the past ten years.
2. Malecontent employees usually are the perpetrators of violence acts in the workplace.

Recommendations

The following recommendations are made based upon the findings from the study:

1. Employee suggestion boxes should be established in each department to encourage employees to submit their concerns about company policies.
2. The Personnel Office should be notified when any employee has a confrontation with his or her immediate supervisor, co-worker, or other employee in the Company.

In an informational report, you would present a summary only as no analysis is needed. However, in an analytical report, you would include conclusions and recommendations.

Physical Appearance of the Report

The physical appearance of the report is just as important as the content. Strive for a neat, attractive appearance. The appearance will help your readers view the report in a favorable light.

The following features of a report are stressed as they contribute to the physical appearance of a report:

Margins. You can use the default margins, usually one inch, in most word processing software packages or you can change them; however, a one-inch left margin and a one-inch right margin are standard for reports that are unbound. A one and one-half left margin is required for side-bound reports.

The first page of each major section of the report requires a two-inch top margin, which is 13 single spaced lines down from the top of the screen or paper. The remaining pages in each major section have a one-inch top margin. Leave no more than a one-inch to one and one-half inch bottom margin on each page.

Spacing. Use double spacing for formal reports, but you should check the spacing in previous reports in your organization to be sure double spacing is acceptable. The organization may want the report single spaced to save paper as well as file space.

Headings. The format of headings should be consistent within the body of the report. Do not use too many different fonts which may detract from the formality of the report. A subheading should have more than one subdivision.

Page numbering. The first page of the body of the report is usually not numbered; but if you put a number on page 1, the page number is centered one-inch from the bottom of the page. Page numbers of following pages are placed in the upper right-hand corner on line 7 from the top to leave a one-inch top margin. Triple space after the page number at the top of the page before beginning the text. Most word processing software have a page numbering feature; some may only allow page numbers at the bottom. To save you time in numbering the pages, particularly if you are preparing a formal report, you may want to turn off the word processor's page numbering feature and input the page numbers yourself.

Paper. A sturdy, good quality white bond paper (20 pound weight) that is 8½ by 11 inches adds to the attractiveness of the report contents. Check to see that the printer ribbon is new to allow sharp and clear print.

Error correction. If the report is keyboarded and you spot an error, do NOT pen in the correction. Make the error correction and print out that page again. If you must use a typewriter, be sure it has a self-correcting feature. Use very little whiteout (correction liquid) on a page; otherwise, retype the page for neatness. Be sure the typewriter keys are clean.

Typing text. Always leave two lines of a paragraph at the bottom of each page and carry over at least two lines of a paragraph to the next page. You may have to insert blank lines or leave extra space at page bottoms to accomplish this feat. Never leave a side heading as the last text on a page without sufficient text following it.

Spacing of text. The body of formal reports is usually double spaced. Paragraphs are indented five spaces. Double space between all paragraphs. The title of the report is typed on line 13, centered and in all-capital letters followed by a triple space. A main heading such as INTRODUCTION is typed in all-capital letters with a triple space before and a double space after. A side heading such as Background is underlined and preceded by a triple space and double space afterwards. A paragraph heading such as the one for this paragraph begins on the first line of the paragraph followed by a period and two spaces. Use initial capital letters on the main words.

Justification of margins. The left margin is always justified, but the right margin is not. You will need to turn off the justification feature of the word processing software. Right justification means that all lines end even vertically; justified right margins are harder on the eyes to read because the eye has to shift between the extra spaces between the words to the next word(s).

The *Supplementary Report Parts* of the report include the Appendix(ces), the bibliography, also called References, and the Index. A blank copy of the questionnaire, a tabulated copy of the questionnaire, along with the cover letter are included in the appendix. Other computer printouts, large, extensive tables, and diagrams or drawings can be included in this section as well.

The bibliography is a list of secondary sources and primary sources actually cited in writing the report and should be listed separately. A list of the interviewees with names, address, positions, and phone numbers should be put in a separate listing along with a list of the interview questions.

An index is not needed in most business reports. However, it is used only for very long, extensive reports or perhaps for a textbook.

Sample of a Complete Formal Report

An example of a Formal Report is shown in 14.6.

Business Presentations and Delivery will be the focus of Chapter 15.

Checklist for Reports

Check Prefatory Parts Needed

Introduction

☐ Is the report title clear, specific, and complete?
☐ Is the purpose of the study or research problem stated clearly and accurately?
☐ Is the scope of the study defined?
☐ Are there any terms needing definition?
☐ Did you state your research methods and statistical analysis used?
☐ Did you provide a report preview?

Body or Findings

☐ Is the review of literature complete? Is the review of related literature complete?
☐ Did provide quotes and paraphrases to lend credibility to the report's contents?

- ☐ Did you document all information in the review of literature and related literature section?
- ☐ Is the analysis free of bias and distortion?
- ☐ Did you indicate what the data means?
- ☐ Did you recheck all calculations in tables, charts, etc.
- ☐ Did you check for percentages adding up to 100 or accounting for why they did not?
- ☐ Did you use correct graphic aids? Are they clear and understandable?
- ☐ Are graphic aids numbered correctly? Are they positioned correctly?

Summary, Conclusions, and Recommendations

- ☐ Is the wording in the summary different from that in the text?
- ☐ Are the conclusions based upon the findings of your research?
- ☐ Are the recommendations based upon the conclusions from your research?
- ☐ Did you check to make sure there are NO new ideas presented in this section?
- ☐ Did you answer all of your research questions?

Appendices

- ☐ Is the list of References complete and in alphabetical order by last name?
- ☐ Is the format correct (APA Style, etc.)?
- ☐ Did you include a blank copy of your questionnaire?
- ☐ Did you include a tabulated copy of your questionnaire?
- ☐ Did you include a list of interviewees?
- ☐ Did you include a list of interview questions?

Writing Style and Format

- ☐ Is the report properly organized?
- ☐ Are the headings, parallel, and sufficient in number?
- ☐ Are the page numbers placed correctly on each page?
- ☐ Does each major section contain a preview, body of information, summary, and transitions?
- ☐ Did you check for correct verb tense throughout the report?
- ☐ Did you check for use of impersonal writing in the report?
- ☐ Did you check for references to all cited sources in the report?
- ☐ Are the quotes and paraphrases formatted correctly?
- ☐ Is the complete report neat and attractive?
- ☐ Are the paragraphs of appropriate length?
- ☐ Is the report FREE of spelling, grammar, and punctuation errors?

References

Blaszczynski, C. and Joyce, M. P. Shane. (1996). Keyboarding instruction at NABTE Institutions: Are we teaching techniques to reduce CTD incidence? DELTA PI EPSILON JOURNAL, Fall, 1996, 38, (4), 195–208.

QUESTIONS

1. Which is formal a memo or a memo report? Why?
2. What is the purpose of reports?
3. How would you classify a research report written by your professor?
4. What is the sample size of the population in Figure 14.6?
5. What is the basis for determining writing style in a report?
6. What are the major text sections of a formal report?
7. What is a limitation?
8. How do Fig. 14.4 and 14.2 differ?
9. Why should recommendations and conclusions be enumerated?
10. Describe the report formats.
11. Who typically request reports in an organization?

APPLICATIONS

1. Input a list of References you have collected regarding your formal research report. Use APA style.
2. Paraphrase 2 paragraphs from different references (#1 above) and include the citation using the author, year format.
3. Input a 6–8 line quote and include the citation.
4. Input a 3 line quote and include the citation.
5. Review the Checklist for reports and list the items you have yet to complete regarding your format report.
6. Make a gant chart of your work remaining regarding the formal research report.
7. Input a paragraph on your analysis and interpretation of the following data:
   sample population—408 students
   ½ of students taught by one professor
   other half taught by another professor
   students enrolled in upper level writing course
   course housed in School of Business and Economics
   course taught Fall quarter 1996
   66% of students used English as a second language
   204 males; 195 females; 7 people did not indicate gender
8. Input a final copy of your introduction to your formal research report.
9. Construct one graphic aid from the data (#7 above). Show at least 3 variables.
10. Construct one overhead transparency from a graphic aid you found in an article dated 1996–1997.

Name ____ Date ____________

JEOPARDY QUIZ #14

1. The answer is: I, we, us, you, and your.

   What are ____?

2. The answer is: Introduction, findings (body) and concluding sections.

   What are ____?

3. The answer is: Similarly, therefore, however, meanwhile.

   What are ____?

4. The answer is: A statement suggesting the solution to a research problem.

   What is ____?

5. The answer is: Christopher, 1993, p. 41.

   What is ____?

6. The answer is: Contains permission for you to do a report.

   What is ____?

7. The answer is: Synopsis, abstract, and executive summary.

   What are ____?

8. The answer is: Choosing a research topic and then narrowing the factors.

   What is ____?

9. The answer is: The margin that is usually jagged, not justified.

   What is ____?

10. The answer is: A listing of sources actually cited in the body (text) of a formal report.

    What are ____?

PART IV

BUSINESS PRESENTATIONS AND DELIVERY

CHAPTER 15

Business Presentations and Delivery

Objectives

Upon reading the chapter and doing the exercises, you should be able to:

1. Determine the differences between formal and informal presentations.
2. Recognize how the purpose of the presentation impacts audience participation.
3. Describe the purposes of presentations in organizations.
4. Use the listener-centered approach in your presentation.
5. Explain the typical organizational plan for making a presentation.
6. Select an appropriate introduction for your presentation on your formal research report.
7. Choose which graphic aids to incorporate in your presentation.
8. Determine how to handle communication in a crisis.
9. Discuss the four basic types of presentation delivery.
10. Give an effective oral presentation.
11. Discuss how communication to various audiences differs relative to presentations.

Speeches and oral presentations are an important communication vehicle in any organization. Business people engage in oral communication daily or routinely at staff meetings, management team meetings, as sales representatives, or as company spokes persons. As a prospective business leader, you will need to hone your presentation and delivery skills to become an effective speaker.

As a speaker, your main goal is to effectively present your ideas from a public rostrum or in a known environment. Sometimes the public rostrum may be a presentation to an outside organization such as a professional organization or an association. Other times the speech may be to your peers, subordinates, or other executives within the company. Of course, as the presenter you probably will be more at ease speaking to audiences within your organization than to those outside your company.

Before preparing your speech, you need to define your purpose, analyze the audience, choose a delivery plan, visit the room or area in which you will be making the presentation, and then make the presentation.

The techniques of effective communication as discussed throughout the earlier chapters apply to making speeches as well. Your speech can be presented in the direct or indirect order. An important advantage of the oral presentation is that you have instant feedback. You can pick up on the audience's nonverbal cues just as they will be picking up on your nonverbal cues. You can receive information as well as transmit it. Your voice quality, facial expression, rate of speaking, diction, tone, and gestures will be certainly evident.

Informal and Formal

When you have to make a presentation, you need to determine whether you will be making an informal or formal presentation. An informal presentation may be made sitting down among others. With this arrangement, you may be more comfortable. Such presentations may be made to subordinates at a staff meeting. Informal presentation usually are made to small audiences. The informality of the presentation does not lessen the need to present your ideas in an effective and convincing manner. Frequently you may be called upon on the spur of the moment to give a short report to others within the company; naturally, you will do well because you are already familiar with the topic or situation.

If you are to make a formal presentation, then extra care and preparation are required. A formal presentation is usually made to larger audiences and may or may not be within the confines of the organization. You could be asked to make a presentation to upper management or to a professional organization or association. In these instances, you may or may not be familiar with the topic. Sometimes you may be invited to present the results of a research study you have completed or you can be asked to speak on a certain topic of which you may not be familiar. You probably would be more comfortable with the former request than the latter request. In any event, you will want to do your best to make a good presentation and to represent the company well. Naturally, you need to organize and plan your presentation.

Organizing and Planning the Presentation

In organizing and planning the presentation, you need to first define the *purpose* of the presentation because the purpose will affect the audience's interaction. Bovee and Thill (1995) p. 592 offer a diagram that illustrates the level of interaction between the speaker and the audience. See Figure 15.1.

As the diagram illustrates, the most interaction occurs when your purpose is to persuade people to take action or to solicit their help in solving a problem or reaching a decision. As the speaker, you present a number of facts and figures to assist the audience in understanding your message. You may also present conclusions and recommendations, and then seek the audience's participation by asking them to express their needs, suggesting solutions, and formulating their conclusions and recommendations. The persuasive or collaborative speech allows you little room for control. Persuasive speeches are often used in sales presentations.

The purpose of your presentation could be to inform or perhaps persuade the audience. If that is the case, then you basically give the audience information and solicit their comments or questions. Bovee and Thill state that such companies use such presentations to implement policies and procedures, to comply with regulations, and to explain the status of work for clients. (p. 593) The interaction that takes place is the sharing, commenting, and questioning between the speaker and hearers of the presentation.

The speech with the least amount of audience interaction is the motivational or entertaining speech. These speeches are usually given at annual conventions or banquets to boost employee morale. Typically, the speaker gives many comical anecdoctal or amusing comments and keeps the audience smiling or laughing while also interweaving a few serious remarks.

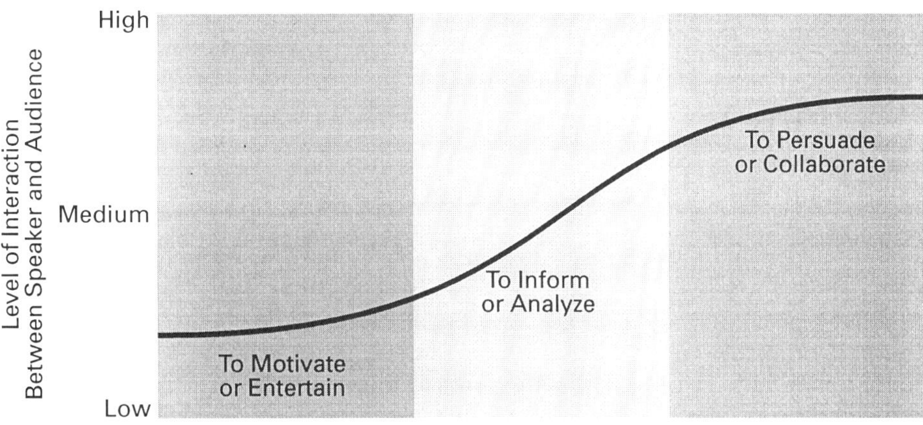

Figure 15.1.

Your next step in organizing and planning your presentation is the make up of the *audience*. If you already know the audience, you can tailor your presentation to their needs. Just as you learned in choosing the writing style based on the reader's reaction, so to do you choose the speech presentation style based on the audience's reaction to the message. You need to learn as much as you can about the audience BEFORE you make the presentation so you can be prepared for the unexpected. For example, if you were just asked to make a presentation on health care packages your company offers and you happen to know your company was chosen because its premiums are lower but offer fewer services, you can certainly expect some hostility or anger. Another example might be your presentation to a group of workers who are to be told they are going to be laid off. Can you imagine their disgust, anger, and indifference? Naturally, you can understand their feelings but you also need to be empathetic if the atmosphere appears to be tense.

The presentation needs structure. You can best achieve structure by focusing on the main idea of your presentation, constructing an outline, estimating the time limit of your presentation, and then choosing the best delivery approach.

The main idea is the overall theme you want to leave with your audience. Use the listener-centered approach by relating the message to the audience's interests. For example, if you wanted to stress the importance of written and oral communication from the viewpoint of an employer, then focus on how such skills will enhance the prospective graduate's opportunities for job promotion, not on degree requirements. Whether you are speaking to individuals or to a group of people, the environment will have an impact.

Before making a presentation, an outline should be constructed. You will need to know what key points you want to cover in the presentation, where and when you will introduce each point, particularly if the message is negative, and how you will end the presentation. Remember to use the direct order if the audience will be receptive to your message and use the indirect order if you expect audience resistance. Organize your presentation like you would reports.

The typical organization plan should include the following:

An Attention Getter (optional if the audience is known)
An Introduction
A Body of Information (secondary sources and primary sources)
Summary, Conclusions, and Recommendations
Question and Answer Period

An *attention getter* is sometimes needed to set the stage for your presentation and to arouse the audience's interest. Some examples of attention getters include stating a rhetorical question, sharing a startling statistic, reading a quotation, or asking a question and asking for an audience's show of hands.

An *introduction* is used to capture the audience's attention, show confidence, and establish the speaker's credibility. Frequently an attention getter is interwoven in this introduction. If you are introducing yourself, mention your accomplishments and background on the topic but keep your comments simple and brief. If you are being introduced, the presenter will choose what to say about you based on a biography you have prepared for him or her. Your listeners are sizing you up along with deciding whether you are worth listening to. As a speaker you need to connect your background to the audience's concerns.

The *body* of your presentation should be limited to three to five main points. Your focus is on making sure your presentation organization keeps the audience's attention. Use of transitional words are necessary to tie the main points together. Stress main points, summarize them, tie them together, and preview what is to come. Use short sentences, concrete examples, and familiar words. You may want to pause to allow time for questions or comments from the audience. Be sure that your time limit will allow this though.

The *summary, conclusions, and recommendations* represent the close of your presentation. The summary is a restatement of the main points. For example, use the words "in summary." This sets the stage for the closing. Make your conclusions and recommendations confidently so that the audience will do and think as you would want. The close of the presentation should leave a lasting positive impression.

The *question and answer* period is usually a short session. You should anticipate questions that may be asked and be ready to answer them. If an audience member becomes agitated or appears hostile, you can best handle it by remaining calm. Just state your opinion and the reasoning behind your opinion. If you are asked a question which you truly do not know the answer, just state confidently that you have no answer at this time but you can research the question and get back to the person at a later time. If you encounter an audience member who seems to be dominating the question and answer period, just state kindly that you would like to acknowledge others in the audience who may have questions as well.

Another major part of the presentation is to know the time limit. Your purpose, subject, and organization should be compatible for the time available. When you are asked to make a presentation, try to find out how much time you are allowed. The average speaker can speak about 125 to 150 words a minute, the size of an average paragraph, or about 8,000 to 9,000 words an hour. For example, if you are one of three people to make a presentation within a 90 minute time frame, you must adhere to your limit of 30 minutes. Otherwise, the other presenters will resent your intruding on their time. If you have an hour's presentation, make sure you have enough material to take up this time period. Or if you are giving a two hour workshop, the participants will expect to get two hours of presentation material. You should practice your presentation, including the use of graphic aids, so you have a good idea of how much time you actually need to do an effective job.

Using Graphic Aids in Presentations

To enhance your presentation, consider using graphic aids or visual aids. Visual aids help the audience to remember the information and absorb the information better during your presentation. The visual aids should be simple which increase effectiveness. According to a recent article, "audiences remember only 10 percent of a speaker's message when it is presented solely through words; however, they remember 50 percent when the information is supported with such visuals as slides and overhead transparencies." (Bovee and Thill, p. 607). Both text visuals and graphic aids can be used in presentations.

Text visual aids consists of words and are used to enhance the presentation. These visuals should be in large type with no more than six main lines and contain five to six words per line. Use grammatical structure such as the following: Student Fees Remain Stable at CSU System or Passage of WPE by Student Soars.

Graphic visual aids can be used to illustrate main ideas. They help the audience grasp numerical data better than speaking the numerical data. Any of the graphic aids discussed in Chapter 14 on graphic aids can be included in a presentation. Graphic visual aids must be readable from a distance and understandable within a few moments.

In presenting visual aids, consider the following guidelines:

1. Include only one main idea per visual
2. Allow enough time for the audience to read the visual
3. Talk only about the main points in the visual aid
4. Do not stand in front of the visual aid
5. Paraphrase the information for the audience
6. Remove the visual aid when finished discussing it
7. Turn off the overhead projector when finished showing overhead transparencies

Visual aids can be produced in many media; for example, one of the most commonly used formal or informal visual aid is the overhead transparency which can be projected on to a screen. A variety of information can be put in a transparency. You need the original or a clear, crisp copy from which to make a transparency. A copy machine and transparency film is needed to make a transparency.

Other visual aid media include handouts, slides, flip charts, chalkboards and whiteboards, filmstrips or videotapes, and computers. Because of the time and effort used to produce slides, they are considered a formal medium.

A handout which is considered an informal medium could be an abstract of the presentation, an outline or agenda, graphic aids, or a listing of key points in your presentation. Listeners usually will write their notes on the handouts, but when the listeners are reading the handouts instead of listening to you, this can be distracting. A solution could be to tell the audience you have a handout for them but not pass it out until you are finished with your presentation.

Slides can consist of pictures, text, or graphics. You may need to operate the slide projector yourself or appoint someone to do it. Be sure to position the slides at the beginning and make sure that the slides are right side up. You should check out the equipment and lighting beforehand to make sure everything is synchronized.

Flip charts work well when there is audience participation. These are large sheets of tablet paper attached to a standing easel. As the presenter, you or someone you appoint will write down key words as suggested by members of the audience. Use a variety of colored markers to highlight key points and limit the items per sheet of paper to five or six points. Naturally, this method is informal.

Chalkboards and whiteboards, although typical for informal situations, are useful. You need chalk and eraser and whiteboard markers and eraser if you use this medium. Both of these methods can be messy—chalk dust flies and whiteboard erasers make the hand dirty. Of course, if would be helpful if you had some hand wipes should you have to use this medium.

Filmstrips really capture the audience's attention because of the color and movement. Likewise, videotapes are useful for showing demonstrations, giving an orientation to new employees, evaluating interviews, or showing sample products and prototypes being produced.

Lastly, the computer is great for incorporating both animation and photos in your presentation. You can create text and modify it at that moment, or you can prepare it before hand and show it on a special projector. Later you can print out hard copies of the visual aids for the audience.

Handling Communication in a Crisis

From time to time, major catastrophes do occur in organizations and society. The public relations department helps management plan for and respond to crises. The way a company handles any major crisis has an profound impact on the future performance of that organization. You may be thrust in the middle of this crisis and have to respond on behalf of the company. For example, suppose you were a professor with a classroom of students and a 6.5 earthquake occurs. You can tell the students are visibly shaken up and some are crying. What do you do? Or, suppose you are riding the Metrolink to school and the conductor announces on the public address system that a bomb has been placed on the train tracks ahead, about two stops away. People are nervous, scared, and some demand to get off the train then but the train is not at a station stop. Of the two crises, one is an act of nature and the other one is a deliberate plot by an individual to reak harm on others. What do you do?

Companies should be prepared for the unexpected and have a proactive plan in reserve for just such a crisis. Regardless of the plan a company takes, a few people will still think it could have been better handled. For established crisis intervention plans to be effective, people must respond as directed. In any crisis, the following guidelines should be considered:

1. Establish a hot-line to handle calls
2. Appoint one company spokesperson who is a good communicator and channel all calls to this person
3. Assess the situation and report on how it is being handled on a daily basis
4. Refrain from publicizing gruesome details
5. Exhibit a sincere concern for the safety of people
6. Develop a crisis management plan
7. Train a crisis management team or response team
8. Issue news updates daily to the media
9. Apologize if the company is at fault and state what is being done to prevent a similar crisis
10. Accept responsibility; do not blame others; and do not invade anyone's right to privacy
11. Handle all crisis with candor, honesty, and concern for human life

Delivery refers not only to your methd of speaking but to your voice quality and body language. The four basic methods of delivery that occur in organizations and in life settings are extemporaneous speaking, manuscript reading, memorization, and impromptu speaking.

In extemporaneous speaking, the person is speaking basically from notes rather than a manuscript. This method permits a conversational message rather than a rehearsed message. Notes can be written on 5 × 8 cards for easy reference.

Because of the complexity of the subject matter, manuscript reading is sometimes feasible. However, this method causes the speaker to focus on the manuscript rather than the audience.

While this situation limits audience feedback, the speaker will need to develop the ability to read a few words, look down at the manuscript and read a few words, and vice versa until the finish of the presentation. At least the audience and the speaker will be establishing eye contact frequently. You will notice that prominent speakers usually read from teleprompters, electronic devices for rolling prepared texts.

The memorization presentation is effective for short presentation like introducing a person or serving as a moderator. This method can be embarrassing, particularly if the speaker suddenly gets stage fright and has no notes of any kind.

Many speakers are able to deliver remarks without advance preparation; this delivery method is called impromptu speaking. You will be called upon often in the business world to speak on the spur of the moment. When this does happen, you will be expected to make cogent, intelligent comments as you face the audience. You should always be prepared to speak whenever the situation dictates.

Multimedia can be used in presentations to corporate executives, in sales presentations, in educating and training employees, in enhancing e-mail messages, in the three basic functions of software—word processing, spreadsheets, database management, and in the windows environment.

Presentation Delivery

If you were to ask people what is their greatest fear, many of them would say giving a presentation or standing before a group of people to give a speech. To deliver a good presentation, you have to have self-confidence. You can gain self-confidence by practicing your presentation. Give your presentation to some one else or before a mirror or videotape yourself. Practice your presentation with your visual aids so you can coordinate where your visual aids are most effective. Don't forget to time the presentation as well.

Guidelines for making a good presentation include:

1. Check out the room before the presentation
2. Get acquainted with the overhead projector and how to turn it off and on; if you use a slide projector or a computer, be sure to check that the equipment is functioning properly. All too often the presenter is ready to go, but the equipment is not.
3. Check the positioning of the podium and the screen and overhead projector and the seat arrangement
4. Get to the presentation at least 10 minutes early to make sure you are ready to begin your presentation on time
5. Establish and maintain eye contact
6. Be sure you have all of your visual aids and note cards, numbered and in order
7. Deliver the presentation with zest, confidence, and a smile

Presentations to external audiences. Concentrate on what you want to say and the audience. Dress professional and speak with authority. As you approach the podium, take three deep breaths. Using the guidelines for giving an effective presentation, you will do well. Remember that some nervousness is all right; in time you will warm up to the audience. The people want you to succeed in your presentation.

Presentations to subordinates. You will probably be a little more relaxed in this environment because you know the people who work under your supervision. Nonetheless, you want to make a good presentation. They are judging you and will usually emulate what you do when they are asked to give a presentation. Above all, dress professional and appear confident.

Presentations to superiors. This environment can be pretty scary because these management people will be assessing your communication skills as well as your presentation skills. Use the guidelines for delivering an effective presentation to the maximum. Practice your presentation; dress professional; exhibit confidence, establish and maintain eye contact, and think positively about your audience. If you encounter tough questions, do your best to answer them, but do not try to be a know it all. Even top management does not always have the answer to every situation. It is good to admit when you do not know an answer than to appear foolish in giving a ridiculous answer.

Chapter 16 contains a discussion on developing effective listening and leadership skills.

References

Bovee, C. L. and J. V. Thill. (1995). BUSINESS COMMUNICATION TODAY, 4th edition, McGraw-Hill.

Questions

1. What are the four types of presentations?
2. How would you dress if you were making a presentation to your superiors?
3. Are oral presentations the most effective type of communication? Why or why not?
4. Is there ever an appropriate use of a memorized presentation?
5. Discuss what would be your strategy if a crisis occurred in a department of which you were the supervisor?
6. If your audience was familiar with your presentation topic, what type of attention getter would you use?
7. What is the highest level of audience participation in a presentation delivery?
8. What are the most important considerations in making a presentation?
9. What is a major difference between the formal presentation and the informal presentation?
10. Discuss the basic parts of a presentation.
11. Should every presentation have graphic aid(s)?
12. Which type of multimedia would you feel most comfortable with using in a presentation?
13. Describe a specific example of how you could incorporate multimedia in a presentation.

APPLICATIONS

1. Analyze the presentation styles of three different professors. What characteristics do they have in common? Which characteristics do they have that are different? How would you change their presentation style?
2. Try to remember the last four formal presentations you heard. Where were they presented? How many people were present? What type of presentation was it? What was the length of the presentation? Do you feel the presenters were effective?
3. Choose a speech from VITAL SPEECHES OF THE DAY. Count the number of transitional words and sentences used in the speech. Applying the concepts in this chapter, determine what type of speech it was.
4. If you are active in a student organization or business student club, list the opportunities you have to make a presentation to the group.
5. You have been asked to make a presentation on a controversial topic such as abortion or euthanasia. What precautions would you take before giving the presentation?
6. Input a list of the number of formal presentations you have made since you began college. List the courses in which they were given and the topics.
7. Select an article of interest to you; summarize it and give a 2 to 3 minutes presentation on the topic to the class.
8. Videotape yourself giving a 3 minute presentation on your formal research topic. Critique the tape for areas of improvement.
9. Prepare a brief biography of yourself to give to someone who will introduce you.
10. Prepare a persuasive 3 minute presentation on a topic of your choice that is a real concern to you.
11. Prepare a persuasive speech for or against the need to have a lower division business writing core course.
12. Critique the next presentation you hear. List the positive and negative qualities of the presentation from beginning to end.

Name ______________________________ Date ______________

JEOPARDY QUIZ #15

1. The answer is: Impromptu, extemporaneous, read, and memorized.

   What are ______________________________?

2. The answer is: A type of presentation made to a large audience.

   What is ______________________________?

3. The answer is: The type of presentation that has little audience participation.

   What is ______________________________?

4. The answer is: Purpose, audience, time limit, and location.

   What are ______________________________?

5. The answer is: The type of presentation that is considered the most effective.

   What is ______________________________?

6. The answer is: An opening, a body, and a closing.

   What are ______________________________?

7. The answer is: To entertain, to inform, or to persuade.

   What are ______________________________?

8. The answer is: Cues that are most evident in a presentation.

   What are ______________________________?

9. The answer is: Subordinates, superiors, customers and clients, and peers.

   What are ______________________________?

10. The answer is: A rhetorical question, a startling statistics, or a quotation.

    What are ______________________________?

CHAPTER 16

John Dallas, Jr. at Career Fair
California State University, Los Angeles—April 10, 1997

Developing Effective Listening and Leadership Skills

Objectives

Upon reading the chapter and doing the exercises, you should be able to:

1. Acquire an understanding of the elements to effective listening.
2. Develop an awareness of effective leadership skills.
3. Recognize barriers to effective listening and how to overcome them.
4. Identify the ingredients of effective meetings.
5. Explain the concept of group dynamics.
6. Define listening.
7. Improve your listening skills.
8. Conduct a formal meeting.
9. Use correct parliamentary procedures.
10. Apply Robert's Rules of Order in chairing a meeting.

Most of our daily lives we are involved in speaking and listening. What cannot be over emphasized is our inability to listen, digest, and interpret the ideas conveyed that ends in an understanding for some form of effectiveness. As a result, in your professional goals or future workplace environment, your ability to express ideas and information could be your key to success. For many people, the idea of communicating in the workplace as well as in public could be a horrifying experience. Thus, the following parts focus on the development of good listening skills for effective leadership in the workplace environment.

Effective listening, assimilating the verbal and non-verbal information presented by another person or persons, will contribute to your personal and professional success. You will be successful if you develop your listening skills because most people develop their listening skills, haphazardly. The difference between an untrained listener and someone who has developed his or her listening skills is like the difference between a hunt and peck typist, and someone who can type 60 words per minute. A skilled listener is more effective and saves valuable time because they listen the first time information is presented and use feedback or requests for clarification to ensure they understand the message.

Successful communication occurs when a mutual understanding develops from the speaker to the receiver. For example, I may disagree with a person who advocates "body-piercing," but if I want to *understand* body-piercing, I will have to carefully listen.

Listening Defined

Listening is defined by Random House Webster's Dictionary (1996)[1] as "to give attention for the purpose of hearing." Dumont & Lannon (1990)[2] define *listening* as "a complex and selective process of receiving, focusing, deciphering, accepting, and sorting what we hear." Timm & Stead (1996) reference *listening* as "the psychological processes that allow you to attach meaning to the patterns of energy 'heard'."[3] Listening may also be defined as (1) paying attention in order to hear; and (2) focusing and concentrating on the conveyed thoughts and ideas of a speaker for some form of your interpreting and reacting to what is said. The focal point in this definition is *"concentration"* because it is by far the hardest part of our listening abilities.

Abrams (1995) says, "Listening isn't a useless tool—it's a vital skill in effective communications and human relations. Listening isn't a trait; it's a quality. Listening improves the quality of communication, thus increases the potential for success."[4] All too often you may find yourself in situations where all you hear is a degree of complaining of individuals around you when you are trying to convey a message of importance. In a frustrating matter, you might just make one of these statements—"Did you hear me?" "I don't think you've heard a word I've said." "What's bothering you; your mind seems some place else? "Let me repeat what I've said because we simply aren't communicating;" or, "I heard you, but I thought 'you said . . . ' so, I did the assignment this way." Usually, our normal response might be that of "being on the defensive" and abruptly responding to an individual at one time or another in one or more of those examples cited. To minimize this behavior, our ability to be an effective listener begins with recognizing how poorly we are at listening to, not only ourselves, but also to those people around us. We need to develop an attitude that says, "listening is somewhat natural, and I'm going to get something out of this speaker's topic that I can use no matter what it takes!!"

So, with this determined effort on your part to focus on the speaker's topic when your mind begins to wonder, you should try mentally to repeat his or her other key points silently, and try to predict his or her outcome.

> "If you sincerely try to understand another person's point of view, then they become psychologically obligated to try and understand your point of view. Through actively listening to the other person, this psychological truth can be established."
>
> —Unknown

Ways to Improve Listening

Consider this question? Are these situational defensive responses outlined reviewed in the same way in the eyes of the "individual" giving the question and that of the "receiver" responding to the question? Although the answers may vary, Abrams's says that when you are asking probing questions, you may discover that the results will not only encourage effective communication but will yield to the discovery of new information. He recommends five stages of discovery and confirmation in the listening process: (See Figure 16.1).

While these stages may prove a success for you in the listening process, it comes to the point of your willingness—personally and professionally—to understand an individual's perspective and exhibit the care in wanting to listen, to understand and respond directly could be ultimate in your workplace success. In the workplace, listening is crucial to effective communication in human relations and in managerial skills. Listening improves these crucial qualities for the potential of your success. Many business successes rely specifically on listening; namely, meetings, oral reportings, teleconferencing, and sales talks as part of its everyday operation. Nothing could breakdown the listening process more than people in the workplace simply failing to listening to others. Not listening causes major problems in human relationships that could ultimately be extremely costly to businesses. Often times in business settings, because someone failed to listen, altered or ignored instructions, actions are not resolved, deadlines are missed, and many opportunities are lost. We know it is important as we communicate the end result to explain ourselves effectively, clearly, and convincingly to people on a subject or point of view they can convey to us. However, the opposite side of the formula is one missing link—*our ability to listen!!*

1. VALIDATE	I understand you correctly!!
2. STABILITY	If I ask you a question again or in a different manner, would I still get the same answer?
3. DETAIL	Do I have enough specific information to decide what to do?
4. COMPLETE	Is the information comprehensive enough for to act on?
5. CURRENT	Have you checked recently enough to ensure that nothing has changed?

Figure 16.1. Abram's Discovery and Confirmation Listening Stages.

The Business of Listening Strategies

To improve your listening skills, some suggested practices may be considered. Ted Pollock (1996) suggests four ways you could consider how to practice your listening skills from his "Most ignored list of communication skills of all—Listening"[5]:

1. *Look at the person who is speaking.* This is a good policy because anybody worth listening to is worth looking at. It helps you to concentrate on what he or she is saying, and by looking at him or her, you may capture certain nonverbal cues—a movement of the head, a narrowing of the eyes and perhaps a smile that helps to understand his or her meanings.
2. *Let the speaker know you are interested in what he or she is saying.* When you nod your head, he or she will know you agree. If he or she tells an amazing story, you smile! If he or she asks a question, you should react briefly!
3. *Provide positive feedback to the speaker.* If you are interested in what he or she is saying, show your reaction by leaning toward him or her! If something he or she says surprises you, raise your eyebrows! Through your body language, you could encourage a speaker to enhance a point, cite an additional argument or to elevate a particular point of view to a different level.
4. *Ask the speaker questions.* If you ask questions of the speaker, this demonstrates to him or her you are following what he or she is saying, and that you are interested in his or her remarks.
5. *Don't interrupt the speaker.* An audience is usually high complimented if you do not interrupt the speaker before he or she completes his or her thoughts. You are evenly more complimenting if you take the time to think through your question before asking. For example, you might try saying, "Could you expand a little on the point you made in your ending remarks about motivating people through merit incentives?" or "I would like to know which government agencies offer the kinds of information you just described." If you happen to engage in these type comments, not only are you demonstrating you are taking the speaker's remarks seriously, you are saying that you have adequately demonstrated good listening skills.
6. *Stick to the speaker's subject.* If you have the notion to change the speaker's topic/subject, do not try until he or she has completed his or her speech. When you seek to do so, it shows your courtesy to the speaker. Additionally, with this level of tolerance, perhaps there is a chance you will learn something from the speaker that you did not know.
7. *Quote the speaker to get your own point across.* You will find that when another person has finished talking—only then—should you repeat some of the things the speaker has said. To show the speaker that you have listened, you might, for example, introduce your remarks with something like, "You certainly defined the hypothetical problem when you said . . . " or, "Your comments on using middle management trainees sparkled a thought . . . ." While you may think of other situations, with these examples, perhaps a speaker can conclude that you listened to his or her ideas.

Effective communication is a two-way street. People in the business world spend many hours obtaining more information than perhaps in transmitting it. To effectively complete job tasks they need to have good listening skills. As customers, we know it is important for our needs and want to be met if a sales clerk listens. According to Tschohl (1994), sixty-eight percent of customers quit buying at a business because an employer appeared to be indifferent towards the customer. Perhaps this indifference is the only reality available to the customer, but it is clear that this does not mean the employee was not listening. A suggested premise here would be that it is far better for the employee to *appear* to listen and to *really* listen to the customer. A good reason for becoming a good listener is: *Listening flatters the customer!!!*

An important question to consider: "Is *listening* important in customer service?" We know the answer could be "Yes," but how can a customer's needs be satisfied unless you know what those needs and wants are?" Most of the time, you can learn what those needs and wants are by listening to the customer describe them.

Tschohl reported in his 1994 article, "Hot Service Tips: Just Listen!, that Arthur K. Robertson, a leading listening consultant, recommends a brief guide to better listening skills in his book, "Language of Effective Listening." He suggests that you remember his technique by recalling the word—**RELATIONS principles**. Each letter in the word represents a key word for better listening steps[6]:

R—"Relaxed tension."	That is, be alert.
E—"Eye Contact, without staring."	Look directly at the customer and listen carefully with a "listen" look on your face.
L—"Lean towards the customer."	This encourages the customer to continue.
A—"Active silence of two-to-three seconds after the customer apparently has finished talking."	This pause, while maintaining eye contact, tells the customer that you've listening and waiting for him or her to proceed.
T—"Tell me more."	Combine your facial expressions, gestures, nods and responses like "uh, hum, oh, and mmhmmm." To encourage the customer to talk more.
I —"Involved feedback."	Repeat some of the words the customer uses, thereby, involving yourself with the customer's feelings and thought process.
O—"Open posture."	Uncross your arms and look directly at the customer to indicate that you are receptive. Arms across your chest create the impression that you're closed to the person's words.
N—"Noise control."	In a noisy store or company environment, either eliminate the noise from your consciousness or ignore it.
S—"Squared off."	Face the speaker directly.

Figure 16.2. Robertson's Listening Principles—"Relations."

Enhancing Effective Listening Skills

Another reason to study good listening skills is that listening does not come too naturally. Many times, we realize that we would rather talk and practice our thoughts in wait of some response as soon as the speaker or a member in a group setting completes a thought or sentence. The latter could occur as the result of a business or organization forming a *"cross-functional work group"* that requires interpersonal, technical and technology skills. Rick Stamm, Consultant, of "The Team Approach," Lancaster, Pennsylvania, outlines competencies that group leaders and members usually bring to groups: (1) *Listening*—Good listening skills have many components; namely, listening to group members within—always finding fault! (2) *Speaking*—Clarity of expression; namely, having the ability to distribute or give to group members information; (3) *Dialog*—Give and take ideas from group members. Do members feel free to ask other group members their opinions, explain reasons for their opinions, or change their opinions as the dialog advances in the decision-making process? (4) *Providing Feedback*—A group's breakdown occurs, according to Stamm, when members are not able to be open enough to each other when they have problems; (5) *Group Goal Setting*—Each member of the group has the responsibility to make contributions and it's his or her right to be taken seriously; (6) *Meeting Behavior*—Each group member has the moral responsibility to attend meetings regularly—on time—, stay focus, and be an effective contributor to the decision-making process; and (7) *Conflict Resolution*—The leader, along with group members, should use a conflict in a positive manner in solving an idea or opinion in the decision-making process.

Listening Skills Benefits

Effective listening skills can be enhanced by considering two distinct benefits. *First*, you should build good rapport with others. *Second*, the knowledge that you gain helps the listener become more influential. According to the 1993 best selling writing "The Leader In You", by Simon & Schuster, "Nobody is more persuasive than a good listener," The question you could consider from this is: "Why is it that many of us are not effective listeners?" Could the answer be that we have been told to listen, or perhaps we have not been taught how to listen, or we have not made the attempt to try to listen.

Robert Reiss (1994) suggests in "Listen Up", three fundamental rules he discovered, as a student, of the listening process. He defines this process as: "The 'WIN' Rules:"

Rule 1: Watch Others. When someone is speaking, you should ignore the voice that gongs, "How can I respond to that?" "What should I say next?" Instead, you should watch others and focus on what they are saying and why they are saying it.

Rule 2: Inhibit Interrupting. As human beings, we have the inclination to interrupt a speaker if he or she takes too long to complete a statement. We feel that they are too boring, wasting our time, or we simply think we know exactly what they are going to say before they say it. So, our ultimate thought is—I'll just interrupt the speaker!! The first thing we should realize is that if we listening effectively, it shows our respect for others. Abraham Lincoln said, "To win a man to my way of thinking, I must first win his respect." Secondly, we need to realize that most people organize their ideas deductively so that their key information is at the end of their statement. If we clip off their statement, then perhaps we may never know what they were going to say.

Rule 3: Numerate Responses. After someone has spoken, you should want to make a list and even itemize the key points made. You may want to summarize what you heard the speaker say to confirm your level of understanding. To respond to such a spoken leader of this kind, perhaps it may be easy for you to try—"So, if I understand you correctly, your three key points are. . . ." This approach will give the spoken leader approval of your listening habits and decreases the likelihood of mis-communication.

After you have read "WIN" Rules, you might conclude, "I've heard these rules before, but they J-U-S-T don't work for me! Then the question becomes, Should I try these rules' concepts the next time I'm engaged in a "real intentionally listening" situation? The answer could become your first step to try to gain control by incorporating the three-rule concepts. Your second step is to interrupt. You may then discover that this step may be annoying to you and to that of the speaker. However, when you become aware of the importance of the exercise, you may just gain control and the habit could become much easier for you to challenge. If you should chose to practice these rules, perhaps one day you may experience someone saying to you surprisingly, "You are a great listener!!" Finally, you'll say, and perhaps it's true, you can "Listen Up" and conclude that YOU and the SPEAKER —— "WIN"

Barriers to Effective Listening Skills

Many corporate managers may state that getting through to people is the most difficult part of the job. As a result, promoting and encouraging good communication on the job is essential. So, these managers should be aware of barriers that could affect listening and how to overcome them. Such listening barriers of "not wanting to listen," "not liking the topic," "lack of patience," and "wanting to be somewhere else" may be experienced at one time or another by employees. As a measure of awareness of these barriers, managers must continually look for and practice avenues to keep the communication channels open with employees in the workplace. In doing so, managers should be informal and available to discuss problems if such occurs.

Listening Barriers Benefits

The most important element of communication in a diverse workplace is the art of focusing on the message—*really listening*—according to four high-ranking food service executives appearing in a 1995 panel, "Can We Talk: Overcoming Communication Barriers." A good understanding of an organization by executives, as well as employees, is a vital link to its success. Lee Channell (1995) says that in any organization "It is important that you become very good at understanding each other, understanding your needs, your perceptions, and your experiences." If this is done, that level of understanding can bring about the actions that you will need to put into place to bring customers "*into*" a business and "*back*" to a business. This kind of benefit could make it worthwhile from a business standpoint to be alert of the diversity of the workplace, as well as in the customer's world[7].

The diverse changing complexity in society continually brings change into the workplace. Virginia Rabata, Vice President, Human Resources, Marriott International, [Nation's Restaurant News, 1995) reports that diversity at Marriott has to do with more than gender. She noted that women and minorities account for 77 percent of Marriott's 100,000 persons in the U.S. workforce. Minority workers make up 40 percent of the workforce, with the largest group African Americans, 24 percent; Hispanics, 12 percent; and Asians, 3 percent. White female groups, as well as women who are included in all these categories account for 56 percent of the workforce.

As a workforce person, perhaps you will experience that a business's success is dependent upon on its manager's leadership and listening strengths. You will also learn that these managers spend many hours communicating with employees—one-to-one or one-to-group/team. Therefore, it is important for managers today and in the future in the culturally diverse workplace to: (a) keep and elevate the level of employee morale; (b) develop group/teamwork; (c) provide for on-going job development of individual employees; and (d) keep employees prepared for the readiness and acceptance of change.

Participation in Meetings and Conferences

Meetings and conferences have become increasingly vital in the workplace environment for most businesspeople to provide an opportunity for the exchange of ideas and information. Rather than interviewing each employee and colleague on a daily basis, a good manager today must maintain skills on how to handle the company's current, 21st century goals, major projects, and problems by organizing, calling, and arranging meetings. This may suggest to you that this trend of interpersonal relationships with others and the encouragement of group/teamwork will probably have you attending more meetings and conferences than you could ever imagine.

Productive Meeting Participation

Meetings consist of three or four individuals in a formal or less than formal setting. These individuals gather to exchange ideas, information, solve business problems, and to "perhaps" establish or clarify policies. Meetings may range from informal to formal meetings in which parliamentary procedures are strictly followed.

Formal and Informal Procedures

An official gathering of members in one area to transact business for a period of time where there is no interruption longer than a recess is defined as a "*Meeting*," says Darwin Patnode, *Robert Rules of Order*, 1989, 21). So, how you conduct a meeting depends on the occasion of the business your are associated with. You will discover that many business persons erroneously assume that conducting a meeting is easy and simple. In fact, meetings can involve a very difficult set of duties/tasks. Many times meetings are conducted needlessly, thereby, wasting too much money and time. Ruch & Crawford reported on these findings relative to meetings:

- About 12 million meetings are held every business day in North America at a cost of about $45 billion a year.
- Approximately one-third of those meetings are considering unnecessary by those in attendance, and 50 percent of any given meeting is considered a waste of time.
- About 80 percent of all meetings last less than 30 minutes; 35 percent for the exchange of information; and, 60 percent that could have been handled through other communication means.
- Executives spend an average of 16 hours per week in meetings, yielding a total of 21 weeks a year.
- Executives paid $45,000 a year earn an approximate $18,500 of that amount just for attending meetings.
- In the last 20 years, the amount of information crossing a single business desk has soared more than 600 percent[8].

Managers faced with any one of these findings may find the distractions to diminish quality management time if there is failure on their part to "control meetings" to be conducted.

Conducting a Meeting

Following are guidelines for business persons to consider in controlling the complex nature of conducting meetings:

Interaction meeting. Two key ingredients for people to adhere to in a meeting are interaction or involvement. Because of the sharing in the decision(s) process, they accept the challenge to seeing it succeed. However, meetings that are poorly-planned and poorly-attended may result in counterproductive bad decisions that could affect the progress of a business. So that you can make the best of these opportunities, here are some fundamental areas for setting up a meeting—*Plan* the meeting; *select* the participants; *prepare* an agenda; *determine* if formal or informal procedures are to be used; *prepare* materials/handouts to be distributed; *choose* a location and the seating arrangements.

1. *Plan the Meeting.* A key to conducting an effective meeting and to save yourself and the participants valuable time is to plan it thoroughly. You should develop an agenda covering the selected items, in logical order, to be achieved during the meeting. Finally, in the process of planning the meeting, you need to determine if the agenda is to be informal—an e-mail or a written announcement, or if the agenda is to be formal—a specified topic to be covered or a speaker to address an approved topic.
2. *Select the Participants.* Consider these factors in determining the number of participants for a meeting: (a) The chair or facilitator for the meeting; (b) The nature of the group(s) to be presented; and (c) The hierarchal level(s) of the participants.
3. *Prepare the Agenda.* As you prepare your meeting agenda, you should think about the "*time limit*" and the "*order of items*" to cover. Usually, a meeting that last over two hours will cause the productivity level of the participants to suffer. A general rule is that the agenda should be made available for participants two to five days in advance. This decision will lend participants sufficient time to prepare for and not prolong a meeting.

4. *Determine Informal/Formal Procedures.* If you decide the agenda is to be informal, a decision needs to be made if it is to be a written announcement via a referenced memo or letter or via e-mail for the meeting. If the decision of the meeting is to be formal, several items are suggested—(a) prioritize specific topics; (b) Attach materials/handouts that are relevant to topics; (c) Identify participants responsible for each topic; and, (d) Specify participants' approximate presentation time.
5. *Prepare Materials to be Distributed.* To avoid information overload for a meeting, it is advisable that you distribute only the materials participants will need in advance of the meeting. Often times if participants receive an over abundance of material, some confusion could very well generate as to what is important and what needs to be and should be omitted. Distributed materials should be made available for participants at least one to two weeks in advance of a meeting. If distributed earlier than one or two weeks, the likelihood of the materials being misplaced, forgotten, or lost by a participant could present a major problem for an important business decision.
6. *Choose a Location and Seating Arrangement.* The location for the meeting is essential in the planning stage. If the meeting is large—i.e., stockholder's meeting of a Fortune 500 company or an international company merger), perhaps an auditorium or lecture hall should suffice. On the other hand, if the meeting is small—i.e., local city or county business alliance or town hall forum, an obvious choice would be to choose a room of adequate size.

Meeting Seating Arrangements

For the meeting to be a success, the following four basic arrangements that are most widely used, according to Rader & Kurth (1988) are: *circular, rectangular, semicircular or U-shaped.* The advantage of using the circular arrangement is that an informal meeting can be most effective, thereby, leaving the leader with less control in the decision-making process. If you choose to use the rectangular arrangement, you may discover that the advantage is unique for formal meetings, leaving the leader with excellent control because communication is directed to the head of the table. Additionally, attendees seated opposite of each other usually find it to be an advantage to talk to each other—agree or disagree—in the decision-making process. The semi-circular or U-shaped arrangement appears to be ideal for a semiformal meeting, thereby, providing an excellent choice for (i.e., six to twelve attendees), with the leader having moderate control in the decision-making process[9].

Conducting a Videoconference Meeting

Videoconferencing has become popular in many business settings of the mid- 1990's with regards to bringing corporate executives and workers from many locations thereby, avoiding the expense of travel. Your ability to carefully plan a teleconference activity for the purpose of disseminating information for your company will require considering some suggested guideline strategies.

Provide instructional and technical details in advance of your conference. Anticipated problems could be with the audiovideo components which connects between the conference site, and should be corrected before the meeting and at the various locations of where meetings are to take place.

Provide written information/materials ahead of your conference meeting time. Participants should know the constraints of their participative part—the material of the topic to be covered and the time limits.

Provide clarity of computer graphics for your attendees. Computer graphics must be made simple for interpretation effectiveness, (e.g., professional, readable, have large size font, and relevantcy to the topic of the presentation).

Prepare your presentation carefully. If your presentation is unorganized, participants in different locations could experience miscommunication. As a result, the presentation process could be delayed. Participants should be encouraged to keep the presentation moving along with direct eye contact into the camera, speaking with clear pronunciation of words from prepared notes or from a teleprompter—if available—and or from cue cards maintained from the screen by an assigned official.

Provide for clarity and proper handling in transmitting remote calls from your conference sites. It is important for you to clarify confused or complex questions by your being able to intervene cautiously and diplomatically. The same applies if you experience a person in the audience calling in and the question is "off track" or "too long."

As the director or moderator, you may find participants will lose interest in the conference if you allow the conference to get out of control. As a result, participants may find it necessary to talk among themselves or leave the room where the conference is being conducted.

Parliamentary Procedure

Parliamentary procedure may be defined as a set of rules established or the purpose of conducting meetings, thereby, allowing for all participants in attendance to be heard in making decisions without a degree of confusion. So, why is *parliamentary procedure* important? These procedures are important because of the many years of this tested method of conducting business meetings and that of other likely public gatherings. You may ask the question: When was the beginning of these procedures? Parliamentary laws was the name given to the original customs and rules many years ago in conducting business in the English Parliament. *Parliamentary procedures* and *parliamentary law* are the same in one, along with *other rules of order* a business chair or facilitator may decide to adopt for the purpose of the meeting.

The making of this process into parliamentary law began in 1867 when Robert Martyn Robert, an army major, transferred to San Francisco, California where he and his wife joined groups to improve social conditions. As the result of early settlers' conflicting ideas, Robert began studying manuals on parliamentary laws, ultimately adopting his findings into rules that he and his wife used in group' and club' meetings. Over a period of time, he edited, refined, and revised the rules to what have become a very flexible, tested method for conducting business that has been enforced for many years.

Understanding Robert Rules of Order

Have you ever attended a meeting and was told the meeting would be very "brief" when, in fact, it lasted "one hour, and twenty-two minutes." Perhaps there is a solution—know "*Robert Rules of Order*!" As reported by some researchers, Robert Rules of Order have been used, underused, or unappreciated in many businesses over a period time. As a result, many of the chairs or facilitators assigned to conduct these businesses' meetings do not know the rules.

In order for you to meet the challenge and set the stage for conducting a first-time meeting, you should inform your participants that you will follow Robert Rules of Orders, followed by any current changes. Examples of recent changes include: (a) after an agenda is introduced, a motion related to it must be made before any discussion beings; (b) any general comments not related to the meeting is to be placed on hold and discussed later in the meeting; (c) the meeting agenda order and the business agenda are to be the same; (d) the adopted agenda is to be followed consistently, and (e) all participants should be familiar with the "basics" and "correct" use of the rules.

Principles of Parliamentary Procedure

In any business meeting setting, abiding by parliamentary procedure can make it easier for participants to work together effectively, to help groups achieve their goals, and to maintain time constraints to accomplish tasks. The chair or facilitator of the meeting has the responsibility to ensure that all participants attending a meeting are treated equally—e.g. equal rights, privileges and obligations. All participants must be assured of complete understanding of any issues, motions and questions raised during the meeting. Moreover, the meetings must be characterized by fairness, with every participant with the right to speak on any issue presented for a yield decision. Therefore, anyone who runs a business meeting would do well to become familiar with the requirements of parliamentary procedure manners.

A majority of businesses using parliamentary procedure follow a fixed order of business. A typical example may consist of the following:

1. Call to Order
2. Roll Call of Participants Present
3. Reading of Minutes of Last Meeting
4. Officers Reports
5. Committee Reports
6. Special Committee Reports
7. Unfinished Business
8. New Business
9. Announcements
10. Adjournment

It is important when called upon to conduct a formal meeting that you know how to carry a motion.

1. A person (other than the chair or leader) will state: I move that . . .
2. Another preson must second the move within one to five seconds.
3. The chair or leader says: It has been moved and seconded that . . .
4. The chair asks: Is there any discussion?
5. The chair allows discussion to take place.
6. The chair asks: Is there any more discussion? If not, then the chair asks: Are you ready to vote?
7. The chair says: All in favor, raise your hand (to count the number of hands). The secretary or minute taker will record the number of "yes" votes; then the number of "no" votes are counted (ask people to raise their hands) and recorded. Finally, the chair must ask: Are there any abstentions? Then, the number of abstentions are recorded as well.
8. If a majority says "yes," then the chair says: The motion is carried.

Make sure the motion is worded exactly and the votes are recorded accurately.

References

[1]Braham, Carol G., *Random House Webster's Dictionary*, 1996, 2 Ed., pgs. 386–387.
[2]Dumont, Raymond A., & John M. Lannon, *Business Communications*, 1990, pg. 644.
[3]Timm, Paul R. & James A. Stead, *Communication Skills for Business and Professions*, 1996, pg. 456.
[4]Abrams, Arnold, "The Art of Listening," *Insurance Sales*. 138(7): 62–66, 1995, July.
[5]Pollock, Ted "Listening Tips," *Production*. 108(2): 10. February, 1996.
[6]Tschohl, John, "Hot Service Tip: Just Listen! *American Salesman*, 39(12): 23–26, December, 1994.
[7]Channell, Lee, "Can We Talk: Overcoming Communication Barriers," *Nation's Restaurant News*, (29)(43):54–84, October 30, 1995.
[8]Ruch, William V. & Maurice L. Crawford, *Business Communication*, 1996, 449.
[9]Rader, Martha H. & Linda A. Kurth, *Business Communication for the Computer Age*, 1988.
Abrams, A. (July 1995). "The art of listening. *Insurance Sales*. 138, (7). 62–66.
Braham, C. G. (1996). Random House Webster's Dictionary, 386–387.
Channell, L. (October 30, 1995). Can we talk" Overcoming Communication Barriers, *Nation's Restaruant News*, 29 (43), 54–84.
Dumon, R. A. and J. M. Lannon, (1990). *Business Communications*, 644.
Pollock, T. (1996). Listening Tips, *Production*, 108, (2), 10.
Rader, M. H. and L. A. Kurth. (1988). *Business Communication for the Computer Age*.
Reiss, R. (1994). Listen Up.
Robert's Rules of Order. (1989).
Robertson's Listening Principles.
Ruch, W. V. and M. L. Crawford. (1996). *Business Communication*, 449.
Timm, P. R. and J. A. Stead. (1996). *Communication Skills for Business and Professions*, 456.
Tschohl, J. (December 1994). Hot Service Tip: Just Listen! *American Salesman*, 39, (12, 23–26).

• • • QUESTIONS • • •

1. Discuss why we have difficulty in listening.
2. What can you do to improve your listening skills?

3. What are some reasons for poor listening?
4. Select what you believe are four or five more important ignored listening skills that affect you in a speaking environment? Explain your selections.
5. Attend a business meeting of your choice. Summarize the "Relations Principles" you observed.
6. What are the major differences between good listening and bad listening?
7. How can a listener keep an open mind about the topic?
8. Describe the five stages that confirm the listening process.
9. Describe some of the duties required of the leader in preparing for a business meeting.
10. Why is the seating arrangement of tables and chairs important in conducting a meeting?
11. Attend a meeting for which you received the agenda in advance. How carefully is the agenda followed?
12. Attend a meeting and observe the participants. What participants were most influential in their presentations? Explain why.
13. The leader—not the participants attending a meeting—should determine the agenda. Discuss.

Applications

1. Study the behavior of the newspersons on the morning news shows—The Today Show; Good Morning America, This Morning, and CNN. How many of their problems result from poor listening?
2. Call the human resource department at your institution to ask what importance they place on good listening skills. Ask this question: Do they have any programs for training employees how to improve their listening skills? If the answer is "Yes," request any materials the institution provides for employees on listening. Write a short report.
3. Break into groups three or four. Assign an activity that requires group participation. Ask each member to observe each other's good and bad listening habits. Summarize your findings and present to the class.
4. Contact a college instructor in your major or minor who often speaks to businesses or community groups. Ask the person to identify the techniques he/she uses to help the audience listen and retain what has been said.
5. Your instructor will divide you into groups of three. The group is to discuss how they would change the graduation exercise at CSLA. Each person is to observe and write down the interaction among the group members.
6. Go to the Library and locate a copy of Robert Rules of Order. Read and outline the steps for motions.
7. Using OPAC, make a list of the current books on Listening.
8. Find a 1996 or 1997 article on Listening skills and share it with the class.
9. You have a meeting to set up based on the following information. What steps would you take to ensure that the meeting is successful?

   a) invite 13 people
   b) information to be discussed concerns impending layoffs

c) need to prepare 3 to 4 visuals on why Company is laying off people (statistics on growth, losses, etc.)

10. Go to an Academic Senate meeting (CSLA) which meets on Tuesdays from 1:35 to 3:30 p.m. in King Hall. Write a short report on what you observe. What things took place, etc? Share your report with the class.
11. Surf the World Wide Web for information on listening improvement. Which skills are perceived as important? Try to apply the listening techniques for three or five minutes. Summarize how much you could recall.

Mini-Case Scenarios

Case 1

Assume that you have been asked to chair a meeting on a topic that is currently splitting your institution and the community: whether the local Business Alliance should consider constructing a $4 billion coliseum adjacent to the institution's coliseum. You are aware that, with both sides represented, the discussion will be heated. The possibility of any type of consensus is unlikely. You have been given the key task of gathering information at the meeting, ending with a vote, and submitting recommendations to the institution's president and his committee officials. As part of your assignment, list ten to fifteen points as the meeting goes on. In preparation of your meeting, select your participants, prepare an agenda, prepare materials to be discussed/distributed, and target a time frame for successful closure.

Case 2

Group project. In groups of three or four, prepare an agenda for a meeting to discuss one current business issue (for example: Trends in Inflation vs. Federal Reserve Policy; Corporate Ethical and Legal Issues, workplace violence, sexual harassment, affirmation action, etc. Once you have prepared an agenda, elect a leader, and conduct your meeting. As a group, arrive at a consensus and submit a memo to your instructor.

Name ____ Date ______________

JEOPARDY QUIZ #16

1. The answer is: To give attention for the purpose of hearing.

   What is ____?

2. The answer is: A leading listener consultant.

   Who is ____?

3. The answer is: Daydreaming, lack of interest, dislike of topic, and desire to be elsewhere

   What are ____?

4. The answer is: An official gathering of members together to transact business at a definite time.

   What is ____?

5. The answer is: People who spend an average of 16 hours a week in meetings.

   What are ____?

6. The answer is: Circular, rectangle, semicircular, and U-shaped.

   What are ____?

7. The answer is: Officers' Reports, a Call to Order, New Business, and Reading of the Minutes of last meeting.

   What are ____?

8. The answer is: I move to adjourn the meeting.

   What is ____?

9. The answer is: A chairperson, a moderator, or a leader.

   What are ____?

continued

10. The answer is: Three items that must be recorded after a vote on a motion.

    What are ____?

PART V

EMPLOYMENT COMMUNICATIONS

CHAPTER 17

Career Day at
California State University, Los Angeles

Career Preparation

Objectives

Upon reading this chapter and doing the application exercises, you should be able to:

1. Determine your short term goals as they relate to your career.
2. Determine your long term goals as they relate to your career.
3. Describe the characteristics of an effective resume.
4. Determine a rationale for choosing references.
5. Analyze your attributes and assets relative to your career goals.
6. Discuss the types of skills needed for Work Force 2000.
7. Analyze your skills relative to Work Force 2000.
8. Critique your strengths as they relate to your career goal.
9. Critique your weaknesses as they relate to your career goal.
10. Analyze the job market as it relates to your career.
11. Distinguish differences between effective and ineffective resumes.
12. Write your own effective resume.

The culmination of your successful academic years of study and hard work will result in a Bachelor of Science degree in Business Administration or a Bachelor of Arts degree. What you must keep in mind is that you are the product that you are now selling. Companies hire prospective employees based on their qualifications and potential value. In other words, they want to know how well you fit their needs. For example, if a company is looking for a manager who has three years of experience in a management position, it is unlikely that the company will hire someone who does not have any management experience.

Just like you choose the central selling point to sell a product or service, now you must weigh what is your central selling point. Perhaps you soon will have a degree in hand and/or you do have some work experience; both of these qualities will be to your advantage. Before you choose a job, you will want to assess your short term goals and your long term goals to see how well certain jobs will fit into your career goals.

Short Term Goals

How does one assess his or her career goals? Well, you first must choose a career path. Consider the following questions:

1. Do you want to be a certified accountant?
2. Do you want to be a banker?
3. Do you want to be an economist?
4. Do you want to own your own business?
5. Do you want to be a programmer?
6. Do you want to be a manager?
7. Do you want to be a marketer of products?

Whatever your career goal which is a long term goal, you will have to take short steps which are short term goals to reach your ultimate goal. For example, a manager usually starts out in a manager trainee position. This person may stay in that job for three to four years and then advance to manager; later that person after three or more years may advance to a middle-level manager. After ten or more successful years in this position, he or she may then move up to an upper-level manager. If your goal was to be a Chief Executive Officer of a company, you can see how these short term goals will eventually lead to that top level position.

Long Term Goals

The point to remember here is that to reach long term goals you must be committed to working hard and to staying abreast of the technologies. The higher you move up in an organization, the more your interpersonal skills, decision-making skills, and presentation skills come into play. Years of experience, people skills, and advanced degrees are usually required for higher level positions in organizations. Along with the higher level positions come more pressures and challenges. Usually your work day does not end after eight hours of work; you sometimes come in early and leave late after all employees have gone home or you take work home. In deciding your short term goals and long term goals, it is best to talk to someone who is in the position you would want to have some day. That person can usually tell you the steps and strategies he or she used in reaching a career goal. As an example, suppose you want to own your own business someday. You would want to talk to a business owner so you can get a sense of time and efforts needed to be successful. Also, a visit to the Small Business Administration Office would be helpful as well. Whatever your qualifications are, they need to be presented in an effective resume format.

Developing an Effective Resume

For now, the focus is on you and your career preparation. You should start your job search as early as possible, perhaps six months to a year before you graduate. To start the job search, you need to begin by preparing an effective resume and letter of application. A resume is a persuasive summary of your qualifications for employment. Treece (1994) says: "A well-prepared resume should be a truly superior expression of your talents and background. It should be a credit to your creativity and to your ability to put ideas and information into convincing words." (p. 322) She further states that the most effective resumes are those that sell ability, talent, and potential as well as education and past experience.

Types of Resumes

Two kinds of resumes include the *chronological* resume which summarizes what you did starting with your most recent positions and going backwards. This traditional resume emphasizes degrees and dates and job titles. The *skills* resume is used to emphasize just that—your skills, not necessarily job titles or offices held. Figures 17.1 and 17.2 are examples of these two resumes.

Information that is included in the chronological resume is somewhat different from that in the skills resume; however, resumes commonly contain the following information:

Name, Address, and Phone Number
Career Objective
Education
Experience
Honors
References

Some other categories of information helpful to a human resources representative are:

Technological skills
Communication skills
People skills
Second language skills

MARI BALDWIN

5002 Stevens Street | Lone Star, TX 75955 | 903/656–2025

EDUCATION

B. S. in Business Education, June 1990, Tyler University, Tyler, TX 75869 (GPA in major 3.7/4.0 scale)

HONORS

Phi Beta Lambda
Beta Gamma Sigma
Dean's List each quarter

ACTIVITIES

Vice President of Phi Beta Lambda
President of Alpha Kappa Alpha Sorority

EMPLOYMENT

Teacher's Aide, Gilroy High School, Tyler, TX 75869
1994 to the present

Student Assistant, Advisement Center, School of Business and Economics; Tyler University, 1993 to the present

PALS Mentor, School of Business and Economics; Tyler University, 1992 to the present

REFERENCES

Dr. Betty Swanson, Assistant Professor, Department of Business Education, School of Education, Tyler University, Tyler, TX 75869

Mrs. Debbie DuFrene, Chair, Business Education Department Gilroy High School, Tyler, TX 75869

Mrs. Lin Aragon, Clerical Assistant, Advisement Center, School of Business and Economics, Tyler University, Tyler, TX 75869

Figure 17.1. A Chronological Resume.

Dr. Damicia Shane
4302 Paris Avenue, New Orleans, LA 70122

Career Objective

To serve as Director of Research and Sponsored Programs
(Write and critique grant proposals)

Education

Ph. D., Organizational Development and Communication,
Rutgers University, New York; June 1995

M. S., Curriculum and Development, Bowling Green State
University, Bowling Green, Ohio; May 1990

B. S., Public Relations, Kansas State University,
Manhattan, Kansas; June 1986

Writing Experience

Wrote proposal for Software Development for $75,000 which was funded by the Xerox Corporation

Wrote proposal for Minority Training Program for Web Sites for $130,000 which was funded by the Johnson Products Company

Wrote proposal for 30 executive workstations for Joyce Corporation for $240,000 which Corporation funded

Wrote proposal for Lock-Step Program for 30 Underprivileged High School Graduates for College Graduates Experience for $275,000 which was funded by the U. S. Department of Education.

Other Writing Experience

Have written over 25 articles which have appeared in refereed and nonrefereed journals

Have published two textbooks on Grantsmanship and Writing Proposal Strategies

Employment History

1992 to present
Assistant Director, Research and Sponsored Programs OFfice,
San Francisco State University, San Francisco, CA 94132

September 1990 to 1992
Researcher, Research and Sponsored Programs Office,
San Francisco State University, San Francisco, CA 94132

August 1986 to 1990
Proposal Writer and Analyst, Loyola Marymount University,
Los Angeles, CA 90082

References

Dan Padilla
Director
Research and
Sponsored Programs
Office
San Francisco State
University, San
Francisco, CA 94132

Robert Cephus Mays
Head, Writer and Analyst
Loyola Marymound Univ.
Los Angeles, CA 90082

Joseph Fang, Managing Editor
Los Angeles Times
Los Angeles, CA 90055

Dr. Marguerite P. Joyce
Professor and Coordinator
Business Writing Courses
CAL STATE UNIVERSITY, LOS ANGELES
5151 State University Drive
Los Angeles, CA 90032

Figure 17.2. A Skills Resume.

Where you place your *complete name, address, and phone number* on the resume, at the top or at the bottom, does not matter as long as you include them.

Although some authorities would suggest the omission of a *career objective,* it is essential to include. The career objective tells what you want to do and the level of responsibility. The objective helps to narrow down the guess work of exactly what job you are seeking. For example, your degree may be a Bachelor of Science in Business Administration; but you do have an option—management, accounting, finance, marketing, and Real Estate to name a few. Can you imagine how broad the job possibilities would be if you did not specify an objective?

You are wise for achieving higher *education.* The jobs of the future will require more and more education. You are to be congratulated if you have just earned or are about to earn a Bachelor's degree. Earning a degree is a real accomplishment. Your education may be your most important credential. If you attended a community college and/or received a degree, be sure to include that information. All courses that you took and certificates earned that are relevant to the job for which you are seeking should be listed as educational preparation.

Human Resource Management representatives differ as to the importance of including your grade point average (GPA). If you had to work to support yourself through college, your GPA may not be as high as you would like; but on the other hand, it should be fairly respectable. For example, some recruiters of Accounting graduates will not look at resumes of students who have a GPA below 3.0. The competition is very keen in this field.

You could include only your GPA in your major, your GPA for the last 50 hours taken, or use an average such as a B-. Use whichever grade is higher. Many Human Resource representatives do check credentials and will ask for transcripts. The important thing to keep in mind is to be truthful. Do your best in your course work. For example, if you saw the transcript of a medical doctor, a surgeon, who earned C's mostly, wouldn't you be skeptical of his or her ability to operate on you?

When listing your education, include specifics such as the complete name of the school, its address, and degree earned and the course work taken at the school.

EXAMPLE 1:

Master of Business Education, August 1978, Bowling Green State University, Bowling Green, OH 43402

EXAMPLE 2:

Associate of Science, Management, June, 1997, Pasadena City College, Pasadena, CA 91105.

EXAMPLE 3:

Bachelor of Science in Finance, May, 1995, Illinois State University, Normal, IL 61761

Course work Related to Finance:
Principles of Finance
Legal Environment of Business
Statistics I
Business Report Writing
Business Communication Fundamentals
Business Presentations
Finance Theory
International Business

EXAMPLE 4:

Bachelor of Science in Accounting, California State University at Los Angeles, Los Angeles, California 90032
40 hours in accounting
12 hours in business communication
8 hours in speech

Experience in related positions is another important criterion in career preparation although some students will complete degrees with no work experience. Any work experience is indicative of your ability to seek and hold a position. Include whatever work experience you have as well as volunteer work. Any experience, including military experience, that shows leadership skills or your ability to work with people is highly valued. If you lack work experience, then you should stress your educational preparation.

Honors and awards. In this section of your analysis, you should list any extracurricular activities, including memberships and offices held in professional organizations as well as offices held in college clubs or organizations. For example, you can list any fellowships or scholarships you have received or any other acknowledgments that show leadership skills or that single out your competitive ability, perserverance, and ambition. Some examples include:

Dean's List for 1996
Alpha Kappa Alpha Scholarship for 1995
Varsity Letter in Volleyball

References. People who can attest to your work habits, skills and abilities should be used as a reference. The name of a reference should not be included in a resume without first getting the permission of that person to list him or her as a reference. Present or former supervisors, professors from whom you have taken 2–3 courses, or professionals are ideal references. Do not list friends or relatives as a reference. You should list three or four references.

Human resource representatives' views vary regarding listing references in a resume. One thing is for sure, if a decision needed to be made quickly regarding hiring someone for a position, the person who listed his or her references would have the advantage. For each reference, you should include his or her name, title or position, organization, complete address, and phone number. If you have a placement file in the placement office at your campus, be sure to include that address.

Some examples of listing references follow:

Dr. Ralph Spanswick, Professor
Accounting Department Chair
California State University, Los Angeles

348 Fine Arts
5151 State University Drive
Los Angeles, CA 90032
213/343–2830

or

Dr. Ralph Spanswick, Professor and Chair of Accounting, California State University, Los Angeles, 348 Fine Arts, 5151 State University Drive, Los Angeles, CA 90032.

Figure 17.3 presents a listing of the numerous ways to locate a job.

Research indicates that the quickest way to get a job is to get a referral from someone you know who already works for that particular company.

How do you know what company you want to work for? Well, you need to relate your job choice to the skills you want to do every day and the company that matches your skills to the job requirements rather than matching the job requirements to your skills. The job you choose should offer a comfortable salary and opportunities for growth and advancement within the company. You should set your salary goals based upon your career goals. Another factor to keep in mind is the work environment.

Competitive Skills

Many applicants may appear equally qualified, but some skills that will help in decision making are technological, communication, teamwork, and specialty skills.

Technological skills. As a prospective college graduate, you should know how to use technology such as MacIntosh, IBM or IBM compatible personal microcomputer and software programs. Ability to use a word processing, spreadsheet, and graphics software is paramount; you should have experience using E-mail and accessing on-line databases as well as using the Internet. Be sure to state the operating systems you have used such as DOS or Windows and the names of the software programs such as Excel, Microsoft Word and Harvard Graphics or Powerpoint.

Referral (by employee, private employment agency, search firm, friend, contact)
Telephone call or Walk-in cold call
Standard resume and cover letter
College Placement Office
Help-wanted Ads
Previous experience with employer
Information interview

Figure 17.3. Job Sources.

Communication skills. You will be exhibiting your speaking and writing skills on a continual basis. In your interview, the interviewer will glean some attributes about you just from how you dress, speak, and how well you have prepared your resume and letter of application. Any speech courses you have taken, this business communication class, as well as other classes in which you exhibited your presentation skills will affirm your commitment to enhancing your speaking and writing skills. While speaking and writing skills are sometimes referred to as "soft skills," they are equally as important as your specialty skills, "the hard skills," if not more important. Specialty skills are not much good if they cannot be communicated.

People skills. Human resource representatives continually stress the importance of being able to work with all kinds of people. The work place is culturally diverse with many different attitudes, beliefs, and work ethics. Showing respect for all people regardless of their backgrounds will certainly help in fostering good human relations. As more and more teamwork is carried out in organizations, having good people skills will make a difference in working with and through people to accomplish tasks and organizational goals.

Second language skills. If you asked the students in your classroom, how many of them speak a language other than English, practically all of them would raise their hands. Many companies are looking for prospective employees who speak a foreign language in addition to English. If you speak Chinese such as Mandarin or Cantonese or Spanish or Japanese or German, you are a step ahead of the competition. The ability to communicate across all cultures is a definite plus.

Job Search Strategies

When you are close to graduation, the pressure is on to find a full-time position. Just like you are eager to find a good job, so are employers eager to find the right match for the company. In fact, United States corporations spend roughly $11.5 billion annually to find the talent they need (McKendrick 1986) You just have to keep searching until you find the employer that is looking for YOUR skills, qualifications, and values.

Where do you look for employment? You can start your search for jobs by keeping abreast of the business world. Read as many business magazines as you can on business and financial news or you may want to subscribe to a professional journal in your field. Some common business magazines include *Fortune, Forbes, Business Week, Harvard Business Review, and Business Horizons. The Business Forum*, published by the School of Business and Economics at California State University at Los Angeles, can be obtained at your campus library or in Room 811 Simpson Tower at CSLA.

You can obtain information about the future of specific jobs in *The Dictionary of Occupational Titles* which is written by the U. S. Employment Service and the *Occupational Outlook Handbook* which is written by the U. S. Bureau of Labor Statistics. Another source is the employment publications of Science Research Associates. You should consider subscribing to the professional journals in your profession and talking to your professors who can give you tips on where to find jobs. Many of them do consulting and could be a valuable source for knowing where the job opportunities are.

Bovee and Thill (1995) cite a recent survey by the American Management Society indicates that 70 percent of the managers interviewed view employee referral as a useful source of job candidates. Personal contacts appear to be the prime source of jobs for job seekers, regardless of whether they have just graduated from college of have been out of school for several years.

Analyze yourself in terms of facing a competitive environment versus a teamwork environment or your role and relationships. For example, does the company have levels of advancement within a job classification? Where does your job fit in the organizational structure? What are the reward structures within the company?

Lastly, where do you want to work? Are you willing to relocate and if so, where? Are you comfortable with making a relocation decision? Have you visited other regions of the United States? Do you know what to expect in terms of weather conditions, housing costs, natural disasters, school systems, social and cultural events? When you are weighing salary offers, you should consider trade offs in terms of fringe benefits and cost of living in different regions of the United States. Figure 17.4 shows a map of the different regions of the United States.

Frequently, you are offered a job that requires your undergoing training at the company's headquarters in a distant state and after training, assume that position in still another region of the United States. For example, you could be recruited in Los Angeles for a position at State Farm Insurance, be sent to the headquarters in Bloomington, Illinois for training, and later assume the full-time permanent position in Texas.

Suppose you were offered a salary of $30,000 and no health or dental coverage? Would you take it? What if you were offered a salary of $25,000 with health and dental coverage? Would you take that? If you have a family and small children, perhaps the lower salary might be ideal because you would have the health and dental coverage for your family.

Figure 17.4. A Map of the United States.

If you like social and cultural events, you would want to be in a city that offered a variety of events or events at least within driving distances. If you like Broadway plays, the New York area is great.

Housing costs are another important factor to keep in mind in relocation. Naturally, the West coast area, California in particular, has extremely high cost housing. Of course, if you are willing to commute long distances, you can find affordable housing in the Los Angeles area. Texas has moderate cost housing, and North Carolina has low cost housing. Every city has its "Beverly Hills" area, though.

Weather conditions are not always ideal in various parts of the United States. If you have never driven in snow or on ice, it can be a frightening experience. If you have never experienced an earthquake, it also can be frightening. Other regions have natural disasters as well whether it is a tornado, hurricane, fires, or flooding. No region is free of disasters.

If you like the four seasons of the year, than perhaps Southern California is not the place; the weather there is really nice all year long for the most part. States like Illinois and Virginia have the four seasons—fall, winter, spring, and summer.

School systems are another consideration particularly if you have children. Usually if you are relocating, a real estate agent can work with you regarding housing and the various school systems in the area.

Once you have made up your mind that you are willing to relocate, you can indicate this on your resume. The job search process requires your analysis of what you want in a job and the responsibilities and opportunities that come with the job you are seeking.

Analyzing Yourself

At this step in your job search, you need to do an audit of yourself and what you have to offer a company. For example, suppose you want a position as a beginning accountant for a large firm. You could start your search by looking in the classified ads in your local newspaper; look for accountant positions. Try to match your skills, what you can offer, to what the ad lists as requirements. If the ad lists requirements which you do not have other than work experience, perhaps you can take courses before you graduate to strengthen your skills.

In analyzing yourself, you also need to look very closely at what are your strengths and your weaknesses. If you were asked what are your strengths, you could rattle them off without much hesitation. Naturally, your strengths are those areas in your major or other courses at which you excel in addition to your personal attributes. For example, for all of the courses in which you earned A's and B's, you could say there are areas in which you show great strengths. On the other hand, for all of the courses in which you earned C's or below, you would classify these areas as your weakness. As an example, suppose you do not like to give oral presentations; rather than say you do not like to do this, you could turn this weakness into an opportunity. You would then say, "Giving oral presentations is an area in which I am continually trying to improve."

You should start a placement file in the Career Planning and Placement Center on campus. The services are free and provide a host of opportunities to help you sharpen your job-search skills. If you are unsure of your personality matching some job responsibilities, you could take the Myers-Briggs Indicator Test or you could take the Strong Interest Inventory Test. Both tests are designed to help you better understand yourself and your traits. The Center also offers internships and cooperative education, student employment, career counseling and mock interviews, and has many books on job hunting and business opportunities in its Library.

Analyzing the Job Market

One important aspect in the job search process is that the organization will offer you sufficient opportunity once you are hired to warrant your accepting the job offer. Here is where you have to show that your qualifications match those of the employer and the job requirements. You should not accept the first job that is offered you; you need to use care in accepting job offers, particularly since you do not want to develop a reputation of short term employment. Should you have to accept a job that is not ideal, resign yourself to the fact that it is just a stepping stone to that more ideal job later on. If you accept a job and later resign after a short period of time because you found that ideal job, that short term employment history does not look favorable on your resume in regards to your commitment to a company. Bear in mind that a company makes a considerable investment in you once you are hired in the form of training.

You should check the classified section of the newspaper, look at professional journals that contain job opportunities, and look at job announcements to see what kinds of jobs are available for someone with your skills. Some other sources that may help are as follows:

Wall Street Journal Employment Weekly
L. A. Times (Sunday edition)
College Placement Annual

Salary Expectations

Many prospective college graduates do not have a clue as to what salary they should expect on their first full-time job. Your spending some time looking at ads in the newspapers and placement annuals will give you some idea so you can make comparisons among the jobs. Also, you could talk to professors in your major to get their views of what would be a comparable starting salary based on their experience and their contacts.

Sample Resumes

Examples of resumes in Figures 17.5, and 17.6 are provided to give you ideas for preparing your own. You should design your own resume to fit each particular job for which you are applying. This "custom-fit resume is called a targeted resume" as stated by Bovee and Thill (p.362). The targeted resume lists related capabilities and achievements after the career objective which show evidence of your capabilities.

When writing your resume, be sure to include all of the important categories as discussed earlier. Remember to tailor your resume to a particular ad or position announcement. Once

Patricia Mays
1228 South 17 Street
St. Joseph, MO 64501

Job Objective: To secure a position as a manager in an upscale clothing store

Education: B. S. in Administrative Management, Missouri Western College, St. Joseph, MO 64501, July 1973

Paid for 75 percent of my college education

Have a heavy concentration in communication courses and management courses

Work Experience: Sales Clerk, Einbender's Clothing Store, St. Joseph, MO, summers of 1970, 1971 and 1972

Cashier, Hirsch's Department Store, St. Joseph, MO, June 1966 to August 1969

Travel Experience: Visited clothing shops along the Champs Elyssee in Paris, France, in 1981

Honors: Was on Dean's List every semester during college years

References: Dr. Tom Haynes, Chair of Management Department, Missouri Western College, St. Joseph, MO 64507 816/279–7000

Mrs. Beatrice Hayes, Designers' Dress, Einbenders, St. Joseph, MO

Mrs. Mary Mays, Bookkeeper, Hirsch's Department Store, St. Joseph, MO

Figure 17.5. Resume of Student with Education as Major Selling Point.

you have tailored your resume to the position requirements, you are ready to begin analyzing what you want to say in your letter of application which is discussed in Chapter 18.

Zachary Xavier Mays'
Qualifications for Convention Manager
in the Los Angeles Area

13353 Lone Hill Avenue
San Dimas, CA 91765

Career Objective

To be the top sales convention manager for a major hotel

Capabilities

Plan and organize large scale events

Manage publicity for major events

Establish and maintain financial controls for major events

Hire employees and coordinate employee work tasks

Supervise staff for various convention events

Maintain effective and professional public relations with convention guests and workers

Achievements

Booked and supervised coordination of a 5,000 participants convention at the Pasadena Hilton, Pasadena

Planned and coordinated Executives Seminar for 50 guests from around the world at the Westin-Bonaventure Hotel in Los Angeles

Managed publicity for two conventions going on simultaneously at the Doubletree Hotel in Pasadena

Organized the 1993 Regional Convention of Property Fund Raisers in Marina del Rey, California at the Doubletree Hotel

Served as the Program Chair for the Western Regional Convention of the Association for Business Communication in 1994 at the Holiday Inn Crowne Plaza in Redondo Beach, CA

Employment History

Sales Manager, Doubletree Hotel, Pasadena, CA 1995 to present

Sales Clerk, Doubletree Hotel, Marina del Rey, CA 1983 to 1995.

Sales Representative, Holiday Inn Crowne Plaza, Redondo Beach, CA, 1980 to 1983.

References

Mrs. Marilyn Atchue, Convention Manager, Holiday Inn Crowne Plaza, Redondo Beach, CA

Mr. Kiang Sung, Manager, Doubletree Hotel, Marina del Rey, CA

Miss Kian Abdoulla, Manager, Westin-Bonaventure, Los Angeles, CA

Figure 17.6.

References

McKendrick, J. E. "Managers Talk About Careers," MANAGEMENT WORLD, September-October 1986, 18–19.

Bovee and Thill, 1995 BUSINESS COMMUNICATION TODAY, 4th Edition, Mc-Graw Hill, 332, 352.

Treece, M. (1995). SUCCESSFUL COMMUNICATIONS FOR BUSINESS AND THE PROFESSIONS, Allyn and Bacon.

Questions

1. What are the characteristics of an effective resume?
2. What should be your guide in selecting people to serve as a reference?
3. What are the attributes you presently possess?
4. What types of skills will Work Force 2000 need?
5. Do you feel you will be a part of Work Force 2000?
6. What are your strengths relative to finding a job?
7. What are your weaknesses relative to finding a job?
8. Are you a people-oriented peson? Why or why not?
9. What are the job opportunities in your major?
10. What type of job do you want after graduation?
11. What would be the ultimate job you would like relative to your profession?
12. Are you willing to relocate? Why or why not?
13. What interest you more about a job—money or enjoyment? Why?

Applications

1. Choose two classified ads in your major and determine how your present skills meet the job requirements.

2. Interview two people in your field and ask them what changes have occurred in the field since they graduated from college?
3. Look up your profession in the OCCUPATIONAL HANDBOOK and write a paragraph on information that you find pertinent to you as you plan your career.
4. Visit the Career Center and find four posted job openings; compare the communication skills needed in each of the jobs. Then write a paragraph on the skills that are required.
5. Go to the Career Center and view a videotape on resume writing or interviewing.
6. Prepare your resume in the skills format.
7. Go to the Career Center and start a placement file; bring evidence of your having done so to your instructor.
8. Prepare your resume in the chronological format.
9. Interview two people in your field and ask them what salary you should expect in a beginning full-time job.
10. Select a classified ad for a full-time job in your field, one you would like upon graduation; then write a resume based on the ad. Keep your ad for use in Chapter 18.
11. Find the DICTIONARY OF OCCUPATIONAL TITLES and look up your profession. What information did you receive?
12. Visit an office print store or a print job and ask what stationery is available for writing resumes.
13. Go to a store like Kinko's and find out what is the cost for typesetting your resume.
14. In reference to #8, experiment with 3 to 4 different fonts in preparing your resume.
15. Prepare your resume and ask another person to critique it in terms of its effectiveness.

Name ______________________________ Date ____________

JEOPARDY QUIZ #17

1. The answer is: Targeted, skills, and chronological.

   What are ______________________________?

2. The answer is: A typical resume for recent college graduates.

   What is ______________________________?

3. The answer is: A specific statement regarding your career goal that is listed on the resume.

   What is ______________________________?

4. The answer is: A document that lists your work experience, skills, and abilities.

   What is ______________________________?

5. The answer is: The resume and letter of application.

   What is ______________________________?

6. The answer is: A book that lists job titles, salaries, and future job growth.

   What is ______________________________?

7. The answer is: Information that can go at the top or bottom of a resume.

   What is ______________________________?

8. The answer is: A former professor or past or present employer.

   Who is ______________________________?

9. The answer is: Punctual, hardworking, and pleasant.

   What are ______________________________?

continued

10. The answer is: A Bachelor of Science degree in Management or a Master's degree in Business Administration.

    What are ____?

CHAPTER 18

Career Day
at
California State University, Los Angeles

Letters of Application and the Interview Process

Objectives

Upon reading this chapter and doing the exercises, you should be able to:

1. Write an effective letter of application.
2. Gain a sense of the purpose of the letter of application.
3. Determine the best strategy for having a successful interview.
4. Use the correct writing style for writing a letter of application.
5. State your strengths relative to requisite employment skills.
6. Develop an understanding of the importance of honesty and truthfulness in the employment process.
7. Discuss the types of employment interviews.
8. Develop answers to frequently asked questions in an interview.
9. Write different types of employment application letters.
10. Determine your weaknesses relative to requisite employment skills.
11. Develop an effective response to illegal questions you may be asked in an interview.
12. Recognize the impact that personal appearance has in the employment interview.
13. Determine a rationale for selecting people to serve as a reference.

The resume and the letter of application should be sent together as a package. Although the resume is a printed summary of a person's education, skills and abilities, and work history, the letter of application is a persuasive letter designed to stimulate the reader's interest in you enough to get you an interview. You want to convince the reader that you satisfy the organization's job requirements. Since this is a persuasive letter, you would use the AIDA approach, the elements of persuasion.

Letters of Application

Purpose of the Letter of Application

The letter of application is a form of advertising; you are selling your skills and abilities. The purpose of the letter of application is to convince the reader to grant you an interview. In writing the letter of application, remember the focus is on the reader, not you. So you want to write with the reader in mind. In other words, show how the reader is going to benefit by employing you.

Preparing the Letter of Application

In preparing the letter of application, you want to first get the reader's attention, stimulate the reader's interest, create a desire in the reader to want to interview you, and then solicit the reader's action—to call you for an interview.

Since the letter of application is about you, it is natural to use the word "I," but do not overuse "I." You can use a combination of the you-approach and "I," "me" or "my" or use a variety of sentences so that the word "I" is not pervasive. Consider the following sentences; which is more reader-centered?

I have five years of experience as a sales manager.
Your Company can benefit from my five years as a sales manager.

I have a Bachelor of Science degree in finance.
My Bachelor of Science degree in finance has equipped me with the knowledge to successfully maintain your financial portfolios.

I have ten years of leadership ability.
Ten years with Harper and Row Company developed leadership ability.

In writing the letter of application, be honest and truthful about your skills and abilities. Do not misrepresent any information. Your letter of application should be original; do not copy one from a textbook. The samples provided in this chapter are examples for you to use in constructing your own letter of application.

Stress your strengths and subordinate your weaknesses. Do not mention unpleasant work conditions in past or present jobs; do not ask for sympathy or apologize for taking the reader's time in reading your resume and letter of application. Do not be overly aggressive or presumptuous. The parties and actions involved in your job search include you, the company, your requesting an interview, and the company asking you to come for an interview.

The AIDA approach is a four-step process. Your first goal is to get the reader's *attention*. You can use a question as an attention getter. For example, "May I work for you as a Senior Buyer and increase your sales goals for the Designer Dress Department?" Such a beginning at least gets the reader to think about what his or her answer might be. Or, you could use a declarative sentence. For example, "I would like to contribute to your further progress and growth as an Accountant for Taylor Corporation." Still another opening statement might be "As a college graduate, I can offer Irvine Company maturity, energy, and flexibility in handling your executive accounts." Notice that in each of the examples, the type of position applied for is mentioned.

In creating reader *interest*, you need to stress what you have done in concrete terms; use good vivid examples. Some examples are:

> My college education has prepared me to handle accounts receivable, accounts payable, and reconciliations.
>
> While supervising the student assistants in the Advisement Center, I coordinated efforts to streamline procedures for Graduation Applications and Reinstatement Petitions.
>
> Earning "A's" in Speech, Business Communication, and Business Presentations and Delivery have sharpened my communication skills; I am able to communicate and interact successfully with all people.

In creating reader *desire*, your focus should be on how you can benefit the company. What can the company gain from hiring you rather than someone else? Here is where you can stress your strengths. Several examples are shown below:

> In my present position as a Systems Analyst, I have implemented new procedures for troubleshooting which have decreased downtime; I can offer your Company this same dedication.
>
> Baldwin Corporation can benefit from my ten years in Marketing Management; I can do your market analysis and product promotion with the same enthusiasm.
>
> My formal classwork at California State University, Los Angeles and an internship at IBM has added to my ability to analyze and solve business problems and to interact with customers and employees. I can bring these same skills to work for your company as a Senior Account Executive.

The main idea in the persuasive letter is, of course, to request the reader's *action*. Several examples of closing sentences are given for your review.

> I would appreciate an interview at your convenience. Please call me at 213-343-2863 after 4 p.m.

> So that we can talk about putting my skills and abilities to work for your Company, please call me at 818/962–1124 to arrange an interview at your convenience.
>
> Please write to me at the address above or call me at 504/288–1533 to arrange an interview. I am excited about the possibility of working for your Company as a Personnel Specialist.

Figures 18.1, 18.2, 18.3 contain letters of applications. Figure 18.4 is a letter of application that is accompanied by the ad to give you an idea of how to tailor your letter of application to the job requirements.

The Interview Process

You want your skillfully written resume and letter of application to result in an interview. When the two-part package accomplishes its purpose, you will be asked to come for an interview. The interview is a formal meeting in which the employer and the applicant ask questions and exchange information to learn more about each other. Bare in mind that most organizations will interview an applicant several times before extending a job offer. The applicant will likely be interviewed by several levels of supervisory personnel. The interview provides a closeup view of the job applicant. The interviewer will be able to glean a number of your talents and abilities as well as your ability to listen and communicate. When the competition is very keen, you may even be asked to write a letter. Of course, you will want to ask if a microcomputer is available so that you can input your letter to show your productivity. You want to give the interviewer a way to differentiate you from the other candidates and at the same time demonstrate your strengths and skills.

Types of Interviews

When you are invited by a company to come for an interview, you may be interviewed in a number of ways. You may talk to human resources department representatives(s), several potential colleagues, and your potential supervisor as well as others.

Types of interviews include the panel interview, the directed interview, the open-ended interview, the stress inteview, the behavioral interview, and the situational interview. Each type of interview is designed to serve a certain purpose; therefore, each type will be discussed in detail.

The panel interview is used quite frequently. Its purpose is to see how the applicant responds to several interviewers asking the applicant questions during one session. These interviewers will be trying to determine based on your answers, attitudes, and actions whether you are a good fit for the company. How you think, express yourself, and listen will help them decide how likely you are to get along with your potential colleagues. According to Bovee and Thill (1995), they state:

"Your best approach during this round of interviews is to show interest in the job, related your skills and experience to the organization's needs, listen attentively, ask insightful questions, and display enthusiasm." (p. 382)

465 Fairview Avenue
Arcadia, CA 91007
July 11, 1997

LA Times
Employment Office
Times Mirror Square
Los Angeles, CA 90053

Ladies and Gentlemen

My experience and abilities parallel the requirements for the Business Analyst position listed in the March 30, 1997, issue of the *LA Times*.

I have three years' experience as a Computer Analyst for Jet Propulsion Laboratory (JPL). My duties include business analysis, testing, and maintenance of advertising billing systems. My numerous presentations and workshops to staff at JPL have enhanced my communication and interpersonal skills.

Mainframe and personal computer experience, along with a Bachelor of Science degree in Computer Information Systems, will enable me to do an effective job at the *LA Times*. During my early college years, I worked part time at the *Star-News* office.

I am personable, articulate, and energetic and would appreciate the opportunity to talk to you. I am willing to come for an interview at your convenience. Please call me at 310/684-1554.

Sincerely

Kim Vargas

Kim Vargas

Figure 18.1. Sample Letter of Application.

2600–71 Street
Des Moines, IA 50433
August 6, 1997

Mr. Larry Mays
Mays Electronics
Highway 36
St. Joseph, MO 64509

Dear Mr. Mays

Congratulations on receiving the Most Promising Small Business Award! Your electronics firm is one I would like to be a part of. Do you anticipate an opening for a management trainee?

I have been employed for the last two years as a part-time manager at Computers-R-Us. I also will receive my Bachelor of Science degree in Administrative Management from California State University, Los Angeles, in June 1997.

My work experience includes my doing employee training, opening and closing of the store as well as making bank deposits. I am bilingual, so I have the ability to communicate across cultures.

I offer you excellent communication skills, decisiveness, and leadership. Please allow me a chance to tell you how I can put my skills and abilities to work at Mays Electronics.

You may call me at 816/279-9795 after 5 p.m. to arrange an interview at your convenience. I look forward to hearing from you.

Sincerely

Binn Ghandi

Binn Ghandi

Figure 18.2. Sample Unsolicited Letter of Application.

515 "L" Street
Atchison, Kansas
September 4, 1997

Providence Seattle Medical Center
P. O. Box 34008
Seattle, WA 981224–1008

Attention: Human Resources Department

Ladies and Gentlemen

Your position for a Central Service Evening Shift Manager in the March 30, 1997, issue of the *LA Times* prompted me to apply. I am well trained in surgery instrument processing and distribution.

My six years as a head surgery instrument processor at Atchison Methodist Hospital Center have well prepared me to assume a management position. In my present position, I have to give many workshops in surgery instrument processing and materials management.

I am quite familiar with hospital operations and have honed my problem-solving and communication skills. I have a Bachelor of Science degree in Hospital Administration. I have attended four special seminars on Surgical Instrument Processing in Washington, D.C.

May I have an opportunity to discuss my qualifications with you at your convenience? I can be reached at 913/576-1819.

Sincerely

Joseph Young

Joseph Young

Figure 18.3. Sample Letter of Application.

10920 Bramblebush Terrace
Boise, Idaho 74113
August 11, 1997

Educational Insights, Inc.
16941 Keegan Avenue
Carson, CA 90746–1307

Attention: Human Resources Department

Ladies and Gentlemen

Your advertisement for a General Ledger Supervisor in the March 30, 1997, issue of the *LA Times* caught my attention. I have the proven skills you are seeking.

I have just received a Bachelor's of Science degree in Accounting from California State University at Los Angeles with an emphasis in cost accounting. I have also passed three parts of the CPA exam. My experience also includes three years as an accountant in a bank.

My proven skills in preparing and analyzing financial statements, doing audits and reconciliations fast and accurately will serve me well as a General Ledger Supervisor at Educational Insights, Inc. I am especially proud of having received the Outstanding Accountant Award in my division.

I offer you experience, dedication, personableness, and resourcefulness.

Please call me at 708/969-9568 to set up an appointment at your convenience. I am excited about the possibility of becoming a General Ledger Supervisor at Educational Insights, Inc.

Sincerely

Tia Ming

Tia Ming

ACCOUNTING
★General Ledger Supv.★
Educational toy & games mfr. seeks exp'd Acctg. Supervisor w/exp in preparation & analysis of Fin'l statements, inventory cntrl, & standard cost acctg. Direct staff of 4. Acctg deg & proficiency w/excel required, Public acctg exp. a +. Casual, non-smoking environ. Please forward resume w/salary hist. (resumes without salary histories will not be considered) or apply in person to:
HR, Onsight, Inc., 1000 Noname Ave, Somewhere City, CA 00001 Fax: xxx–xxx–xxxx.

Figure 18.4. Sample Letter of Application with Ad.

The directed interview is a screening device; the employer controls the interview by asking a series of questions of the interviewee. The interviewer writes down the applicant's responses. The series of questions are usually asked within a set time frame. This method is rigid and usually is not a good determinant of a prospective employee's personal qualities.

However, the open-ended interview is a method designed to make the applicant feel relaxed. This type of interview is used to encourage applicants to talk freely; an applicant's personality type can be assessed using the open-ended interview.

The stress type of interview is designed to see how the applicant operates in certain environments. You are purposely asked irritating or unsettling questions to see how you would respond. Or you are asked to do something on the spot. You could be asked to step into the interviewer's office, and he or she says nothing for five minutes. How do you respond? You can rephrase the irritating or unsettling questions into requests for information and then respond. If you are applying for a sales job or teaching job, you must have the ability to sell a product on the spot or teach a mini lesson on the spot. These tasks are attributes of the trade. When there is silence, just keep a smile on your face and know that this is a test of your endurance.

Locker (1995) states that many companies are now using behavioral or situational interviews. The behavioral interview asks the applicant to descibe actual behaviors, rather than plans or general principles. For example, instead of asking, "How would you motivate people?" the interviewer asks, "Tell me what do you do to get other people to do something." Such questions that ask specifically for what prospective employees have done in the past provides better insight into how they will actually function as employees in their firm. (p. 590)

Situational interviews put the applicant in a situation that allows the interviewer to see whether he or she has the qualities that the company is seeking. For example, the situation might be as follows:

> Suppose you are the supervisor of your information systems department, and you have a report to get out today. The computer system goes down, and no one seems to be able to get it up again. What would you do?
>
> You are the Assistant Vice President of Academic Affairs, and a faculty member has come to you because her department chair and dean have not solved a problem she is having. What would you do?
>
> You are an instructor. A student is unhappy with his grade and has come to you. You have gone over every thing with him and his grade is as you calculated it, but he insists that you raise his grade. You later discover that this student has gotten other students to sign a letter accusing you of discrimination, unfair grading, and defaming your character. A copy of the letter was given to you by your Dean; you were not sent a copy of the letter. What would you do?

Bovee and Thill (1995) have developed a list of frequently asked questions that are categorized by College, Employers and Jobs, Personal Attitudes and Preferences, and Work Habits.

Questions about College

1. What courses in college did you like most? Least? Why?
2. Do you think your extracurricular activities in college were worth the time you devoted to them? Why or why not?
3. When did you choose your college major? Did you ever change your major? If so, why?
4. Do you feel you did the best scholastic work you are capable of?
5. Which of your college years was the toughest? Why?

Questions about Employers and Jobs

6. What jobs have you held? Why did you leave?
7. What percentage of your college expenses did you earn? How?
8. Why did you choose your particular field of work?
9. What are the disadvantages of your chosen field?
10. Have you served in the military? What rank did you achieve? What jobs did you perform?
11. What do you think about how this industry operates today?
12. Why do you think you would like this particular type of job?

Questions about Personal Attitudes and Preferences

13. Do you prefer to work in any specific geographic location? If so, why?
14. How much money do you hope to be earning in five years? In ten years?
15. What do you think determines a person's progress in a good organization?
16. What personal characteristics do you feel are necessary for success in your chosen field?
17. Tell me a story.
18. Do you like to travel?
19. Do you think grades should be considered by employers? Why or why not?

Questions about Work Habits

20. Do you prefer working with others or by yourself?
21. What type of boss do you prefer?
22. Have you ever had any difficulty getting along with colleagues or supervisors? With other students? With instructors?
23. Would you prefer to work in a large or a small organization? Why?
24. How do you feel about overtime work?
25. What have you done that shows initiative and willingness to work?

Preparing for the Interview

Every interview has three parts—an opening, a body, and a close. Usually in the opening, the interviewer will try to set you at ease by asking you questions you can easily answer. Practically all job interviews are a little unnerving, but that is to be expected. That is why the skillful interviewer will do his or her part to provide a comfortable atmosphere.

You may be asked to take certain tests before the interview or after and then some tests before you are finally offered the job. These pre-or post-tests consists of aptitude tests, honesty tests, situational tests, essay exams and sample job tasks; other tests include a routine physical exam and a drug test. Once you are offered the position, you are asked to complete an employment application and or sign a contract depending upon the job itself.

Conduct research on the company. Before you go for the interview, you must do your homework. Do a little research on the company itself. What products or service do they sell? What is their financial standing? What is their corporate culture? How large is the company? All of these answers can be found out by reading a copy of the company's annual report. Just like you would not buy a product or service that you new nothing about, you would not want to work for a company that you knew nothing about either.

Present the asset side of you. Here is where you will want to present your strengths for that particular job. State your skills, abilities, and qualifications; then give concrete examples of how you have accomplished tasks using these strengths. For example, maybe you have implemented a new procedure for a task. You could say, "Using the skills learned in a market analysis class, I was able to conduct a market analysis for a small business in my hometown." Another example might be that you increased sales by 15 percent for a company. You could say, "Using a variety of sales tactics such as anticipating a customer's negative reaction to a product, I was able to convince most of them to buy our product."

Minimize your weaknesses. You will undoubtedly be asked what do you consider your weaknesses. Do not state that you do not have any weaknesses. Everyone has a weakness or weaknesses. What you can do is to rephrase the weakness into an opportunity for improvement. For example, maybe you do not like to work in teams. You could say, "One area that I am continually trying to improve is my ability to work effectively in teams." Having said this, you have admitted that you are not perfect. At least you have recognized the need for improvement in oral presentations.

Frequently Asked Interview Questions

One very important aspect of the interview process is that you will be exhibiting your communication skills. The interviewer will be sizing you up in terms of how well you react to questions and gleaning some aspects about your personal qualities. Listen very carefully to the questions asked before you respond; that is, think before you answer. The time you use to think through your answer may be reflective of how you react in stressful situations. Some of your traits will be displayed in the interview process.

Figure 18.5 is a list of frequently asked questions in the interview process. Although you will be asked questions about your work experience, qualifications, and previous education, these questions are designed to test your ability to think quickly and to react positively and confidently under stress.

Handling Illegal Questions in the Interview

Most interviewers who are up do date on questions that can be asked in the interview and will not ask you illegal questions. However, some interviewers may not be. If you are asked one or more of the following questions, you may or may not want to answer them:

1. Do you have children?
2. Who takes care of your children?
3. What are the ages of your children?
4. Do you think your career will interfere with your marriage?
5. What kind of job does your spouse have?
6. What is your native language?
7. Can you work on Friday, Saturday, or Sundays?
8. What do you do in your time away from work?
9. Do you have any impairments that are not job related?
10. Would your spouse contest your promotion or transfer?

Bear in mind that should you refuse to answer the question, the interviewer may say that your refusal will not be held against you. Actually, you have no guarantee that your refusal will not be. Some times female applicants are asked questions not typically asked of men. For example, consider the following question being asked of a female applicant: "Who will take care of your children while you are at work?" Clearly, this question is illegal as the caretaker of your children has nothing to do with your ability to perform the job. What you could say is "Although that question is not reflective of my ability to handle the job, I will gladly answer it for you." Remember if you really want the job, you probably should answer the question even though it is illegal.

Tips for the Successful Interview

First impressions are lasting impressions. You never have a second chance to make a good first impression. Your appearance and mannerisms will come into play during the interview. You must look like a business person if you are interviewing for a position in an office or a store. You must look inconspicuous; that is, blend in with that company's culture. So if you are male and have long hair, a pony tail, or an ear ring(s) you will look conspicuous; that is, you will stand out.

1. Tell me about yourself in five minutes.
2. Why did you choose your major?
3. What are your long-term goals?
4. How do others describe you?
5. Can you work well under pressure?
6. Can you work without close supervision?
7. Why do you want to (did you) leave your job?
8. Why do you want this job?
9. Why should we hire you?
10. What are your greatest strengths?
11. What are your weakness(es)?
12. What salary would you expect?
13. Do you have plans for continued education?
14. What is the one most important factor you are looking for in a job?
15. Can you forget your education and start from scratch?
16. Are you willing to relocate?
17. Are you willing to travel?
18. What extracurricular activities did you participate in when you were in college?
19. Do you belong to professional organizations? Which ones and why?
20. Do you have any impairments, physical, mental, or medical, that would interfere with your ability to do the job for which you have applied?

Figure 18.5.

Business attire. Men should wear a 2- or 3-piece dark solid color suit; all pieces should be of the same fabric and color. A white shirt with a conservative tie is appropriate. The socks should be the same color as the suit. Women should wear a 2-piece dark solid color suit with a no ruffled white blouse; both pieces should be of the same fabric and color. Stockings should be a natural color or the color of the suit. John Malloy's *Dress for Success* (men's clothes) and *The Woman's Dress for Success Book* make good reading for business fashion tips. Visiting two to three expensive stores for business suits will give you a flare for what is trendy; then you can go to a store in your price range to buy a similar suit.

Hair. A business woman's hair should be pulled back and tied with a bow or barrett rather than long and loose. Loose long hair can get caught in an office machine. Men's hair should be short and conservative looking. Hair styles for both men and women should be conservative.

Shoes. A woman should wear a low heel pump, preferably one to two inches high; no heel or toes should be seen. The shoes should match the color of the suit and, of course, the shoes for both men and women should be shined with no worned down heels.

Fingernails. Men's fingernails should be cleaned and trimmed. Women's fingernails should be short and trimmed as well. With the acrylic nails that women now wear, the length should be short enough to suggest that you can keyboard without getting the nails caught in the keys. Remember you are going to work, not a party.

Jewelry. Men should wear no ear rings in their ears for the interview. To do so may label you as nonconforming to the corporate culture. Women should wear small hoop earrings or small studs—one in each ear if they have pierced ears, or they may elect to wear no earrings at all if their ears are not pierced. Dangling bracelets that make noise should not be worn.

Cologne. The commerical adage that "a little dab will do you" is appropriate here. Be cautious not to wear heavy scented cologne or perfumed aftershave lotions. If your scent is still in the room after you have left, you have overdone it.

Makeup. Women's makeup should be understated. They are going to work so their eye shadow, lipstick, and blush should be subtle. Women should not outline the eyes or lips.

Communication Interplay Between Prospective Employer and You

When you appear for the interview, bring a small pad on which to write brief notes. You may have several interviews, so you want to keep the information separate. A good idea would be to develop a fact sheet on each company with space to fill in the answers to your questions and to write in specific information about the job. Figure 18.6 is an example of a fact sheet.

You may want to bring one to two copies of your application package so you will know specifically what you have included in each letter of application and resume. You should carry a small brief case for these items as well as information the prospective employer will give you. You may need the resume to complete an application form if requested.

You should practice answering the frequently asked questions so you will not be mumbling and/or stammering through your responses. You can go to the Career Center to arrange for mock interviews or have a friend practice interviewing you. Perhaps the friend can videotape you or maybe you will be videotaped during mock interviews in your Business Communication class. It is best to see yourself in action so you will know what areas you need to improve. Irritating speech mannerisms include using fillers at the end of sentences such as "you know" and "um." You should avoid using them. The way you speak is just as important as what you say during the interview.

Try to arrive 5 to 10 minutes before the interview. If it is a windy day or you had to walk a distance because of parking, you may want to go to the restroom to compose yourself. At the interview, you want to look your best, present your best self, and appear interested in the position and energetic. If your interview is a luncheon interview, do not order alcohol even if the interviewers are having a drink. If a drink is ordered for you anyway, do not touch it. Order a light, nonmessy meal. For example, you would not want to order crab legs or barbeque although either may be your favorite meal. Try to exhibit good table manners.

The communication interplay between you and the prospective employer is designed to see how compatible you would be with the organization. In other words, you must be a good fit for the organization. Your academic preparation, job-related personal attributes, work experience, appearance, communication skills, and attitude will be key areas that impact an employer's decision making.

You will likely be asked questions that determine what you know about the company, so present your research on the company. Employers will usually gear their interview questions to specific needs of the organization, your present and past work relationships, and your willingness to accept change and flexibility. You will want to communicate your strengths so that you differentiate yourself from the other applicants.

During the interview, you want to look confident, appear poised, establish and maintain eye contact, smile often, and look attentive. A male interviewer will extend his right hand for a firm handshake to another man; however, the woman should extend her right hand first to the male interviewer to help set him at ease. Similarly, a female interviewer will automatically extend her hand to a female for a firm handshake. It is highly possible that the interviewer may be nervous as well. Nonverbal behavior come into play as well. Keep your nonverbal behavior and words in sync. Remember the nonverbal behavior wins out every time.

Bovee and Thill (1995) have developed a list of Marks Against Applicants (in General Order of Importance) p. 391.

Marks Against Applicants (in General Order of Importance)

1. Has a poor personal appearance
2. Is overbearing, overaggressive, conceited; has a "superiority complex"; seems to "know it all"
3. Is unable to express self clearly; has poor voice, diction, grammar

JOB SEARCH
COMPANY FACT SHEET

Name, Address & Phone No.	Contact Person	Date Resume & Letter of Application Sent	Acknowledgment Received	Other Communication Received	Follow-up Letter(s) Needed	Other Communication Needed	Interview Date	Miscellaneous Information	Other Issues	Decision

Figure 18.6. Job Search Fact Sheet.

4. Lacks knowledge or experience
5. Is not prepared for interview
6. Has no real interest in job
7. Lacks planning for career; has no purpose or goals
8. Lacks enthusiasm; is passive and indifferent
9. Lacks confidence and poise; is nervous and ill at ease
10. Shows insufficient evidence of achievement
11. Has failed to participate in extracurricular activites
12. Overemphasizes money; is interested only in the best dollar offer
13. Has poor scholastic record; just got by
14. Is unwilling to start at the bottom; expects too much too soon
15. Makes excuses
16. Is evasive; hedges on unfavorable factors in record
17. Lacks tact
18. Lacks maturity
19. Lacks courtesy; is ill-mannered
20. Condemns past employers
21. Lacks social skills
22. Shows marked dislike for schoolwork
23. Lacks vitality
24. Fails to look interviewer in the eye
25. Has limp, weak handshake

Listen carefully to the questions you are asked. For example, if you were asked the question "Are you eager to please?" how would you respond? Perhaps here you may want to ask for clarification. You would not want to ask a question during your time for questions that has already been answered directly or indirectly. What kinds of questions should you ask? Well, here are some for thought:

1. What is the organization's corporate culture?
2. How will I be evaluated? How often? By whom?
3. What other training will be needed in this job?
4. Are there employee-educational assistance plans available?
5. Will the job be in this area? Or is relocation expected?
6. Will I have to travel? How often? Where?
7. What are the major job duties?
8. Will I be working individually or with teams?
9. What are the organization's major strengths?
10. Does your organization plan to merge with another company? Or relocate out of the state any time soon?

The interviewer will signal when the interview is over. You need to watch his or her verbal or nonverbal cues. The interviewer will ask you if you have any other questions and then sum up the interview. At the close of the interview, the interviewer may tell you that other applicants are being interviewed so that he or she will get back to you. However, you can ask if you can call back within two weeks to find out a decision. At this time, you can ask for the interviewer's card. It is a good idea to ask if you can call back because you are indicating that you are interested in the job plus you want to know so that you are not waiting one to two months later expecting a call and the decision was already made to hire someone else. If the interviewer prefers to call you, then just thank him or her for the interview and express the fact that you will be waiting for a decision.

All stages of the interview are crucial. If you present yourself well, you may be asked to comeback for a second or final interview. If you are, remember the techniques discussed and stress your personality traits.

If you are asked back for a final interview, the culmination of the interview may result in a job offer. At this stage, you can either accept the offer on the spot or ask for time to think it over. Assuming that salary has already been discussed, perhaps the best decision is to ask for a couple of days before giving your answer.

If salary has not been discussed, do not bring up the subject. Let the interviewer start the salary discussion. A part of your job search strategy was to look at comparable jobs in the classified ads or talk to professors in your field to get ideas on salary. If the salary is not quite what you expect after having done your research, you can always ask if there is any room for negotiation. Many organizations have relatively rigid salary practices so they are unable to offer any negotiation. Only accept the job offer if you are truly interested in the job, the salary is acceptable, and you would be satisfied to work for the company for some time.

Follow-Up Letters in the Employment Process

You can show your appreciation after an interview by sending a thank you message. Many applicants will not think to make this gesture, but you show your interest in the job with this goodwill message. Sending a thank you message keeps your name in front of the interviewer and really gets the message across that you are sincerely interested in the job. If you have other information relative to your qualifications for the job you want to share with the interviewer, you can include it in this thank you message. A thank you letter is illustrated in Figure 18.7.

Other letters in the employment process include a follow-up letter, a job acceptance letter, a letter of refusal, and a letter of resignation.

A follow-up letter is written when you have not heard from the interviewer within a reasonable time after the interview. If you have not heard from an interviewer within two weeks, you need to follow-up. Surprisingly, many companies may never contact you. A follow-up letter shows that you are still interested in the job and that you are diligent in trying to secure employment.

A Follow-up Letter is shown in Figure 18.8.

A job-acceptance letter is an easy good-news message to write. You may want to restate significant information relative to the position, salary, and the date you are to report to work. The acceptance should appear in the first sentence. A Job-Acceptance Letter is illustrated in 18.9.

In a job refusal letter, you should try to keep the goodwill of the reader and of the organization. Remember to thank the employing company for the job offer. Since this is a negative letter, you need to couch it in bad-news message format. See Figure 18.10 for an example.

7890 Wyandott Avenue
Kansas City, MO 64571
July 9, 1997

Mr. Robert Cephus Wu
Vice President of Customer
Services
Joyce Bank
St. Joseph, MO 64501

Dear Mr. Wu:

I really appreciate the time you spent with me in discussing my qualifications for the Senior Customer Services Representative position at Joyce Bank.

I am excited about the possibility of working with a team of representatives in delivering the best services possible to your customers and to be involved in developing new customer services.

I look forward to hearing from you soon.

Sincerely,

Mary Louise Mays

Mary Louise Mays

Figure 18.7. A Sample Thank You Letter.

You will at some time during your career need to write a letter of resignation. You must remember that this letter is an important letter and that you should not use this letter to expose your problems or personality conflicts. If you need to resign, you should do so gracefully. You never know if some day you will want to work again for that company. Also, your past and present employers will surely be contacted to verify your employment, so this letter of resignation could be used to influence a recommendation for you. This bad-news letter should be written within a month or two weeks of your leaving. Use care in writing as you will want to maintain friendly relationships.

An example of a Letter of Resignation is shown in Figure 18.11.

Completing Application Forms

One formal procedure of the employment offer is for you to complete an application. You should have experience in filling out applications which you can get by collecting four or five from various companies and practice filling them out. You want your employment application to be neat with legible writing or type the application; make sure you use a typewriter that has a correcting ribbon. Too many whiteouts stand out and may suggest carelessness.

Figures 18.12, 18.13, 18.14 represent three different types of application forms. Compare the differences in the space allotted for information and the questions asked.

Soliciting Letters of Recommendation

In asking people to write you a letter of recommendation, you usually ask those who you think will write you a positive letter of recommendation. You should always seek a person's permission before you list him or her on your resume or give his or her name as a reference.Usually these persons will write you a positive letter, but you should always ask the person to send you a copy for your file. Surprisingly, one applicant thought a person he listed as a reference would write him a positive recommendation letter. Unfortunately, the writer wrote a negative recommendation letter; naturally, the applicant did not get the job.

In today's litiguous times, people are sometimes reluctant to write letters of recommendation. Any thing that is printed in a letter can be used against the writer. As a result, you should not be too surprised if a person chooses not to write a letter of recommendation.

Securing that first full-time position takes patience, perserverance, and confidence. Just keep reminding yourself that you have some great assets to offer an employer. You just have to find that great employer who wants to put your great assets to work.

6580 Bralorne Court
Stone Mountain, GA 30083
June 6, 1997

Mr. Alfred Chuang
Walker Printing Company
616 South 17 Street
Atlanta, GA 30077

Dear Mr. Chuang

I sent you my resume and letter of application for the Advertising Manager position on May 10. I am really interested in the position.

My business communication skills have been further enhanced by the course work I have taken in three business writing classes. I had to incorporate artwork in newsletters and news releases.

Since your receipt of my application package, I have been involved in a two week internship with NBC studio doing some advertising artwork. I would be happy to show this artwork to you.

You can telephone me at 770/645–6461 any day after 4 p.m., or you can write to me at the above address.

Sincerely

DeJevan Shane

DeJevan Shane

Figure 18.8. A Sample Follow up Letter.

1412 Wooster Street
Bowling Green, OH 43402
July 11, 1997

Mr. Clifton Iwatsu
Human Resource Manager
Wirerope Corporation
36 Belt Highway
St. Joseph, MO 64501

Dear Mr. Iwatsu

I gladly accept the Office Systems Supervisor position at Wirerope Corporation.

I will report to work on August 15, 1997 at 9 a.m. My salary of $35,000 is acceptable, and I will submit receipts for my moving expenses not to exceed $3,000 after my arrival.

I have been in touch with the real estate agent, Ms. Karen Cook, who is getting me a list of houses I can lease. I appreciate your efforts on my behalf.

Thank you for all the information you have sent me about the St. Joseph area. I am excited about my move to the mid-west.

You can contact me at the above address until August 1.

Sincerely

Marilyn Wang

Marilyn Wang

Figure 18.9. A Sample Job Acceptance Letter.

3 Sutherland Road
Montclair, New Jersey
October 10, 1997

Miss Renee Martinez
Director, Student Housing
Hampton College
Richmond, Virginia

Dear Miss Martinez

Thank you for offering me the Residence Hall Administrator position.

Hampton College is a well-known school with beautiful surroundings. I was impressed with the students and the curriculum.

During my interview, I informed you that I was trying to move closer to my parents who are getting up in age. Since I have been offered another position in the New York area at a comparable salary, I have decided to accept it.

Again, thank you for offering me the position. I do wish you and the College well in your efforts to fill the position.

Sincerely
Judy Haynes
Judy Haynes

Figure 18.10. A Sample Job Refusal Letter.

2510 Vista Laguna Terrace
Pasadena, CA 91107
November 2, 1997

Mrs. Tiffany Xia
Senior Clerk
Municipal Court House
Pasadena, CA 91103

Dear Mrs. Xia

I have enjoyed my five year tenure as a Junior Clerk at the Municipal Court House.

The staff has been most supportive of me and my efforts to learn the real estate property records procedures. I owe them a great deal of gratitude.

As you know, I have been going to school at night to attain my Master's degree in Business Administration. I have finally accomplished this endeavor which has opened up another exciting opportunity for me. I will be leaving to accept a position as a Manager of the Real Estate Property Division for the County Assessor's Office in Columbia, Georgia.

My last day will be November 30, so you will have time to find a replacement for me; I would be glad to help in training that person.

Best wishes to all of you at the Municipal Court House, and thank you for many lasting friendships and your support.

Sincerely

Patricia Gorman

Patricia Gorman

Figure 18.11. A Sample Resignation Letter.

Application for Employment

POSITION

Position Title and Job No. desired:____________________

Name (*Last*) (*First*) (*M.I.*)	Social Security # (*optional*)
Address (*Number & Street*) (*City & State*) (*ZIP Code*)	Home Phone ( )
Are you over 18 years of age? Yes ☐ No ☐	Message/Office Phone ( )

Do you have current authorization to work in the U.S.? Yes ☐ No ☐ If yes: Full-Time ☐ Part-Time ☐

If you are related to anyone employed by us, please supply the following:

Name *Relationship* *Department*

____

ADDITIONAL INFORMATION You are required to give information on all convictions. Minor traffic citations and incidents which occurred before your 18th birthday will be excluded.

Have you ever been convicted of a crime?________ If yes, please explain: ____________________

(NOTE: A conviction is not an automatic bar to employment. Each case will be considered on its own merits.)

EDUCATION List schools attended other than high school (include military training and/or related courses):

Name and Location of School	Major	Credits Completed		Degree/ Diploma	Date Received
		Semester Units	Quarter Units		

PROFESSIONAL ACHIEVEMENTS/PUBLICATIONS ____________________

____

____

____

SKILLS Valid Licenses/Certificates: ____________________

Keyboarding WPM:__________Computer Programs:____________________

Office Machines:____________________

Languages: Speak__________Read__________Write__________

Applications will be evaluated on the basis of information provided. It is the applicant's responsibility to insure that this information is thorough and complete. Failure to provide sufficient information which shows evidence of meeting minimum qualifications will result in disqualification or nonconsideration. Providing your social security number at this time is voluntary based upon 20 CFR 4104.1242-3. Only the Division of Human Resource Management is authorized to extend offers of employment.

We are an equal employment opportunity, affirmative action employer subject to all state, federal and our regulations pertaining to non-discrimination based on sex, sexual orientation, race, national origin, religion, disability, marital status, age and veteran status.

Upon request, reasonable accommodation will be provided to individuals with protected disabilities to (a) complete the employment process and (b) perform essential job functions when this does not cause an undue hardship.

Employment History

(List present or most recent employer first, attach supplement if necessary.)

Relevant volunteer experience will be considered as qualifying experience on an hour-for-hour basis.

Dates (Mo/Yr)		Total No.	Firm Name & Address	Duties:
From	To	Yrs/Mos		
Salary		No Hrs		
Start	End	Per Wk	Supervisor	
Position Title			Phone Number	
Reason for Leaving				

Dates (Mo/Yr)		Total No.	Firm Name & Address	Duties:
From	To	Yrs/Mos		
Salary		No Hrs		
Start	End	Per Wk	Supervisor	
Position Title			Phone Number	
Reason for Leaving				

Dates (Mo/Yr)		Total No.	Firm Name & Address	Duties:
From	To	Yrs/Mos		
Salary		No Hrs		
Start	End	Per Wk	Supervisor	
Position Title			Phone Number	
Reason for Leaving				

List people who would have knowledge of your qualifications for the position. Do not list relatives.

Name	**Business or Home Address**	**Occupation**	**Phone**

Special Job Information: Briefly describe your qualifications for this postion by virtue of your education, experience, and interest.

Past employers will be contacted for references. May we contact your present employer? Yes ☐ No ☐

Have you ever been discharged from any position(s)?__________

If employed under other name(s), please list:__________

I affirm that all answers and statements in this application for employment are complete and true to the best of my knowledge and belief. I understand that any false statement or omission may be cause for rejection of my application or for my discharge after appointment. Employment offers are contingent upon willingness to sign the loyalty oath and be fingerprinted. I also understand that if hired, I must provide documentation attesting to my identity and current authorization to work in the United States, as required by the Immigration Reform and Control Act of 1986.

SIGNATURE DATE

Figure 18.12. Sample Job Application for educational institutions.

TODAY/S DATE | SOCIAL SECURITY NUBER | EMPLOYMENT APPLICATION

WE ARE AN EQUAL OPPORTUNITY EMPLOYER.

NAME (FIRST) (MIDDLE) (LAST)

DRIVER'S LICENSE/STATE ISSUED I.D.
STATE NO.

ADDRESS (NUMBER, STREET, CITY, STATE & ZIP CODE) ☐ PERMANENT ☐ TEMPORARY ☐ MAILING ADDRESS

HAVE YOU EVER WORKED OR ATTENDED SCHOOL UNDER ANOTHER NAME THAT WE NEED TO KNOW TO VERIFY OUR RECORDS? IF YES, NAME:
☐ YES ☐ NO

HOME PHONE NUMBER
( )

BUSINESS OR TEMPORARY PHONE
( )

PREVIOUS RESIDENCE

CURRENTLY EMPLOYED
☐ FULL TIME ☐ PART TIME ☐ NOT EMPLOYED

HAVE YOU EVER BEEN CONVICTED OF A CRIME (MISDEMEANORS OR FELONIES) BY A CIVILIAN OR MILITARY COURT?
☐ YES ☐ NO
Conviction Of A Crime Will Not Automatically Prohibit Employment

POSITION DESIRED (Check only one)
☐ OFFICE ☐ STOCK ☐ OTHER (SPECIFY)
☐ SALES

MINIMUM SALARY DESIRED

SCHEDULE PREFERRED
☐ FULL TIME (6 or more hours daily)
☐ PART TIME (3 - 5 hours - days)
☐ PART TIME (evenings and weekends)

LIST ALL TIMES YOU ARE AVAILABLE TO WORK (Full Time must be available any 5 of 7 days)

SUNDAY	MONDAY	TUESDAY	WEDNESDAY	THURSDAY	FRIDAY	SATURDAY
FROM	FROM	FROM	FROM	FROM	FROM	FROM
TO	TO	TO	TO	TO	TO	TO

HOW WERE YOU REFERRED TO US?
☐ EMPLOYEE ☐ AD ☐ AGENCY
☐ OTHER (SPECIFY)

HAVE YOU EVER APPLIED FOR EMPLOYMENT WITH US OR ANY SUBSIDIARY OF OURS?
IF YES, INDICATE DATE AND LOCATIONS.
☐ YES ☐ NO

HAVE YOU EVER BEEN EMPLOYED BY OUR CHAIN OR ANY SUBSIDIARY OF OURS? ☐ YES ☐ NO

IF YOU WERE EMPLOYED UNDER WHAT NAME WERE YOU EMPLOYED? STORE LOCATION?

RELATIVE IN OUR EMPLOY? NAME DEPARTMENT
☐ YES ☐ NO

WHERE ARE YOU AVAILABLE TO WORK. LIST THE STORES BELOW.

EDUCATION

SCHOOL	NAME & ADDRESS OF SCHOOL	COURSE OF STUDY	DATE FROM MO YR	DATE TO NO YR	CIRCLE LAST YEAR COMPLETED	LIST DIPLOMA/DEGREE
HIGH SCHOOL					1 2 3 4	
COLLEGE					1 2 3 4	
OTHER (SPECIFY)					1 2 3 4	

PREVIOUS EMPLOYMENT — LIST IN ORDER OF EMPLOYMENT STARTING WITH YOUR PRESENT EMPLOYMENT. PLEASE ACCOUNT FOR ALL TIME, INCLUDING CURRENT EMPLOYMENT, MILITARY SERVICE, PART TIME JOBS, AND PERIODS OF UNEMPLOYMENT. IF YOU HELD TWO JOBS AT THE SAME TIME BE SURE TO LIST BOTH JOBS.

DATE FROM MO YR	DATE TO MO YR	NAME OF BUSINESS	ADDRESS/PHONE OF BUSINESS	JOB TITLE OR NATURE OF JOB	SALARY START END	REASON FOR LEAVING

IMPORTANT (PLEASE REVIEW AND SIGN)

The facts set forth in this application are true and correct. I understand that if employed, any false or misleading statements, omissions or failure to fully answer any question will result in my immediate dismissal, regardless of when such information is discovered. I further understand and agree that I may be bonded if employed. I agree to submit myself at any time upon request for medical examination and/or testing (including drug testing). I understand that should I be found to be unable to perform the essential functions of the job, with or without reasonable accommodation, to the extent required by law, my employment with this store will be subject to termination. I authorize this store to secure a consumer report from consumer reporting agencies (i.e. Credit Bureau Inc., Stores Protective Association, etc.), and verify employment and educational references in connection with my application for employment and subsequently as the store deems appropriate. Upon written request from me to this store I will be informed of the name and address of each consumer reporting agency, if any, from which the store has obtained a consumer report relating to me.

I understand and agree that nothing contained in the store's handbook, manual, rules or regulations, practice, policy, etc., shall be deemed to create an employment contract between myself and the store. It is further understood and agreed that my employment relationship with this store may be terminated on any day by myself or the store's for any reason, or no reason, without liability. I represent that I am not relying upon any promises or representations regarding either the nature or duration of my employment in accepting employment if it is offered to me. I understand that no supervisor, manager or other representative of the store has any authority to enter into any express or implied contract. I further understand and agree that no promise, representation, inducement or agreement contrary to the above is binding unless it is in writing, expressly states that it is a contract, and is signed by the Chairman of the store.

Following An Offer Of Employment All Applicants Will Be Required To Supply The Following:
A - WORK PERMIT
B - SOCIAL SECURITY CARD
C - PROOF OF CITIZENSHIP OR AUTHORIZATION TO WORK IN U.S.
D - NAME AND ADDRESS OF 3 REFERENCES
E - PROOF OF AGE

I CERTIFY THAT I HAVE REVIEWED THE ABOVE, UNDERSTAND IT AND AGREE TO IT

SIGNATURE OF APPLICANT (*DO NOT PRINT*)

REASON FOR NON-HIRE
☐ MORE QUALIFIED PERSON NECESSARY/HIRED
☐ NO SUITABLE OPENINGS AT THIS TIME
☐ HOLD FOR FURTHER CONSIDERATION (one month)

☐ CANDIDATE NOT INTERESTED IN JOB AVAILABLE. GIVE REASON - SALARY, SCHEDULE, ETC.

INTERVIEWER'S INITIALS AND DATE

Figure 18.13. Sample Job Application for department store.

We are an equal opportunity employer committed to a diverse work force. In order to assist in our efforts we invite you to voluntarily provide responses to the following requests for information. Failure to respond will not subject you to adverse treatment. This form will be kept strictly confidential and will not be retained with your application. Information provided will be used only in accordance with law and for equal opportunity purposes.

SEX
☐ Male
☐ Female

RACE, COLOR, NATIONAL ORIGIN
☐ American Indian (1) ☐ White (4)
☐ Hispanic (2) ☐ Black (5)
☐ Asian American (3)

VETERAN
☐ Disabled Veteran
☐ Vietnam Era Veteran

EMPLOYMENT APPLICATION

SOCIAL SECURITY NO. ____

NAME ____ STREET ADDRESS ____
FIRST NAME MIDDLE INITIAL LAST NAME

APT. NO. OR BOX ____ CITY ____ STATE ____ ZIP ____ AREA CODE ____ TEL. NO. ____

ARE YOU 18 OR OLDER? ____ ☐ YES ☐ NO, IF NOT, BIRTH DATE ____

EVER WORKED IN OUR RESTAURANT BEFORE? IF YES, DATES, ADDRESS AND REASON FOR LEAVING ____

AVAILABILITY:

TOTAL HOURS AVAILABLE PER WEEK ____

HOURS AVAILABLE	M	T	W	T	F	S	S
FROM							
TO							

ARE YOU LEGALLY ABLE TO BE EMPLOYED IN THE U.S. ☐ YES ☐ NO

HOW DID YOU HEAR OF JOB? ____

HOW FAR DO YOU LIVE FROM RESTAURANT? ____

DO YOU HAVE TRANSPORTATION TO WORK? ____

SCHOOL MOST RECENTLY ATTENDED:

NAME ____ ADDRESS ____ CITY ____ STATE ____ PHONE ____

TEACHER OR COUNSELOR ____ DEPT ____ LAST GRADE COMPLETED ____ GRADE POINT AVERAGE ____

GRADUATED ☐ YES ☐ NO NOW ENROLLED? ☐ YES ☐ NO SPORTS OR ACTIVITES ____

TWO MOST RECENT JOBS: (IF NOT APPLICABLE, LIST U.S. MILITARY, WORK PERFORMED ON A VOLUNTARY BASIS OR PERSONAL REFERENCES)

COMPANY ____ ADDRESS ____ CITY ____ STATE ____
PHONE ____ JOB ____
SUPERVISOR ____ DATES WORKED FROM ____ TO ____
SALARY ____ REASON FOR LEAVING ____ MGMT: REFERENCE CHECK DONE BY:

COMPANY ____ ADDRESS ____ CITY ____ STATE ____
PHONE ____ JOB ____
SUPERVISOR ____ DATES WORKED FROM ____ TO ____
SALARY ____ REASON FOR LEAVING ____ MGMT: REFERENCE CHECK DONE BY:

The Secretary of Health and Human Services has determined that certain diseases, including hepatitis A, salmonella, staphylococcus, streptococcus, giardia and compylobacter may prevent you from serving food or handling food equipment in a sanitary or healthy fashion. An essential function of this job involves handling and serving food service equipment and functioning in a sanitary and healthy fashion. Is there any reason why you cannot perform the essential functions of this job? ☐ YES ☐ NO If yes, why.

DURING THE PAST 7 YEARS HAVE YOU EVER BEEN CONVICTED OF OR PLED GUILTY TO A CRIME, EXCLUDING MISDEMEANOR AND TRAFFIC VIOLATIONS?
☐ YES ☐ NO IF YES, DESCRIBE IN FULL *A conviction will not necessarily bar you from employment.

NOTE: Employees working in Massachusetts and Maryland—see reverse side for information.

1. I verify that the information contained in this application is correct to the best of my knowledge and understand that any omission or erroneous information is grounds for dismissal in accordance with our policy. 2. I authorize the references listed above to give you any and all information concerning my previous employment and pertinent information they may have, personal or otherwise and release all parties from all liability for any damage that may result from furnishing same to you. 3. I acknowledge that the restaurant reserves the right to amend or modify the policies in its handbook and other policies at any time without prior notice. These policies do not create any promises or contractual obligations between the restaurant and its employees. At the restaurant my employment is at will. This means I am free to terminate my employment at any time for any reason with or without cause, and the restaurant retains the same rights. The Senior Vice President of Human Resources of the Corporation is the only person who may make an exception to this, and it must be in writing and signed by him. 4. If applicable to my employment, I have read and understood the notice regarding polygraph tests and my rights under state law.

The restaurant is an Affirmative Action and Equal Opportunity Employer. Various Federal, State, and Local laws prohibit discrimination on account of race, color, religion, sex, age, national origin, disability or veterans status. It is this restaurant's policy to comply fully with these laws as applicable, and information is requested on this application will not be used for any purpose prohibited by law.

I understand that as a part of the procedure for my employment application an investigative consumer report may be made concerning my character, general reputation, personal characteristics and mode of living. Upon written request additional disclosure concerning the complete nature and scope of the investigation will be provided. If I am denied a job based either wholly or in part because of information contained in an investigative consumer report, I will be provided the name and address of the reporting agency that supplies the information.

SIGNATURE ____ DATE ____

Figure 18.14. Sample Job Application for fast food restaurant.

References

Bateman, D. N. and N. B. Sigband (1989). COMMUNICATING IN BUSINESS, Scott, Foresman, Glenview, Illinois.

Bovee, C. L. and J. V. Thill (1995). BUSINESS COMMUNICATION TODAY, 4th edition. McGraw-Hill, p. 382.

Locker, K. O. (1995). BUSINESS AND ADMINISTRATIVE COMMUNICATION, 3rd edition, Irwin, p. 590.

Questions

1. What is the purpose of a letter of application?
2. How should you state your weaknesses when asked in the interview?
3. Is it improper to use "I" in a letter of application?
4. Why is the AIDA approach more effective in a letter of application?
5. What is the purpose of an interview?
6. Should the resume and letter of application always be sent together?
7. Which is the most effective type of interview?
8. What are the different types of interview and their features?
9. Should the interviewee ever bring up the subject of salary?
10. How would you characterize the interview process?
11. What things should you keep in mind when selecting someone to serve as a reference for you?
12. How does the situational interview differ from the behavioral interview?

Applications

1. List work tasks that come easily for you. List work tasks that are difficult for you.
2. Think about how you obtained your first job. Do you see any techniques discussed in this chapter that you used or were used? If so, list them.
3. Visit the Career Center on campus and view a videotape on interviewing. List the features you learned.
4. Pretend you have just finished interviewing for a job in your major you really like; you want the job badly. Input a thank you letter to the company (your choice).
5. Visit a professor in your major and ask him or her the pressing issues and concerns they have for the progression of their field in the 21st Century.
6. Visit the Career Center on campus and set up appointments for you to have one to two mock interviews. Bring to class a critique of your interviews.
7. You have not received a response to an ad for a job for which you applied ______________ (fill in a job title in your major). Write an inquiry letter seeking confirmation of their having receiving your application for the position.
8. Locate a copy of the book DRESS FOR SUCCESS for men or THE WOMEN'S DRESS FOR SUCCESS BOOK. Input a paragraph on the features you liked about the book.

9. Go to a bookstore and make a list of the current books out on interviewing and job search skills. Be prepared to share your list with the class.

"As Southern California's leading information provider for over a century, the 123 News is continuing its excellence in print media while expanding into alternative technologies to become the information partner of choice for its readers and advertisers in every market and medium it serves."

Computer

BUSINESS ANALYST

The 123 News has an exciting opportunity for a **Business Analyst** in our Advertising Financial Services department.

The **Business Analyst** will participate in requirements definition, design, development, testing, implementation, and maintenance of the advertising billing systems. The ideal candidate for this position will perform the following duties; business analysis and design work as required, prepare test scripts and business scenarios, executive function and application testing and analyze results, and system administration of codes, rates and security.

THE SUCCESSFUL CANDIDATE WILL HAVE:

•Bachelor's degree

•Minimum 2-5 years related experience

•Mainframe and PC experience

•Strong communication and interpersonal skills

•Packaged software experience

•Testing and implementation planning experience

•Demonstrated ability to meet deadlines

•Project administration experience and newspaper industry experience a plus

The 123 News offers a competitive compensation and benefits package. Qualified candidates should send a resume with salary history indicating **Position #12G** to:

123 News

Employment Office

123 Highway

Los Angeles, CA

You may also fax to (xxx) xxx-xxxx or send via the Internet.

Equal Opportunity Employer

COMPUTER

NETWORK COMPUTING

XYZ Medical Center seeks a dedicated information services professional with the following expertise to act as a Computer Operations Supervisor. Our environment offers the latest technologies available and a high degree of autonomy/opportunity for personal/ professional development.

Requirements include:

- Strong supervisory experience in a computer operations environment
- Excellent oral, written and interpersonal communication skills
- Extensive experience with MVS operating system and SMS financial system
- Working knowledge of JCL, abend project coordinator/team member

We offer a competitive salary commensurate with education and experience, along with an excellent benefits package. Please forward your resume, indicating Job #MU965, to: Human Resources, XYZ Drive, LA, CA.

XYZ Medical Center

Management

CIRCULATION MANAGER

(OPMA-Outside the Primary Marketing Area)

The circulation Manager (OPMA) will develop home delivery and single copy circulation strategies, tactics and goals for outside the primary marketing area, establish a distribution network focused on customer needs; negotiate rates and evaluates and responds to competitive influences. Requires extensive travel.

THE SUCCESSFUL CANDIDATE WILL HAVE:

- 3+ years demonstrated success in managing sales and distribution.
- Competitive newspaper market experience a plus.
- Excellent oral/written communication skills.
- Strong organizational, analytical and strategic planning skills.
- Demonstrated ability to develop and implement superior customer service programs.
- PC skills (including Excel, Microsoft Word) required.
- Bachelor's degree preferred.

The Los Angeles Times offers a competitive compensation and benefits package. Qualified candidates should send a resume with salary history indicated position number 97H055 to:

Los Angeles Times
Employment Office
Times Mirror Square
Los Angeles, CA 90053

You may also fax to (213) 237-4962 or send via the Internet to jobs@latimes.com

Equal Opportunity Employer

Accounting

Growing co. has the following F/T immed. openings. We provide a competitive salary and benefits package.

SENIOR FINANCIAL ANALYST

Work on special projects for Controller, CFO & CEO. Must have strong analytical, PC & communications skills. Acctng degree req'd. Cost acctng/pricing knowledge pref'd. Min. 4 yrs exper.

LOAN PROCESSOR

ABC Funding Corporation, a National Mortgage Lender, has an excellent opportunity in our Corporate Office for a Commercial Loan Processor with minimum 2 years' experience. The successful candidate will have strong knowledge of title and loan documentation; understanding of real estate and lending terminology; ability to identify requirements for proper loan underwriting; cognizance of clouds in title, adverse title exceptions, appraisal and environmental report findings, and/or other issues that may inhibit the successful collateral of the loan; able to produce high quality work in a fast-paced team environment; proficient with Microsoft Word and Excel. Experience with Conduit Lending preferred, but not required.

We offer competitive compensation and excellent benefits, including 401(k). Please mail or fax your resume with salary history to

ABC Funding
Corporation
Attn: HR Director
1800 Ventura
LA, CA
FX xxx-xxx-xxxx.

Equal Opportunity Employer

Marketing

SALES/MARKETING ASSOCIATE

Children's Health Foundation, affiliated with ABC Medical Center, has an immediate opening for a Sales/Marketing Associate. The ideal candidate will possess strong interpersonal skills, be a motivated self-starter and have the desire to work collaboratively in an dynamic team environment. Minimum qualifications include 3 to 5 years direct sales experience, preferably in an Occupational Health or other healthcare service-related field. Strong oral and written communication skills and the desire to build and maintain close relationships with a diverse client base required. Bachelor's degree in Marketing or a related field is desired.

Qualified candidates may apply in person or direct a resume to: Children's Health Foundation, ABC Medical Center, 123 Highway, LA, CA or fax xxx-xxx-xxxx. EOE

10. Visit the Career Center and list in a paragraph all the services that the Center provides for students. Turn this into your instructor.
11. Visit the library or use OPAC and print out a listing of the current books available on interviewing. Check out one to two books to bring to class for discussion.
12. You have to resign from your present position. You have been having personality problems with your supervisor for quite some time now about three years. You cannot handle the tensions between the two of you any longer. Also, he tries to belittle you in front of other s even though you have the most education. Nothing you do seems to please him or her although other executives in the company have complimented you on your work. Write a letter of resignation. You choose a company and position.
13. Write a letter of application to accompany the ad that you selected in Chapter 17. The ad and letter of application are to be turned in as a unit.
14. *The LA Times* lists the preceding classified ads; choose two and write a critique on how your skills match those listed in the ads. The following ads are adopted from ads that appeared in the March 30, 1997, issues of *The LA Times*.

Name ______________________________ Date ____________

JEOPARDY QUIZ #18

1. The answer is: The process of interrogating prospective employees.

   What is ______________________________?

2. The answer is: An effective method to persuade someone to do something.

   What is ______________________________?

3. The answer is: A person who can attest to one's skills and abilities.

   What is ______________________________?

4. The answer is: A questioning technique that ferrets out your reasoning ability.

   What is ______________________________?

5. The answer is: An interview consisting of two to five people asking the interviewee questions.

   What is ______________________________?

6. The answer is: An opening, a body, and a closing.

   What is ______________________________?

7. The answer is: Tell me about yourself in five minutes.

   What is ______________________________?

8. The answer is: Do you have children?

   What is ______________________________?

9. The answer is: Author of the book entitled DRESS FOR SUCCESS.

   Who is ______________________________?

continued

10. The answer is: A document that will hopefully merit the applicant an interview.

    What is ____?